A BOOK FOR "US"

This is a parenting book only in the sense that parenting is familying, something that children and adults should be doing together, not to or for one another. It is more a how-to-see-it book than a how-to-do-it book, and it is more an us-help book than a self-help book. This is a book for "us," for people who want to rediscover who they are, and who they can be, by rediscovering their family within them.

I hope the five families I will use for examples will help you find a wider and safer path to spiritual fulfillment and help you learn how to walk alongside everyone in your family on that path, not just run as a gang of individuals along the precarious path to self-fulfillment. Perhaps, if the path we choose together is wide enough, clear enough, and safe enough, the entire human family may join us.

THE POWER OF THE FAMILY

Paul Pearsall, Ph.D.

BANTAM

NEW YORK   TORONTO   LONDON   SYDNEY   AUCKLAND

*This edition contains the complete text
of the original hardcover edition.*
NOT ONE WORD HAS BEEN OMITTED.

THE POWER OF THE FAMILY
A Bantam Nonfiction Book/published in association with Doubleday

PRINTING HISTORY
Doubleday edition published January 1990
Bantam edition/October 1991

ISBN 0-553-29435-0

Published simultaneously in the United States and Canada

---

*Bantam Books are published by Bantam Books, a division of Bantam
Doubleday Dell Publishing Group, Inc. Its trademark, consisting of the
words "Bantam Books" and the portrayal of a rooster, is Registered in
U.S. Patent and Trademark Office and in other countries. Marca
Registrada. Bantam Books, 666 Fifth Avenue, New York, New York
10103.*

PRINTED IN THE UNITED STATES OF AMERICA

RAD   0 9 8 7 6 5 4 3 2 1

914497

For my son Roger,
for all the loving energy
he brings to our family

Contents

FOREWORD
xiii

CHAPTER ONE
Family Forever
1

CHAPTER TWO
A Portrait of Your Changing Family
24

CHAPTER THREE
Family Ritual:
The Cure for Family Jet Lag
37

CHAPTER FOUR
Family Rhythm:
Learning to Move Together
60

vii

CHAPTER FIVE
Family Reason:
Reasonable Families at Irrational Times
85

CHAPTER SIX
Family Remembrance:
The Keeping of the Family
115

CHAPTER SEVEN
Family Resilience:
Together Through It All
152

CHAPTER EIGHT
Family Resonance:
Making Good Family Vibes
200

CHAPTER NINE
Family Reconciliation:
Getting Back Together Again
225

CHAPTER TEN
Family Reverence:
Protecting the Dignity of "Us"
272

CHAPTER ELEVEN
Family Revival:
Quick Recovery from Family Feuds
314

CHAPTER TWELVE
Family Reunion:
Celebrating Life Together
349

EPILOGUE
386

BIBLIOGRAPHY
389

INDEX
397

Acknowledgments

I had cancer, and my family saved my life. Just as I completed the manuscript for this book, doctors discovered that a seven-month back pain was, in fact, lymphoma. Everything in this book has taken on a deeper meaning for me. The courage, energy, endurance, patience, and love from my wife Celest has been without limit. She is my life. My sons Roger and Scott have given me the gift of life, hope, and sense of the future every day. My mother Carol and my brother Dennis gave me their support and assurance. Through our shared tears as we sat around the family table, trying to make sense of this sudden and terrible news, I have found a new strength, a family strength that has saved my life. No matter how optimistic I may sound about families in the book you are about to read, I now know that I have underestimated the power of family love. If I were to write this book over again, I would talk even more than I have of the magic of the meaning of "us."

I owe much in the preparation of this manuscript to the theorists you will read about in this book and to the patients I studied, but I now know more than ever on a personal level the true meaning of the miracle of "us," the power of a family to love you to health and to help you make sense of your living and your mortality. As with all of my books and books to come, I will forever be indebted to my friend and agent, Susan Cohen, who always shows such personal and professional faith in my work. My editor, Loretta Barrett, has shared with me not only her skills but her feelings about her own family love. The president of Doubleday, Nancy Evans, has provided an atmosphere where I can feel comfortable to work as I heal.

As I feel my body return to health, I can feel my family within and around me always and everywhere, crowding out the disease with its power of healing. I regret the times I took "us" for granted. I never will again, and I hope this book will help you discover this same miracle.

Foreword

"Between experiencing cosmic joy and alleviating local pain, there is a path that each can follow. If it is a narrow path, it is at least wide enough to walk on."
HAROLD MOROWITZ

Every day, you make the most important choice of your life. Whether you are aware of it or not, everything you do, say, think, or feel reveals whether you choose to see your world in terms of "I, me, and mine," or "we, us, and ours." You choose between coping with life on an individual basis, reacting to the local laws of our immediate world, or interpreting your life experiences from the point of view of an ultimately connected human family and the broader laws of our ultimate connection with everyone and everything in the cosmos. This book teaches you and your family how to choose lasting family loving over the day-to-day struggle to survive as one person against the world.

You may decide to think and behave as if you are alone, trying to cope with a world that operates under the influence of the simple laws of separateness, competitiveness, and survival of the fittest. The main character in the movie *An Officer and a Gentleman* states, "You're alone. Once you get that straight, nothing else matters." His choice was to see himself as without family, disconnected, isolated, and ultimately a success or failure based purely on his own individual strength.

You may see yourself as exclusively affected by the cause-and-effect, see/touch world, governed only by concrete rules that leave each of us ultimately lonely victims in our attempts to get the best job, the most money, the biggest house, or the most security. You can choose to see yourself as a small reactive part of an automatic, arbitrary, insensitive, machinelike world and universe described several hundred years ago by the scientist Sir Isaac Newton. It was Newton who discovered the concept of gravity and the mathematical predications of our everyday living, and his mechanistic view of the world has been the dominant explanation for our daily living.

Newton explained that, like apples falling from a tree, we all independently react to mathematical laws of life's motion, that grind on without purpose and without regard for the human spirit or the strength of our collective humanness. Newton's world is the local world, the here and now of our experience without consideration of the possibility that the whole is not only much more than the sum of its parts, but that both parts and whole affect each other.

On the other hand, you may decide that life is much more than reacting alone to day-to-day events. You may choose to see yourself as more than a solo player in a type of life lottery of good and bad luck randomly dispersed by a Newtonian gearlike spinning of planetary roulette. You may decide that your world, the cosmos, is governed by forces we cannot always see or touch, by forces that go beyond our local experiences; that we are as much the tree as the apple; that apples grow not "on" but "with" their trees; and that we are nurturing and nurtured by our interrelatedness with every star and every soul in the cosmos.

You may decide that you have a potential to influence your world and those around you by thinking and behaving as if you are a part of one family developing together. You can choose to look for your life explanations not in the simple local laws of daily living, but to search for meaning with Albert Einstein and other modern physicists, who went beyond local explanations of life to search for the power of our relationship with the cosmos.

You can choose to believe, as Einstein proved, that we are each representations of the whole and that we each profoundly affect the whole. Einstein and scientists who followed him demonstrated that we contain the elements of the stars in our bones, that we are more energy than mass, more process than "stuff," and that we are all a part of, cared for by, and mutually influenced by all humankind now, before, and forever. The family view is the cosmic view that we are never alone.

I will show you that, just as the beauty and tranquillity of tropical islands owe their life to the rage and turbulence of volcanoes, the more severe your family problems, the more the potential for your development of a warm and enduring sense of family peace. You can convert the energy of family conflicts into powerful energy for family growth, but first you must decide on your point of view: family or self.

Perhaps you live alone and draw energy from occasional family visits, phone calls, the special memories unique to your family, and the comfort that your family is always there even if they are not physically with you. Perhaps you live as a tightly knit group of parents, children, and extended family, taking on the daily challenges of an increasingly complex and cruel world. Perhaps your family is struggling to cope with and help a chronically suffering family member. Perhaps you are a single parent making a family that sometimes seems too small and almost overwhelmed by an insensitive society that defines away what family really means by its overemphasis on the traditional view of a family as two problem-free adults and two perfect children. Perhaps you are living with persons that have seemed to become your family even without legal or blood relationship. Perhaps you have experienced abuse, manipulation, or have seen your own parents or other family members struggle with the most terrible of problems in their own life. No matter what form your version and experience of a family may take, there is something about your family, your being an "us" with people who will always be a part of you, that can carry you through life's most difficult moments and teach you how to experience life's most meaningful and enduring emotions. It's your chosen point of view, whether you think "family" or "self," not a head count, that makes a family a family.

When I started the Problems of Daily Living Clinic in the Department of Psychiatry at Sinai Hospital of Detroit in 1972,

I decided to study family system instead of individual dynamics. Like most of my colleagues, I had been trained to expect sickness in the family. I had been taught that the family was where an almost constant parental seduction and child rebellion took place, where symbolic sexual interactions and infantile competition over who would be allowed to love whom the most resulted in a lifetime of individual psychological upheaval, resolved only by the final independence of each family member from their smothering family ties.

My studies revealed that even the most disturbed families had powerful healing potential, enormous recuperative resources, and that, in spite of continuing social pressures against "us" and in favor of "me," the family continued to be the spiritual center for every one of my patients. I found that persons who enhanced and protected their dependence on family and saw events from the perspective of connection, rather than isolation, were healthier in all respects than those who spent their emotional energy "breaking away" to chase self-fulfillment.

The entire cycle of life is contained, experienced and explained within the family, and those persons who are able to stay family throughout their lives, to call one another, to remember one another, to gather at emergencies and remember the family at times of crises, and to extend their sense of family to their everyday life, were the healthiest and happiest persons I ever saw. Being family seemed to be causing psychological and physical hardiness, not pathology. It was not independence, but family dependence and the mutual personal responsibility viewpoint throughout life, that was the ultimate measure of wellness.

I noted in my clinical work that those persons who rebelled against their family and had lost the family point of view, who were, or felt, evicted, rejected, or blamed by their family, or felt that they had "outgrown" their need for family, tended to suffer more illness, anxiety, and depression than those persons who maintained the family view. I saw persons who held the family view heal faster after surgery than persons who saw themselves as alone. It was seeing oneself as "out" of the family that caused distress, not being immersed "in" the family view of things.

The major premise of this book is that the rediscovery of

the miracle of "us," of family power and a family way of understanding daily living, is the most important step in human development. The failure to make such a rediscovery will allow us all to continue down our solo paths to what we delude ourselves as being self-fulfillment while true "us" fulfillment is ignored.

I have chosen five families from my clinical work to serve as guides through an exploration of the family system. Each of these families came to me for help with a transitional life crisis. One family came because of problems in re-forming a family group after divorce. Another came because of trouble adjusting to the empty-nest syndrome as their children grew up. Another family came because of the failing health and impending death of a grandfather who had been the center of their family group. Another came because their daughter was seriously ill. Another came because the father had been killed.

The five families I have selected for this book are no different than your family. I did not select them because they are unique, but because they are not unique at all. I selected them because they were representative of the thousands of families that have been seen in my clinic over the years. I hope you will be able to see how each family struggled to keep their family choice alive and to find meaning in their times of crisis through their faith in their choice for the family way.

Each of these families are continuing to learn and implement what I call the "ten Rx's," ten factors that serve as prescriptions for healthy family living and learning the family way of understanding the world. These ten factors resulted in each of these family's endurance, growth, sense of unity, and mutual responsibility that survived the difficult challenges that all families will face.

Each of the ten Rx's of family life are related to the laws of the universe, the cosmic laws described by Einstein, and not to the limiting and mechanistic laws of Newton. All of these families maintained their family orientation to life through the most challenging of the local laws of living, the disease, death, and suffering that are the taxes for the gift of life.

As you read this book, think about your own family. Don't think about how it "ought to be" or how it compares with other families. Think instead of how your own family can be, and of the strengths that your family may have that have not yet been actualized. Look for the ten Rx's in your own family, no matter how impatient you may feel with your family at this time in your life. You will see that you have within your grasp a magical family healing power.

This book is the first family care book. Each of the twelve chapters contains specific steps you can take with your family to help you learn what the miracle of "us" is, and how that miracle will help you come to understand more about what your life means and what it means to be alive with everyone else. There are tests in each of the chapters to help you assess your family ability and to help you write your own prescription, your own Rx's, for happier and healthier family living and loving.

This is a parenting book only in the sense that parenting is familying, something that children and adults should be doing together, not to or for one another. It is more a how-to-see-it book than a how-to-do-it book, and it is more an "us" help book than a self-help book. This is a book for "us," for people who want to rediscover who they are, and who they can be, by re-discovering their family within them.

Within the small homeless family clustered against the cold inside a cardboard box and the family living in the utmost luxury, there is the common element of a sense of the power of "us." I hope the five families I will use for examples will help you find a wider and safer path to spiritual fulfillment and help you to learn how to walk alongside everyone in your family on that path, not just run as a gang of individuals along the precarious path to self-fulfillment. Perhaps, if the path we choose together is wide enough, clear enough, and safe enough, the entire human family may join us in the joy of this journey for joining.

CHAPTER ONE

Family Forever

"I really don't know where I'd be without my family. They are my life. I wish it didn't have to take a crisis to teach me that."

MS. BONNER

A FAMILY RESCUE

The little girl looked pale, weak, and frightened. She closed her eyes with each stroke of her mother's hand on her forehead. The family was gathered together for a meeting with the doctor. In spite of the most extreme medical efforts, a rare blood disease was taking the girl from her family.

"She just is not responding to the chemotherapy," said the doctor to the girl's parents, Mr. and Ms. Anders. His almost accusatory words betrayed his unconscious blaming of the patient for his own sense of helplessness and inability to rescue the four-year-old. "She's getting weaker and weaker, and the medicine we're using only seems to sap her energy. We just aren't sure how to proceed. You must prepare yourself for the worst."

I was called in as a consultant to sit in on this family meeting, to speak with the little girl about her disease, and to

1

help her accept what some of the doctors labeled as a "hopeless" situation. I was asked to help "the patient," as if it is ever possible to separate the hurting person from the hurting family.

"You both have to accept the reality that this girl is dying," said the child's doctor to the parents. "However painful it is for all of us to face, she just is not responding."

When it was my turn to talk, I asked the parents how they felt. They described their sense of despair and devastation.

Ms. Anders said, "We're losing her. I know it, I sense it. Don't you think she knows it too?" As if to rub away the sting of her words, the mother's hand stroked more rapidly on her daughter's forehead.

Mr. Anders cuddled both of his young sons closer to him and said, "We're losing her. We're just watching her die, and we can't do a thing about it. I just wish we could help her take her medicine, get inside her to help her to use her medicine to make her well. She's just drifting away from us."

"Why don't you?" I asked. "Why don't you join together around her when she gets her treatments? Why don't all of you go right in to the treatment room with her and join hands with her while she gets her medicine? Why don't you give her a family energy boost right while she takes her medicine? Don't just sit outside in the waiting room. She's no more separate from you now than ever. You're all together. Get in there with her."

"Do you really think that would work?" asked Mr. Anders. "It sounds a little strange. Do you really think there is hope? I mean, you just don't see that done in the hospital. No one but the medical staff is allowed in the chemotherapy room. I don't even know if they would let us in the treatment room."

"In the absence of certainty, all we ever really have is hope," I answered. "And I think your doctor will agree that there is nothing in medicine that is absolutely certain. I know you can help your daughter get more from her treatments and even more from all of you. And I'll tell you something else. She can help all of you. You all look like you're running out of energy, and you need that energy as much as she does. This isn't something that is happening to your daughter. It's happening to your family. Don't allow this disease to separate you. Don't let your daughter's illness take your family strength away. You can help her maximize her own healing powers to fight this disease. There's a healthy and an unhealthy way to be sick, and the healthy way is to try to use every ounce of your family's healing strength. I'll see to it that you get into the treatment room with her if you are willing to try this approach."

The next week, the chemotherapy for their daughter's blood disease continued. This time, the daughter was not wheeled alone into a cold and distant treatment room to be administered to by strangers. This time, her entire family went with her. The family joined hands as the medicine was given. They closed their eyes, prayed, and tried to send their family member all of the loving energy they could muster. They could feel their daughter's energy coming back to all of them, and they could feel their collective energy flowing to their daughter.

The parents cried, the little brothers peeked to see what was going on, and the little girl squeezed her parents' hands tightly as she anticipated the usual burning as the medicine entered her veins. But this time, there was less burning. This time, there was less fear. This time, the lie of certainty was replaced by renewed hope for healing. The burning from the chemical seemed to be overwhelmed, dissipated, and dispersed by the collective strength of the family.

As you will read throughout this book, the little girl continues to struggle with her illness, but the family is with her, energizing her and being energized by her. She is doing much better, and all medical tests indicate that less medication can now be used with more positive effect. The family had come to the rescue by reversing the direction of family alienation that too often accompanies catastrophic illness and other life crises. The family had regained their "us sight," their view of connection and unity at this time of crisis.

HOW WE FAIL OUR FAMILIES

One of the biggest mistakes made by modern medicine is to separate the patient from his or her family. One of the biggest mistakes made by our society is the accelerating isolation of each of us from our own primary family systems. We walk, drive, jog, work, eat, pray, sleep, and too often die alone. At the very time we need each other most, we find ourselves detached, isolated from the most powerful source of healing and happiness in the universe. The family system is our strength, yet we too often make the wrong choice. We try to "go it alone."

Families aren't failing; we are failing the family. We have been taught that independence is strength, that families are temporary places for preparation for real living, and that maybe once in a while we can get together as a family "just for old times' sake," for "special occasions," or for that one last visit before a relative dies. We have not learned the skill of family maintenance as we grow through life, of re-familying when the family is torn apart, or learned how to make our family life the number one priority in our interpretation of our world.

When our own family seems to fall short of the illusion of "the perfect family model," we tend to accept defeat, assuming that our family is "dysfunctional" or no longer of significant value to us. We assume that we must face the world on our own, find other sources of support, and that "the family just isn't the same anymore." We have not learned what I will attempt to teach throughout this book: that being a part of any family can be the most important privilege of being human, the most healing experience of being alive, and the source of a lifelong and evolving understanding of what it really means to live. But first, we must learn to raise our families instead of our children.

THE WISDOM OF "WE"

Our most basic instinct is not for survival, but for family. Most of us would give our own life for the survival of a family member, yet we lead our daily life too often as if we take our family for granted or consider our family as if it has outlived its usefulness. Child neglect, abuse, exploitation, and most family problems are in fact family neglect, the lack of the establishment and maintenance of family aptitude and attitude.

As I write this paragraph, the two most powerful nations in the world have combined forces to save two whales trapped in thick ice near Alaska. Russia and the United States have worked for days to save the lives of these wonderful animals. Mammals are trying to save mammals, just two whales and hundreds of humans struggling together to save the connection between all of us.

Why are these two whales so important? In the overall view of life, they are a part of us, a part of our family. There is something within us that is telling us that only "we," not "me," will be able to help our world survive. Your own family is a microcosm, your everyday chance to experience your fundamental humanness, your inner sense of the power of "us."

We must work now to save our emotional environment, our families.

FAMILIES FOR LIFE

The next time you see a family, any group of beings "doing" life together, remember that such a group is the basic building block of our world, the place where the miracle of "us" takes place. Any researcher who has spent time actually living among animal families in the wild is comfortable imparting what we arrogantly call "human" feelings to what we refer to as "lower" species. The trapped whales have been described by the most cynical news reporters as "anticipating" their freedom, "trusting" in their rescuers, and even acting as if "they're packing their bags to head south once we free them."

Researchers have seen the actual joy of family life in the animals they study, the evolution of the principle of "survival of the family-est." Cynthia Moss has studied elephant families for more than sixteen years. Her experience with these large and long-lasting families (elephants can live sixty years) taught her that the elaborate family greetings she observed among the elephants signaled that the elephants were ". . . experiencing joy . . . It may not be similar to human joy or even comparable, but it is elephantine joy . . ."[1]

Dian Fosse, in her studies of mountain gorillas, often commented on the closeness of their family units and the apparent

1. Moss, Cynthia. *Elephant Memories: Thirteen Years in the Life of an Elephant Family* (New York: Morrow, 1988).

expression of caring and celebration within the gorilla family. She noted such behaviors as cuddling and comforting of the young and the mutual protective interaction among the family members.[2] Ms. Fosse herself felt intimately connected to the gorillas, spending her life in an attempt to protect them.

The work of these scientists, and others, supports the universality of the family drive, nature's mandate of the family unit as the socially manifested genetic glue of our existence. Families are the one dimension of the human experience that can be seen in a cluster of cells on a slide under a microscope, a bouquet of plants huddled together in the sun, a herd of wild beasts roaming the plains, or three whales clinging together in a fight for life.

Even though the so-called "sex drive" or the "survival drive" have been given the status of the most basic of all instincts, these drives pale in comparison to the drive for family, for grouping together to live, to love, and to become. The drive for "collecting," for "grouping," is more influential than the drive for procreation. Perhaps God sees to it that we will reproduce, but leaves it to us to solve the mystery of how to evolve together for spiritual growth. God provides for the start, but the journey is ours.

THE "CONNECTION" RESPONSE

One of my patients was flying between two islands in Hawaii when the unthinkable happened. More than half of the top of their airplane blew off. Had their seat belts not been fastened, most of the passengers would have been sucked out of the plane and fallen twenty thousand feet to smash against the ocean. As the wind rushed in, there was no word from the cockpit. Was it possible that the cockpit itself was torn away? Was the plane going down?

At this dreadful moment, several passengers risked their own lives to reach out to grab the hand of a flight attendant being blown from the plane. With the woman strapped in a

2. Fosse, Dian. "More Years with Mountain Gorillas," *National Geographic* (1971) Vol. 140, pp. 574–85.

seat, some of the passengers cheered the rescue and began to sing together. They sang every hymn they could think of. Another passenger began to write a note to his family, reminding them of his love for them.

My patient was alone on this flight. She was sitting in a seat next to a person she had not spoken to, when something inside her made her reach out and take the stranger's hand. He in turn took the hand of the person across the aisle. They began to sing hymns, even as the wind prevented them from hearing one another. Within this threatened airplane, people were "refamilying," acknowledging their infinite connection with one another.

At times of crisis, the first instinct is not exclusively for individual survival. The first instinct is for the establishment of an "us," a cluster or group of caring people trying to be together more intensely than ever. Only when that initial sense of connection is replaced by individuality and selfishness does senseless panic, helplessness, and "mob" replace the sense of "us."

When the flight had safely landed, the passengers did not want to separate. My patient recalled, "We just wanted to laugh together, to cry together, just sort of stand around and be together. We would never really be apart again. We were forced together in something only we knew, that only we experienced. We would share that crisis and our survival together forever."

Think of your own life experiences and times when you were alone and without friends or relatives. Think of times when you were under stress and among strangers. You will note that within you is a need to bond with those around you, to talk, to sing, to joke, or to share mutual complaints. When we hurt, we tend to "herd." We want to tell someone else and have them know what we feel and hear how they feel. The "cluster response" is a drive for "herding," for grouping together, for becoming a system, for tapping into a universal energy shared in communal ownership by each of us and all of us.

We distort our natural drive for family when we mistake the intensity of protecting turf or artificial boundaries, nationalism, and ethnocentrism for the true meaning of being a family. We think that defending a boundary, denying someone else their space, blind loyalty to a collective cause, or striking out against a perceived threat to "our" territory is protecting ourselves and our family. We are wrong. Every division we create between any of us eventually impacts on all of us.

Familying is much more than living under the same roof or blind clinging to our narrow view of what constitutes our blood-related group. Familying is "us-ing," learning to re-awaken the archetypical "we" of the human community. Familying is a chosen point of view of how we will lead our life and give meaning to all that happens in our life. Our own family is where we experience and learn the family view, and our loving of everyone in the world; a place that allows us to be connected to millions of persons by loving intensely with several family members around us.

THE IMPORTANCE OF NOT BEING NUMBER ONE

We live in a society that worships the individual. We spend a great deal of our time trying to avoid family formation. We keep our distance, avoid getting too close. We talk about finding a lover, a "one and only," or "the" one perfect lover intended for us, but we talk very little about intense and continued family effort, about finding and keeping family love for a lifetime. We have mistaken our innate need for everyone for an intense erotic need for someone, as if having one person completely and fully will somehow compensate for our conscious or unconscious need for family.

Being number one is seen as much more desirable than being one of the group. The family is now seen as a form of cultural "foreplay," preparing the individual for intercourse with the real world. The family is viewed as little more than a temporary training ground, to be used and even abused until the nest becomes empty or a parent "gives away" their child to someone else in a marital ceremony that speaks of forsaking all others while the respective families of the new marital partners sit divided on opposite sides of the church and temple.

"When does life begin?" goes the old joke. "When the dog dies and the kids move out" is the punch line. Independence is seen as much more desirable than dependence, and staying too much a part of the primary family is viewed as immaturity, even failure to be "psychologically healthy."

THE DEATH OF THE OEDIPUS FAMILY

Much of psychotherapy conceptualizes the family as the primary source of neuroticism or mental illness. With absolutely no evidence to support it, the psychological assumption continues to be that every man has sexual desires for his mother and every woman has sexual desires for her father. Only narcissistic freedom from primal striving for Mommy and Daddy, from the necessary but potentially evil family system always lurking to trap us in a perpetual eroticized childhood, is viewed as true psychological health. Therapists too often urge us to work to be free of our family, not to learn to maintain our interdependence with them as a means of moving toward a universal family of human beings.

Psychotherapists and psychologists are not typically trained in the workings of the family as a system. Instead, the family is broken down into "dyads," pairs of two that are forever sentenced to a primal dance of love and hate that is culminated only in the lifelong guilt that inevitably follows the loss of or separation from a parent or a child. Therapists often advise "freeing ourselves" from the influence of a parent, as if breaking the ties that bind us to our family is healthier than strengthening them.

Psychotherapy has failed to recognize the "whole," the entire family system, the line of ducklings swimming with their parents in order to learn to cope with the threats to their lives. Most psychotherapy is a narcissistic exercise for both therapist and patient, engaging in an "as if" game of hours of talking about a symbolic, even delusional, family, without the real family present.

Therapy time is spent in discussions about the father or mother or siblings of the patient, but such talk is historical, metaphorical, and filtered through the murk of psychoanalytic misassumptions, distorted patient recollections, and therapist selective listening. Very seldom does psychotherapy include real life discussions with the family all seated together on the couch. Even when family therapy is attempted, there is often an "identified patient" who is the focus of the process.

Psychologist Bernie Zilbergeld writes, "Many therapy students take courses on family therapy—where they learn about families in trouble, how they got that way, and what to do with them—but few take general courses on families: their history, functions, and strengths as well as their weakness."[3] Psychological theories have profound influence on our society, and the view of the family in these theories takes little account of the strength, love, and caring of the family. The therapist comes to see only the potential harm done by the intense intimacy of a family system gone wrong. It may be better to select a therapist based not on her or his training but on the answer to the question "Do you get along well with your family?"

THE INFLUENCE OF THE "MESS" MEDIA

Movies and television programs tend to portray families as either delightfully benign "Ozzie and Harrietisms" or centers for continual family conflict. Most families in movies, plays, novels, or soap operas are either a mess, and the source of endless conflict and tragedy, or a mirage of perfectly peaceful and delightfully benign daily living. Somewhere in between is where the most of our families really live.

Few of the heros and heroines of our media are family people. The "real" movie hero has long ago left his parents. He saves the town or the ranch, is tempted to settle down, but is naturally driven by the need for freedom and rides off on a horse, for whom he shows more concern than for the people around him. A potential love looks wistfully at his back as the almost always male hero rides into the sunset.

The message is clear. Women can stay on the ranch with the family, where the skies are not cloudy all day, while the almost always male hero goes out to start and fight new wars.

3. Zilbergeld, Bernie. *The Shrinking of America: Myths of Psychological Change* (Boston: Little, Brown and Co., 1983).

The family means female submission to what must be done to keep the family going, and freedom from family means adventure and hero status for the male, who may drop in on one of his several families once in a while.

The television family situation comedy is often about a father's futile and comic attempt to keep some semblance of order and control over "his" household while he tries to carry on in his "real" work, his career. The wife is seen as guardian of the family, a stable and mature officer in charge of supplies, cleaning, and caring. If she has a career, she is expected to add this work to her obligations without requiring changes toward a new system of sharing family tasks. The mother may wink in toleration of the well-intended bungling of the father who has more important things to do than really get involved with the day-to-day family life. The inference is that families are "women's things" to be "settled for" once we have established ourselves at the "really important things" of our individual living. We much more often struggle to make time for our family because we are so busy at work than we try to find some time for working because we are so involved with the joy of our family life.

THE FEAR OF FAMILY LOVE

In a society that sexualizes everything from socks to cars, the family has not escaped the sexual immaturity and insecurity of our culture. Fears of incest and sexual abuse are common, and stories about these emotionally disabling events are frequently on television and in newspapers. As a result, we have come to fear the intense feelings we have for our family members.

"I would like to hug my daughter every day," said one father. "I don't, though. I'm afraid, I guess. I'm afraid of what people might think. She's a young woman now. She's fifteen." At the very time when our young people need holding and hugging the most, we withdraw our contact for fear of the corrupted psychological and now cultural view of the potentially abusive family. When our young people need us most, we are busy trying to redo our own youth and answer our own questions about career, relationships, and the meaning of life.

Many families are being frightened away from intimacy by the publicized pathology within some families.

The family is generally not a sick place. The family is just suffering from severe neglect. The family can be the healthiest of places, and families are where we learn what "us" means. Instead of fearing our intense family feelings, we can learn to recognize them for what they are, the internal signals of a strong need to stay connected with our family and with everyone forever.

While pain and sorrow and terrible tragedies can take place in the family, this does not mean that even the hurting family does also not offer some solace, safety, and security to its members. Even when a family member is scared by the sickness of another family member, they are also influenced by some of the good of that same family member. We must not allow our family view to be abandoned because of the pathology and pain of a part of our family life.

The crises in families are usually related to failure to identify and offer help to one member in that family who is disturbed, who is hurt, confused, and as a result, can hurt others by their inability to learn what "us" means. To look at sickness in the family and say that the family itself is sick is to forget the miracles of the family that you saw in the Anders family, to miss out on the most powerful healing agent in our society.

FIVE FAMILIES FOREVER

Meet five families whom you will follow throughout this book as they show aspects of healthy family living. I selected these five families from my clinical work in the Problems of Daily Living Clinic at Sinai Hospital of Detroit. I selected each of them from families who came to me for help over the years.

You have already met the Anders family. They came because they were seeking help in coping with their sick daughter. The Bonner family came to me because they were attempting to cope with the sudden loss of the father. The Steiner family came because of the parents' sense of loss and emptiness as their children moved out of the home. The Johnson family came because of problems dealing with a son with severe learning disabilities and difficulty in forming a new family from two families left over after a divorce. The Muller family came because Ms. Muller's father was dying, and his presence in the home seemed to be causing a severe strain on all family resources. Many other families sought my help during this time, but these five provided a broad representation of transitional life problems that could be used to learn about the power of the family to overcome life challenges.

These families did not come for "family therapy." They each came for help with a specific problem that all of us might face in some form. As you will see throughout this book, all of the families became stronger as they rediscovered their "usness," the power of their family system to energize and cause growth even at times of suffering.

I selected these particular five families because they represent somewhat of a cross section of family types, including the more traditional Mom-and-Dad-and-two-kids type family, the single-parent family, and the extended family. Certainly there are many other types of family systems, families who will never come to a clinic for help, and families struggling together as they huddle against the cold in cardboard houses or subway stations, or line up to receive just one cup of rice for the day's meal. I write about the five families in my clinic only as a point of departure. I am sure you will be able to find some features of your own family life and see some lessons that you can take into your own family circle.

These families were not extraordinary, at least not any more extraordinary than your own family. They were doing their best to deal with the challenges to the evolution of the human spirit, the disease, sudden loss, disabilities, and infinite pressures that all families face at one time or another.

I have followed each of these families for nine years. I still see them periodically for follow-up appointments, and a member of each of these families has a special message for you at the end of this book. I have seen these families experience birth, death, conflict, joy, change, and challenge. I have seen them go through the same daily life challenges that your family encounters, and as a result, each of these families has found a transcendent energy of our collective human spirit. I hope this book will help your family find this spirit in your own life

together. To help you get to know these five families, here are
the five families as they experienced Thanksgiving Day in 1980.

FIVE FAMILIES ON THANKSGIVING DAY

Do you remember your own Thanksgiving dinner with your
family when you were a child? Do you remember the sweet
odor of roasting turkey that was so strong you could actually
taste the turkey itself? Did the odor of that turkey or other
traditional family meal seem to touch that part of the nostrils
that lead directly to the family memory centers of your brain?
Do you still get strong family memories when you sense particular odors or experience various events of a holiday time? Try
to think back to your own early Thanksgivings as you visit with
each of the five families on their own Thanksgiving days.

THE ANDERS FAMILY

First, meet the Anderses. This was the family who rallied
around their ill daughter. The father is an accountant with a
successful financial firm that required, or at least the father felt
it required, that he be absent from the home for more than fifty
hours per week. The mother seemed to be in charge of almost
everything else. Her favorite saying was pasted on the refrigerator. "If wives had wives, things would be easier for wives."

You have already read about the three children in the Anders family, including the two little boys, ages eight and ten,
who snuck a peek during the family treatment experience, and
a brave little girl of age four. The little girl was born with her
severe blood disorder, and it was accompanied by severe
breathing problems. From time to time there was a family
emergency requiring a mad dash to the hospital, or at least a
frantic late-night call to the doctor.

No one knew the stress this family experienced. From the
outside, it looked as if this was a "typical American family,"
free of problems and enjoying a comfortable middle-class life. If
I have learned anything from my years of clinical work, it is
that there is no such thing as a problem-free family. We are

taught to present a good family image, but behind that image, all of us struggle with the transitional life crises that are our shared human burden. If you are jealous of one of your friends' families, it is only because you don't know their true daily family experience.

The little Anders girl's physical problem is a constant emotional and financial drain on this family, but she is also a source of inspiration through her courage and refusal to let her physical problem limit her. Recently, the daughter has become a catalyst for family energy rather than a burden draining the family energy. The family's success at joining together for the daughter's medical treatment made this Thanksgiving dinner a very special occasion.

The Anderses prepared to eat their Thanksgiving dinner, brought to the table with great dignity by the wife's mother, who was now turkey consultant, by way of long-established seniority. Tradition dictated that Grandma would now ask Grandpa to carve the turkey. He would refuse at first and suggest that Mr. Anders do the job. Mr. Anders knew better. It was not his time to be the carver yet. This carving assignment ritual was only one of many such rituals that were long established in the Anders household. The Anderses will serve throughout this book as an example of the magic of family healing, not only for the daughter, but for the whole family group that managed to learn about family living through their struggle for their daughter's life.

THE BONNER FAMILY

Next, meet the Bonners. Ms. Bonner had been widowed for three years in 1980. Her husband had been a fire fighter and was killed when the roof of a burning house fell on him. All of his fellow fire fighters had survived the fire, but Ms. Bonner had received a terrible phone call late one evening that meant she would be raising her two children alone. All families will receive some form of a call of loss, a terrible instantaneous blow to the family heart, and the Bonner family was trying to regain its breath.

The Bonner daughter was twelve and the son was fifteen. The son had not gotten over the death of his father, and was

angry much of the time. The daughter seemed to be withdrawn
and seldom spoke of her feelings about the loss of her father. As
the Bonners prepared to eat their Thanksgiving dinner, Ms.
Bonner struggled to hold back her tears. This was a much
smaller turkey than at prior Thanksgivings, just enough for the
three of them. She bought it frozen like a rock and, because she
had to work overtime as a teller at the bank, she had not allowed sufficient time to defrost the turkey.

Ms. Bonner's son was upset with her, but the two of them
always seemed to be upset with each other lately. In fact, there
seemed to be something seriously wrong when the two of them
were not struggling with one another over something. Their
constant conflict was their way of being together, the way they
were "familying" at this time of change. In fact, every family I
have worked with seemed to show a strong correlation between
intensity of conflict and amount of love.

Ms. Bonner had spent most of Wednesday night trying to
beat the solid turkey into submission. She had laughed and
cried as she hit the turkey, thinking how silly it was that she
felt each blow was a blow against the injustice she had just
endured. She was too tired now to really want to eat a big
dinner, but she felt she must carry on for the children. After all,
they needed each other now more than ever. The Bonner family
will serve as an example of the survival of the family through
times of loss.

THE STEINER FAMILY

Now, meet the Steiners. Mr. Steiner and Ms. Steiner are both
executives and work at least fifty hours a week. They both often
bring their work home. They have three children, their first two
from the prior marriage of Ms. Steiner. Two of the children are
now married with their own families, and their third child is
now away at college in London. They will eat their Thanksgiving dinner in a restaurant, and then hurry home to await phone
calls from their children.

Mr. and Ms. Steiner had both worked throughout the raising of their children. "I really think we missed something," Ms.
Steiner reports. "I wouldn't have wanted to give up my career,

but I just feel like I never really was with my children enough. A black woman today has to carry a real burden."

Mr. Steiner agrees, but adds, "In this day and age, and being black, we have both had to work. Our kids wouldn't be in the position they are today if we had not both worked. There's no sense looking back on that now. Black people have to work at least twice as hard just to stay even. When she was alone with her two kids after her first marriage, she might forget how bad that was. Her husband just up and left. At least she's been able to give them a lot more than she would have ever expected."

Mr. and Ms. Steiner are trying to maintain a long-distance family. They feel the tug of multiple obligations and their childrens' increasing responsibilities and distractions, but they have managed to keep their sense of family alive. The calls came in as expected. No one said anything about their distance from one another, about the fact that they would each cry after hanging up the phone, but everyone knew there would be tears. They still missed each other and they still needed each other, if only sometimes to hear one voice that represented their history of life together. The Steiner family will serve as an example of the permanence of the family even as its members grow and become independent.

THE JOHNSON FAMILY

Next, meet the Johnsons. This was their first Thanksgiving dinner as a new family. Mr. and Ms. Johnson had each been married once before and were now attempting to combine their two children each from their prior marriages into a family with a new set of parents. Mr. Johnson had custody of a son, eight, and a daughter, ten, from his first marriage. His former wife had legal custody of his other daughter, fifteen, who was spending this Thanksgiving with her mother. Ms. Johnson had two children from her prior marriage. One son was six and the other ten. Her first husband shared custody with her, and they alternated holidays with their children.

Mr. and Ms. Johnson noticed that this was the quietest Thanksgiving they could remember. Everyone seemed to be watching everyone else. Ms. Johnson's oldest son said, "Dad would always let us have a taste of wine before we ate the turkey." Ms. Johnson answered, "Well, we are starting some new traditions of our own now."

Her son looked down and said just loudly enough for everyone to hear, "I don't want new traditions. I want Dad." Mr. Johnson wasn't sure what to say, so he just smiled at his wife. She smiled back and said, "It's just going to take some time." They began to eat their first holiday dinner together as Mr. Johnson secretly pushed his almost-empty wine glass toward the hand of his stepson. "Just one sip for old times' sake?" asked the stepfather. His stepson sipped tentatively as he smiled over the top of the glass.

This same stepson struggled with a severe learning disability that resulted in continued pressure on the Johnson family to deal with school problems and their son's frustrations, exacerbated now by the formation of a new family system. The Johnson family will serve as an example throughout this book of the need for constant reconstitution and strengthening through change required of all families.

THE MULLER FAMILY

The fifth family, the Mullers, were busy cleaning up the traditional Thanksgiving gravy spill. It seemed that someone always had the job of spilling something at Thanksgiving, especially since the kids were promoted to the big table from their corner-card-table status. This cleanup was more awkward than others, because Grandpa had done the spilling. He was very old and very sick. Sometimes, he behaved and talked like a child. Instead of laughing at the spill as they had always done before, the family seemed embarrassed and confused.

This was the one tablecloth used for holidays. Failed attempts at destaining the cloth left a road-map history of holiday spills. As Mr. and Ms. Muller worked to clean the spill, Ms. Muller hoped that this stain would be the worst. She hoped that they would always remember Grandpa's stain and see it every holiday. She wondered if he would be at the next family holiday dinner.

The Mullers children were a boy, twelve, and a girl, sixteen. They were able keepers of the traditional and universal brother/sister hatred. This was their own private hatred, and interference with it led to their immediate unification for its protection. If any outsider said or did anything to either of them, the brother/sister hatred changed instantly to blind loyalty and protective rage on behalf of the welfare of their sibling.

Ms. Muller's father had failed badly this past year. He was unable to control his bowels now, and the family took turns cleaning him. "Look. We all catered to our babies. They soiled themselves more often than Grandpa. Nobody objected," said Ms. Muller. "Grandpa has a lot more seniority than a newborn baby. He's earned our help and love. We sure don't like doing it, but we will continue to do it. He's ours and we're his."

The family began to eat. The granddaughter cut Grandpa's turkey as the grandson automatically moved Grandpa's water glass at just the right moment to save it from Grandpa's shaking hand. Even as they silently anticipated Grandpa's leaving, they all felt closer together than ever. This Muller family will serve as an example throughout this book of the resilience of the family even when the bitter realities of aging, illness, and a society unprepared to meet the needs of an aging population impact upon daily family life.

FIVE FAMILY FEATURES

As I pointed out earlier, families are much more than a pack of coresidents going through life together. My clinical work indicates that families have five features unique to them as a group —features which, if extended to the world at large, can save us all from our own self-destructive, shortsighted self-enhancement. Check these features against your own family, and you will see just how powerful the family system really is.

1. FAMILY FIRST AND FOREVER

Families are dedicated to the primacy of the family point of view. While they nurture and encourage the development of each member, their primary goal is to make sure everyone is given a chance to live and love happily within a group system. If you are in a family, you are supposed to give in, to sacrifice, to sometimes put other family members' needs before your own. Even the Anderses' daughter was expected to give to the family even as she needed to take from the family strength to survive.

We talk more about supportive families than supporting the family. Our society is interfering with the family-first feature. Scheduling demands make family Thanksgiving dinners as described earlier more and more difficult. There just doesn't seem to be enough time to get together. We may promise over and over to visit and to spend more time together, yet we seem to find less and less time to do so. We confront difficult decisions between career and family, and when families do get together, the result is a rapid attempt to solve problems rather than enjoy each other. Should I skip this meeting just to go home to eat with the family? What really comes first?

I warn you that if your family does not come first, your family will not last. We are in familial bankruptcy and have fallen into the hands of receivers such as schools, businesses, recreational pursuits, and numerous institutional demands. The issue is not one of setting priorities; the issue is one of making difficult choices for the family. There can only be one number one. Is it your family?

"You'd think that, with kids as young as four, eight and ten, they wouldn't be busy all the time," said Ms. Anders. "Somehow, there's always something to do, someone to pick up, some school thing to go to, some appointment, something that makes the day sail by without our finding time just to sit. We have to go to the doctor's with our daughter almost three times a week, and if one other kid gets sick, we are really in a mess. We have to intentionally make the time, just say that's it. We come first. It isn't easy to just skip something for our family, but we've learned to do it. We take the time to sit down and do nothing instead of always trying to solve some problem."

2. TOLERANCE OF FAILURES

The family forgives. It is the one place in our life where we can receive unconditional acceptance for just being us. All families have their real characters, those family members who have idiosyncracies that can stretch patience to its limit. Even at the most difficult times, the family is the place where we can be forgiven, accepted, and given a fresh start. Families accept even the loud aunt, the crazy uncle, the selfish brother, the arrogant sister, and all family members, just because they are family members.

"I can't stand my new stepdaughter. She whines all the time. Her clothes are ugly, her hair's too straight, and she complains that it's too hot, or that it's too cold. She can make a disaster out of a dream," reported Mr. Johnson. "But when her teacher caught her cheating on a test and embarrassed her in front of the class, we all just hugged her. No one said, 'I told you so.' We knew how upset she was and we're getting used to her showing her pain about the divorce in funny ways. We talked a lot about it, but I don't think she ever thought we didn't love her or that our love for her was affected one bit by what happened. She's a pain in the neck, but she's our pain in the neck."

3. FAMILY-BODY BUILDING

When a family forms, something biological happens beyond the biology of conception and birth. Families are not just social institutions but physiological processes shared by all of the family members. Families are as much physical body as social body.

Something biochemical happens when families live together over time. Each family member's physiology begins to mirror the physiology of other family members, much as menstrual periods tend to follow similar patterns when a group of women live together for a long period of time. Being family means becoming more and more connected with one another on every level of our humanness.

A classical study by John Bowlby described the importance of attachment and the three stages of emotional adjustment to disruption in attachment.[4] Anxiety, disbelief, and a searching for the lost person or persons to whom an attachment was formed is first, followed by depression, despair, and a gen-

4. Bowlby, John. *Attachment and Loss,* Vols. 1–3 (New York: Basic Books, 1969).

eral surrender and withdrawal. Finally, usually because some form of attachment is finally reestablished, there is recovery. Is our society so characterized by anxiety and depression because we have failed to maintain our family bonds? Is our health and immunity disrupted by our failure to maintain our family unity?

"We already feel Grandpa's beginning to leave us," said Ms. Muller. "We began to feel frightened, and we even tried to pretend he was not going to die soon. Then, we all started to feel sad. I even started to ask myself about the meaning of life, why we should go through all of this anyway. I think we are finally seeing that the more we stay a family, the more we stay together, the more we see that Grandpa will always be a part of us, the more we can accept what is happening. It all wouldn't be so sad if it all has not been so very, very happy. He's a part of us, an irreplaceable part. When he's gone, he will be here with us just like a phantom limb on the family tree."

4. THE FAMILY SOUL CENTER

The family system is uniquely designed to help solve the problems of daily living. Within the family system are historical precedent, multiple generational resources, a collectively developed and pretested appraisal system, and the ability to rally around a family member in distress or having trouble coping. The family is a soul center, the apex of spiritual energy and the place we learn what everything means and how to make everything meaningful.

I have always been suspicious of the person who tells me that they do not bring their work problems home with them. I wonder where their work problems go when they go home. The family is the place where problems must be taken for appraisal, for solving, for discussing, for learning about why problems happen and what can be done to prevent them.

"I would have never made it," reported Ms. Bonner. "When my husband was killed, everything seemed to go blank. Everyone wanted something from me. What about insurance? Where are his records? What about taxes? Have you checked with Social Security? I was drowning. My family saved me. My uncle, my aunt, my mother, my own sister all helped. I just don't think one person can lead a life. It takes a whole gang of people just to make it. It takes a gang who is on your side. It takes your family."

5. FAMILY SENSATIONS

Someway, somehow, families develop a special sense for and of one another. They can feel one another, sense when something is going wrong, read family members for clues that no one else could see, and even detect early signs of illness before any medical test would be effective.

Mr. Steiner reported, "I can tell when she's upset. It doesn't matter what she says and it's not just how she looks. I've learned to sense how she is, and she can sense how I am. It's beyond words. I can even do it at a distance. I can sense when things might not be going well for her at work, and she can do the same."

There is such a thing as "FEP," or family extrasensory perception. It isn't mystical or parapsychological at all. Such perception is simply the result of loving sympathy, of caring deeply and broadly enough about others to take the time and make the effort to really see them, to feel "us," to understand them, to touch and be touched by them.

The family features of special bonding, family priority, tolerance of family members for one another, strong and unique family problem-solving capacity, and a type of family extrasensory perception that grows from the deep and demonstrative love of all family members for one another, are characteristics of family life that extend from the Anders family's attempts to combine individual energies to save their young daughter to our consuming interest in saving whales tapped hundreds of miles away. This book is about ways to maximize each of these five family features for the health of each family member, how to keep the family view of living alive no matter what the challenge, and ultimately for the enhancement of the health and well-being of all of us.

CHAPTER TWO

A Portrait of Your Changing Family

"Mystics and schizophrenics find themselves in the same ocean, but the mystics swim whereas the schizophrenics drown."

R. D. LAING

TOGETHER IN SICKNESS AND IN HEALTH

Divorce, mental illness, child abuse, alcoholism, workaholism, child neglect, teenage suicide, family violence, drug abuse, adultery—each of these problems dominate our media as signs of the faltering family. There are, however, millions of families who are flourishing, who are loving and living together in happiness and joy, even as they struggle with the complexities of life in today's world. In fact, some of the strongest and happiest families I have ever seen have been families that have been made stronger than their pain.

If we define a healthy, happy family as one with no problems, then there are no happy families in the world. It is the purpose of families to help their members learn and love

24

through the sometimes bitter cruelty of life. Families are for teaching us that we can survive our local pain through our sense of our cosmic connection with one another and the fact that we are never as alone as we may be frightened into thinking we are.

"It's remarkable, when I think about it," said Mr. Muller. "So often, we've been trying to get things done. I mean, it's like getting things done is more important than doing things and experiencing them. I really wonder if there would be any need for families if everything was already done, if kids were born already educated, graduated, and employed, and all parents started out in their last house instead of their starter house."

Mr. Muller is describing the erroneous assumption that the goal of a "good" family is to be problem-free. The purpose of family life, all life, is the development and evolution of the collective human spirit. If that task were "done," we wouldn't be here to continue our evolutionary work. Families exist because we are always in process, always growing, and always becoming.

REAL FAMILIES AND SHARED PROBLEMS

Our health care system has always focused on sickness and pathology. We try to learn from sickness and suffering about how to be healthy and hardy. As a result of our pathology focus, we have very few models of the extremely healthy person other than someone who shows no obvious symptoms of illness. This "health as the absence of illness" view has been applied to family living.

We have tended either to create an unrealistic, idealistic model of the family from which we all fall short, or to talk about the terrible examples of family love gone wrong, the murders, abuse, and desertions that fill our newspapers and television screens. We have failed to identify universal principles of healthy and hardy family living that carry most families through the worst of times and give each family member their most loving times.

Every family I have interviewed has told me that the most

stressful times in their family life are still remembered as some
of the most loving times. "Now that the kids are gone," said
Ms. Steiner, "We talk about the old times. And we noticed that
we talk a lot about times when crises struck, as if those were the
times when our family ties tightened up and bound us more
tightly together."

The family can be a greenhouse for the growth of pathology. The mental disease of schizophrenia is related in part to
failure on the part of the individual to function successfully and
rationally in social interactions. Psychiatrist R. D. Laing reports that studies of schizophrenics indicate that mental illness
is the result of a network of extremely disturbed patterns of
communication within the primary family.[1]

Genetics and biochemical factors play a major role in
mental illness, in determining vulnerability to whatever toxic
family factors may exist in a person's life. For reasons we do
not yet understand, some of us are born vulnerable to the distortion and corruption of family power. It is not in the family
itself, but in a complex interaction between predisposition to
mental illness and the family system, that the problems lie. We
should be busy looking for clues as to why some families can
help the most troubled person become healthier, rather than
focusing on why some families seem to make some people sick.

Instead of saying, "See what damage a dysfunctional family can do," we should be asking, "How could this family do so
well under such trying circumstances?" or "How could he or
she have come out so well from such a seemingly bad family
experience?" We must learn to look for explanations of health
rather than excuses for illness.

WARNING! NORMALCY CAN BE DANGEROUS TO YOUR HEALTH

Our society now views the concept of "normal" as equivalent to
"majority." A daily life-style of stress, hurrying, lack of exercise, unhealthy diet, alienation from one another, from life and

1. Laing, R. D. *The Politics of Experience* (New York: Ballantine,
1978), p. 1.

spiritual purpose, of being blind to meaning and our place in the cosmos and our shared responsibility with all persons, is becoming the majority life orientation, the "neurotic normal."

Allowing life to lead us rather than making the choices necessary to lead a healthy, family-oriented life, is becoming the common adjustment, the "normal" way to be. In our society, normalcy is the description for the striving and successful individualist. We continue to applaud aggression, success, self-sufficiency, and the autonomous person, labeling such an orientation normal without concern for whether or not this behavior is healthy. We have deluded ourselves that we are "setting priorities," but in fact we have made a choice against the family and for the "successful individual" as the "normal" way to be.

Too many people seem too tuned out or turned off to real meaning in their lives, recognizing sometimes far too late that they have mistaken an intense, active, self-success-oriented life of acquiring more and more goods, status, and "things," for the life they really wanted, a life of meaning, of loving, of family, and of a daily sense of "us." In effect, normalcy is becoming increasingly the number one risk to our health.

Dr. Laing writes, "A child born today in the United Kingdom stands a ten times greater chance of being admitted to a mental hospital than to a university . . . This can be taken as an indication that we are driving our children mad more effectively than we are genuinely educating them."[2] Families are where a genuine education can take place, an education for loving, meaningful, mutual responsibility between parent and child, and hopefully the lesson of shared responsibility of all and for all of us.

Physicist Fritjof Capra writes, "The symptoms of cultural madness are all-pervasive throughout our academic, corporate, and political institutions, with the nuclear arms race perhaps its most psychotic manifestation."[3] The family that realizes its potential to help its members break free of this cultural madness, of the "normalcy" of disease in living, is the single greatest hope we have for a cure for our societal self-sickness. If a family seems distressed, perhaps it is only because it is trying to

2. *Ibid.*, p. 104.
3. Capra, Fritjof. *The Turning Point* (New York: Bantam Books, 1982).

cope within itself with the insane world within which it must try to survive. Alone, we are ultimately powerless. As family, our power is limitless.

When you attempt to implement any of the ten Rx's I will be presenting in your own family, you will first have to take the risk of making your family life "abnormal." You will have to help your family learn to live in, but not with, the cultural flow of stress, alienation, and the general disregard for loving that has come to be accepted as "normal." You will have to make an active, committed choice to making your family "abnormally healthy" while most families around you will continue to live "with" the cultural trend to a madness of self-centeredness, stress, and a minimum of active caring and time to be together.

THE EVOLUTION OF THE CARING FAMILY

No matter what you may hear, the family is not, in fact, gradually outliving its usefulness and is not in a state of decay and demise. Our evolution as human beings has made the family even more important today than it was thousands of years ago.

When humans evolved to the point of being able to stand, this evolutionary change allowed freedom for our front limbs to hold weapons, tools, and hopefully each other, to manipulate more efficiently than any other species. Unfortunately, the ability to manipulate has resulted in our manipulation of one another, in a distant and mechanical interaction between people.

This change to being upright also resulted in severe pressure on our hind limbs, our legs. The back pain and varicose veins that are so frequent today are reminders of the price we pay for standing on our own two feet.[4] The pressure on our lower back and pelvis also resulted in compensatory changes in the human pelvis. It grew thicker, resulting in the shrinking of the birth canal.

As our brains and heads grew larger and larger, over thousands of years, there was less and less room for babies to make

4. Ornstein, Robert, and David Sobel. *The Healing Brain* (New York: Simon & Schuster, 1987).

their way through the birth canal. Nature compensated by having our young born very, very early in their development. In effect, we are all born as quite unfinished products into family finishing centers. The evolving family is nature's way of adjusting to us, of providing us with social support as we attempt to stand on our own. Without the family around us for support, we will all remain unsure and unsteady on our own two feet.

This "unfinished product" characteristic of human beings results in two major factors that make the family the most important social and biological institution in the world. First, unlike the brains of other animals, the human brain is not even near completion at birth. Most of our brain development takes place after birth and is strongly influenced by the people we live with and the environment we live in. The family is our brain baker, the place for a leavening of our spirit, and the creator of how we will see our world, how we will interpret it, and what we will choose to do about it.

Second, because the human newborn is so incomplete and so helpless, the infant will always require at least one consistent caretaker for his or her survival, and perhaps two consistent caretakers to thrive. I suggest that two caretakers may be needed because, contrary to cultural myths and baby-food commercials, taking care of a human baby is the most time-consuming, complex, fatiguing, sometimes angering and overwhelming task imaginable. Being placed in charge of God's unfinished product and assuming the sacred and awesome responsibility of providing a place for spiritual development is a task that requires more human, physical, and emotional energy than any other human or animal activity. Babies emphasize in the most sobering and awesome way that we ourselves are far from "finished" in our own development, that we still need raising, and that family is a necessity.

To work on the ever-unfinished human product, and considering that this unfinished product is in turn being taken care of by persons who themselves are products still in process and constantly entering new stages of their own life, somebody has to, at least temporarily, "drop out" of some of their own social activities and make radical personal sacrifices to do the primary personal human product finishing. In the process, someone has to make profound changes in their own life development.

There is no such thing as "parenting." When our society

made the word "parent" into a verb, it suggested that parents do something to children. In fact, there is only "familying," parents and children sharing development together and raising each other. The debt of personal sacrifice from our family development requires that we be family forever, that we care for our family throughout our life.

The extent of this "family debt" is becoming more obvious as our population ages. Parenting our older parents is a difficult task that few of us are prepared for, and our social institutions offer little help. We are dangerously close to "parent abuse," to a societal neglect of our extended family system. As a result, we attempt to drug our older people, isolate them, and work hard to deny the inevitable fact that we too are heading where they are.

Mothers have done most of the child rearing in our human world. Even in other species, however, the mother has trouble taking care of her own sustenance while she cares for, feeds, teaches, and protects her young. Teamwork is needed, someone to go out, get food and bring it back. Someone is needed to help repair the nest, to protect the young and to make sure the mother survives in the process.

Families are nature's teamwork for the continuance of our human development, and even though humans have an infinitely wider set of options than other animals as to who hunts, who feeds, who cares for, who works, or what combination of these factors is established, the family is needed not only for the continued development of our unfinished young, but also for the perpetual maturing of all of us.

Children are the catalyst for the further growth of all of us, the constant reminder that we are all evolving spirits visiting earth through the vehicle of the family system. Children are not, however, the reason for families. We are all the reason for families. We must learn to raise "us," not "them."

REPAYING THE FAMILY DEBT

The sacrifice and complexity of caring for our unfinished young demands much from the primary caretakers. Our society at the same time expects us to put our children first and put ourselves first, to be a successful parent and successful worker, a lover, and a learner in our own right. This is an impossible societal requirement unless our children, unless all of us, are indebted to the family system forever. Families must teach that we are all forever caretakers of each other, and that the family is the best place for this mutual caring to take place, over time and across generations. The family debt is never paid off, and we are required to pay forever, for we can only borrow from our family.

Our society incorrectly assumes that whatever debt we owe for the time, effort, and giving of our parents will be paid back through our caring for our own children. This is an overly restrictive view of the family system. It is just not enough to offer a family IOU to our primary family to be paid back in some symbolic currency by caring for our future family. The family debt is to the whole family system, to future children and to past parents, grandparents, and everyone in the family.

Parenting our own parents may be the one silent challenge that we will all struggle with alone until we realize that this debt does not just come due when our parents are ill or dependent. We have a major deficit within us, a deficit of caring enough about our own parents, of giving back for all the taking we did and all that our parents gave.

Our guilt regarding our parents is like the pain within an injured body, and it signals that something is strained and needs attention. Therapists should be less busy trying to get rid of parental guilt and much busier guiding us to a concept of "good guilt," of mutual and perpetually interactive parenting throughout our life. When parents themselves experience guilt at not having done enough, such guilt may come not from what they have failed to do for their children, but how little they continue to do with their own parents.

The debt I am talking about is a debt of mutual responsibility for everyone in the family and a responsibility to develop as a family for the overall human family. We have many parenting classes and programs, but I have never heard of a "childing" class, of instruction in developing with our parents and our whole family. Our own development is greatly enhanced when we understand this obligation and pay this family debt, for we invest in our future, and the future of everyone.

We cannot expect of ourselves the automatic ability to care

for our parents only when our parents reach their final years. The debt can not be paid back in one lump sum, when our parents are thrust upon us as dependent, helpless persons, deserted and shown disrespect by the very society they helped to build. Our children must be taught from the very beginning that they too are "parenting" even while they are "childing," learning to give care as well as receive it. Our children are not our future; we all are.

One reason that so many people I have seen in my clinical work have a sense of life's futility, even life's absurdity, is that they failed to develop a true sense of family. They have failed to understand the nature of the debt they owe, feeling strangely guilty and unfulfilled. They have often mistaken wealth, goods, activity, several friends, and intense life experiences for a true meaning of "us" in process through ageless parenting. When I work with single persons without children, they sometimes sound like the following patient:

"I'm on my own. I mean, I really don't have a family anymore. I'm not going to have children, so I really don't have anyone to care for but myself. Even when I get together with my mother, we just either tolerate each other or fight. We really can't relate on any comfortable or significant level."

This woman, president of her own corporation, has mistaken tradition or social expectation for the true meaning of family. We all have family, no matter what we say or how we behave. Some of us have just not developed our family aptitude, our capacity to care for those who cared for us, once our total physical dependence on their caring is over.

Caretaking is not maintenance, it is the prolonged showing of respect and the continued effort to share with someone else in their struggle to live well and live healthily. Paying back our family debt is directly related to our development of equanimity, of being able to show an unqualified love for those we come from and have been through life with. In a society that stresses achievement and self-fulfillment, we would all be better off "loving" our families and only "liking" our work. Far too many people have reversed these two priorities.

LOSING OUR PARENTS BEFORE THEY DIE

We lose our parents long before they die. We separate from them, and we may become angry and impatient with them. We feel overwhelmed by other obligations, and our parents' needs seem to be just another load on our already overburdened back. We may come to see caring for our parents as a form of punishment rather than opportunity.

I hope this book will draw your attention back to your family debt, a debt not of obligation but of opportunity—the opportunity to learn and love for life with those who gave you life and lived with you, as you learned how to maintain a family view of living. Mr. Steiner's statement reveals this viewpoint:

Mr. Steiner said, "I can't stand my mother. She's opinionated, self-righteous, and demanding. She's terribly immature. But then, just when I'm ready to disown her, I remember that I had exactly the same characteristics as a child, just like all children. She wasn't a great mother. I don't even know what that would be. But she's my mother, and I know that even though I struggle, I feel a lot better when I work hard to love her, to care for her, to stay her son. When I do that, I seem to be better with my own kids, and I feel free from the constant guilt and needless aggravation of petty battles, power struggles, and some unconscious need to think of my mother as not worthy or deserving of my caring anymore so I can get on with my life. If she had done that to me, I wouldn't be what I am."

AN INSTANT FAMILY PORTRAIT

I have already defined the family as two or more people attempting to develop together in every area of life and doing so for a lifetime. At work, we develop with our colleagues only in a few areas, and the same is true at school and in all of our other social institutions. But in a family, every member shares responsibility for the development of every other member in every single aspect of living. It is this all-inclusiveness and permanence that makes the family system unique.

Families go far beyond blood relationships. Families are as

much a choice we make as they are a genetic assignment. To be the biological father or mother of a child requires only one single act. To be a family member requires an endless array of complex behaviors, personal growth, sacrifices, and commit- ments to the welfare of others.

List the names of your family. Who are your parents, brothers, sisters, husband, wife? This is not a geographical re- port of who lives with whom. Families' ties are not physical but metaphysical, transcending time and place. As you will learn later, the memories of deceased family members are always a part of the family system, so I hope you will include their names on your list if they seem to you to be a part of your psychological family portrait.

Who do you choose to make a part of your family image, the imprint that will forever be with you? Do you add in-laws? Remember, this is the most important choice you will ever make, the choice of the system within which you will lead your life, remember in your life, and be remembered forever.

Many families find this family-identification assignment difficult. It requires much thought, decisions about mutual re- sponsibilities, tolerance, acceptance, patience, and, most of all, the willingness to make a major decision that you as an individ- ual will be returning to "familying," and making this familying a part of your everyday life, to make payments toward your lifetime family mortgage, the basic principal of which will never be erased. I am asking you to reidentify those persons in your life who mean everything to you and with whom you share a spiritual indebtedness.

Ms. Johnson reported, "I was amazed when I did the fam- ily-identification assignment. I thought I was just going to have trouble with putting together our two new families, now that we are remarried. I never realized until I sat down to write the list that I had to confront whether or not my former husband would be on the list. I hated to put him there, but somehow I had to. He's a part of me and guess he will always be a part of me. I put my grandpa on the list, and he's been dead fifteen years. My grandma's still living, so she was easy to put on the list. So I ended up with the six of us, my husband and our four children, plus my ex-husband, my grandma and grandpa, Mom and Dad, and, for some reason, my Uncle Bill. He just seems to be a part of my family to me. I didn't put my new in-laws on the list, but I added my former mother-in-law. Would you believe it? I just got close to her, and how she feels, what she thinks, and what she means to me, is still a big part of my life."

You will learn, as did Ms. Johnson, that your family list is not static. It is a dynamic group image that you carry with you whether or not you pay attention to that image. You will add and subtract names as life goes on, not because of death or geography, but because your choice of whom you will allow to matter, whom you will share developmental responsibility with, and whom you will experience life with in everyday living and in your dreams, thoughts, and images will change. Your needs and goals will change, and your psychological family portrait will change right along with you.

In fact, the list does not really change at all. Your awareness of or focus on specific aspects of the evolving and ever-growing family is what does the changing. We are all very narrow in our view of "our family," often seeing only the here and now, those persons we deal with every day, or the immediate memories of those persons in our family that seem to be affecting us at a given time in our lives.

Your family identification list is really less a portrait than a snapshot, a quickly developed photograph in time, your camera turned inward. The lens only catches a part of the whole image, aimed by your needs and feelings at a certain time or passage in your family life.

None of us are alone or without family. Some of us are just blind to the family ghosts all around us, the spirits of our infinite link to every person with whom we choose to take on the total challenges of spiritual development.

There is only one type of family; the extended family. If the family is not extended, if it is limited, it is limited because we fail to focus on our family as integral to our lifelong development, seeing it only as a part or phase of our life rather than our whole life itself.

Your family-identification assignment, your psychological family portrait, is an imprint, an indelible image within your very soul. You can try to deny it, even try to hide and compensate for this image, but you are forever a part of that image, and that image is always a part of you.

"I was stunned when you asked me," said Mr. Anders. "I had a complete psychological family portrait of my wife, my three children, my parents and grandparents and my in-laws. But someone was missing. Me! I realized that I was so busy trying to make a family, take care of my sick daughter, and support a family that I wasn't seeing myself as a part of the family itself."

Don't forget to put yourself in the psychological family portrait. Don't allow anger, pain, resentment, or guilt to block out the image of family members who should be in the picture with you. All development is not positive and happy, and the true definition of family is "ultimately together," sharing all of life's joys and agonies.

The picture of the family is one of inclusion and caring, of awareness that we can quit our jobs, drop out of school, and move to another city, but our family will always be with us. The family, after all, is us.

CHAPTER THREE

Family Ritual:
The Cure for Family
Jet Lag

"With my husband gone, the little things we all do together mean even more. The hugs good night and being sure we all get in bed for the night makes us all feel safe. There's something sacred about it all, and before I used to think it was just bedtime routine."
MS. BONNER

A FAMILY TEST

At the core of every family I have seen in my clinic are ten components, ten characteristics that allow the family to grow together forever. The more aware the family is of these components, the more the family puts these ten factors into daily practice, the more enduring their family orientation to life and the healthier their family system. Here is a test for you and your family to take regarding what I call the "ten Rx's," ten prescriptions for maximizing the power of your family.

Each of the following items is based on the family view of life and the concept of lifelong mutual caring for the family system. If possible, have all of your family members take this test along with you, and then discuss the scores and the items as I will describe them. The chapters listed beneath each question will describe each family factor in detail. Remember, this is not a self-test, but an "us" test, and all of your scores on the tests in this book are only clues, indicators of areas that you can begin to strengthen your own family.

The Family Test
The Ten Rx's of Family Life

Assign a score of from zero to ten on each of the following ten items. Use the following scale to help you decide on your score. I have made the test brief so that you can call family members who no longer live with you and take the test together over the phone or take the test by correspondence.

0	1	2	3	4	5	6	7	8	9	10

ALMOST NEVER   SELDOM   SOMETIMES   A LOT   ALMOST ALWAYS

RITUAL
Chapter Three

1. ———— Does your family eat at least two meals together, with every family member present, every day? If some of your family no longer lives with you, do they attend holiday meals with regularity and without encouragement or pressure?

RHYTHM
Chapter Four

2. ———— Does there seem to be an even rhythm to your family's daily life, with things going smoothly, on schedule, and without panic and pressure? If your family is separated, do you all regularly interact at predictable times and with ease and smoothness?

REASON
Chapter Five

3. ———— Is everyone in the family rational and logical and does everyone try to be fair when conflicts occur? Do fam-

ily members assume equal responsibility for reducing family blowups and arguments?

REMEMBRANCE

Chapter Six

4. ——— Does everyone in the family show respect for the history of the family, for the older people in the family, and for the idea that family seniority has its privilege?

RESILIENCE

Chapter Seven

5. ——— When society seems to cause the family problems, or when things seem to get out of hand and go against the family, does every member of the family attempt to rally around the family and help get things back on an even keel?

RESONANCE

Chapter Eight

6. ——— Does everyone in the family seem to contribute a positive energy to the family? Is there an absence of family members who seem to use up the family energy?

RECONCILIATION

Chapter Nine

7. ——— Does everyone in the family take the initiative when it is necessary to "make up" after a family conflict? Is there an absence of grudge holding?

REVERENCE

Chapter Ten

8. ——— Does the family share a common belief system that unites all family members in some form, a spiritual system for explaining what life means?

REVIVAL
Chapter Eleven

9. ——— Can the family quickly get its energy back after major family setbacks such as severe arguments, death, major illness, divorce, or the leaving of a family member?

REUNION
Chapter Twelve

10. ——— No matter what happens to the family and within the family, does the family always seem to get back together and move on? Does the family seem to be getting to be a happier and happier place to live?

——— TOTAL SCORE

Now, add up your total score. Remember, on all of the tests in this book, just taking the time to take each test has strengthened your family orientation, so your score will always be changing and improving. Don't use the tests to label or classify your family. Use the tests in this book as a way to strengthen your own and your family members' sense of what family really means. To help you select starting points in your efforts to develop your family power, a score under 90 indicates that your family should look carefully at the item or items on the family test where points were lost.

ROUTINE IS NOT RITUAL

FAMILY RITUAL: The family is able to develop its own sense of permanence and continuity by taking the time to fully attend to the simplest of family activities; by going beyond just "getting things done" to enjoying the sharing of doing things together; by acting with a sense of the honor conferred by the basic activities of family life, which are not chores or obligations, but opportunities to "be" together.

This chapter focuses on the first family Rx, the concept of ritual as basic to healthy family living. The diminishing of family ritual today is disrupting the time frame in which family members live together, resulting in each family member living in their own unique time zone. Unless we are able to reset our family clock and synchronize our family watches, family members will continue to move further and further apart. They will succumb to a chronic jet lag that leaves little energy or vigor for the enjoyment of daily life.

The day-to-day routine of family life has come to replace true family ritual. Family routine refers to an individually experienced set of obligatory procedures, a "going through the motions" in order to get things done, so that each family member can focus on what are assumed to be more important things later. The batter in a baseball game may go through a routine of warm-up and maneuvers in the batter's circle and in the batter's box, but such routine itself is only a superstitious and isolated dance in preparation for the real game.

Routine is born of superstition and selfishness, and is intended for individual preparation and self-efficiency. Ritual is born of a celebration of family togetherness, through attention to and enjoyment of shared life activities. Routine is designed for getting "on" with life, while family ritual is intended for getting "with" life and for the solidification of the family bond. Routines are done quickly, automatically, and without thought. Rituals are done slowly, intensely, and contemplatively.

Family ritual is making the effort to impart dignity and symbolism to the simple acts of eating together, going to bed, and rising in the morning. Family ritual is attempting to "share" rather than just "do" what life requires. Family ritual is not just saying grace at the dinner table; it is making the effort to help all of the family experience grace together, through the simple act of attending fully to being together for a meal, slowing down the process of preparing to eat and eating, and using what must be done as a means of giving meaning, significance, and context to what we are doing. When a family keeps their rituals alive, they do not "do lunch" or "have dinner." Instead, the family shares a meal.

Family rituals represent what pediatrician and researcher Thomas Boyce and his colleagues refer to as "the belief or perception that certain central, valued elements of life experience are stable and enduring."[1] Dr. Boyce collected data on

1. Boyce, W. T., C. Schaefer, and C. Uitti. "Permanence and Change: Psychosocial Factors in the Outcome of Adolescent Pregnancy," *Social Science and Medicine* (1985) Vol. 21, p. 1281.

families who employed rituals in their daily life, and found these families to be healthier and happier than those families who lacked such rituals.

The Family Ritual Test

Before reading further about the importance of family ritual, take this test for the presence of ritual in your own family life. Most of the families I have worked with use the individual test items below as "family assignments" for developing more ritual in their own life. Score your family from zero to ten on each test item, using the following scale:

0	1	2	3	4	5	6	7	8	9	10
ALMOST NEVER		SELDOM		SOMETIMES		A LOT		ALMOST ALWAYS		

1. ———— Does your family move as one unit when it walks as a group, instead of walking like a long parade with one or two marchers dragging far behind and a family drum major or majorette in front?

2. ———— Are mealtimes almost always at the same time in your house?

3. ———— Does everyone eat meals together as a family?

4. ———— Is there a ceremony before each meal, such as a moment of silence, a prayer, or some form of acknowledgment of what is special about this family being together?

5. ———— Is most of the family "stuff" kept in a special place? Are gift wrappings, holiday decorations, family candles, and the things which the family values kept in a family place in the house that no one bothers?

6. ———— Does everyone in the family go to bed at

about the same time and say good night to everyone else when they turn in?

7. —— Does everyone in the family get up at the same time in the morning and say good morning to everyone else?

8. —— Does your family have an unwritten seating chart that is honored by family members when sitting at the table?

9. —— Does your family have a cooperative and mutually honored system for loaning clothing and other goods, a code of family conduct regarding who can use what, when, how, and for how long?

10. —— Are there "family phrases" that are said to one another "just for luck," such as "Be careful," or "Don't forget to call" or "Do you have your comb?"

—— TOTAL RITUAL SCORE

The higher your score, the more ritualized your family life, and the more likely it is that your own family is behaving in keeping with one of the basic principles of healthy family living. The arbitrary "cutoff" score is 90, meaning that a score under 90 should be a signal that your family would benefit from attention to ritual in your life.

FIVE FAMILY RITUALS

The five families you are reading about in this book had each their own rituals. Here is one example from each family as described by one of their members:

"We always have to hug good-bye," said the eight-year-old brother in the Anders family. "Even if I just go outside to play, my mom makes me hug her. Maybe it's because my sister is so sick and we all worry about her, so we have to hug. I just got used to it, so I say 'Hug' while I'm getting my coat on so she's ready when I need her."

"You never, but never, in our house, go to bed without saying good night," said the teenage son in the Bonner family. "Now that Dad is gone, we still do it. There's just three of us now, but I think we all three say good night to Dad still."

"We have never ended a phone conversation without saying the words 'Take care of yourself, now, OK?'" said Mr. Steiner. "We never answer, but if one of the two people talking forgets to say it, somebody will speak up. The older the kids get, the more they are on their own, the more this little message seems to mean to all of us."

"It's hard to get your patterns going with two new families together," said Mr. Johnson, the father in the stepfamily. "But already, it's an unspoken rule. You never leave the house without telling everyone where you are going. I know it sounds dumb, and sometimes it takes a long time to get out, but you have to get the message to everybody that you're going to the store."

"We have our seats in the house," said the sixteen-year-old daughter in the Muller family. "I mean, in every room, there's a place for everybody. You can sit in someone's seat anytime, but when the family is together in that room, you have to go to your spot. It's going to be sad when Grandpa's spot is empty."

These five examples of ritual illustrate the sameness and the predictable patterning of family ritual that, in spite of the scoffing and joking of some family members about these rituals, become ingrained in the way in which the family interacts day-to-day. As you will see, family health and the health of every family member ultimately depend on the viability of these rituals.

The Anderses problems with their sick daughter, the Bonners' struggle with the sudden death of the young father, the Steiners coping with their newly empty nest, the Johnsons efforts to make one new family of two prior families, and the Mullers preparation for the loss of the grandfather are all problems that each of our families have in some form, and each of these families has turned to ritual as an important strategy for keeping the family growing and alive through these difficulties.

PERMANENT LIFE ASSURANCE

Dr. Boyce refers to the concept of family ritual as "a sense of permanence," implying that ritual is the tangible acting out of the shared belief that even ordinary family activities are meaningful and significant in their own right, a form of family life assurance that the family is reliable and steady. Dr. Boyce and his colleagues suggest that true meaning in daily living is only accomplished and maintained by family ritual, and that such concrete ways of acknowledging life's meaning are a prerequisite for the physical and emotional health of every family member.

Aaron Antonovsky's book *Unraveling the Mystery of Health* emphasizes the impact on our general health of a sense that daily life can be structured, predictable, and explicable. He writes of what he calls "a sense of coherence," the sense that daily living activities are worth investing in, paying attention to, and significant in the overall scheme of things.[2] I suggest that the family system is the place where such a consistent sense of coherence, of structure, of control and predictability, begins.

"Just when everything seems to be falling apart, we sit down together for our Saturday popcorn snack," said Ms. Muller. "It's funny how the house can be a mess, everybody can be arguing, and then we pop the popcorn and sit down together for a snack. It seems to give a sense of control back to us and gives the feeling that we are running our own life instead of life running us." Ms. Muller, whose father is seriously ill and requires hours of care daily, is describing the "coherence" of family life, the family glue that ritual provides for holding the family together under the strain of constant change.

"We all get very, very quiet when we sit down to dinner," said Ms. Johnson. "Even when our children come to visit, we always get very quiet. No one ever said we should do that, but it is a ritual for us. It's a way of saying we love and value each other even without words. No one eats until it is completely

2. Antonovsky, Aaron. *Unraveling the Mystery of Health: How People Manage Stress and Stay Well* (San Francisco: Jossey-Bass Publishers, 1987).

quiet. We are even uncomfortable at other people's houses when they are so noisy in preparing for dinner."

Ms. Johnson is describing her family's ritual, the symbolic act of using the mealtime as the quiet time. This is something the whole family can count on, every time, as a sign that the family system is still intact, that family means something, and that there is at least something in this changing world that can be relied upon. The quiet meal reminds the family that they are in charge.

PSEUDOFAMILIES AND PSEUDORITUALS

"We're bad, man," said the young gang member. He couldn't have been more than twelve years old, but he had a knife in his pocket, a studded leather jacket, and a large scar running down his left cheek. "We're blood, you know. We're together, man. If somebody does one of us, he does all of us, man." He seemed to use the word "man" as a challenge from his own insecurity.

It is a mistake to assume that these or other gang members come from homes without families or always from homes with dysfunctional families. Many of the gang members I have interviewed had, at least on the surface, an intact family system of mother, father, and siblings. While many gang members were from financially deprived homes without a parent or with a financially and emotionally overwhelmed single parent, others lived in at least adequate financial situations with a stable family system.

The common denominator driving the gang members to seek out the pseudofamilies was that their own families did not include the ten Rx's, the factors of healthy family living described in this book. There was almost never a family ritual system in the home, and the gang's own rituals became substitutes, filling, at least temporarily, the individual gang member's needs for predictability and control. The young people had clustered together for safety, for some sense of ritual, significance, pattern, predictability, order, and meaning in a life full of terror, helplessness, and lack of meaning.

In prisons, pseudofamilies form among the inmates. Criminals form "families" within which a "code among criminals" and crude honor among thieves is maintained. These pseudofamilies are all based on fear and anger, fake families of rebellion against a world that seems to be made up of real families that exclude or ignore them.

There is a dangerous counterfamily movement in the world, a movement of terrorism and threat centered on pseudofamilies competing with one another for territory, for recognition, status, or power. The decline of stable-family-system rituals, based on good, on trust, on love, and on the enhancement of everyone, is being compensated for by the emergence of the pseudofamily ritual of violence and false unity imposed by panic to survive.

Perhaps gangs and peer groups gain such control over, and seem to demand such precocity from, our teenagers because of the decline in basic family-system reliability, the absence of the consistent rituals that symbolize sameness and sanity in a world that doesn't seem to hold still long enough to understand. What the other kids say and do can become much more obvious and easy to copy than what a father or mother "thinks" is right while at the same time the family so seldom "shows" and gives repeated credence to these beliefs through shared rituals with their children. Family ritual is the bringing to life of the family words about what the family stands for, and without these rituals at home, peer groups can provide at least the illusion of meaning.

Maybe we are mistaking adolescent rebelliousness for our own unconscious exclusion and neglect of our developing young people. If we don't have time to do things with them, to ritualize their daily life with us, they will find others who will. Drug use, alcoholism, and the sometimes general disregard for the value of life shown by the senseless risks our young people occasionally take may be a symptom of lack of the consistency of ritual I have been describing. All of adolescence in the United States may be seen as a mass cultural ritual evolving to fill the void of intimate family rituals.

If we truly want to confront the crime, drug, and sexual promiscuity problems of our time, we must start with a focus on the eroding family system, not just in the ghettos of our land, but everywhere where people are failing to attend to the ritual of shared life activities, the safety and comfort of knowing that things will get done, that they will get done together, and that those things that are worth getting done are worth doing together.

HEALTHY RITUAL OR SICKENING ROUTINE?

E. W. Jensen states, "Observable, repetitive behaviors which involve two or more family members and which occur with predictable regularity in the day-to-day and week-to-week life of the family are conducive to child health."[3] Studies of children's patterns of colds and sore throats indicate that the single most predictive factor in such illness is the presence or absence of family ritual. There is something intrinsically healthy in patterns, in predictability, something that may even help our immune system pattern itself for better defense of our wellness. It's as if the family develops its own ceremonies in celebration of the family system, a family shamanism of regular family tribal rites left over from our ancestry.

When families begin to lose their rituals and are unable to establish replacement rituals for aging and changing families, the family and its members become lost, trying to establish rituals in other areas of their life. The family member may become a ritualistic worker, lover, drinker, or recreator, trying, usually in vain, to find something in their life that can replace the family ritual. Like the baseball batter I mentioned above, who does the same things every time he steps to the plate, a family member may mistake superstitious gyrations and compulsive repetitions for significant, meaningful ritual that celebrates the wonder of sharing life processes together.

"I used to go out jogging," reported Ms. Bonner. "I would run at 5 P.M. every day. It became an addiction. I would get angry if anything got in the way of running. It wasn't the exercise, it was my ritual that was messed up when someone asked me to do something during 'my time.' Then I realized that I was getting further and further from my family, just running

3. Jensen, E. W. "The Families Routine Inventory," *Social Science and Medicine* (1983) Vol. 7, pp. 210–11.

away from them. We weren't eating together anyway, so I started running at dinnertime. Then everybody else in the family started to do their own thing, and we stopped doing our thing, almost anything, together. Once we got back to family dinners and family walks, I noticed that I began to run only three times a week."

I wonder if the thousands of people running around in circles, doing their exercise repetitions, doing aerobic tribal dancing, are not seeking as much from the ritual of this activity as they are from the exercise. I wonder if sweating, running, or exercising with a group of strangers is a form of replacement for more basic family ritual. After all, these people could sweat, jog, and bounce alone at home, but this does not seem to offer the support they need, the group ritual that keeps an exercise program going. I have learned from hundreds of families that ritual within the family is one of the most important aspects of sound human development, physically, mentally, emotionally, and spiritually, and if we don't get our ritualism at home, we will probably find it somewhere else.

There seems to be an ebbing and flowing of a family tide, a family biorhythm that must be acknowledged through our family rituals if we are to discover the power of the family. Crisis, sickness, and loss are a natural part of this family tide, and especially when crisis strikes, the enduring family ritual becomes even more important, a way of getting family members back into the family flow.

OUT-OF-FAMILY EXPERIENCES AND THE RE-EMBRACEMENT RITUAL

Ms. Johnson said, "My son was terribly, terribly disturbed. I took him to every doctor I could find. We were told that our marriage, our family, myself, my then-husband were causing his problems. Then a doctor said he was 'EI,' I mean, emotionally disturbed. They put him in the hospital. Everything seemed to fall apart. He was away from us, and we felt relieved for a while because he wasn't disrupting things. Then, we all felt disrupted. He was supposed to be with us, a part of us. His therapy was taking him away from us. That's why we came to you for family help. We didn't know how to get him back into our family again, how we could get together again. We seemed to need the disruption he provided somehow. It had become a way of life for us."

When a family member becomes disturbed, physically or mentally ill, there is no substitute for good and holistic medical treatment. But such treatment is never enough. Medications, staying in a hospital, visits to doctors and clinics, all disrupt family and life ritual. In fact, being hospitalized is a cultural rite in itself whereby the "hospitalized" must surrender prior family rituals in favor of the "hospital routine," typically useless and superstitious acts of wearing open-backed robes and eating and sleeping in the most unhealthy of patterns. At a time when we require our patterned rituals the most, we are required to give them up for new ones not related to the family system.

Problems are family soul food that help families grow. Problems and setbacks are the stimuli around which new rituals are formed. If one of your major family problems has been solved, hurry up and find another one! If you don't, life may create one for you.

Whenever the family is disrupted by illness or pain that takes a family member away from the system, a family re-embracement ritual is necessary. There must be a consistent way of allowing the family to "re-collect," to get the family herd rounded up again and to gather and group together in health following a disruption.

One example of a family member leaving the family group is mental illness. Writing about the serious mental illness of schizophrenia, Gregory Bateson writes that the patient has ". . . embarked upon a voyage of discovery which is only completed by his return to the normal world, to which he comes back with insights different from those of the inhabitants who never embarked on such a voyage."[4] Bateson is describing the journey from family that some family members must take, and the positive perspective of such a journey that can allow the family to learn and grow together even at times of crisis.

Families must be able to ritualize the return of the chal-

4. As quoted by Fritjof Capra in *The Turning Point* (New York: Bantam Books, 1982), p. 383.

lenged and distanced family traveler, or that traveler will never feel safely returned. The family must be able to reestablish for itself and for its challenged member a sense of control and meaning in all that has happened.

THE FAMILY RE-EMBRACEMENT RITUAL

Whenever a family member is hurt or ill, whenever a family member becomes emotionally distraught or experiences serious illness or other life setback, they become separated from the family system. Their own problems are so severe that they seem for a time to be gone, departed for their own private journey that can teach them even as it stresses them. They become focused away from family, in toward their own issues. The family member returns from such quests a different person, with different feelings and perceptions of the world that can help the family grow only if all of the other family members can come to understand some of these experiences.

Like a traveler returned from a long and arduous voyage, the returning family member can help the family grow by bringing new and challenging experiences back into the family system. But to do so, the family requires a return to family ritual to allow a smooth reentry. Sometimes, the family must learn to establish new rituals by taking time every day to sit as a group to discuss the conflicts encountered by the returning family member.

The son or daughter who returns from college, duty in the armed forces, a failed marriage, career problems, or from any transitional life problem requires a reentry family ritual. Time is needed for all family members to be together to talk with and share feelings with the family member, who also must hear about the family system that he or she has missed. The family should not try to "carry on as if nothing happened." Instead, the family should share an acknowledgment of what happened and the impact of the family member's problems on the whole family.

The returning family member must be guided home, returned to the system with sensitivity and caring ritual, not just with maintenance routines, overcompensation, or tentativeness. Every time a family member is hurt or stressed or leaves the family system, a re-embracement ritual must take place that acknowledges that this one family member's "vision quest," however problematic, may have been undertaken on the part of the family. The absent family member may have gone in search of something the family needed to learn. Repeated meetings, to share with the returning member, not only solidify that member's place within the family but help the family grow, change, and learn from the individual problems of one of its members.

Repeated sitting together, holding together, talking over what happened and what lessons and experiences and feelings the hurt member may have had are all aspects of a re-embracement ritual. Just taking time to be with the returning member, without inquisition and pressure, can be a form of the re-embracement ritual; but too often the family tries to deny the crisis, carrying on as if nothing significant, nothing remarkable, human and spiritual, has taken place.

The key is not to ask the member "why" they were hurt or what happened to them as they experienced their individual odyssey. Instead, the emphasis must be upon the family system learning from the hurt member what that member experienced and felt during this phase of their life, their journey outside the system of the family. This family traveler can bring back messages that only such travelers can learn, serving as a family shaman for those who have not yet journeyed outside the system. The family can share the experiences it had while the traveler was gone, and provide him or her with necessary family history to prevent the exclusion of the traveler from a place in the evolving family capsule.

R. D. Laing wrote that a ceremony of reentry is necessary at the end of an extrafamilial journey, an "out of family" experience caused by illness or other life crisis. He referred to an ". . . initiation ceremonial through which the person will be guided with full social encouragement and sanction into inner space and time, by people who have been there and back again."[5] Even if the family system does not currently contain members who have traveled such journeys themselves, who themselves have been there and back again, a family ceremony

5. Ibid., p. 384.

of communal learning can help each family member tune in to their own innate sense of the importance and significance of such journeys.

"When I got home from the hospital after my surgery, I felt strangely out of place," said Ms. Anders. "The family had one set of experiences together, and I had my own. We had to make a lot of time to just sit and talk things over. I sort of had to be guided back into the family. I had to let them know what happened to me, how I felt, and I had to hear what happened to them before we got back in our flow again."

Ms. Anders describes the importance of ritual in providing for consistency of family even as new lessons and experiences are integrated into the family pattern. There is not much use to flying if we can't have some system for bringing our experience of flight back to those who would learn with us about what it means to fly. Family ritual provides the time, pace, and purpose not only for welcoming back a family member, but also for strengthening the family through integration of the family member's experiences with the family history.

Family ritual is a way of acknowledging life's transitions and challenges as much as it is a way of celebrating the day-to-day living of the family itself. The family has the capacity to learn together, even in a society that almost exclusively emphasizes the importance of "individualized instruction." Family ritual is one way of moving beyond coping to commemoration, beyond "carrying on" to learning new ways of "pulling together," when someone in the family has had an out-of-family experience.

SIX STEPS FOR ESTABLISHING FAMILY RITUALS

Here are six steps that I have used in my clinic to help families restore meaningful ritual to their lives. Try to implement one step at a time, and give your family plenty of time to make the changes necessary to establish or reestablish family rituals. Don't become impatient with yourself or the family if getting the rituals started is much more difficult than you may have imagined. Just making the effort together to start or return to family ritual is already a major step in tapping into your family power.

STEP ONE. TURNING IN TOGETHER TO STAY TO-GETHER. Begin by trying to arrange for the entire family to go to bed at about the same time. Even if there are very young children, try to approximate their schedule of early-to-bed and early-to-rise. Of course, work and school schedules will have to be taken into account, and you will have to confront the threat of what I call the "weekend coma." Some families try to "sleep in" on weekends. They don't really sleep, but just try to get away with staying in bed much longer than even they think necessary as some type of protest against a demanding world that already dictates too much of our living. We hide in our bedding cocoon, attempting to summon our courage and strength for another day.

I have found that many of the families I work with suffer from "family jet lag." Because there is very little ritual or pattern to their sleeping, they actually end up feeling as if they have traveled across time zones. In effect, they have. Unless we go to bed and get up at about the same time every day, including weekends, we begin to tamper with our body's biological clock. The body becomes confused, never really knowing for sure if it is night or day. Some family members begin to behave as if it were early morning for them while another family member feels like it is lunchtime, even though the clock might say it is 10 A.M.

Mr. Anders said, "I feel so much more energized when we are all on the same schedule. I used to wait until everyone else was in bed, and then I would watch late-night television or work on my computer. I thought I was getting in some great quiet personal time. What I was really doing was distancing myself from my family. I was actually living in a completely different time zone than the rest of the family. When I was tired, they weren't. When they were tired, I wasn't. It works so much better to just go to bed all at one time."

When I treat patients who are working in shifts or who regularly travel across time zones as a part of their work, I sometimes ask these patients to try to alter their sleeping pattern temporarily. I will request a medical leave of absence for the patient and ask them to identify the times they used to go to bed and awaken when they were a child. I have found that there is something primal, something innate, in those old sleeping patterns that is healing. Sometimes, just a few weeks of returning to the old childhood pattern of sleeping can have measurable positive effects on these patients. We cannot deny the existence and impact of our early family patterns, and when we wander too far from them, we often pay a physical and emotional price.

You have to try this ritual of going to bed at the same time slowly, because it is likely that all of you in your family will be readjusting your biological clocks. Try to diminish the differences in bedtimes between family members by increments. I promise you that you will begin to feel a new family energy, but it may take weeks to feel the effect. When a family sleeps, it is still together, perhaps communicating in ways we will only be able to understand in our dreams.

STEP TWO. GETTING UP AS A FAMILY. The demands of our world have caused the family to rise in the morning at different times. The father or mother may be gone by the time the children get up, and the family may never see each other as a group, as they disappear one by one to scatter themselves throughout the community. Not only does getting up at different times contribute to the family jet lag I have described, it also results in more distance and missed opportunities for closeness between family members.

"When my husband was killed, the one thing I was always thankful for is that all of us had said good-bye in the morning," reported Ms. Bonner. "We always did that. We always said, 'Good-bye and drive carefully,' or 'Good-bye, have a good day in school.' We were always all up together and were able to start the day together. It wasn't easy, either. My husband was on those ungodly shifts that firemen have. We really had to work at changing shifts right along with him. We never knew how important that effort would be."

If someone in your family has an altering work or school schedule, the family will have to adjust, changing along with the time changes. If not, one family member will end up in an entirely different time zone, spaced out from the family. Researchers know how disruptive shift work and night work can be, and the general health of the family can suffer severely. Of course, the whole family cannot go to bed and sleep during the day, just because one member must do so. However, there can be an effort to get up together, to see each other off, even if some members of the family must return to bed to get sufficient sleep to fit their own individual schedules.

Starting the day together, greeting the morning as a unit, is a basic step in establishing a ritual for family living. If you are thinking that it will take more discipline than you have at your disposal to maintain a schedule of going to bed and getting up as a family, remember that you will come to feel as you behave, actually be energized by such behavior. It's beginning the process and maintaining the process for just a few weeks that will be the most difficult. Soon, the ritual will become an automatic and strengthening part of your family life.

STEP THREE. BREAKFASTING TOGETHER. If there has been any one consistent change in family life in the recent past, it is the disappearance of the family breakfast. Rural America typically focused on this first meal of the day, the beginning of the workday during which everyone gathered together in ritualized preparation and nurturing for the pressures and problems that each family member would encounter.

Now, families have the mobile breakfast. Most families seldom sit down for breakfast, searching instead for their equipment for the day, dressing, drinking, and nibbling on the move. Mr. Johnson said, "We noticed that we had to rearrange everything now that we were a new family. All of us were used to different schedules. It was really tempting to isolate ourselves into each of our own little schedules, but the best thing we ever did to start out our new family on the right foot, to merge two families together, was to at least turn in for the night and greet the morning as family. When we took the time to eat together in the morning, we seemed to have more of a feeling of being together through the whole day. It was easier to come home and be together at night, and it was even easier to be apart. We seemed to have established a group that wouldn't be stressed when we had to be apart. At least when you eat breakfast together, you have to start the day sitting down together first. It even smells good to wake up to something cooking for all of us."

STEP FOUR. SMOOTHING OUT FAMILY LANDINGS.
There comes a time at the end of the day when the family reunites and the workers and students return home. Many families allow this reentry time to become problematic. Mr. Muller reported, "I remember in my own home that we had a rule. When Dad came home, all of the kids got together, and Mom would make us all sit down with Dad for a few minutes. Everybody just sat down and had to share one good thing that had happened that day. We shared pretty quick sometimes, because the kids were eager to play or get back to whatever they were doing. But sitting with Dad when he came home was a ritual. Even if we made something up, at least we were taking the time to talk."

Much as the family tends to leave one another in spurts in the morning, with different schedules, different breakfasts, and different obligations, many families return together at day's end in much the same fashion. There is no ritual to the reentry, or worse, everyone checks in for messages, or even first asks the dreaded question "Any problems today?" One of the most obvious symptoms of family failure is the fact that, as soon as the family sits down together for a period of time, problems and conflicts immediately arise. Soon, sitting together creates a conditional response in which family unity is associated with having a problem. An "If we're all here together sitting down, there must be trouble" viewpoint can evolve.

Some families become addicted to "problem communication," unable just to talk casually and comfortably. Mr. Anders said, "I used to come in the door and right away I would ask if anything had gone wrong. I don't know how that started, but I just always asked if anything had gone wrong, was there any mail or were there any phone calls. I never really said hello other than to brush my wife's cheek with a kiss and ask what was for dinner."

Many of the families I have worked with paid more attention to how they said good-bye in the morning than how they said hello again in the afternoon or evening. As strange and awkward as it may sound, I suggest that, as soon as everyone is safely back home at the end of the day, everyone should sit down, join hands and share a moment of silence. Some families may choose to say a prayer at this time, others may choose to meditate. Others may choose just to sit quietly. What is important is to ritualize a reconnection of the family unit, a "we're home" celebration.

Some of my patients resist this assignment. They find it contrived or phony. "Why do we have to go through all this stuff? We love each other. We don't have to fool around with this Eastern religion nonsense," said one man. It is important to remember that our families are at least as important as any other part of our life, and, I suggest, more important. We seem willing to jog, do aerobics, learn the latest lovemaking technique, purchase mantras, and engage in the latest self-improvement craze, but when it comes to family improvement, some of us shy away. I hope you will give this opportunity for a smoother reentry to the family a chance. You will find any self-improvement efforts you are making in other areas of your life greatly enhanced by better reconnection and by adding this reconnection ritual to your daily family life.

STEP FIVE. MANDATORY ATTENDANCE AT THE FAMILY DINNER.

Family dinners too often become small-claims courts. Problems and complaints are raised, criticisms are leveled, and very often many of the family members miss the dinner entirely. The ritual of a family dinner to end the day, a time to eat in peace and quiet and the comforting support of the family, is one of the best things anyone can do for their own health. I suggest you make every effort to return to a real family dinner. The time and effort will be well worth it.

One basic ground rule should be followed: absolutely no negatives during the dinner. Later, I will suggest ways to conduct productive family problem-solving sessions. The family dinner is not the place to solve anything, and the only reason these dinners have become so problematic is that, for many families, the dinner is the only time everyone in the family ever sits down together.

Setting up a different time to sit together to look at problems will take the pressure off the family dinner. I also suggest a moment of silence, perhaps saying grace or having one family member give thanks to everyone else in the family with heads bowed. Such a pause will allow time for the family to change gears and relax for the meal ahead, allowing everyone to rediscover the art of the meaningful and stress-free meal.

STEP SIX. A FAMILY PRAYER. You will be reading later about the value of a common family belief system. Taking time at the end of the day to pray briefly together as a family, or just to sit together quietly for a minute or two before going to bed, can do wonders in helping the whole family to sleep better and live more peacefully.

"No matter how much we may have argued, we never, but never, miss our quiet time before bed," reported Mr. Muller. "Sometimes, we are all angry, and we really just sit quietly and tolerate each other, but it's like a time to let our engines idle down and turn off for the night."

The total extra time involved in these six family ritual steps is probably less than an hour a day. Your family probably spends much more time than that trying to solve the problems created by the lack of such family rituals. Everyone has to sleep and to eat anyway, so the only change is to ritualize and share these activities as a family.

A healthy family life requires more than routine, more than special social ceremonies for weddings, funerals, birthdays, and graduations. Hardly anything has changed our world more in the last decades than our increasing obsession with getting things done at the expense of remembering and acknowledging why we are doing things. This "doing" obsession has made it difficult for our family just to "be" together. Establishing your own family rituals is a major step to being a family again.

CHAPTER FOUR

Family Rhythm: Learning to Move Together

"In the future elaboration of the new holistic world view, the notion of rhythm is likely to play a very fundamental role."
FRITJOF CAPRA

FAMILY RHYTHM: Living in harmony with and being constantly aware of the family's natural cadence, its pulse in accordance with all natural life processes, and allowing the family to dictate its own pace of living rather than responding to external and accelerating pressures of daily life.

THE PULSE OF FIVE FAMILIES

All families, all living systems, have a rhythm to their existence. We breathe in and out, night follows day, and seasons change. When families feel "on beat," functioning within a comfortable rhythm of their own choosing and in a flow comfortable for all family members, they tend to have less conflict, more joy, and better health.

When the family finds itself merely responding to a pace established by a society that stresses the value of hurry, worry, hustle, and scurry, the family functions like a 33⅓ rpm record being played at 78 rpm. Nothing seems clear, everything seems forced, and there is little joy or appreciation of life.

When the family allows itself to become depressed and lethargic as a group, the result is similar to a 78 rpm record being played at 33⅓ rpm. Everything seems dull, sluggish, and without energy. Healthy family rhythm happens when the family becomes aware of its own speed and works as a group to maintain that speed, even when pressures from outside the family call for a different rhythm.

Here are members of each of the five families as they describe the rhythm of their own families when these families are playing themselves at the wrong speed.

"When these damn emergencies happen with our daughter, we get all off our pace," said Ms. Anders. "Just when things are humming along, her illness might act up, and everything gets out of whack. Somebody has to be at the hospital, somebody has to shop, we never get together as a family, and everything just seems off."

"After my husband was killed, our family just dragged along," said Ms. Bonner. "We were such an up group, then we got sluggish and slow."

"Now that we have two of our children married, with kids of their own, and our son gone to college, we have to sort of start all over," said Ms. Steiner. "We didn't realize how much the kids set the pace in our house. Now we have to set our own pace, and it hasn't been an easy adjustment. It's as if we haven't got the beat yet."

"It seems as if we have too many songs that are being sung," said Mr. Johnson. "Trying to put two families together is like trying to make one choir out of a hundred singers, each singing a different song. We haven't found just the right chord yet. Everybody is not only marching to their own drummer, they have entirely different drums."

"It's like we have two ways of living," said the twelve-year-old boy in the Muller family. "When Grandpa isn't acting crazy, things go pretty smoothly, but when he gets nuts, we get all screwed up. Nothing goes right. Mom doesn't pack our lunch, homework doesn't get done, and nobody gives phone messages right. You just have to wait until Grandpa quiets down, and then things get going back to normal. Until then, even the phone ringing causes everybody to jump."

Each of the above examples illustrates the negative impact on the family of a loss of natural rhythm and of the ability to synchronize together as a group rather than to respond as individuals struggling to adapt to stress.

The Family Rhythm Test

Before reading further about natural family rhythm, take the family rhythm test. As with each of the ten tests for the ten Rx's described in this book, each test item may be seen as a family assignment, an opportunity to get your family rhythm back.

The same scoring system will be used for all ten family Rx tests.

0	1	2	3	4	5	6	7	8	9	10
ALMOST NEVER		SELDOM		SOMETIMES		A LOT		ALMOST ALWAYS		

1. ———— Can you sense an even flow to your daily family activities, with everyone seeming to feel a part of that flow?

2. ———— Are times of family-member returns and leavings smooth and easy as opposed to hectic, loud, and disorganized?

3. ———— Does your family seem to be synchronized most of the time, with everyone knowing what is going on, when things are supposed to be happening, and what family plans are?

4. ———— Does "the word" get out clearly in your family, with everyone hearing what time and where something is supposed to be happening and what is expected of each family member?

5. ——— No matter what family members are around, does your family seem to run as smoothly and easily when everyone is present as compared to when only some family members are present?

6. ——— Does your home feel calm, easygoing, and comfortable?

7. ——— Do all family members feel peaceful and safe in your home?

8. ——— Are there times when there are no radio, television, or other appliance noises serving as constant family background?

9. ——— Is your phone quiet, not ringing most of the time, with most phone conversations brief?

10. ——— Are family members moving slowly and easily through the house, without knocking things or people over, spilling things, or sending pets scampering through the house?

——— TOTAL FAMILY RHYTHM SCORE

Remember that it is not possible to have a static score on any of these family tests. Just by taking the test, you have changed your family. For discussion purposes, however, if your score was over 90, your family has a good sense of rhythm. If it is under 90, your family should pay attention to the items that lowered your score. The first two Rx's of family life, ritual and rhythm, are closely related and require constant vigilance if they are to become a healthy part of your family's experience.

RUSHING PAST OUR LIFE

I have already described the importance of ritual to family life. These rituals serve as the "behavioral myths," the acting out of the family belief system. When these rituals are hurried because of attempts to comply with self-created time pressures, or when these rituals are skipped because there is "too little time," family rhythm suffers.

"Well, we used to always say grace before our meals," said Mr. Steiner. "But as the kids got older, we seemed to develop this speed-grace thing, where the words rushed together, nobody really listened, somebody was on the phone, and it really started to lose its meaning."

While family ritual is a prerequisite to family health, family rhythm allows the time and priority for such rituals to evolve and continue. Try slowing down some of your own family rituals and see what happens. Try sensing the beat of your own family. The next time you say good-bye to a family member, really take the time to say it slowly. Look the family member in the eye, take their hand, and say a meaningful good-bye. Try to get some of your family rhythm back by helping everyone in the family become aware of the rhythm in which they are living.

THE FAMILY RHYTHM METHOD

One of the major scientific discoveries of our time is that all of the universe, and everything in it, exists in the form of rhythmic waves. In our day-to-day life, we are consumed by the illusion of solid objects, bones, bodies, the things we describe as real because they are in our local world, and "real" in the sense that we can see and touch them. When we choose to see and react only to this limited, local world, we fail to develop our own sense of a universal rhythm of life, influenced by things and events we can not always see and touch. We begin to think that our clocks "are" time instead of arbitrary measuring devices. Our health depends upon our making the active choice to develop our awareness of the more cosmic laws that reveal that we are vibrations, not objects; that we are processes and not structures. You make the choice as to which rhythm you will attend to: the local rhythm of day-to-day pressures or the more cosmic rhythm of life that emanates from within you and your family.

STRUCTURE VS. RHYTHM

To take the family point of view is to be aware that we are more than skin and bones. There is a rhythm to everything. Within a stone there is a constant dance of energy that we can feel if we take the time, sit down on the beach, be very quiet, and try to tune in to universal rhythms rather than local noise. If you choose to pay attention, you can feel the rhythm of the tides, the winds, the growth of the trees and the growth of your own family.

"It's funny how at night, late at night, when I get up for a snack, I can sort of feel our house," said Mr. Steiner. "Because nothing else is driving me on, I can feel the pulse of our home, the way we are together. I can sit and actually feel my own heart beating almost with the way our home is, our family is. I guess we're too busy to pay attention to that feeling most of the time, but now that the kids are gone, I can feel it more and more. I wish we all would have taken more time to feel it before."

Try Mr. Steiner's experience for yourself. When the house is still, when everyone is in bed, sit quietly and try to feel how your family is. I promise, if you wait long enough and try hard enough, you will begin to feel the heartbeat of your family. You may notice that the beat of your family is similar to the natural cadence of all natural processes, such as the waves and the winds, rather than the humming of traffic or the buzzing of jet engines.

We all have our own unique movements, ways of talking, breathing, listening, and making love. We are "ways of living" more than types of people. If we can see ourselves and our family members in terms of how we, or they, are currently moving and changing, rather than labeling or categorizing them, we begin to coordinate the family system with the overall universal system. We begin to develop a tolerance for the imperfections of our family members. We learn to see them "in process" rather than as established personalities.

"I tried to get organized," said Ms. Bonner. "I tried and tried. I wanted so badly to make life predictable, controllable, even almost perfect for my family. Every time I tried, something else happened. Just when I was up, something would bring me down. Just when I thought I had it together, that was when my husband was killed. It seems that when things are going well, it is always a signal that something will change. It just goes on and on. I was so interested in later that I regret how many 'nows' I missed."

Ms. Bonner is correct. The "it" that just goes on and on is our "us rhythm," the total rhythm of the cosmos playing through our family. Try as we might to see ourselves as individuals, as separate from one another and in control of our own little worlds, we will never succeed. No matter how hard we may try to cling to a special moment, the natural rhythm of life insists that the living process cycle in its evolution. A guaranteed prescription for unhappiness in the family, or anywhere, is to expect perfection instead of change, to get ready for, instead of get with, life.

SOLO AND ENSEMBLE

Family rhythm not only involves a "tuning in" for the subtle and universal aspects of living as a family. Family rhythm also involves the oscillation between individual development and family growth. Healthy human development depends upon our innate sense of self/other, I/thou rhythm, and upon our sense of the growth—and rate of growth—of self, that accompanies the growth of someone else, and of a collection of "someone elses."

We are too often taught how to grow as individuals rather than with others. As the soloist emerges and then disappears to join again with the orchestra, the family symphony is a composition based on individual excellence contributing to the good of the group.

If we only think of "self" and our own sense of life rhythm, we become numb to the rhythms of others. We function as a second hand ticking through a faceless clock. We fail to see and experience people as systems shared with us, as collections of experiences and histories that cycle through a mutual development with us. We fail to experience the life rhythm, the family rhythm, that we all share. We become solo players without accompaniment, and without the ability to direct our talents to the group and for the enjoyment of the audience. As skilled as we may be at singing our own song, many of us seem unable to join the chorus of life because we can not seem to sense the beat and fall into a rhythm with others.

THE MOST BASIC RHYTHM OF ALL

All life and all families are based on the basic rhythm of sex and death. Joining, experiencing life, and ending life are the most obvious cycles of the family experience. Whether a family exists in the more traditional forms, of parents and children and husband and wives, or in the form of families of people electing to live together without blood relationships, as groups of senior citizens, students, or other group arrangements that fit the criterion of family I described earlier (elected sharing of and mutual responsibility for development in all areas of life over time), there is always connection, bonding, and ending, some form of the rhythm of sex and death.

Without the natural rhythm of living I have been describing, without the ultimate rhythm of sex and death, of connection and separation, life would be boring and insignificant. Only in the last two thirds of our evolution, when multiple-cell life and death developed, has there been any true variety and uniqueness to the experience of living. Leonard Shlain wrote, "Without sex, there could be no variety, without death no individuality."[1] He was referring to the fact that all individuality and variety depend upon combining as people and accepting the end of that physical combination, even as we remember our infinite spiritual connection with one another.

Sex allows for a pairing and mixing of our genes. Aging and death allow for physical and psychological individuality even in a system where all of us are connected. Sex allows for a variety of spiritual experience through a form of genetic rou-

1. Shlain, Leonard. Lecture at College of Marin, Kenfield, California, January 23, 1979, as quoted by Fritjof Capra in *The Turning Point* (New York: Bantam Books, 1982), p. 283.

lette that gives the spirit an infinite number of forms with which to experience earth.

When one-celled organisms were the only living things, they lived forever, multiplying by simple division, with no variety and no uniqueness. There was no aging, because the one-celled organisms were immortal, living on through their own divisions. Cancer cells are immortal, dividing on and on until inevitably they kill the system in which they exist.

Cancer cells have no sense of rhythm, just one-directional, mechanical self-development and multiplication. Like a selfish family member, never attending to the sensitivities of other family members or behaving as if their pace of living were unrelated to the family pace of life, the cancer cell eventually destroys its own home. The cancer cell simply reproduces and never dies, never taking into account the system in which it exists. In effect, cancer is a metaphor of the nonfamily, here-and-now, local point of view of life; do your own thing, survive, and keep on going as long as you can until the system which surrounds you is eventually destroyed.

Sex, aging, and death are the major beats of the rhythm of life, and families are where these processes are shared and given meaning. Families that talk openly about sex and death, and share their most intimate feelings and fears of sexuality and dying, are allowing the natural cosmic rhythm of life to evolve within their family system. Family denial of these two natural processes causes each family member to live and die alone.

Like the immortality of the cancer cell, physical immortality would ultimately rob us of our life, for there can be no true system and rhythm of life without death. The evolution of the human spirit, which is the main job of the family, depends on our soul's enjoyment of the variety and cyclicity that sex and death signify, the beginnings and apparent endings of our physical existence.

When we become impatient with the natural rhythm of life, when we fail to communicate intimately and openly with our family about these fundamental aspects of our humanness, and when we are aggravated or intolerant toward the individual expression of the sexuality of our family members, we are trying to block out a natural beat that dictates all of our lives. When we curse death or attempt to mask death's reality through denial or routines disguised as ceremonies, we are really showing our deafness to the local and personal effect of life's rhythm.

"I cursed the fact that my father was getting senile," said Ms. Muller. "I even started to hate him for it. It was very difficult to come to see this whole thing as a part of life. I always thought death and dying was the opposite of birth and living. I learned, we are all learning now, that death is not the opposite of living. It is a part of life. Instead of waiting for it, instead of waiting for Gramps to die, we are living with him through this part of his life and ours."

Ms. Steiner said, "I became more and more angry that my kids were growing up and moving away. I knew it had to be, but I actually started to get physically sick, maybe as a way to get my kids' attention and sympathy. Maybe they would stay home forever and take care of me. It's been the most difficult thing in my life to accept my children's leaving."

Ms. Muller and Ms. Steiner are trying to cope with the key point about rhythm in the family. Both women have come to see that fighting or fleeing from the natural flow of life only makes us sick, both physically and emotionally. Learning to pay attention and be at peace with natural life rhythms, even though that life is difficult and stressful in itself, is the only antidote for the pain of life.

We would not be able to experience the family celebration of birthdays, the special talents and skills of each and every family member, the marriages, graduations, and religious ceremonies of family living unless life had invented sex and death, unless life had given us the ultimate and dominant sense of what seem to be beginnings and endings, but are really only points on the infinite path of life.

THE DANGER OF TRYING TO BE PERFECT

We will never be in tune with our natural life rhythm unless we can overcome one of society's biggest obstacles to a happy family. Our society believes that perfection is something to be achieved. Even though we give lip service to that fact that "no one is perfect," we seem to spend our lives trying to disprove that statement by trying to do more and get more than we are or have. We are driven toward a perfection that can never be.

We are taught in school that "A" is better than "B" and that anyone who tries hard enough can get an "A." We are taught by advertising agencies that, if we will only buy the right things in the right amounts at the right time, get enough of the right "stuff," and use this stuff intensely and often enough, we can at least fool other people into thinking that we are perfect.

We suffer from the collective "virgin syndrome," of always being "on the verge" of where and how we feel we ought to be. When we externalize perfection and seek this idealistic and perpetually illusive image, we become blind to the miracles within our own daily family life and to the fact that perfection is process, not product, a way of traveling and not a station to arrive at.

THE IGNORANCE OF LOOKING FOR MIRACLES

Psychologist Abraham Maslow wrote, "To be looking for miracles is a sure sign of ignorance that everything is miraculous."[2] When we "work for perfection," we fail to accept our natural perfection, our basic value as human beings. There is no such thing as the perfect job, the perfect husband, wife, son, or daughter if by perfection we mean a finished and flawless personal product. We are perfect just because we "are." We can hope and work for our own contribution to the evolution of the human spirit, and to the development and change for the better of everyone, but we can not attain what we already are: perfect beings in process, adapting to a challenging and changing world.

We must start from a point of celebration of who we are and move toward the ability to rejoice with others in who and how we are together. Family rhythm is disrupted when, in the

2. As quoted by E. Hoffman in "The Right to Be Human: Abraham Maslow," *East/West: The Journal of Natural Healthy Living* (May 1988), pp. 68–69.

interest of trying to be something, we fail to enjoy how we are doing things right at this very moment.

Consider one example of how our search for perfection disrupts our life rhythm. A major obstacle to the stability of marriage is that we forever seem in search of the perfect spouse. If a marriage is not happy enough, sexual enough, entertaining enough, or growing enough, we may assume that we have failed to find the perfect mate. We have become so industrialized and product-oriented in our approach to living, choosing a point of view that emphasizes an assembly-line, final-product, and bottom-line orientation, that we even speak of our selves and relationships in automotive terms. We are "driven away" by our partner, or we become "drained" or fail to "get a charge out of" him or her. Thinking that the loudest squeak will get the most grease, we try to make that loudest noise. Our relationships seem to "run out of gas," "crash," or get "burned out." We too often fail to see marriage as a process; instead we look for just the right person to "make a marriage."

"I think my marriage now is much better than my first marriage, because I'm much better," said Mr. Johnson, the father struggling to form a new stepfamily. "I was always looking for the perfect girl to marry, then I expected the perfect wife, sex partner, friend, and housekeeper. I think I am finally learning that I have to make my life, my relationship, what it will be. I have to learn to accept instead of seeking perfection. I have to learn to wait and feel instead of always criticizing and complaining."

As Mr. Johnson did, we tend to see something wrong "out there" that needs a tune-up, rather than working to tolerate differences and change, and committing to development and to the natural rhythm of growth and maturation that can happen between people. Too often, divorce is failure to show the patience and sensitivity we need in order to learn the sometimes subtle rhythms that can evolve between two people and within whole families over time. Marriages, families, all relationships are more a process of learning the dance rather than finding the right dancer.

If we stop looking for miracles and perfection and start paying attention to the miraculous within and between us as we develop together, we can celebrate living life rather than working toward an earned reward of celebration when we have neared perfection in the future. We find a natural family rhythm when we realize that our family is already miraculous, and has the capacity for changing, helping, forgiving, and growing from a point of family acceptance and strength rather than doubt, self-abuse and insecurity.

The student is not flawed because he or she does not yet know. All learning problems are a form of disconnection. The troubled student has not yet connected with a system, learned how to adopt the family view, and therefore has failed to see himself as an important, effective, needed, and meaningful part of his or her world. If we see each of us as perfect processes, we begin with optimistic tolerance and acceptance because we see our full potential for connecting with others.

"When will the world be perfect, Dad?" asked the little boy, looking at the glacier. The tour bus had stopped along the edge of the road, and as the family looked out at the burning blue light that radiated from the glacier that moved before their eyes, the boy was told that the world is always in process, always in change. "Will it ever be done, Dad?" asked the boy again. The father's answer showed an understanding of the concept of perfection through acceptance of the natural rhythm of life. "Well," he said. "The world is perfect, really. But it's always changing, and that's why it's perfect. Perfect things are perfect because they are always changing."

"When you told me that my learning disabled child was perfect, I thought you were crazy," said Ms. Muller. "I had always been taught and told that he was broken and needed fixing. It was an almost impossible concept to learn at first. But once I saw it, that we are perfect, he is perfect, then I stopped trying to fix him and remake him and began to live and grow with him. I could accept the fact that he was who he was, and that the changes he would make throughout his life wouldn't be because he needed fixing, but because he had to fit in with all of us and everyone in his way. I just started from a different place, by accepting him now instead of waiting for some time later when he was 'better' and more deserving of my love."

Ms. Muller's statement indicates her understanding that, even in the face of illness or impairments, we should begin with the premise of the perfect and miraculous in all that characterizes the actions of this wonderful life system. It is being a part of that system that makes us perfect. We are all classmates in the advanced training center for the human spirit, and we only continue to matriculate. We will never graduate.

"I just had to learn not to fight it," said Ms. Bonner. "I couldn't really grieve, I couldn't even cry when my husband was killed. I was too angry, too eager to find out why, who did it, and what I should do to make it right. Death is so profoundly real that it forces you to accept it, or you die yourself. I have learned to cry, to weep, to go on. I have learned to laugh with my son and daughter again, to realize that life is all of these things, the terrible pain and the remarkable glee of my children."

Ms. Bonner was grappling with the concept of life's natural rhythm, the cosmic perfection of life even at times of local pain and suffering. She has learned the difficult concept that things don't "happen to people," families are not "jinxed" or broken. Everything is a part of our swinging with the beat of our living.

To fully understand the concept of family rhythmicity, we must understand the fact that, when something seems to go wrong, something is actually going right. Listen intensely to the troubled family member, for he or she is trying to get the family's attention back to some problem in family rhythm.

Serious illness, disabilities, even death are changes and processes within the system. Our medical establishment is embroiled in an inflationary disaster of war against disease, not yet learning that all sickness is a form of adjustment. We will never defeat illness, but we can learn from it, comfort those who are sick, strengthen and support the body's and mind's own natural healing capacity, and attempt to learn more and better ways to live healthy lives. We can learn that illness, like all human problems, is an archetypical life challenge for further human development, a way of adjusting our family rhythm. In the sense that illness results in life adjustments, being "sick" can ultimately be good for your health.

There are always counterthemes occurring within family systems, the fact of constant adjustments taking place. Instead of blaming or trying to correct a family member who seems out of step, perhaps the whole family should be looking instead at the way they are dancing. There may be clues in their dance that reveal a rhythm that the whole family should hear.

Someone in the family will always try to get the rhythm

back. If we try to learn about the family system from the member or members who seem out of step, we will all be better able to adapt as a family. We have become more successful at fixing, soothing, and seeking professional help than we have at learning from those who would teach us through their own actions about the family's needs for an alteration in its rhythm and about how it is living and loving day-to-day.

When a family member is angry, depressed, and afraid, try thinking of their behavior and feelings as signals rather than hassles. What is the distressed family member trying to say about the rhythm of the family? Is there depression because this family is going too fast, agitation because this family is going too slow, alienation because this family is too scattered or too distant from one another? Look for the metaphor of a family member's distress, and you will find clues for adjusting the family rhythm to a healthier beat. When a family problem strikes, ask first, "What does this say about our family rhythm? Are we responding to our own healthy family rhythm, or have we lost our beat?"

I have chosen four major problems in family living as examples of the disruption of family rhythm. There are no easy solutions for these complex problems, but one unifying principle underlies the first steps to dealing with these problems. When children run away, talk of suicide, have problems becoming independent, or are hurt or impaired, the family system must look even more intensely for its own rhythm rather than for what is wrong with the distressed family member.

WHEN FAMILIES CAN'T BREATHE: THE RUNAWAY

When young people run away and desert their family, perhaps because they feel out of step with their family and the world their family lives in, the family system may have failed to contract, to contain, comfort, and embrace, to counterbalance the premature expansion or sensed isolation on the part of one of its members.

On the other hand, running-away behavior may relate to the family system's restriction, overwhelming, and stifling of the runaway's sense of independent growth (however misguided, immature, or premature such a need may be). The run-away sees no other choice but to leave. Runaways leave because they feel they can't breathe, and ultimately they only find more restriction and entrapment in a world ready to take advantage of young and immature persons.

"When our son went through a time when he just pulled away from us, we didn't know what to do," said Ms. Steiner. "He wanted to be left alone, but then he was mad at us because he said we didn't pay enough attention to him. We just couldn't get it right. He left one day, and we went through hell. We finally found him at his friend's house. We went to family therapy and learned that we all were getting too far apart from one another. We were all taking each other for granted. He didn't just need more attention. We all needed more family attention."

Ms. Steiner's son now has a family of his own. He states, "I remember that time I ran away. There just didn't seem to be any place for me. It was like I couldn't breathe. I didn't know what to do. I can see it now in my own kids. When we're not a family, when we get all caught up in getting busy and just doing, doing, doing, everyone gets all confused and starts acting up or out. Kids just do things more obviously, and we've learned to see the kids' actions as a sign rather than a problem."

These reports by Ms. Steiner and her son show the difficult vacillation between self and family, the rhythmic alterations between needs for autonomy and the need for interdependence. It is a challenge all families face, but being aware that such a rhythm is taking place is a good beginning for promoting both self- and family communication about the process of interdependence balanced with dependence.

As I mentioned in Chapter One, the ritual of re-embracement, of intense welcoming back to the family even before actual physical absence takes place, can help get the family rhythm back. When someone in your family is going to run, it is time for the whole family to stop, listen, and get back in step together. Remember, the runner is running for the family, driven by a rhythm that the family may be too busy or too numb to hear.

"Sure I ran away," said one little girl. "But my dad ran to work, my mom ran to work, my brother ran to school and football practice, and even the dog ran in the neighborhood. I just ran away in a way that people could see more easily." This girl is describing the way in which a family member may demonstrate a disorder of family rhythm to which all other family members are deaf. Her next statement illustrates the correction of family rhythm that can take place when a family problem occurs.

The little girl continued, "I told my mom that I would come home if she and Dad and Bobby would. She was confused at first, but then she saw that everyone in the family was running away. Now we are together more. We slowed down. We even went to a show together last night."

TAKING THE BREATH OUT OF THE FAMILY: SUICIDE

When any family member attempts to end his or her life, there may be a sense of desertion and helplessness, a loneliness and hopelessness experienced by that family member. It is also possible, however, that the family member in distress is feeling so close to the family, so contained, so stifled, so overwhelmed and perhaps so overwhelming, that he or she feels a need, however inappropriate, to "help" to free the family from these pressures by leaving it. The family is left in a state of not knowing how much support to give, trying valiantly both to be supportive and at the same time to grant the freedom and privacy the family member seems to need.

"Our daughter went through a time when she talked about killing herself," said Ms. Muller. "She wouldn't even let me touch her, hold her, or hug her. We didn't know what was wrong, and she wouldn't or couldn't seem to tell us. In therapy, we saw that the burden of Gramp's illness made her feel that her own needs as a developing young woman were going to be too much for the family to handle. We had to let her know we could all handle it."

Ms. Muller describes the complexities of the issue of suicide and the differing motives related to this tragic human crisis. Suicide and all life-threatening behavior in families are manifestations of feelings of being disconnected, out of sync, without clear purpose and meaning. If someone in your family talks of ending their own life, think first of how well connected the whole family is with one another, not just the individual dynamics of the person threatening suicide. Suicide is not always an act of depression. It can also be a misguided attempt to correct a system gone wrong, a signal that family life is going by too fast, without meaning, and without purpose.

THE REFILLED NEST: HOW MUCH DO YOU PUSH?

The "refilled nest" phenomenon reveals the problems the family is having with the closeness and independence dimension of their interaction. False and exploiting expectations of our young children may result in the young person "missing out" on needed age-appropriate containment, safety, and nurturance. They may suffer from a form of parental deprivation during their childhood, and as a result, as a young person or young adult, may return to the nest in an attempt to "redo" what was done wrong, to reexperience a childhood interaction with their parents that they may feel they never had. We do sometimes make our children too old too quickly by marveling at their precocity instead of celebrating their immaturity and dependence.

Young persons may return dependently to the family system at a time in their life when they should be establishing new family branches, and when the original family should be undergoing its own changes and acclimation. Once again the family struggles with its rhythm, with its natural breathing, with whether or not to inhale and contain the family member or exhale and allow, or even force, the family member to find their own independent life.

"One of our sons kept coming back home," said Ms. Steiner. "We thought we were moving toward an empty nest, but we ended up like a family motel. He kept coming home, and we didn't know if we should parent him, or treat him like a renter. It was a real conflict to decide how much to push and how much to just provide a safe place for him."

The Steiner family struggled for years with various of their children in terms of the issue of independence from the family and support of the family. They had to learn that they themselves as parents had not established a clear concept of a bal-

ance between continued interdependence with their children
and required independence from them. Parents become as dependent on their children as their children become on them,
and these parents, as all parents, had to develop a new system
of interaction with their offspring that was a more age-appropriate system for their family at this time in its evolving rhythm
of growth.

The family can learn to breathe freely much of the time,
contract and expand in a rhythm that seems suited to all of the
members. "Every time we open the door to let a child go, we've
learned to leave it open just a crack for their return," reported
Ms. Steiner. "And that crack gets wider, then smaller, wider,
then smaller yet, but they can always get back in. One thing
though—getting back in isn't so easy as it was." Ms. Muller's
statement reveals the establishment of a family rhythm that
allows for each family member's growth while still providing a
family base for everyone.

"We have to let him go," said Ms. Muller, speaking now of
her father. "We know he is dying, and we vacillate between
pretending he's not going and then making the changes necessary to let him go. It's painful, like breathing with broken ribs.
We just all have to do it together. When somebody in the family
won't let go, someone else helps him out. When somebody is
too ready to let go, gets angry or just gives up, somebody else
always seems to help get the hope back to keep us going." This
ultimate contraction and expansion, of living and dying,
stresses family rhythm to the maximum, but the healthiest of
families seem to develop even a better ability to cope, through
their adjustment to their transitional crises.

HURT CHILDREN AND SUFFERING FAMILIES

When a family has the added burden of a hurt child, a child
who is impaired physically or mentally, the rhythm of that
family can be severely disrupted. Verbal and even physical violence can occur as a symptom of the absence of family rhythm,
a rhythm that should be soothing instead of unsettling everyone
in the family. Our schools and our psychotherapy offer little
help to families in such distress, too often prescribing drugs to

impart an artificial rhythm to the child or sending the family off to one therapist and another with little consistency or follow-up.

Financial pressures on these families can be severe, and even simple daily activities require enormous amounts of energy. Such families must establish a rhythm of daily life that allows for reenergizing, private time for every family member, and the acknowledgment that not only the impaired child but the entire family must make time for celebration as well as remediation.

"We have to do so much for her all the time," said Ms. Anders. "Our daughter demands so much of our time that we used to be exhausted, no matter what time of day it was. We resented families who didn't have impaired children, until we learned that such resentment only tired us out even more. Then, in therapy, we learned to stop thinking of our daughter, of us, as broken. We started to think of us as perfect, just our own unique form of perfect. We learned that our challenge was not our daughter's problems, but us. We had to get our own rhythm back, and not let our daughter's problem be the whole focus of our life. That wasn't good for her or for the whole family. It was like a breath of fresh air when we all saw our own family without comparison to other families, when we saw our family as not broken but as special, strong, and together."

SIX STEPS TO GET BACK INTO STEP

Here are six steps that the five families used to help them find and keep their own family rhythm. Remember to take your time with these steps. As I warned in Chapter Three, about establishing or reestablishing family rituals, the idea is to begin to harness even more of your already abundant family power, not to pressure your family to be "the perfect family."

STEP ONE. RESETTING THE FAMILY METRONOME. It is hypocrisy to attempt to meditate twenty minutes twice a day, and then hurry, worry, and scurry the rest of that day. Returning to a healthier family rhythm requires active responsibility for the family schedule. It seems to be a fact that all families need more time, so I ask the families I work with to create more time for their family. They do this by getting up at least one half hour earlier, together, every day. They may not find a full day of extra time, but rising just one half hour earlier every day usually allows the family an easier, less hurried pace and adds three and one-half hours of time a week for the family to use.

"Leaving early for work has stopped that mad dash during rush hour," said Mr. Johnson. "I used to cut it so close that I was always trying to nudge the guy ahead of me to move up just an inch in traffic jams. Leaving fifteen minutes earlier took all the pressure off, not only on the way to work, but at home when I was getting ready to leave. I left in a better mood, and I came home in a better mood. We also had more time together in the morning. We actually sat down together for breakfast."

STEP TWO. CONQUERING APPLIANCE ADDICTION.

Are your automatic appliances automating you? Do you find yourself rocking and rolling to the beating drum of your clothes dryer? The modern conveniences that some families have can take over the entire family. "The dishwasher and the clothes washer and dryer are supposed to save me time," said Ms. Johnson. "Well, somehow, I just end up doing more dishes and more clothes more often. It seems like I am feeding my appliances instead of using them. They keep calling to me to keep them full, to keep them busy. It's like I'm working for them now."

Although it may seem strange at first, I have asked some of the families I work with to try not using one of their modern appliances for a period of time. I ask them to wash dishes by hand, wash clothes the old-fashioned way, or make some modification that frees them from their appliance addiction. Most of the families report experiences similar to Ms. Anders.

"We started to do our dishes by hand. All of us. One washed, one dried, one put them away, and my youngest cleaned off the table and put other things away. It became a time together. Of course, little battles started at first. Somebody missed a spot or somebody splashed somebody. Finally, though, we noticed that we had to stop to just do the dishes, instead of turning on the washer and each of us spreading out all over the world."

I am not suggesting that a return to washing our clothes in a nearby stream is going to return a more natural rhythm to the family, but I am suggesting that some attention to the basic tasks of life, the basic experiences of life maintenance, can result in some return to a more fundamental, even primal rhythm of life activity.

Ms. Anders reported, "Once we started using the dishwasher again, I noticed for a while that we all stood around watching the darn thing. We didn't know what to do with our time. Now, we go on a family bike ride while the dishes are washed." By taking control of our automatic devices, we may learn that they have been accelerating us as much as, or more than, they have been helping us. If these devices are to really be timesavers, then we must ask what and who they are saving the time for.

STEP THREE. BRINGING IN A GUEST CONDUCTOR.
"There was something unbelievably settling about sitting around the radio and listening to a radio show," said the Bonner family's mother. "I remember just sitting around sort of staring at the dial. We would smile at one another when something funny happened. We would react together. It was a way of settling down."

Today, we spend little family time just sitting together. I suggest that families spend some time each week listening to music together. Each family member gets to pick the music when it is their turn, but the rule is that, at least sometimes, everyone sits down to listen to a tape or album. Such an activity seems to slow the family clock and reestablish a beat that can be more comfortable. No fair watching television. The idea is to experience, sense and share, not gaze, gawk, and become entranced.

Mr. Johnson said, "Nothing like sitting around listening to hard rock music. It wasn't what I would call restful, but you know, it was kind of nice just sitting and listening even to that junk. We finally found a compromise with some albums. You know what, though? When the album was over, we all felt more mellow, even after the lousy music. It just got us back down and steady somehow. We had to look at each other instead of the television screen, and we even nodded together with the beat." Many of the families reported this same response of the common listening to music providing a refocusing for the family.

STEP FOUR. LOOK TO THE CLASSICS. Most family picture albums, souvenirs, posters, and memorabilia suffer from drastic neglect. Pictures and slides may be paraded out for the occasional slow torture of an unsuspecting dinner guest, but seldom do families make the time to look at old pictures together, to relive trips, or get out "the old family stuff."

"It used to be that when I got out the family slides or videotapes, the kids would disappear after groans of disgust," said Mr. Muller. "Now, we spend every Sunday after dinner, for just a few minutes, looking at slides, films, or albums. The kids look forward to it, and it really reminds us of what matters. When I see my dad, the kids, a family trip, and we all begin to discuss it and share memories and remind each other of memories, it really feels great." This step does not have to be in the form of a major theatrical production, but just a few minutes of looking back can help the rhythm of the family.

STEP FIVE. THE FAMILY MEMBER OF THE WEEK. I asked the families in the clinic to pick one family member each week who would be given "extra attention." I didn't ask for major concessions, breakfast in bed, or a complete holiday for this special candidate. I only asked that the family keep a different family member in mind each week. I asked that the family listen more, do more, and try to care just a little more for that member. I asked that the member's name be put in a place of prominence, and that every other family member make the extra effort to enhance the life of that member for just one week.

"The funny thing was that we always have an employee of the week at work, so I don't know why it was so strange to have a family member of the week," said Mr. Johnson. "Everybody rebelled at first. Then we fought over the selection procedure. Now, it is just alphabetized turn taking. It's no big deal, but I did notice that when a conflict arises, a chore needs getting done, we do have a tendency to defer to the family member of the week."

Mr. Johnson's family and the other families found that

this fifth step drew their attention to the fact that the family was sometimes out of step, focusing too much or too little on one member. Just thinking about a family member of the week helped to call attention to this imbalance and to reestablish a more equitable rhythm of attention and caring.

STEP SIX. THE "AND THEN WHAT HAPPENS?" QUESTION AND THE CAUSATION CIRCLE TECHNIQUE. One of the biggest mistakes families make when they are trying to solve problems, trying to get their rhythm back, is to ask "Why did you do that?" or "Why did that happen?" I suggest that family problem-solving sessions be spent drawing "causation circles." I ask the family to start with the problem, any problem, and then ask, "And then what happened?" Without argument or agreement, I ask them to write down the various answers and then ask, "What happened after that?" I instruct them to keep asking the "and then . . . ?" question and to draw a large circle, until they discover that these causation circles always end by coming back upon themselves.

"My son said my daughter hit him," said Ms. Anders. "I used to always ask 'why?' when that happened, even while they argued about whether it ever really happened and who was the hitter and who was the hittee. Now, we just grab a big piece of paper, or we use a chalk board. I write down what was said, then keep asking, 'And then what happened?' Usually, things quiet down. Just listening to them, letting everyone be heard, and focusing on what happened next instead of trying to find the culprit or fix blame, seems to really help."

I have seen causation circles help families at very trying times. Just be sure that the rules are clear. It doesn't matter what really happened. The idea is to look at sequence, at the important family principle that what follows a behavior is what ultimately causes that behavior. Everything that happens to and in a family is a matter of rhythm, of sequence and cycle. By attempting to understand problems by looking at their natural family rhythm circle, family discord can be better understood.

Ms. Anders said, "My son and daughter were both surprised by the question 'And then what happened?' When we started this causation circle thing of yours, they were both used to 'Why?' and 'Who did it?' After my daughter hit, or just brushed, my son, they would argue. Then they wouldn't talk to each other. Then they both ran to me. Then I would try to figure out what happened. Then, at least usually, they would reluctantly apologize to each other out of pure fatigue or because one of them needed something from the other. Then they would stay away from each other as much as possible and sulk. Then, somebody hits, pushes, rubs, or looks at somebody the wrong way, and the circle goes on and on. Once we looked at the circle, we saw what we thought was happening. We were trapped in this thing. They had no way they could see to relate with one another, they tended to keep their distance, and then they would crash together. We had to come up with something they could actually do together instead of fight. We're still trying to figure that one out, but at least we can see the system in action. I actually heard my son say the other day that he felt he was circling with his sister again. I guess they're beginning to see it."

The causation circle described here, and the hundreds of similar circles I have seen in my clinical work, reveal the patterning, the rhythm of family life that can control us unless we decide to be the conductors of our own family symphony. If we can learn to see and sense the circle of family life rather than see our life as a one-directional, static line along which we are helplessly dragged, we will hear and move to a much sweeter music.

CHAPTER FIVE

Family Reason: Reasonable Families at Irrational Times

> "None of us are a genius. Some of us are just less damaged than most."
> BUCKMINSTER FULLER

FAMILY REASON: Understanding that we create our own world by how we choose to think about that world, and that rational family living requires self-responsibility for our own feelings and thoughts, and the awareness that we are not reactors to but interactors with events and people in our life.

PERSONAL POWER VS. FAMILY POWER

What we think is what we get. Our perceptions of the world are our interpretations of that world, our choices about how we think life is or should be. What we think is happening "to us," and our interpretation of our effect on others and their effect on us, are merely reflections of our own theory of life turned outward. In all that we do, we react to images that we ourselves project, creating our own life circumstances.

When we choose to see our life individualistically and to see ourselves as mere reactors to our everyday, local world, family members seem to "make" us angry or happy, we have "bad luck," and we trust only our personal power to be an effective "reactor" to a world "out there," over which we choose to have little or no control.

When we choose to see life in a family way and from a more cosmic, universally connected point of view, we are never separate from other people or events, so people and events can not "happen to us" or "make" us do or feel anything. Instead, we "happen" with people. We experience not just the local impact of limited natural laws of life, but become aware of a broader view of life in the context of our shared power, through our connection and shared responsibilities with everyone and everything.

Being family is more a way of thinking about life than it is a genetic assignment to a group of people, more a choice of how life will be than just a place we live. Reasoning in the family perspective is a cosmic cognitive style based on our ultimate connection with the cosmos and with the person walking beside us on the sidewalk.

The Family Reason Test

Take the family reason test to assess your own self-responsibility in your family for thinking and feeling about daily living in a family way. Use the following scoring system:

0	1	2	3	4	5	6	7	8	9	10
ALMOST NEVER		SELDOM		SOMETIMES		A LOT			ALMOST ALWAYS	

1. —— Are your family arguments short?

2. —— Do family members take responsibility for their own conduct, making an attempt to remain rational during arguments?

3. ———— Is there an absence of sulking and withdrawing after family arguments?

4. ———— Is there an absence of raised voices and hollering in your family?

5. ———— Is there an absence of accusations and blaming in your family?

6. ———— Is there an absence of name-calling in your family?

7. ———— Do family members see behaviors as inappropriate or destructive rather than finding fault with the family member himself or herself?

8. ———— Can your family maintain their sense of humor even when there are conflicts?

9. ———— Do family members listen to one another and show their listening by head-nods, attention, and immediate response to questions?

10. ———— Does everyone in the family take shared responsibility when things go wrong, believing and acting as if the family is in control of daily living, rather than a victim of random events?

———— TOTAL FAMILY REASON SCORE

If you scored more than the arbitrary 90 points on this test, your family is showing the ability to take responsibility for feelings and behavior, rather than ascribing what happens to external events or other people. If you scored less than 90 points, your family may be falling into the trap of "externalizing" their world, with family members viewing themselves as reactors to, rather than creators of, their daily family life.

BLAMING THE MIRROR: THE DIFFERENCE BETWEEN KNOWING AND PERCEIVING

PERCEIVING: Seeing what's out there and trying to make sense out of it. ("If I see it, I'll believe it.")

KNOWING: Looking within yourself, sensing who's in there, and making decisions and choices about how your world will be. ("If I can believe it, I'll see it.")

We tend to mistake what we project for what is real. There is a world of difference between knowledge and perception, yet we continue to confuse these processes in our everyday family life, fighting windmills that we build even as we criticize their builder, their construction and their worth.[1]

True knowledge is always rational, clear, logical, and truthful. It is not based on what we think or see as outside, but on the constant awareness of processes going on inside us, the choices we are making about our life and what our life means. Knowledge is awareness of our learned false assumptions of who and what we are, and the ability to free ourself from these assumptions to interact with the world actively and rationally, rather than passively and irrationally. Knowledge, first and foremost, is total self-awareness that humans make choices and that we are all responsible for our thoughts and feelings.

Perception, on the other hand, is mere intellectual reflex by an undisciplined mind that mistakes itself for "us." Perception is seeing things as happening to us, existing "out there," a simple mechanical reflex between a brain addicted to intensity and to stimulation. Perception is based on materialistic, sensory, narcissistic survival needs, and the false principle that love and living is "out there somewhere," to be sought and accomplished by being a powerful person who can master his or her world.

Perception is the surrender of your mind, allowing it to serve as mere automatic individual reactor to images you create from a set of universally accepted yet totally false assumptions

---

1. A difficult but detailed exploration of the concepts of perception and knowledge can be found in *A Course in Miracles*. (Tiburon, California: Foundation for Inner Peace, 1985).

about living in our world. Most family arguments are based on disconnection, on false assumptions made by an individual family member, which, in effect, cause the family to become irrational, illogical, and to collectively lose its sense of reason and most of its family power.

BENT FRAMES OF FAMILY PERCEPTION

Here is a list of completely false projections, perceptions of the world that can dictate the daily living of the family. They are based on the central false assumption that we are all separate entities, floating helplessly through life, while a series of random events happen to us. I have included a comment from tapes of family arguments of the five families to illustrate how these errors in thinking, these errors in family reasoning, play themselves out in everyday family life.

Ten False Family Perceptions

1. Life is short, and time goes by quickly, so we had better crowd as much activity and intensity into our daily living as we can.

Mr. Anders to his ten-year-old son: "We don't have all the time in the world, you know. Don't just sit there while time passes you by. Do you expect us to wait on you forever? You're starting to take up all of our time."

2. We are all really alone, on our own against a difficult and evil world.

Ms. Bonner to her teenage son: "You will never understand all I have to do. You just have your simple things to take care of, but I have to take care of everything. You have no idea what I have to put up with in my life, and you never will."

3. Being an independent person who doesn't really need anyone else is a sign of ultimate maturity.

Ms. Bonner's son in response to Ms. Bonner's statement

above: "Why don't you butt out of my life? I'm on my own now, and you don't need to be taking care of me. I take care of me. I'm my own person, and I don't need anybody else to help me or try to run me. I'm not a kid anymore. I'm independent."

4. Everything ends.

Ms. Steiner to her oldest son: "You know, we won't be a family forever. At least you can spend some time with us now. You'll be sorry when it's too late. All good things end, and then they are gone forever."

5. Anger happens to us when people or things go against us.

Mr. Johnson to his teenage stepdaughter: "I'm sure you know just how angry you make me. You can get me angrier than anyone I know. You are making me into a monster."

6. Love happens to us. It is rare, magical, and requires only that we let it happen.

Ms. Muller to her sixteen-year-old daughter: "Now listen. I know you think you're in love with this boy, but you're not. If you were, you would feel feelings like you never felt before. You would hear bells ringing. Give it time. Love takes time. You just have to let it happen, like a butterfly landing on your shoulder."

7. Death is the end of the self.

Ms. Bonner to her son: "Look, when you're dead, you're dead. Gone is gone. Your father is gone, and someday I'll be gone, and you'll be gone. You just have to face this and move on. When you're gone, you're gone for good."

8. Self-worth is determined by external criteria.

Mr. Anders to his eight-year-old son: "You used to be a very good student, and now look. Your grades stink. You've really lost it, buster, so we're cracking down on you. You're grounded until your teacher tells us you've improved."

9. No one is perfect.

Mr. Muller to Ms. Muller: "Nobody's perfect, OK? I'm

going to have a better year at work next year. I've really stunk up the place this year. Don't you think I feel bad enough without you getting on me? I'm a failure, OK? Now, are you happy?"

10. The world is made of opposites; good and evil, happy and sad, and now and then.

Mr. Johnson to his son: "Your friends are the wrong friends. They're just bad kids. I'm sorry to say it, but it's true. You're either a good person or you're not, and they're not, and if you hang around with this bunch, you won't be a good person either."

The above statements were made during the heat of family battle, and they reflect the local, individualistic view of life that is always at the root of family fights. If you look carefully, you will note that each statement reflects three major errors. First, there is a general passivity and surrender to what the family member sees as an inevitable universal truth over which no one has control. Second, each statement reflects externalization of life events, as if the person himself or herself is being led by life, instead of leading their life. Finally, each statement reflects a static, fixed orientation to life processes, as if "the way things are is the way they will be" or "that's how it goes" or "that's just the way it is." Ultimately, the individual view is a pessimistic, powerless view of living.

CHOOSING A FAMILY WAY TO KNOW

The family view of life is an optimistic, empowering view, because this view places everyone right in the midst of all life processes, instead of leaving people spinning outside of "the way things are" and trying to make it alone. Consider the following list of principles, based on a family view of living and on the laws of our infinitely connected cosmos. Once again, I have included statements by the five families to illustrate how these principles apply to daily living, but this time each family member chose the connected, family way of dealing with their problems.

Ten Facts for Family Knowing

1. Life is infinite. Our physical body and the see-and-touch world are not life, but only one step on our spirit's journey. Infinity cannot be "short," but we can create our own world, one that seems to be running out and running us down. We perceive life as short only in order to defend our unhealthy pace of activity and our spiritual laziness for taking responsibility for our world.

Ms. Muller to her twelve-year-old son: "Look, you have all the time in the world. I know you get frustrated trying to do everything you want to do. You're pressuring yourself to get all of your living done too quickly. Take your time, because you have all of it you will ever need. When you don't think you have enough time, it's only because you're not taking enough time. Time isn't running, you are."

2. We are never alone. We exist as a part of a universal system. We have only to look inside to sense our ultimate connection with everyone and everything. We feel we are alone only when we actively and always unsuccessfully try to separate ourselves from others.

Ms. Johnson to her new stepdaughter: "I know you feel very alone right now, but you're not. I know how confused and frightened you are without your first family around you. But remember, your first family will always be a part of you, and now all of us will be with you too. The more alone you feel, the more something inside you is trying to tell you how much a part of all of us you are and have to work to be."

3. It is impossible to be an independent person. Maturity is not separateness, but complete merging with and shared enduring responsibility with everyone, particularly family members. This merging is what a family means. We perceive independence as maturity only to defend our fear of being vulnerable and dependent with others.

Mr. Muller to his son: "If you think you can make it, or

anybody can make it, on their own, you're wrong. I'm nothing without you, and you will see for yourself that the most grown-up people are those who are close to other people, take care of other people, and try to make their life with other people."

4. Nothing ends. There is no such thing as time, only mechanical measures we use to segment our life. Change, not ending, is the principle of new science. We perceive things as ending to defend our narrow and limited concept of self as beginning and ending.

Mr. Anders to his wife: "We have to learn to get free of this time thing. We are so worried about what's next, we don't even know what's now. We always talk about later, about the kids growing up, about retirement. We're even starting to reminisce about things we haven't done yet."

5. Anger does not happen to us. We make a choice to become angry. We perceive people and events as angering only to defend our perception that we are emotionally irresponsible and reactive.

Mr. Johnson to his new stepson: "Nobody makes you angry. You always have a choice, even when you don't feel you do. You make yourself angry. It's not 'You make me angry.' It's 'I'm making myself angry.' "

6. Love does not happen to us and has nothing to do with magic, emotion, spontaneity, or meeting the right person. Love is spiritual awareness and commitment, a profound sense of self, the "self" of others, and accompanying behaviors which show the awareness of connected "selfs." We perceive love as happening to us or not happening to us only to defend our fear of total loving of everyone through our daily actions. If love happens to us, we perceive that we are free from the responsibility of having to "do loving."

Ms. Bonner to her preteen daughter: "I remember myself how these crushes on a boy felt, but believe me, love is not something you feel. Love is something you do. It's commitment, caring, and effort to make each other better. Doing loving takes a long, long time, so I hope you will slow down and not let yourself get all consumed by these feelings you are having. They're just the beginning of love, like the sniffles when you are going to catch cold. The real thing takes time."

7. Death is not the end of self, because there is no ending. The social self is highly vulnerable, but the spiritual self is infinite. Death is change. We perceive death as the end of self only to defend our own concept of scarcity, that everything is limited and quantified and running out.

Ms. Muller to her daughter: "We all are sad about Grandpa dying. We should be sad, because he's leaving us physically. Now we have to learn to love him for who he really is. He's a permanent part of us and of our spirit. We're all more than just our bodies. You know that, because a part of you, down deep inside, is listening to me right now. That part of you will never die, even when your body dies. Grandpa is forever, just like all of us. It's just hard to go through these changes from the easy ways of relating to someone to the challenge of loving Grandpa for who he really is, the part of him you can only feel and not see and touch."

8. Self-worth is not established by external assessments. We are all naturally worthy. We perceive self-worth as established by the evaluations of others only to defend another aspect of what is called the scarcity principle, that we are all lacking and seek in others what we lack in ourselves.[2]

Mr. Anders to his ten-year-old son: "I don't care if your teacher called you a C student. Nobody is a Steiner student. You're you. Don't let that teacher, don't let anybody, put limits on who you are. You got a C in her class. Getting a grade does not tell you what kind of person or student you are. It just tells you what you did in one place at one time."

9. We are perfect because the human spirit is perfect. We perceive people as imperfect only to defend our fear of our own potential for greatness and love. As long as we perceive the world and ourselves as naturally flawed and in need of perfect-

2. The concept of the scarcity principle has a long history in psychology and psychiatry. Attempting to make up for our own perceived deficits by seeking compensation through others, or how we see others seeing us, is described from the spiritual dimension in *A Course in Miracles,* op. cit.

ing, we feel excused for our own neglect of the welfare of others, and our own higher purpose.

Ms. Anders to her sick daughter: "You're not broken, darling. Your body is going through changes and trying to heal itself, but I don't want you to wait until you're all better for you to feel how great you are. You're a special, special person inside. That's where you have to start. Inside you. You're perfect in there, even though your body needs some repair. Start with feeling just how perfect you are and how perfect we all think you are, then your body can try to catch up with how great and healthy you are."

10. The world is one. We are one. Unity and wholeness is the governing principle of the universe. We see the world as divided and opposed only to defend our perception of our self as separate from others and to excuse our anger and hate as automatic reactions to others' behaviors. The ultimate principle of the universe is the principle of "us."

Ms. Johnson to all of her new stepfamily: "All we have to begin with is all of us. We're a group, an 'us,' and if we remember that we are always together, then nothing can ever cause us to hurt one another or feel alone. That's what families are for, so people can be 'us.' "

The above statements by members of the five families I am describing in this book, the same five families that made the errors I mentioned earlier, show the potential for rational thinking about life, even when there is severe conflict and stress in the family. The five families that were capable of the irrational, powerless statements you read earlier were the same families who also showed such wisdom, power, and peacefulness in their comments above.

FAMILY FUSES FOR FAMILY EXPLOSIONS

The narrow, individualistic view about daily living creates the fuse for almost every family argument. Based on the general views of life described above, there are ten "family false assumptions" that lead to irrational family interaction and destructive arguments. The clue to discovering the irrationality in your own family is to look for statements of surrender, loneliness, and helplessness that reflect one or more of the following assumptions about life—false assumptions that can cause us such suffering and fatigue in our family life.[3] Remember, you are the one who decides how to use your mind. You can turn your mind over to the role of perceiver, serving as a reactor to data you blindly project outside of you, or you can take control of your mind and use it as a tool for connecting with your family. You are the one who aims your brain.

THE MALIGNANCY ASSUMPTION: GOING FROM BAD TO WORSE AND WORSE

The "This is another indication of how bad things are and how much worse they're going to get" argument:

When we have no consistent and enduring positive image of our own perfection as a human spirit in progress, we feel out of control, and become victim to the malignancy assumption, the perception that any negative event or behavior we experience is a sign of impending and ultimate disaster, or a verifying symptom of our own flaws finally exposed.

When we embrace this assumption of repetitive negative testimony to our self-worth, our mind selectively magnifies every event in order to keep such false assumptions alive. An envelope with the letters "IRS" on the outside is bound to be a summons to federal prison. An argument with our mother is a sure sign that she never loved us anyway. The defiance of a child is an indication that we have failed as a parent. When we perceive the world in this way, we see the world through a cognitive magnifying glass that distorts reality much as the mirrors in a fun house exaggerate our image, only if we choose to cast our image to the mirror.

3. For a discussion of negative believes about daily life and the new field of cognitive restructuring therapy that has evolved to help correct this belief system, see A. Beck, et al., *Cognitive Therapy of Depression: A Treatment Manual* (New York: Guilford Press, 1979).

Mr. Anders said, "When the teacher called, he said that my oldest son was having some trouble in school. I thought immediately that I knew what was wrong. I had been working more hours lately, and I thought that I wasn't really paying much attention to my kids. I thought that I was leaving my wife with too much to do. I got angry at me, at her, at my boy, at work, at the school. I thought that this world just asks too much, to work and to raise a family. I thought that I still had years and years of this pressure. I got a headache and had an argument with my wife."

The Anders family went into a severe family crisis at this time of the school call. The parents began to argue, the son felt responsible for the problems, and everyone seemed overwhelmed and exhausted as the day of the meeting with the teacher approached. The family too quickly abandoned their family self-concept, the image of themselves as a good family doing their best. They failed to see this call as only "this call." They all began to project and perceive, rather than to try to know who they were and what would now be needed to make sure who they were would not be threatened.

Ms. Anders continued, "By the time the school conference came, I wasn't talking to my husband. I thought he was mad at me, and I was mad at him for playing hockey and sleeping instead of trying to help. When the teacher told us that our son had a reading problem that would require a tutor, we didn't hear him. We took the report as criticism. When we stopped and asked more questions, the teacher told us that our son has a form of dyslexia that required expert intervention. The problem had nothing to do with all the things we had been arguing about."

The Anders case above illustrates the importance of family "detoxification" of events. We must learn to contain ourselves and our thinking, remembering again the importance of family and life rhythm. Before families attempt to deal with any problem, I ask them to write the problem down in one clear sentence, without using the name of a family member and without labeling anyone or the family. I want them to be able to see the problem as a natural part of family life rhythm, rather than as "someone's problem." Here is a sequence of the attempts of the Anders family to write down the school problem.

ATTEMPT ONE: "Philip is having trouble in school because the father is working too many hours and is too tired to help with schoolwork, and the wife has to do it all."

ATTEMPT TWO: "Our family is disorganized. The father and mother are not communicating well enough to pay attention to the kids' school issues."

ATTEMPT THREE: "Philip has a reading problem. We have to find him some help."

FINAL ATTEMPT: "The family has to learn something new about reading."

At first, the Anders family rejected this process of problem writing. They thought that the final attempt was too simple, too incomplete. They, as many of us, were used to finding out "who did it," rather than starting with the assumption that "we all did it." They were finally able, however, to see that by seeing the problem as a shared problem, by not labeling Philip as the source of the problem or the only victim of that problem, and by stating something they could all do about the problem, a collective plan of action could be established. Within the limits of each family member, they all began together to learn about reading and reading problems, and about what they could all do about the problem the teacher had identified. The ultimate result was the seeking of further evaluation of reading skills, more family reading, oral reading together, and ultimately the finding of a tutor who not only helped Philip but gave some ideas to the whole family about reading skills.

You may find the above problem-solving process awkward. It may sound strange, too good to be true, or in some way phony. This is the case because we do not live in a society that starts from an optimistic assumption of "us" and the importance of inner knowing. We do not live in a society that sees problems and problem solving as a process involving the whole family. The examination rooms in doctors' offices are seldom large enough to hold a whole family.

We see our therapists alone. We label and diagnose people, which only serves to promote the malignancy prophecy, rather than identify a group way to cope with and try to solve a problem. All family problems are ultimately benign but significant challenges to spiritual development, unless we make these problems malignant by our own fear and overreactions to our own distorted perceptions.

Another effective way to learn the process of family detoxification is to avoid labels for individual family members, learn to focus on one issue at a time, and remember the difficult concept that we create our world more than we live in and react to it.[4] The difference between the first attempt at detoxification and the final problem-solving step shows how we can shrink problems by enhancing each other and the family unit.

THE ABSOLUTE ASSUMPTION: NOBODY SEEMS TO BE A PARTIAL FOOL

The "Some people are nice and some people are jerks" argument:

"He's a good son, but she's a lousy daughter-in-law," said Mr. Johnson's mother. "My first daughter-in-law was a goddess. This one is a devil."

Such exaggerations as the statement by Mr. Johnson's mother are not unusual. We are not conditioned to be qualifiers. Our world makes few allowances for the "in-between," yet almost all of us are "in-between." In our day-to-day living, things may be either black or white, but in the cosmos, everything is in process and beyond labeling. By the time a star is identified and named, it is typically dying or dead. You must choose whether you want to live in a world of the illusion of "either/or" or in the world of "maybe," "sort of," "sometimes," and "it depends" that characterizes the life of the universe.

In our day-to-day world, we want to know who is number one, who is the leader or the best, who is the worst or last. As soon as the outcome of an athletic event is clear, the crowd heads for the exits. Their interest was in who won and lost, not how the game was played. The undisciplined brain, that thinks it is alone in this world, is addicted to the intensity of victory

4. For a discussion of rational emotive therapy and ways to dispute and alter irrational belief systems, see A. Ellis, *Reason and Emotion in Psychotherapy* (New York: Lyle Stuart, 1970).

and the fear of defeat. It is not sensitized to the process of interaction and the game itself.

"I listened to my daughter's violin teacher," said Ms. Bonner. "He said that he wasn't working with her to make her just another violin player. He said he didn't want her sitting with all the other violin players. He wanted her on the end seat, the first chair, the concertmaster. It really bothered me, because I just thought she would have fun learning to play a violin. I guess the words 'play an instrument' should be changed to 'master the instrument.' "

Like Ms. Bonner, I wonder how we would ever have orchestras if none of the musicians would sit anywhere but in the end chair, the so-called "first chair." Things are seen as black or white, good or bad, in or out. Each year we have the Super Bowl in professional football, because few fans have been taught to show interest in the "pretty good bowl." We pay most of our attention to the extreme ends of the human experience, what we label as the worst and the best. In fact, almost all of us cluster somewhere near the middle of the range of human accomplishment, never being total failures or unqualified successes.

It takes a great deal of practice to learn to qualify our thinking and speaking. When families in my clinic listened to tapes of their discussions, they were asked to count the words that were either "absolutes" or "qualifiers." Words such as "always," "total," "complete," "hate," "lazy," "incompetent" and dozens of other words were more frequent than "often," "sometimes," "partial," "sort of," and "occasionally." I seldom heard someone called "somewhat of a fool." All foolishness seems to be complete.

One of the major risk factors in heart disease and heart attack, a factor as important as lack of exercise, poor diet, high cholesterol, or hypertension, is the relentless pursuit of "absolute success," of being number one, outdoing someone else, or avoiding, at all costs, being "less than we should be." Self-acceptance is as important as self-improvement, and healthy families give themselves permission to settle sometimes, to accept adequacy and to celebrate just "being."

"I asked you to cut the grass, not press it down," said Mr. Muller. "You didn't cut it right. When you cut it right, you cut first in one direction, overlap, and then cut in the other direction. You just pushed the mower all over the grass in all directions."

"Yes," answered Mr. Muller's son. "I got all of it, though. I just looked for where it was high and then I went over to that spot and cut. You asked me to cut the grass, not organize it."

This father and son were able to laugh about this minor disagreement, but it does illustrate how a family problem could arise when arguments over the "absolutely right way" to do something take place. A family system of qualifications, of in-betweens, of toleration of "sort ofs" and "OKs" can result in much more peace and gentleness than attempts to live up to arbitrary standards of the one and only way to live.

"If you want a good example of absolutism, how about this one?" said Ms. Johnson. "My first husband never made love with me, he made love on me. I was a project. He was working for my orgasm. Making love was only a way to work to what he called 'completion.' It's so beautiful now to not make love. Now with my husband, we share loving. Orgasms aren't accomplished. They happen to us."

Family absolutism can turn family life into a project rather than experience. If we are consumed by all or none, we usually end up with none. If we pay attention to process, to how we are traveling instead of just our destination, we end up getting at least some of what life is really all about.

THE GENERALIZATION ASSUMPTION: A LITTLE SELF-DOUBT GOES A LONG WAY

The "Now I've really done it" or "Now you finally did it" argument:

Some persons make prophecies about their entire future and self-esteem based on one report from someone else or one impression regarding their own or another person's behavior. They form images based on limited data, creating entire artworks from just a few negative strokes. A dropped plate means we are clumsy, a failed exam means we are a poor student, or the slightest flaw in one area causes us to devalue ourselves in all areas.

The generalization assumption tends to follow three steps. First, one negative report or event is personalized and seen as a general personal characteristic. Second, the report is seen as a forecast of social limitations because of the characterization. Finally, the person who generalizes predicts their entire future and views their self-worth based on one piece of usually exaggerated, inaccurate, and highly selective information.

"When my oldest son was turned down by the college he wanted to go to, it really took everything out of him," reported Mr. Steiner. "He was such a confident kid before. He did great in school, but not great enough for the college he wanted. The next thing I knew, he was thinking of himself as a failure, as not college material anyway. Then he started to pull away from his friends who were going to college. He said he didn't think he was smart enough to be with them. He started to hang around with some real losers. Then he started to talk about never going to college and about just taking different jobs to survive. It was very sad to watch the change from an optimistic and even arrogant high school senior to a dejected and helpless kid."

Our tendency is to see everything in terms of a lifeline, a vision that what is said to us or done to us today directs us helplessly down that line in one way or another. We seem to have trouble thinking of life, and of living our lives, in terms of "now."

We are looking for any signs of the direction of our lifeline, and when we experience rejection or criticism, we feel that an indelible mark has been made for us to follow. Our self-esteem is damaged, and we refuse to alter our family support system to serve us just when we need support the most. We begin to live out a self-fulfilling prophecy in keeping with the original rejection, and our family becomes a screen for negative projections rather than a process for personal growth.

Family members will continue to have fragile self-esteems just as long as they see their worth as external, and based on criteria established by the outside world rather than on the love of the inside family. A major family error is taking place. We are, in not-so-subtle fashion, teaching our children that their worth depends first and foremost on what they accomplish, much more than on who they are. "What a good boy you are! You cleaned your room" teaches that you are good because you clean well. Too seldom do we tell each other within the family that we are good boys, girls, men, and women, just because we "are." Certainly, socially constructive and compliant behaviors are important to our society's survival and to the welfare of everyone, but we must not lose sight of personal worth just because we miss the mark drawn by someone else.

I asked the families in the clinic to use as many family affirmations as they could in their everyday life. A family affirmation is acknowledgment of personal worth without a criterion. "Gee, you're really great" has come to sound phony except when we talk to very young children. When we talk to older family members, we seem to need some documentation before we give praise. "Good job" seems easier to say than "great person." We seem embarrassed to celebrate just "being."

Try this assignment, and you will see just how awkward personal rather than task acknowledgment in the family really is. Tell someone in your family that they are really a very wonderful person. Just say the words when they least expect it and especially when they haven't done anything for you or accomplished any major feat. Just affirm someone in your family, remembering that the affirmation is the process of acknowledging someone's worth for just being. You will probably notice that the family member will ask why you affirmed them. They will ask what it is they did that deserved this. We will never have families that can just "be" together if our affirmations are based solely on what family members "do."

THE SELECTIVE ASSUMPTION: ELECTIVE DEAFNESS

The "You never said that and I never said that" argument:

Even when we praise and affirm our family members, some of them will seem unable to hear us. They seem to select what they choose to hear, and such selection is often based on firmly entrenched negative self-concepts just waiting for verification.

"I only asked him why he had a B in science," said Mr. Steiner. "He hit the roof. He yelled at me and said I never appreciated how well he does in school. He said he doesn't drink or do drugs, and here I am attacking his report card. He never heard me say how proud I am of him, how great his report card was, how really super I think he is. He just got right on the B thing and sulked for days."

The selective deafness shown by Mr. Steiner's son is a deafness of seeming to hear only that part of a message which seems to affirm a preset notion of self-worthlessness. The sender of a message feels misunderstood and may resent the lack of appreciation and responsiveness shown by the person who is not getting the whole message. The receiver of the message seems only able to collect data for defense of prior conclusions he or she has drawn about himself or herself, or the nature of his or her specific interactions with a family member. The selectively deaf family member is looking for love in all the wrong places, just waiting for further evidence that seems to confirm their own low self-esteem in some area of their life.

The best way out of the selective listening problem is to assume that the receiver of any message is a perfect listener. Assume that what they heard was indeed what you said, even if it wasn't. The accuracy of a message rests with the efforts of the sender. "You didn't hear what I said" should really be seen as "you heard what I didn't say, so you must be hearing something I didn't mean to say. Let me try again." Amend, apologize, and assume, for the improvement of communication and enhancement of everyone's self-esteem, that the listeners did hear what they think they heard. Work hard to correct the message, for it is this effort, this reassurance that you care enough to send your very best, that the selective listener is really listening for.

The five false family assumptions described above, irrational ways of thinking about and forecasting what events in our lives mean, block the rational approach to family life that is necessary for preventing escalation of family conflicts. Ultimately, these assumptions generate a family life philosophy based on irrational thinking, and lead to eventual emotional conflict and family helplessness.

THE IRRATIONAL CORE OF FAMILY THOUGHT

We tend to mistake our reactions to events for the actual events themselves. When someone cuts us out in traffic, we may choose to become angry. We may think that the person who cut us out made us angry, when it is really our choice as to what emotion we will experience in any situation. We become upset that the person who drove in front of us "made us angry," and our reaction to our reaction is one of even more anger. Bad moods are only choices we keep making that we wish we wouldn't make and think we can't help making.

The only way to think logically about our daily life is to be aware of the fact that our thinking about events takes place in three phases. First, something happens to us. Then, we quickly interpret what happened. Then, we react emotionally. We are actually reacting not to the facts of the event, but to our reaction to the event. We are reacting to ourselves. When our heart quickens, fists clench, and face grimaces in anger, we are really responding to an interpretation, not an event.

Mr. Muller said, "My neighbor dumps his grass clippings on my property. I saw him do it. He thinks he can just do whatever he wants. He ignores my rights and just does whatever pleases him. It really gets my dander up. I'd like to collect the clippings all year and dump them under his Christmas tree for a nice gift." Even as Mr. Muller discussed this issue, he looked angry. His face was reddened and tense, and his fists clenched. Unfortunately for Mr. Muller, he often reacted much the same way to problems in his family, and he was incurring a health debt to be paid back someday in the form of real physical stress-related symptoms.

Mr. Muller was reacting to his perception of events. What he didn't know is that his neighbor really didn't think that dumping the clippings was significant at all. He thought the clippings would just disintegrate, even serve as fertilizer. The fact of the matter was that the neighbor really meant well by dumping the clippings. Mr. Muller interpreted this action from his own perspective, gave his meaning to the event without clarifying what the neighbor was thinking, and became angry at his chosen interpretation. Mr. Muller was reacting to his own reactions, was driving himself to anger, and he himself was at the wheel.

Mr. Muller became angry at what he thought was taking place, not the actual event. He was doing his thinking too late and with too little rationality. He should have been thinking clearly when he saw the clippings being dumped. He should have been thinking, "Well, my neighbor dumped his clippings on my property. I am sure of that fact, because I saw him do it. I cannot possibly know his motives for doing so, so I will ask him why he did it." Such clear thinking would have saved several drops of adrenaline from pouring in to Mr. Muller's bloodstream.

The reason we react to our reaction, rather than to actual events, is that we are constantly projecting our views and motives onto others. We operate within a set of irrational beliefs about how the world works, or is supposed to work, and our family life is burdened by what become firmly entrenched but invalid "ought tos" of daily family living.

THE FOUR INVALID "FAMILY OUGHT TOS"

CHILDREN "OUGHT TO" COME FIRST. Children have been viewed in different perspectives through the decades. From neglect to total indulgence, our view of the role of children has reflected our view of ourselves, our view of responsibility and of the priorities we set for our daily living. In recent times, the central irrational belief has been that children should always come first, should be the most important members of the family, and that their needs should always come before any adult family member's needs. As a result of this belief, many parents find themselves trying to raise their children rather than develop with them. We cannot raise our children when we assume an emotional position distant from or in deference to them. We must be able to pull them up with us, not push them over us.

"We used to do absolutely everything for the kids," reported Ms. Steiner. "We would almost totally sacrifice our own life for them. Then we realized that we really were not doing them any favor. In fact, we were pressuring them to be happy as a way of showing us that we were doing a good job."

Ms. Steiner's comment shows how family life can become obligatory for both parent and child when any one member of the family becomes the total focus and purpose of that family. Children don't come first, because nobody in the family comes first. The individual needs of any family member at any given time should determine who gets attention and who gets cared for. Parents who neglect their own development only leave their children a legacy of guilt.

WE "OUGHT TO" KEEP OUR FAMILY LIFE SEPARATE FROM EVERYTHING ELSE.

"I thought I didn't bring my work problems home," said Mr. Anders. "I tried to keep my job separate from my family. Then I learned that it was just an artificial separation. I could see that the kids could see when I was upset or pressured. It worked much better to share all problems openly, instead of pretending that life can be compartmentalized."

Mr. Anders had made the common mistake of trying to lead his life as if parts of this life could be opened and closed at will. It is irrational to think that how we feel at home or at work does not influence us everywhere we are; and family communication should reflect the totality of life, not some pretense of control by denial.

WE "OUGHT TO" GIVE OUR FAMILY MEMBERS UNQUALIFIED SUPPORT.

The worst thing anyone in the family can do, in terms of long-term family health, is to offer blind loyalty and support when a family member is under pressure. Studies of executives who suffered physical symptoms of stress indicate that those workers who had the least social support at work and the most social support at home were the worst off. What is needed at home is not only support, but problem solving, large doses of reality offered up with plenty of guarantees of unqualified love, and sufficient faith in the strength of the family that criticism and corrections can be offered when needed.

"No matter what happened, I used to always support my wife when she came home," said Mr. Steiner. "She would really complain about work, that somebody had really messed her up.

No matter what she said, I would tell her how right she was, and how unfair everyone else seemed to be. Sometimes, I thought that the other workers were probably home telling their families about how my wife was driving them crazy, and sometimes I thought my wife was totally wrong, but I would never tell her. I finally learned that what I was doing was just creating more distance between my wife and her work problems. We had to learn to really solve her work problems and my work problems, not just be therapists who listened."

The irrationality of blind family support was one of the most difficult family belief systems to correct in my clinic. "If you can't get support at home, where are you going to get it?" asked one frustrated man. He had to learn to get support everywhere, not just at home. He had to learn to use his family for reality testing, not escape from reality. The difference between work support and family support is only that, as much as it may want to sometimes, your family will never fire you.

There is total safety and security in the family system, with guaranteed "family union contracts" containing clauses of no dismissal or rejection. Such family contracts, however, carry with them the nonnegotiable responsibility of all family members to do much more than support one another. Family members must also help each other grow, change, and come to see their own flaws in an environment where such flaws will never result in rejection.

WE "OUGHT TO" LET OUR EMOTIONS OUT. Human emotions have received undue status and freedom. We think that emotions "just are." We think we "fall" in love, "become" depressed, are "made" upset, or should "get things off our chest." If it's an emotion, we think that we "just can't help it." In fact, we ultimately choose and are responsible for every emotion we will feel. This is a very important fact for achieving a rational family life.

Family members and other people don't "make us" unhappy or angry, and if you often find yourself feeling that somebody in your family is "getting to you," you must learn that you are choosing to let them get you. If we are aware of our ability to clearly understand what is happening, to understand that the world is what we make it and how we choose to see it, we can find the greatest freedom of all, the freedom to make choices about what emotions will fill our life.

"My dad drives me nuts," said Mr. Anders's youngest son. "He's always on me about something. He gets me upset and he just keeps going after the same thing. He causes me to get sarcastic with him, and then he gets mad at me when it was really him who caused it."

Mr. Anders's son's error is the same as that of any family member who attributes causation of their feelings to someone else. The time to intercede is following a behavior, a communication, any event. We must learn to pay much more attention to what is happening when it is happening, to ask ourselves, "How am I feeling about that, and do I really have to and want to feel like this?" We must learn to tune in and see what is happening inside, rather than ask about the motives of others whom we wrongly think have control of our emotions. When we make the choice for a family view of living, we choose to see ourselves as interactive, not reactive.

We do not have to let our emotions have us, to be victims of our emotions or slaves to automatic thinking based on irrational assumptions about life. We do not have to let our family interactions be reactions to our reactions. If we pay more attention to our connection with others, we can learn that no one upsets us. Instead, we may be behaving in an upsetting way with someone, equally responsible for the interaction.

Six Steps to More Rational Family Living

STEP ONE. A TIME-OUT FOR THE FAMILY. If you are arguing, you are irrational. Although I have heard therapists describe the art of fair fighting and how to have constructive arguments, I have never seen a rational argument in a family setting. There seems to be just too much emotion, too much closeness, too much investment by everyone concerned for an argument to be rational.

An argument may sound rational and polite, but I have never talked to a family member after a real argument about something that really mattered who was not upset and, at least to some degree, temporarily irrational. Instead of arguing, I suggest that, when possible, the occurrence of an argument should be an automatic call for a family time-out. A twenty-four-hour cooling-off period should be required, and an appointment should be set for a discussion or a planned argument. Unplanned arguments are the ones that really get irrational.

I am not suggesting that family life can be all structure and planned communication. Nor am I suggesting that we can always avoid irrational arguments, hurt feelings, and just plain old-fashioned family blowups. Family arguments are as much a sign of loving and growing as they are of frustration and impatience. I am suggesting that some effort to allow for a more rational approach to conflict by granting a cooling-off period whenever possible can be a big step to more rational living.

"When our family fights, we really fight," said Ms. Muller. "The only thing we do sometimes to keep some semblance of control and rationality is call a time-out. We have a rule that whenever someone calls time-out, that person must set up the time for time-in. It doesn't always work, of course, and we have had arguments about who and when to call time-out, but sometimes it gives us a chance to collect our thoughts."

Ms. Muller's statement reflects the realistic approach the five super families used to resolve their problems. Rational family living is an attempt to remember the difference between knowledge and perception, between looking at what we ourselves have projected outside ourselves and looking deep within ourselves and our families for how we really feel and think.

STEP TWO. FAMILY LOVE IS ALWAYS HAVING TO SAY YOU'RE SORRY. Never, but never, let anyone leave the home or go to bed angry or hurt without at least letting them hear the words "I'm sorry." Of course, these two words will not solve the problem or heal the wounds, but they will acknowledge that, even though we may feel ready to evict a family member forever, we will never be able to do so. We will always be family, whether we pay attention to our familying or not. What we are sorry for is the pain, the hurt, the family conflict. Saying "I'm sorry" does not admit defeat, assume responsibility, or excuse a family member's behavior. "I'm sorry" only gives the assurance that we are still family, even if we or someone else has acted like a complete fool.

"You should see the thousand and one ways we can say 'I'm sorry' in our house," said Mr. Anders. "Each of us has a way to say it which makes it sound like one more criticism or getting in the last word. But there is something about it, just saying it even if you don't mean it."

Mr. Anders is only partly joking about the more serious elements of never letting our irrationality cause us the ultimate pain of losing a family member to anger. Ms. Bonner, the widowed young mother, said, "I can still remember the nights we would argue and go to bed mad. What a waste. I'm only glad we didn't do it more than we did."

STEP THREE. THINKING FUNNY. Humor is the one saving grace for any family, for any conflict. Comedian George Burns said, "Happiness is having a large, loving, caring, close-knit family in another city." He was joking about the persistent conflicts that are one and the same with a close and loving family. If we are able to realize that our battles in the family stem from our closeness and caring, we can sometimes make time to let humor heal our wounds.

The Muller family told me that they have a rule that never fails them. Whenever an argument or conflict starts, someone in the family times the argument. The Muller family rule is that the family will find something funny—a book, a videotape, an audiotape or record album—to listen to or view together that is equal in length of time to the time spent fighting.

"This hasn't always been easy," said Mr. Muller. "We really have to search for something funny, because sometimes we fight a lot. We have found, though, that we have our favorites that we never seem to get tired of. We love to watch a Bill Cosby tape or listen to one of his albums. They have a lot of family stuff on them, and we can laugh at them a thousand times."

Laughter is the first and best of the three ways to shed tears. Cutting onions and crying can't compete with communal laughter. I suggest you get the family together for a group intestinal jog as soon as possible.

STEP FOUR. PATTERN AWARENESS. All families have certain areas of conflict that constantly repeat themselves. "I can't tell you how many times we have fought over the clean-room issue," said one of the children in the Bonner family. "You can count on at least one good battle a week, or more, about the same old thing. Mention your room, any room, and the 'Why is your room a pigsty?' argument starts. I wonder if my mother ever really saw a pigsty, because she sure seems to know a lot about them."

I asked the families in the clinic to keep a list of what they argued about most often. For a while, the list grew and grew. Then, the family members started to see patterns and duplications. Finally, just a few major conflict areas became obvious. The family was then asked to invest their full energy in coming up with some mutually acceptable plan or compromise to avoid the redundant and nonproductive conflicts.

"We finally declared my room not a room anymore," said the Bonner daughter. "We sort of passed a constitutional amendment. All rooms in the house have to be clean every day, and I finally agreed to that. Now that my room isn't a room, I'm exempt. I just keep my door closed. Of course, there were two subclauses in our amendment. I can't ever have anything in my room that I can eat or that gives off anything that could be considered crumbs. Second, no forms of animal life are allowed in my nonroom at any time."

As silly as the Bonners daughter's story may sound, the conflicts over the clean room stopped, allowing more time for attention to other and more significant family areas. It is my experience that it is seldom the big and important conflicts that aggravate the family over time, but the socks left on the bathroom floor that cause family heart rates to soar.

STEP FIVE. OLDER IS WISER, BUT NOT NECES-SARILY SMARTER. Every family at one time in its life has had the parents ask the question "Isn't there any respect for age anymore?" Many family arguments center around control and individual family member's rights to individuality. Attempts to make and enforce rules can result in rebellion and testing of the family laws. I ask the families to allow some deference just based on age alone. I ask them to allow more tolerance, more time, more listening to the older members of the family, simply because they are older.

Rational discussion can be enhanced by having at least some sense of deference to age. Such deference does not imply that the older family members, a parent or older brother or sister, know more or are likely to be more rational than a younger member. Age deference only helps establish some order in the communication system, some implied rules for who shuts up more often and who gets to talk the most.

"We don't have the parents talking all the time, but we do have an implied rule that when the older person wants to talk, they get the first chance. We also have the rule that the older person may, just may, have learned something through experience. Of course, experience can just be doing the same thing incorrectly over and over again, but the idea that older people get listened to a little more seems to help just a little."

This was a statement by Ms. Johnson. It reflects what some family therapists consider to be a radical departure from the idea of total family equality. I have not found that democracy works in the family setting. There have to be leaders, hopefully gentle and caring high-family-aptitude-type leaders, who lead by example and through toleration and consideration of everyone's views and feelings. Families that try to give everyone equal status and an equal say will find themselves arguing over even the most simple of family decisions.

STEP SIX. NO "SSAADD" TALK. SSAADD stands for surrender, sarcasm, assumptions, accusations, demands, and demeaning statements. All of these communication errors lead to irrational interactions in the family system. Here are examples of such statements from the five fantastic families:

SURRENDER: "That's it. I give up. The house is yours. Go to bed when you want to, do what you want to. I resign as a parent."

SARCASM: "Good. Good. Just go and come as you please. We love to wake up in the middle of the night worrying about you. It keeps us alert and reminds us to go to the bathroom."

ASSUMPTIONS: "I'm not naming names, but someone who shall be nameless probably is the one who put the rubber doorstop in the dishwasher. Now we have a nice set of spoons all melted together in one group. This will save us time setting the table. I can't imagine who could have done that, can you?"

ACCUSATIONS: "I know you did it. I saw it. You walked right by and spilled it. You did it. Admit it. You did it. You always are the one who shows no respect for the carpet in this room."

DEMANDS: "Do it. Just do it. This is your father talking now. Get up and go do it. Now. Move!"

DEMEANING STATEMENTS: "Nice going, Mr. Kind-and-Gentle. The next time I'm upset with you, I'll just act like little old immature you and punch you like you punched your brother. You are such a child. Really!"

Do any of these statements sound at all like something that might have been said in your family? They all show how irrational we can be when we live with a group of people for a long time. They all show the generalizations, magnifications, selectiveness, and absolutism I described earlier as the central cores of family irrationality. Remember, these things were said in families that were strong, healthy, and growing together. I have included them here so that you will not think that your family is much different from any other.

We all struggle to maintain our sanity in families whose very intensity of loving causes occasional lapses of love and an irrationality that stresses the family system. By making some effort to attend to the rational aspects of family life, the conflicts we all have at home can be reduced, ending up as parts of the family history we can celebrate together when the problems are long past and replaced by new family challenges.

CHAPTER SIX

Family Remembrance: The Keeping of the Family

"I wish I would have put as much emotion into my relationships with my mom and dad as I do now in my memories of them. We should pay more attention when we are making our memories. If we did, we wouldn't have so many regrets when all we have is memories."
SIXTY-YEAR-OLD WOMAN

FAMILY REMEMBRANCE: Never forgetting our family heritage, and being able to look to the family future while giving credence to the seniority of family members, respect for the history of the family, and value of and learning from the developmental stages and conflicts family members have already passed through for us.

THE GENESIS OF FAMILY

There are numerous theories of the development of the individual person. Sigmund Freud's theory of psychosexual stages, Erik Erikson's concept of the individual's struggle to resolve what he called psychosocial conflicts, Erich Fromm's theories of the individual's attempt to resolve the conflict between the

115

need for and the fear of individuality, and Alfred Adler's focus on the child's battle to overcome an inferiority derived from a family system governed by the powerful world of adults, are only some of the classical views of individual development.

The individual person's battle for self-expression and love has dominated the history of psychology and the content of countless psychotherapy hours spent on "individual life histories." Every family experiences its own life history, its own genesis, that profoundly affects each of its members. Although each family experiences a unique cycle of its own evolution, there were some patterns of family growth that emerged from my clinical work with hundreds of families and the five families you have met in this book. The individual family member who has a clear perspective and awareness of these phases and patterns, the common familial maps and main roads that make us who we are, is better able to overcome family crises, experience family hardiness, and maintain the family view of life.

The Family Remembrance Test

To discover to what degree your own family possesses the characteristic of family remembrance and a strong sense of its own genesis, take this test. Each item represents one way in which families show a respect for what has been, even while they are busy with what is and will be.

0	1	2	3	4	5	6	7	8	9	10
ALMOST NEVER		SELDOM		SOMETIMES		A LOT		ALMOST ALWAYS		

1. ———— Do your family members show respect for older family members, deferring to them just because of their seniority?

2. ———— Is there a shared concern and discussion in your family regarding what your family has experienced together, with everyone showing interest in the family history?

3. ———— When family pictures are shown, does every-

one in your family show an active interest beyond pained toleration?

4. ——— Can everyone in your family identify all of your relatives by name and relationship?

5. ——— Do your family members show a toleration for your family's most difficult relatives?

6. ——— Does everyone in your family show a concern for the future of the family and how it will be able to stay together throughout the years?

7. ——— Are favors and caring acts remembered and reciprocated in your family?

8. ——— Do you sense a deep sense of family loyalty between all family members?

9. ——— Do family members try to protect one another from disappointments and emotional pain?

10. ——— Is it easy to get the family together, and for family members to make time for family events, dinners, holidays, birthdays, weddings and other family occasions?

——— TOTAL FAMILY REMEMBRANCE SCORE

Again, on this family test, use the arbitrary score of 90 as an indication of how well your family is doing on this Rx of family life. If you scored over 90, it indicates that your family is doing very well on the remembrance factor of family life. Remember, however, that you are not categorizing or comparing your family to others, but trying to establish priorities for family enhancement and to identify which of the ten family factors deserves your most immediate attention.

OVERCOMING THE "INDUSTRIAL-STRENGTH SELF"

Psychologist Karen Horney, in her classic book *The Neurotic Personality of Our Time,* discussed the problems engendered by a society in which our focus on acquisition, achievement, and the tangible causes difficulties in our development of an ability to give and receive the less tangible but more important aspects of our humanness; true loving and affection. She suggested years ago that a society that places almost exclusive value on individual competitiveness will de-emphasize and ultimately neglect our needs for love and friendship.

Dr. Horney's predictions were accurate. We have developed what I call an industrialized sense of self, based on working, accomplishments, acquisitions, and personal growth. In the process of the evolution of "self," we have left an underdeveloped and impoverished sense of the collective body human and the emotional security that a sense of loving "us" can bring.

Modern psychology focuses almost exclusively on the "motivated individual," seeking to explain and enhance our ability to want, have, get, do, and achieve. Goal-seeking behavior is highly prized by goal-setting psychologists working in a goal-oriented society. When we spend our lives trying to "do" and trying to be motivated or to find more motivation, we forget how to "be," and how to enjoy how we are being with others. We too often neglect the powerful qualities of the human experience such as playfulness, awe, wonder, esthetics and the enjoyment of what went before. Instead, we work to excess, become cynical, seek to know rather than enjoy our wonderment, and fail to fully experience the beauty of daily living with our family.

If you stop to appraise your own life, you may notice how little priority you assign to the present and the past and how much time you spend on getting ready for later. Only when illness or age forces us to slow down do we seem to do what we should be doing all along, to look back and enjoy what we have done. Perhaps it is not an accident that it is always our short-term memory that fails us first. Older persons who forget the simplest of day-to-day things are often able to remember decades back to the specifics of family events. Perhaps this is nature's way of telling us that a phone number is less important than a personal conversation.

A Test of "Just Being"

We have been taught to be introspective and prospective, but we are less skilled at being retrospective and experiential. If we focus on being constantly motivated, we will have little time to sit down and pay attention to the making of memories. To see just how strongly our society emphasizes a motivated and accomplishment orientation to living, the "self do and fulfillment" mode of living instead of the "us be and experience" way of life, score yourself on the "Just Being Test" below.

On a scale from zero to ten, place your own orientation in each of the following categories:

The Unmotivated Test

1. Acquiring Things——————Not Having Things

    0————————————————————10

    2. Individuality—————Belonging

    0————————————————————10

3. High Achievement—————Being Average

    0————————————————————10

4. Tangible and Measurable—————Mystical

    0————————————————————10

    5. Independence—————Dependence

    0————————————————————10

6. Completion—————Accomplishment

    0————————————————————10

    7. Power—————Vulnerability

0————————————————————10

8. Aspiration—————Reflection

0————————————————————10

9. Status—————Anonymity

0————————————————————10

10. Concrete—————Abstract

0————————————————————10

The closer your score is to 100, and the more your score exceeds 50, the more "family remembrance"-oriented you tend to be, because you are more involved in enjoying the here and now rather than getting ready to accomplish something in the future.

THE FAMILY CENTER: THE BASIC BOND

To begin the process of family remembrance, try to think of the name of your first teacher or some teacher you had in elementary school. Now, use this name as the mental landmark to think back to your own childhood family at about the same time you were with that teacher. Try to remember the nature of the relationship between your mother and father, or between your brother or sister and your mother or father. Try to remember the one relationship within your primary family, your beginning family, that seemed to dictate the family ecology, the way in which the family felt and interacted in their day-to-day life.

Think back to the arguments, the loving, the relationship that seemed to be always "on," always influencing how everyone else in the family behaved and felt. Think of the relationship that seemed to control your family. Most of us can remember one particular relationship in our family that seemed more intense, more influential, than the other relationships within the family. This relationship is what I call the "basic bond," the core of the family unit. It is this bond that is the centerpiece of your family memories.

No family is stronger than the weakest two-person relationship within that family, and family remembrance depends upon the clear understanding of where the strongest and weakest links in the family system existed before, and may exist now. The family system and the living style of the individual tend to reflect interactive style, the style of loving and conflict resolution that is modeled from within this basic bond.

When the basic family bond is characterized by bitterness, distrust, and hostility, the family system itself begins to feel these negative emotions and the family becomes an unhappy place to live. When this basic bond is loving, trusting, and modeling of a sense of competence and effectiveness in daily living, the family itself develops these positive traits, generating a type of family optimism and family coherence that results in the family confidence that "we can make it."

ELECTIVE AND REACTIVE BASIC FAMILY BONDS

The strongest families are directed and influenced by elective bonds between two family members who have chosen to be the basic family captains, who have chosen to relate with one another in a way that intentionally influences and directs the family for good and growth. A mother and father who have actively chosen each other for family, and who work to make their relationship grow and last, can be a powerful influence for good within the family. A mother and daughter, father and son, or other combination can also direct the family effectively, if both partners in the bond make an active and communicated choice to do so.

If two persons in the family find themselves forced to take over the family and serve as its center, or if two persons in the family unknowingly are seen by other family members as the basic bond and the center of the family by default, trouble in coping with daily living can arise. The family system is much too complex to fall under the control of receivership, assigned persons who are either unaware, unready, unwilling, or incapable of family centering and direction.

"I can see now that when my wife and I were arguing, we were still trying to run the family, but we really were too consumed by our own problems," said Mr. Johnson. "I can see that we left the family on its own, leaving someone else in the family to take over. We defaulted."

Mr. Johnson is describing one of the dangers of the divorce process, the fact that what is seen as the basic family bond is no longer able to direct and energize the family. Usually unknowingly, some other relationship in the family takes over, and the family finds itself struggling to adjust to new emotional leadership.

When the basic family bond is one that has been forced upon its twosome, perhaps by the leaving, death, parental separation, psychological absence or abdication of a family member who would seem to be the more logical or traditionally accepted basic bond member, the family system falters for lack of strong leadership. A pseudobond can come to dictate family life and, as a result, everyone in the family feels insecure.

Strong, healthy families are always a matter of active choice, not surrender. It is healthier for the basic bond to be one that elects this central role, rather than being assigned to it, a bond that is consciously choosing to take responsibility for the family direction. Even if a family bond has been thrust upon two family members by crisis or other factors, the clear identification of the fact of that bond, its new role in the family, and active acknowledgment and effort by the family to enhance that bond are necessary if the family is to grow and the members of the bond are to remain healthy.

Many families today are ruled by bonds that are doing the job of family direction only because no one else seems to be willing or able to do it. A young brother and sister, a father and his son, a grandmother and her son-in-law may find themselves in an uneasy and awkward alliance as the only relationship available to keep the family going. Eventually, this bond itself will tire, come into conflict, and even mutual resentment, as the two persons struggle to fulfill requirements that neither of them understand, is ready for, or have chosen, and may even resent.

"After a time, my first wife's mother and I started to be the center of the family," continued Mr. Johnson. "It never worked, though, because my mother-in-law resented me, and I never wanted to be raising a family with her. We started a silent war, and everyone suffered."

Mr. Johnson's statement illustrates what can happen when bonds are assigned, forced, or unknowingly evolve to take over family leadership. One strong bond must lead all families, and the key to that strength is the choice to be that bond.

In this chapter I will describe some of the types of basic bonds that I have noticed in the families I have worked with. There are many more than the few I discuss here, and some of the variations of the basic bond are courageous, workable units that carry families through difficult times. Remember, the key for a successful central family bond is active choice by the twosome to fill the basic bond role, active communication within that bond about this role, and support and understanding by the extended family system, and even by society as a whole, regarding the role of this basic family bond.

The family is always changing, and so is the basic familial bond; so the following examples of basic family bonds refer more to behaviors than to types of people, and more to interactive styles than to a style of one person's behavior. The struggles faced by each of these bonds are the struggles that constitute family living in our increasingly antifamily, even nonfamily, world.

THE ENDURING PARENTAL BOND

This is the traditional mother-and-father relationship at the center of what is seen as the typical family configuration. Changes in our society are resulting in more frequent variations on this parental bond theme, but my years of work with families indicate that, modern and liberated or not, we have to face the fact that it is better if a committed father and mother are the basic bond of the family system. Courageous single parents carry a big load on behalf of our world, but a healthy two-parent bond at the head of the family provides the best chance for healthy individual growth of the family members.

The mother/father bond is probably the most workable basic bond in terms of fit with most of our social institutions and cultural expectations, and it is more appropriate for our articulated and publicized cultural objectives and morals. While other forms of relationships can guide the family, the least awkward and most efficient basic bond is still between a mother and father who choose to take mutual responsibility for the life, loving, and daily living of the family. All other bonds remain experiments.

The further we get from the father/mother bond as the center of the family system, the more problems we seem to encounter within the family group and with the family group fitting into the overall social structure. In our eagerness to develop long-overdue tolerance and understanding for alternative life-styles, we are sometimes afraid to say out loud what almost everyone feels; if possible, a mother and father living together in love and modeling a relationship of equality and mutual respect should be in charge of as many families as possible for as long as possible. Divorce, separation, and custody battles are forms of attempts to compensate for failures in human interaction and toleration, not alternative life-styles.

The Chinese family system has strictly forbidden divorce. Alasdair Clayre writes, "Society and the family come before the individual, the family must be maintained, whether husband and wife like each other or not."[1] The first communist Marriage Law emphasizes the duty of husband and wife to stay together, to protect one another, and to protect their family. Article XIII of this law reads, "Parents have the duty to rear and educate their children; the children have the duty to support and assist their parents."[2]

This reciprocity within the family, the obligation of parents to children and children to parents, is centered on the integrity and permanence of the basic husband-and-wife unit, and relates to the concept of the reciprocal family debt I mentioned earlier. All family members owe each other lasting love, the volitional, behavioral commitment to one another to support, nurture, protect and try to keep the "us" of family living alive.

Certainly obligation, laws, and communistic sanctions do

1. Clayre, Alasdair. *The Heart of the Dragon* (New York: Houghton Mifflin Co., 1985), p. 108.
2. Ibid., p. 80.

not serve as a model for healthy family life, but the ancient tradition of the sacredness of the Chinese family that gave birth to such laws says something about the role of endurance and commitment that was so cherished by the Chinese. Our society considers "staying together for the children" to be one of the worst motives of all for maintaining a marriage, but I suggest that we need to look at divorce as much more than a two-person decision.

The basic husband-and-wife unit creates, takes place within, evolves and is evolved by the family system. When we behave as if courtship, marriage, affairs, divorce, and failure to invest in family life are somehow separate from the family itself, we delude ourselves into thinking again that the family is place instead of a process within each of us.

The sexism of the Chinese system contained its own sources of severe pain and suffering. Husband and wife were allowed to divorce only with complex governmental interference, and in compliance with a few rigid "laws of divorce." Our system of giving priority to the individual, of looking for the right partner through serial marriage, ignores the fact that much more effort, commitment, toleration, and endurance is required of our husbands and wives if the family system is to maintain stability. We should be busy looking for a family, not a lover.

Our own legal system is one built on the assumption that divorce will be frequent, faultless, and should be made easy and fast. Swift divorce, so-called open marriages, legal and para-legal separation, day care, summer camp, separate vacations, daily schedules that preclude any real time together as husband and wife, and an array of "self"-improvement books and seminars are key aspects of our society now, and each of these factors is designed with an emphasis on the priority of individuality and not on the survival of the unit of family.

Why Parental Bonds Fail

People who get divorced are all wimps.
COMEDIENNE ROSEANNE BARR

The quote from comedienne Roseanne Barr is an exaggerated way of pointing out that maintaining relationships is much more difficult than ending them. Most parental bonds fail because husband and wife just did not try hard enough to stay together. Staying together as a basic parental bond may be one of the most difficult of human challenges, requiring maturity, sacrifice, just plain "putting up" with idiosyncracies and aggravation, maintenance of the family view, and constant awareness of a responsibility and tolerance for "us" rather than an exclusive pursuit of "self"-fulfillment.

As anyone who has divorced will tell you, divorce is not as simple and painless and "for the children" as some people would have us believe. We need to be looking to our development of our own marital aptitude, on being the right participant within a unit, more than we look for who we think will be a better partner.

When the father and mother consider divorce, the question should not be "Is this good for the children?" or "Is this the right thing for me or us?" The first question regarding divorce should be "Is this worth ending our family for?" Legal issues of custody, the maintenance of friendship outside of the marriage contract, and references to the "truly mature divorce" notwithstanding, the end of the basic bond is the end of the worldly and physical aspects of the particular family upon which that bond was built.

Divorce is always a failure, a failure to keep the system together. Divorced persons should understand why and how they failed, not explain away the marriage's end with statements such as "It was better for both of us." Divorce is often something done to our family and children rather than for them. In our hectic and delusional search for the perfect partner and a successful, fulfilling life, we are running right past the most important issue of all; sticking it out, making it work, and staying together for the children are still viable options.

We are encouraged to divorce by images of the so-called "mature divorce," where everyone loves everyone, respects everyone, and still remains lovers and friends even after the divorce. If there is such respect and love, why haven't these divorcées used some of this love and respect to try to keep the system intact? Is the process of divorce without its own demands for physical and psychological energy? Where do we choose to spend our energy, and why are we sometimes so quick to choose to invest that energy in a new beginning, rather than attempting to maintain an established family? Do we invest for separation and potential personal growth in the future, or for unity, survival, and growth of our family now?

I have not seen evidence that living together, divorcing, serial marriages, shared custody, visitation rights, and open marriages really work for large numbers of persons. I see instead that divorce is much more difficult than Hollywood tells us it is. I see that custody becomes more of a legal term for distributing parental claims to what they see as their natural birthing right, with children held "in custody" more than loved within a growing relationship. The healthiest family, the goal to work for, is still a mother-and-father-centered family. Everything else is, however courageous and however necessary, an approximation of a growing family.

Ms. Johnson, the wife who is sharing a second marriage with her husband who is also married for the second time, says, "I love my new husband. I love him deeply. I don't think I could have ever stayed married to my first husband. We just could not get along. But I wonder. I have to tell you that I wonder sometimes if I should have, if we should have, tried harder. The divorce ended our family. As many and as serious as the problems were, it was our family. I know it hurt the kids at least as much as it may have helped, if not more. I miss it, and I know my second family is unique to itself, but my first family is over. I will never get it back. The visitations, the sharing of our children at holidays, the false 'hello and how are yous' every time my first husband comes to get the kids are things I will never get used to."

Mr. Johnson adds, "I said to myself that I had to get a divorce. I could see no choice, but an easy divorce probably means you never really had a strong family in the first place. If you can get an easy divorce, than you weren't in a relationship. If you were in a relationship, the divorce will be difficult, and maybe you should put the divorce effort into a relationship effort. I don't know. I can tell you for sure that divorce isn't as easy as everyone seems to tell you it is. I feel free from the arguments and the distrust with my first wife, but I grieve for what we did have, for the family we started but never finished. I do feel like a failure in some ways."

Mr. and Ms. Johnson's reports were typical of reports from hundreds of men and women who divorced. When many of the persons I interviewed divorced, they were looking "out" and not "in." They assumed that something was missing in someone else or that some need within them was not being met by someone else. These persons too often saw the decision for divorce as a step to self-fulfillment rather than major and irreversible family change. Almost all of them paid too little attention to their own family's unique history and how much a part of them this history had become.

All divorce is compromise, and an attempt to fail a relationship gracefully. A society that worships the self, that worships motivation and accomplishment of goals, is often too quick to promote the surrender of the "us" for a gamble for the attainment of happiness for "me."

WHY CAN'T WE "COME" TOGETHER?

The problem of premature divorce is much more common and malignant than the popular sex diagnosis of "premature ejaculation." The popular sexual-dysfunction diagnosis of "inhibited sexual desire" is much more accurately described as inhibited sense of commitment to volitional and enduring loving behavior beyond genital interaction. If we are failing to come together, it is not in our sex lives where the problems lie. We fail to come together because we sometimes make insufficient effort to "be" and stay together. We show a family fatigue and become too lazy to try to make the family work.

Many of our current psychotherapists were trained in the times of the "me" generation. Their teachers, the theorists they read about, themselves did not maintain strong family ties. A check of the heroes of psychiatry and psychology reveals that almost every one of them failed in their own relationships. Many therapists themselves are divorced or have abdicated family responsibility.

Psychologists are trained that cultural relativism is fact,

and that we are, first and foremost, what our culture makes us and secondly, what our psychosexual influences leave us. Cultural relativism, the idea that we are first what our culture makes us, is incorrect. We are first humans. Differences between us are minimal, existing in shades of experiential difference rather than different colors of life. However, modern psychology sees us as different, and driven by egocentricity and ethnocentricity. Psychology thinks that health is individuality, perhaps because so many psychotherapists themselves have been so individualistic in their approach to life. The philosophy seems to be "if your marriage is broken, get a new part" rather than "if your marriage is broken, fix it."

Psychologists Johanna Shapiro and Deane H. Shapiro write, "The pursuit of transcendent or transforming experiences is often posited as antithetic to relationship. Indeed, great lovers of humanity in the abstract, such as Mahatma Gandhi and Albert Schweitzer, have not always been overly successful in their most intimate family relationships."[3] Our psychoheros have almost all been rugged individualists who made little investment in their own family.

The first sex, the first love, is not of, from, or to self, but between parent and child. Even in utero, a bond is established. It is pure psychological myth that we must first love ourselves before we can love anyone else. Love is a behavior we learn to do together, a shared commitment for the mutual welfare of another person. Try as psychologists and pseudopsychologists might, they will never overcome the reality that we are not separate beings. We are "us."

As I pointed out earlier, the extremely healthy person is often seen as someone who doesn't need anyone else, someone who has broken the bonds of the immature and regressive family ties. In fact, some prescriptions for the extremely healthy person advise against intimate family relationships. Gandhi became an ascetic to give more of himself to others, and Catholicism still requires that a priest have no primary intimate family of his own. The assumption seems to be that a loving commitment to a family is somehow less or different than a love for

3. Shapiro, J. H., and D. Shapiro. "Well Being and Relationship" in *Beyond Health and Normality,* R. Walsh and D. Shapiro, eds. (New York: Van Nostrand Reinhold Co., 1983).

personkind. It is assumed that high-level development is ultimately a lonely struggle, yet there can be no true development at all until we learn the endurance and commitment necessary to keep a real family alive.

Ms. Bonner, a single parent now, because of the sudden death of her husband, said, "I really have trouble putting together what I think with what I feel. What I think is that the old Mommy-and-Daddy relationship is not the only way to raise a family. I think that a woman or a man can raise their family well alone. I think, as a woman, that using day care centers and focusing on career, working out some strategy for being two parents in one, can still result in a strong family and happy kids and parents. I think that serial relationships with many partners can be fulfilling. But I feel, or should I say I fear, that there is something basic, something almost required, about having a mother and father raise the kids. I know that there are millions of happy parents and kids who come from families that did not have one consistent set of parents, but I'm just beginning to feel that, given the choice, a Mom-and-Dad basic relationship for the family is the best in the long run. God, I hope I can make another one. My kids need, and I need it."

I am certain that the general unhappiness, the continued and too often frustrated and unrewarding search for meaning, for love, for intimacy and closeness that characterizes our society today, is related to disruption in the basic family system. I am certain that such disruption is, in large measure, due to the absence of a persistent and consistent basic parental bond at the helm of the family system. Because we are so motivated, so driven for self-fulfillment, we have left our families to fend for themselves.

THE FORFEITURE PARENT

Because the basic parental bond fails so often in our society, more than eighty percent of our children will not be raised by the same mother and father to their eighteenth birthday. Divorce, separation, desertion, death, and what I call the "forfeiture parent," result in most of our children being raised in families that are not directed by a mother-and-father basic bond. The "forfeiture parent" is the mother or father who, while staying in the marriage and filling the ascribed role of parent, really does very little parenting or familying at all.

For the forfeiture parent, the family is only a place to be, somewhere to go after work and before recreation, some place around which financial accounting, retirement systems, life insurance, and taxes are organized. "The only time I think he realizes he is in a family," said one mother, "is when he checks his Form 1040 on the income tax return for number of dependents."

The forfeiture parent often brags that "I haven't missed a school play or a school conference one time." Forfeiture parents will describe how important the family and the children really are to them, but if you listen carefully, you will hear obligation rather than caring and family enjoyment in their voices. The forfeiture parent doesn't really experience family life; he or she attempts to survive it, doing things for the family much more often than really doing things with the family.

I was touring Disneyland with my own family when we spent more than an hour waiting in line for the Space Mountain ride. The father in front of me complained the whole time. "I hope you kids are going to enjoy this. We've been waiting here for hours. I hate these rides. You'd better enjoy this." This poor man was about to be shot through space as a prisoner rather than as a part of a family enjoying the excitement of life. He was forfeiting his parental right of loving his life with his family, because he was too busy doing life for his family.

Of course, just having a mother and father present and together does not mean that the mother-and-father relationship is truly the basic bond. A true basic bond is behavioral and active, not symbolic. Freud was wrong. It is not our unconscious images of the family that cause the trouble in some people's development; it is the real and present danger of parents who never wanted to parent, who didn't really parent at all, parents who feel obliged rather than flourishing in the family, and children who are never given the opportunity to truly "child." The best of all basic bonds is suffering severely in our society, and the following bonds are filling the void.

THE IMMATURE PARENT/ EXPLOITED CHILD BOND

This is a family's central bond made up of one child and one parent who have assumed the directional responsibility for the family. An adult may actively or unconsciously enlist, for life, the help and support of a child in the family, in order to keep the family or the parent alive and as well as possible. When one adult is missing from a pair that could direct the family, one of the children will almost always be assigned the role of surrogate parent.

When a child becomes a parent, the potential for exploitation of the child always exists. The child can come to be resented by other children in the family, be robbed of his or her opportunity to be a child, and become overwhelmed with feelings that are happening much too soon and without sufficient preparation. The resentment from this experience can be lifelong and continue to show itself in future relationships, where the adult cannot seem to be nurtured by another person because they know only the role of nurturing.

"I never had a chance to grow up," said Ms. Steiner. "I seem to have always been grown up. More was always expected of me. My father never did anything, and my mother turned to me for support and for help with everything. She never seemed to even think about it. She just assumed I would listen to her complaints, do the work my father never helped her with, and be her husband or sister instead of her child. I felt sorry for her, and I still do. But I resent her for it. I resent my father for it. I feel like I have already led more than one life. I feel like I missed out on being taken care of, and now I overdo it with my own children. I probably spoil them because I'm afraid to use them like I was used. I never respected my mother. I just felt sorry for her. God, I hope my children will be able to love me and not pity me."

Ms. Steiner's comments illustrate the pervasive and lasting influence of the parent/child primary bond at the center of a family system. The positive aspects of such a relationship are a strong and permanent bond between the parent and child who struggled together to help the family survive. There can be a communication, an understanding and an empathy between this parent and child that few people will ever know and few relationships can parallel. The courage and emotional resilience of parent and child together often carry the family system through the most difficult transitional life crises.

"My mother and I had to pick up the pieces," said the young daughter of Ms. Bonner, the widow who lost her fireman husband. "We just sort of started doing things together, talking more and differently than before. She needed me. She needed me in a different way. She was still my mother, but we were more now. Much more. We fought differently. We argued and fought, but we were different and closer than ever, once I started talking about how I felt about Dad being killed."

Ms. Bonner's daughter's statement gives evidence of the potential strength of the parent/child bond taking over control of the family. The same issues were raised by comedienne Joan Rivers in a recent television interview regarding the impact of the loss of her husband on her relationship with her daughter. Ms. Rivers said, "We are closer now than ever before. We would have never been this close without this terrible crisis. Don't get me wrong. We argue, and we are trying to learn from one another. We're trying to grow through this thing together. I need my daughter, and she needs me in a totally different way now."

My clinical experience indicates that there is seldom a midground in the parent/child primary family bond. This arrangement never just "works out." There will either be permanent scars for the child and guilt on the part of the parent, or the closest of bonds that will last a lifetime. The best step a parent/child family bond can take is to acknowledge that bond, talk about it openly, and share the pain and conflicts that such a bond will always contain. When the bond is assumed, ignored, or taken for granted, both parent and child will leave much unfinished emotional business that will forever interfere with their relationship together as adults and their capacity to "family" with others later in life.

One of my woman patients reported, "After I finally divorced, I could never find a man to even date. Every one of them seemed totally inadequate, even worse than my husband. In therapy I learned that my relationship with my daughter had been my basic relationship, not my relationship with my husband. We had raised the family and I had come to depend on her. It was a strange form of adultery. I mean, I made her an adult because I needed one to help me get through my life and take care of my family. No man could ever meet the needs or be what she was to me."

This woman's daughter, who was joining her now in family therapy, said, "I just never saw it. I knew that I cleaned the house, got dinner ready, and even put the little kids in bed. It just seemed to be what I was supposed to do. I thought kids like me always did that kind of stuff. I would listen to my mother's complaints about my dad. I would listen to her cry in her bed at night, and I would cry too. Then I would go to her room and hold her and comfort her. She needed me. Now, I don't seem to have any caring left in me. I guess it was all used up much too soon."

This discussion with this mother and daughter illustrated the potential danger of the parent/child primary family bond. While such bonds can save the life of some families, and result in a lifelong love between the parent and the child, based on their sharing of a struggle to love, the bond between an under-developed adult and an undeveloped child can influence both persons, consciously and unconsciously, throughout their lives.

Our society continues to count on women to keep the family going, so the parent/child family primary bond is most typically between a mother and one of her children. Such a bond may evolve between the father and one of his children, and again it is most often a daughter who becomes the surrogate parent, because of the continuing dominance of the matriarchal model, homophobic characteristics of men, and sexist dependence on women for family care. Just as men too often enlist their wives as housekeeper rather than partner, some men enlist one of their children as caretaker, causing a lack of more appropriate parent-child interaction.

Some men may turn to one of their children for the meeting of their own corrupted and distorted needs for intimacy, an intimacy the man has never invested in with his wife. Sexual abuse or incest may be related to deficit-based bonding. If the man sees his wife as caretaker and maid, assigning her out of his romantic interests because of fear of closeness or sexist depersonalizing of his wife, and perhaps all women, he may turn to a child for these needs. He may immaturely genitalize the deeper needs for love and caring that he has been unable to acknowledge, share, and develop with an adult woman.

Mothers may choose their daughter for the primary family bond out of their fear of being alone and an inability to develop autonomy. Fathers may choose their daughter for the primary family bond to compensate for their inability to maintain intimacy on an adult level. Sons may be chosen by a parent because of false images of the strength-and-protector model of the male in our culture. The only hope for success in such bonds is open and vulnerable discussion of the adult's motives and awareness of the child's primary nurturing needs.

The parent/child family bond may continue its influence through impact on the future selection of partner and subsequent marriage of the child, when he or she becomes an adult. Parental interference, whether real or symbolic, in the new family of the grown-up child, who must now himself or herself be concerned with a new family group, can result in family conflict or competition between father- or mother-in-law and the new spouse.

Remembrance as a positive family characteristic depends upon keen awareness of this parent/child bonding process and its chronic impact. The healthy functioning of such a bond depends upon the clarification of that bond, acknowledgment of the bond by both persons and by the family system in which it is functioning, and on efforts to reestablish new relationships free of exploitation and overdependence.

THE CHILDREN-AS-PARENT BOND

When the adult bond fails a family, or when even one parent is unable or unwilling to take on responsibility for the primary direction and survival of the family, two of the children in a family may take on the central bond role. If there is only one child in the family, that child may turn to another adult outside the family, or to a peer, to serve as a partner in the bond to offer at least some direction to the family system, some sense of centeredness, direction, and control. In effect, children begin to take care of adults and other children.

"My sister and I were the family," said Ms. Steiner, as she

described her own child bond as center of her primary family. "When economic problems almost ruined us, and my dad and mom had to work, my sister and I took care of our brother and the house. We even took care of my parents and my grandmother. We have been close ever since, but just like before, my sister and I argue all the time. I guess it's like a sister marriage. We love each other, but we get into fights."

Many of the families I have worked with over the years have been under the direction of a two-child bond. The parents may either be too busy or too self-consumed to pay attention to the direction of the family unit, and two of the children, or a child and someone other than one of the parents, carry the day-to-day burden of family life maintenance.

The danger in this type of child/child central family bond, even though a lifelong mutual caring can develop, is the danger that underlies all of the central family bonds except a stable two-adult bond. When a bond evolves by reaction, surrender, or default, the central bond is not in place by choice, but by survival. To "drive" a family, to be at the center of the family system, serving as the consistent source of direction and stability, is one of the most time-consuming and demanding of personal tasks. It requires maturity, self-confidence, and an evolved and tested sense of direction, born both of experience and of the wisdom of knowing what really matters from what doesn't really matter too much at all. When children must parent, their energy for their own development is drawn from them.

A single parent will require a bond, a relationship with another mature person, as friend or lover, who can help with the direction of the family unit. One person can not direct a family alone, and active choosing of someone to help with familying is a key step in single-parent family survival.

In collecting data for this book, I classified the family systems I saw into twelve categories, twelve forms of family system within which the bonding I have been describing took place. Before I describe the stages of the family development cycle, consider each of these twelve types of family system to see which system most closely resembles your own primary family and the family system in which you are living now. To do so is to begin the process of family remembrance, of knowing how sets of two people move beyond mere grouping to healthy family life.

TWELVE VARIATIONS ON A FAMILY THEME

I have listed the twelve types of family system in order of their frequency as seen in my clinic. As you consider each category, remember that no one category applies to any family. All of our families are parts of each of these categories, and all of our families change over time. This list is presented only as a point of departure for your own remembrance of your own family systems, as some "types" of systems to replace our more typical emphasis on "types" of people. I have included a brief statement from various members of the five families, regarding their own primary family background, to illustrate each category.

TYPE 1. THE MATERNAL REACTIVE FAMILY. This is the single-woman family that may have resulted from unwanted divorce, widowhood, separation, neglect, male sexist default of equal family responsibility, or the chronic debilitating physical or mental illness of the husband. Self-doubt, financial pressures, fatigue, and disillusionment may be noted on the part of the woman carrying the full load of this family system. Our world is not only still a man's world, it is also a couples' world, and a great deal of energy is needed to direct a family alone for a woman who must confront discrimination and exploitation in her daily life. We expect our women to protect the family, and we do not commend or reward women for what we think they are supposed to do and are genetically designed to do anyway.

"I was raised by my mother," said Ms. Bonner. "She had everything just dumped on her. My father seemed to think that being there was all that he had to do."

TYPE 2. THE PATERNAL REACTIVE FAMILY. This is a single-man-directed family that may have resulted from unwanted divorce, widowerhood, separation, attempts by his partner to compensate for years of what she sees as a lack of autonomy, or the chronic debilitating physical or mental illness of the wife. As in the case of the maternal reactive family system, the partner may in fact still be present, but is not for some reason able to fill the role of coparent or codirector of the family system. Self-doubt, resentment, uncertainty, and a tendency to overcompensate through overindulgence or rigid discipline may be noted in such a family. Our world is a world of woman-run families, and the man who finds himself in charge of his own family may find himself without clear role models, social support, or rewards for his efforts to keep the family going. We applaud our men for working and achieving, not for loving and familying.

"I was always amazed by it," said Mr. Anders. "My uncle raised the family, made the money, cooked the food, and gave the parties. My aunt got all involved in this women's movement group, and she stopped doing anything. She didn't even come to family parties any more. We all sort of felt sorry for Uncle Steve, but now that I think about it, we wouldn't have felt sorry for Aunt Angie if she did it all. We were sexists even then, I guess."

TYPE 3. THE MATERNAL ACTIVE FAMILY.

This is the family directed by a woman who has chosen divorce or separation or to raise her own family as a single person. Since our society expects women to care about and care for family, this type of family system is better supported by our social institutions than some of the other family systems among the twelve listed here. Women in our society are expected to behave like a man, act like a lady, and work like a dog. Society expects a woman to be able to direct a family alone, particularly when she makes a choice for her own independence. As one woman said, "All woman have to raise their families alone. Some women just have a man around and others don't." The woman directing this type of family may find several other women with whom to bond for support in directing their families, because statistics favor the chances of a woman meeting other women in charge of their own families.

"I was proud of me," said Ms. Johnson. "I chose to take on everything, and I proved I could. Then I started to get so terribly tired. I realized it wasn't so much what I was doing, but my constant effort to do things even better than before the divorce. I was trying to prove something instead of just getting on with living."

TYPE 4. THE PATERNAL ACTIVE FAMILY.

This is a family system directed by a man who has chosen divorce or separation or to take solo responsibility for a family system. Society tends to wink at such arrangements as novel and somehow courageously original on the part of the man who attempts to direct his own life while taking exclusive responsibility for a family system. Such a pattern is still seen as somewhat of a cultural experiment on behalf of male liberation. There are few support sources for a man who chooses this role, for men are supposed to have "more important things to do" than take total responsibility for the most important social institution in the world, the family.

"It was really novel then," said Mr. Muller. "My next-door neighbor divorced, and he got custody of all four kids. We never thought he could do it, but he did. Everybody kept trying to find him a woman. We thought sure he would die from the strain of what he was trying to do. He never remarried. He raised the whole bunch alone. We were amazed."

TYPE 5. THE COMPLIMENTARY FAMILY.

This is a family with two adults in charge. Typically, one partner does almost everything while the other does almost nothing. The assumption is one of complimentarity, of each adult's tasks fitting to the tasks of the other. In reality, there is often a sexist division of responsibilities, with minimal or token family time or task contribution by, usually, the man, who may see his role as family financier while his wife takes care of everything else.

"My parents had such a system," said Mr. Muller. "It was like a dance. My dad would start the coffee, hand my mom her cup, and she would cook the breakfast. Then he would clean off the table, and she would do the dishes. They had the thing down pat. Neither one of them ever, but ever, did what the other one was supposed to be doing, and when one of them was sick, the whole system fell apart until the illness passed."

TYPE 6. THE SYMMETRICAL FAMILY.

This family system is characterized by an intentional and continuous effort on the part of both family adults to share the responsibility of family direction and maintenance. An attempt is made to keep the primary adult family bond one that is egalitarian, nonsexist, and balanced. Competition and overlap of responsibility can cause some conflicts in such a family system, and society does not strongly support or reward such an egalitarian relationship. Symmetrical families are efficient in day-to-day adaptation, but can suffer from a sense of being trapped in a problem-solving rather than life-enjoyment mode.

"I can still remember my grandfather and grandmother arguing over who waxed the floor the best," said Ms. Anders. "They tried to outdo each other on everything. One day, the kitchen floor got washed three times because they both thought the other one had left watermarks."

TYPE 7. THE PARALLEL FAMILY. This is a family system that vacillates between the complimentary and symmetrical family pattern. Symmetrical and balanced as to role and responsibility for daily family life, this family system can become complimentary in pattern when major family problems arise. One partner will take on certain tasks and the other partner will do something key to the crisis management. This is a transitional pattern that lasts only through the crisis or problem period. Then, following crisis resolution, the family returns to a more symmetrical pattern. This is a rare but highly adaptable form of family system, and there are often problems in returning to a symmetrical pattern of family life following a prolonged family crisis that may solidify task assignments that were designed to be only temporary.

"I think what made my parents so special was how they could adapt to anything," said Ms. Johnson. "Nothing slowed them down. They both did every task. Heck, they ate problems for lunch. They never missed a beat."

TYPE 8. THE COMPENSATED FAMILY. This is a family system dedicated exclusively to problem solving rather than loving and living. Typically, one major chronic challenge dictates the daily life of the family. An impaired child or parent, the challenge of dealing with an aging parent or parents, coping with substance abuse, workaholism, or mental disturbance on the part of one family member may be the primary task and accepted reason for existence of this family pattern. When and if the problem that dominates family life is resolved, this family may find itself without direction, clear purpose, or lack of role definitions for each family member.

"We had to be careful at first," said Ms. Anders. "We started to devote every moment to our daughter's illness. That's right, to her illness and not her and not our family. I even started to wonder what in the heck we would do if this illness suddenly went away. We wouldn't know where to start."

TYPE 9. THE RECONSTITUTED FAMILY. This is a family system in transition between a prior family pattern and a new family arrangement. Second marriage, stepchildren, adjustment following financial crisis, illness or death may result in a prolonged adjustment period. My clinical experience indicates that a family system requires at least two to three years to develop its own new system and that impatience or premature attempts to "do it like we used to in our other situation" can cause alienation, scapegoating, or surrender by one or all family members within the new system.

"Let me give you one warning about stepfamilies," said Ms. Johnson. "It takes a long time to get in step. Don't ever rush it."

TYPE 10. THE CUSTODIAL FAMILY. This is a family system that attempts to fill roles neglected by society, but which seriously overextend family resources almost to the breaking point. The family system may spend almost all of its money and time on the care of one family member who in fact cannot be maintained by the family system without considerable family disruption. Sometimes, the family has fallen into this pattern as a means of avoiding difficult decisions regarding other approaches to their problem, such as institutionalization of a seriously impaired or disruptive family member. The family begins to nurture and even foster the problem rather than confront and attempt to deal with the disruption itself. Living with an alcoholic, a chronically ill person, or a narcissistic, abusive family member who refuses professional help can result in the family trying to do what it will never be able to do and society chooses to ignore. As a result, the family begins to support pathology rather than to cope with and confront it.

"With Gramps' illness, we were starting to become a hospital instead of a home," said Ms. Muller. "We started to give him much more care than we had to. We had to get by what I called preventative guilt behavior. I think we were doing so much so we wouldn't feel guilty later when Gramps died."

TYPE 11. THE COMMUNAL FAMILY. This is a family system that transcends many of society's arbitrary role definitions. Gender does not direct role assignment, and the number of family members is typically much larger than more traditional family groups. The purpose of the group is to promote a political or religious philosophy or to master some major task. Religious cults and socially experimental communes based on religious or social policy are examples of the communal family, but intact and extended biologically based families may function as large, communal groups, able to embrace persons who are not family by biology.

"When I was a graduate student, I heard about a commune outside of town," said Mr. Anders. "They were trying to prove that they could live on a totally reinforcement-based system, like B. F. Skinner's *Walden Two.* I don't know if the thing ever worked out, but they all seemed very committed to the whole idea."

TYPE 12. THE OPEN FAMILY. This family system is amorphic and dynamic, responding to one direct and clear objective. It exists for purposes of achieving a goal, and then changes or ends once the goal is achieved. A group of students in a long training program, patients in a hospital ward, or workers for a company may coalesce as an open family system. Especially during times of crisis similar to the airplane accident I mentioned earlier, groups of people may form into a transitional or open family system, with parental and leadership roles and other features of a more traditional family system. Often, groups of families of survivors of victims of major catastrophes will form themselves into such an open family network.

"When I was going through nursing school, I lived with four other girls," said Ms. Muller. "We became a tightly knit family, and we cried like babies when we graduated and our group disbanded. I still think fondly of those days. We talk to one another once in a while."

You may find your own family system in one or more of

these family arrangements. Try to think about your family pattern, its purpose and its evolution. You will soon learn that how you are is very much due to how your family was and is, and to how you remember your family life.

WHAT A FAMILY IS AND ISN'T

The stages of family development are based on my work with hundreds of families as they attempted to cope with daily living. I discovered early on that many people cling to myths about what a family is or should be.

A FAMILY ISN'T   A FAMILY IS . . .

A FAMILY ISN'T	A FAMILY IS . . .
A group of people	An ever-changing set of interactions between sets of two's

FAMILY FACT: Families don't function like large groups. They function like collections of two-person relationships that combine into an ever-changing system that looks and acts like the weakest set of two.

Happy people sharing life	Persons of ever-changing moods trying their best to share and survive life together

FAMILY FACT: "The Adventures of Ozzie and Harriet" is over. Families have as many bad times as good times, and families are the one place where you don't always "have to be" anything.

An economically efficient unit	An economic compromise for the financial protection of everyone

FAMILY FACT: Our economy is not set up for the family or

by the family. Four can live as cheaply as sixteen, and much family strife is related to financial issues.

People who will be together always	People moving toward ever-changing relationships with one another and the eventual experience of leaving one another

FAMILY FACT: All behavioral love ends. Only spiritual love is forever.

A place where everyone loves everyone else	A place where persons are committed to mutually shared responsibility for the development of each other and the tolerance and forgiveness of everyone

FAMILY FACT: It's a lucky thing some family members are family, or their family would never let them in the door. Being family is only a guarantee of toleration. Many family members will not like other family members, but they must decide to love them.

As a summary of the remembrance factor of the family system, and to move beyond the myth of family to the realistic view of the daily life of families, consider the following eight stages of family life, a model for the genesis of "us."

PASSING THROUGH THE FAMILY CIRCLE: THE PERPETUAL EVOLUTION OF "US"

Based on my interviews with families in my clinic as these families experienced the transitional life events that characterize our day-to-day living, eight phases of family development emerged. As in the development of the individual, the stages are not discrete steps, separate from one another. Each passage represents a phase of family life experience that may be repeated several times. Think about your own family experience as you consider each of the eight phases of family living.

1. PRIMARY ATTACHMENT

During this phase of family life, family members are establishing the basis of their relationship. Dependence on one another emerges, and there is a requirement of the evolution of trust among family members. The key question that must be answered by every family member is "Will my needs be met by these people, and am I willing to invest my time and my energy in helping each family member meet their own needs?"

Family life requires several returns to this part of the circle of family development. "With Gramps dying, we all seem to be testing each other," said Ms. Muller. "It's like we are all starting all over again in some ways. We're all trying to reconnect with each other now that Gramps is leaving us. It's like a circle of people trying to rejoin hands after someone has left the circle."

2. BONDING

To bond is to establish a dependence on someone else for our emotional and physical survival. Every member of every family must establish their own bond with every other family member, not just to meet each other's needs, but to allow another family member to become a permanent piece of one's internal emotional furniture. While attachment is based on needs, bonding is based on wants, on wanting to love, to survive, to enjoy, and to make the most of life.

When a child is born, the parent attaches to the child, deciding to attempt to meet the needs of the child. The new child begins eventually to bond with the parent, seeing the parent not only as someone who can meet her or his needs but as someone who embodies the way to be happy, safe, and successful. The parent becomes someone who not only keeps you alive, but helps you make life worth living. All family members must learn to move beyond attachment to bonding, from meeting each others' needs to promoting and facilitating the satisfaction of everyone's hopes and dreams.

Mr. Anders said, "It's funny how you start to talk with your family about wishes and dreams. You spend so much time early on just getting things done, just washing, eating, getting people in bed on time, getting to work and to school, that you hardly notice when you start to talk about why you are doing all these things in the first place. You start to talk about where everyone is really going and why, about what we all want." Mr. Anders's statement shows the change from need meeting to wish fulfillment that characterizes the change from attachment to bonding.

The key question of the bonding phase is "Will my family members help me identify my wants and dreams, and am I willing to help my family find their direction and work to smooth the way for each of them?" If the trust of attachment is in place, then the autonomy of knowing that the family is there for much more than survival is the next turn in the family circle.

3. INCORPORATION

Phase three of the family circle of development is incorporation, the ability of family members to keep the family alive while each member begins to strike out on their own. Once a family member enters this phase of development within the family system, he or she senses sufficient self-esteem, family trust, and self-autonomy to begin the initiative of broadening the limits of friendship, and the risk taking of self-enhancement.

The key question during the incorporation phase is "Am I ready to take some chances in my life with the knowledge that my family will let me try my wings, and am I willing to be there for other family members when they return from their own flight or perhaps crash in need of more support and direction?"

Mr. Steiner said, "My son has tried three different careers. I hope this one will stick. He has tried some really risky things. He moved up North to be a writer until he found out he didn't like to write. He came home to us, and he tried to start an art gallery until he found out he didn't like art. He wants to be a musician now. We're behind him, but this time we're kicking him just a little harder in the ass. But he knows we'll be there." Mr. Steiner typifies the member of a family that has incorporated, joined together to allow its members the opportunity to take risks for self-growth and discovery.

4. EXTENSION

During this phase of family development, all family members try to establish a wider view of who is family. Grandparents, uncles, aunts, and cousins now play a bigger role in the family system, and the core family becomes strong enough to tolerate the individual quirks and idiosyncracies of relatives.

"My mother is probably the most obnoxious, opinionated, hostile person I know," reported Ms. Johnson. "We all used to let her get to us. We would fight over what she said or didn't say, whether she was happy, sad, angry or just plain ignoring us. We're stronger now. If we're strong enough to go through a complete Thanksgiving dinner without a total war, you know we are finally able to keep Mother at least on the outer fringes of our family without her tearing the main garment."

Ms. Johnson's statement illustrates the sense of competence a family can develop, a sense of confidence in itself that it can broaden its scope without overextending its emotional resources. Today's family is simply too small to handle the demands and complexities of daily living. We need bigger and broader families, and must be able to include those family members who demand the maximum of our familying skills and toleration, without impeding the progress of those who are asked to give so much for so long.

The key question to be asked at the extension phase of family life is "Can I see more and more of my family as worthy of my loving and tolerance and am I able to see their love for me even when some of their behaviors and characteristics are difficult to accept and understand?"

5. RESILIENCE

The fifth phase of the family's development is the establishment of resilience, the capacity to rebound from even severe family crisis and conflict without destroying the basic family matrix. "I know we are getting stronger even as Gramps is getting weaker," said Mr. Muller. "It's been totally fatiguing, and during some of our arguments, we have said some dreadful things. But we know who we are. We know no matter what we say, we love each other." The resilience typified by the Muller family as they attempt to cope with the dying of one of their members illustrates the clear establishment of their family identity, a resilience that I will describe in detail in the next chapter.

The key question at the phase of resilience is "Do I know how I fit into the family, how I contribute to and stress the family, and am I able to make the effort, do the forgiving and forgetting necessary to protect our family identity, even if I have to yield on some points that seem major to me?" Phase five is a high level of family development, and requires progress through the first four phases, the establishment of family trust, family members' autonomy, a feeling of family competence and value of the family identity sufficient to produce a sense of invincibility of the family system.

6. INTEGRATION

The sixth phase of family development, integration, requires that each member be able to bring back to the family the fruits of their own successful development. Instead of seeing success as individualized, the integration phase requires a balance between individual accomplishment and family enhancement.

The key question at the sixth phase of development is "Am I willing to share my success and accomplishment to make my family stronger, or am I investing my gains in myself and in new or future relationships?" In essence, this question asks whether or not we have to care about our primary family anymore, once we don't really "need" that family to survive.

"It was so intoxicating to be so successful," said Mr. Steiner. "So many promotions, so many positive strokes. I was like a hero at work. I almost forgot what got me there. I wasn't really sharing with my family anything I had gained but my money. I really started to wonder what my success brought to the family but more things, more trips, and better schools. I almost didn't give them me anymore, my happiness, pride, and confidence. My wife, my kids, all loved it when I began to share these parts of me with them again."

Mr. Steiner is describing the integration of self-growth with family enhancement. Our society doesn't emphasize the "family-izing" of its individual member's successes. Too often, the family is where we go when we fail. There is more to family integration than watching the graduation ceremony of one of its children. Integration means the emotional and spiritual sharing of what the graduation means for the family as well as for the graduate. "How will your success help the family grow together more?" is an appropriate question of the family of a successful family member.

7. MATURATION

During the seventh phase of family development, the family begins to identify its own traditions. There is an increasing sense of pride, of celebration of the family, a feeling of "we did it!" The key question at this phase is "As I look at my family now, can I see what it has done for all of us and what I have done for each family member?"

"We know that we have been through it all now," said Ms. Bonner. "The loss of my husband and the kids losing their dad was the obvious crisis, but we have been through so much more. We have a sense that we can do anything now. We are actually arrogant about us."

Ms. Bonner is describing the solidification of family identity that takes place at the maturation phase. There are no longer questions about family survivability. The family has established its direction, its values, and its purpose. In effect, the family is reborn and seems to sense that it is family forever. Each family member feels productive and important to the family, a part of the birth of a new and stronger sense of family.

"Funny thing—" said Mr. Anders, "when we bought that wood sign at the fair with our family name on it, we never used it. Now, we have it on the door. The Anderses. That's us. We're family."

8. TRANSCENDENCE

The highest and rarest level of family evolution is the eighth phase, transcendence. At this phase, every family member feels that the family is forever a part of them. Each member can communicate on a special level with every other family member, and each member can communicate far beyond words. Family members seem to know each other completely, and are able to sense one another in a type of extrafamilial perception.

"I can tell when any one of my family is in trouble," said Ms. Anders. "I can dream it, sense it, feel it. I can tell when they need me, and they can tell when I need them. Be sure you tell the people who will read your book that something magic happens when the family grows together. You all begin to be able to go beyond this world. You have your own ways of being a family, and time or distance doesn't matter."

"Most of us are scattered now," said Mr. Steiner. "We're miles apart, but we just know when we need each other. It's very, very special. We don't need to be physically together to sense our togetherness. We just sense it."

The question that assesses the presence of the eighth phase of family development is, "Have I allowed myself to sense beyond my basic five senses, to feel for my family wherever they are?" When a family is transcendent, it goes beyond what our present science and psychology will ever be able to measure. When the family is transcendent, it has discovered the miracle of "us," and it will forever be connected beyond time and body.

SIX STEPS TO FAMILY REMEMBRANCE

To include the remembrance factor in your own family life, try some of the six steps that follow.

STEP ONE. Start a family emotional diary. In addition to the usual entries of significant family events, record an emotional time line, the key emotional factors that influence your family. Take time at least once a month to sit down as a family and make a brief entry as to how everyone is feeling at this time in the family's development.

STEP TWO. Make audio recordings or videotapes of the senior members of the family. Interview them, don't just record them at a party or family gathering. Ask them what matters to them, what events in the family history have significance to them. Start your own family archives of tapes of the senior members, the true historians of your family.

STEP THREE. Make time for the youngest and the oldest members of the family to talk and listen to one another. A subtle division along generation lines can evolve within a family, and most people are familiar with the clustering of different-age family members in different rooms at birthday parties and holidays. Make the effort to break these generational clubs in favor of some cross-generational sharing.

STEP FOUR. Try to focus on the family's extrafamilial perception. Listen for each other beyond words, and try to sense the feelings of family members beyond the psychological cliché of "communicating." Try to tune in to each other beyond the everyday requirements of hurrying, scurrying, and worrying.

STEP FIVE. Discuss with your family what all of you consider to be the major family "imprints." What common memories of events, problems, pain, and joy seem to have emerged as major events in the history of your family? What common event is seen to be reemerging in the life of the family? What lesson is God trying to get your family to learn?

STEP SIX. Try to learn, as a family, about the family history of significant persons. Study and read together just a few minutes each month, and focus that study on the family system of the great leaders of the world. What were the strengths and weaknesses of these families? How did the person help her or his family and what role did the family play in the life of that person? Are there any messages in someone else's life story that have implications for your own family?

The next chapter focuses on the resilience factor of families. How do families survive troubled times and major crises? Before reading the next chapter, however, take some time to look back at your family's life map. Don't wait until the end of the journey to pay attention to the family voyage together through life. Part of being a resilient family is remembering where your own family's strengths and weaknesses are.

CHAPTER SEVEN

Family Resilience: Together Through It All

"Life is not a matter of holding good cards, but of playing a poor hand well."
ROBERT LOUIS STEVENSON

FAMILY RESILIENCE: The existence of a shared and unanimously accepted family system for explaining even the most stressful of life events, the ability to tolerate and grow through prolonged uncertainty and insecurity, and the faith that the family spirit is invincible.

UNFAIR WINDS AND FAMILY FIRES

"He was so young, so alive, so here. Then, just like a door closing, he was gone," said Ms. Bonner, the young widow who lost her fireman husband, "like a door slammed in your face by the wind. We wanted to scream at somebody, but there's nobody to blame, nobody to even talk to. It's so final, so over. I never thought I could make it. I never thought that we could make it. Two teenagers to raise, and I had never worked. I had been totally involved in my kids, in him. Now, he was gone. We were gone. The kids and I just cried and cried, until our eyes burned with dryness and ache. I decided that the kids would have to go and live with other family members, and that I would go back to school to learn something to do. What happened didn't make any sense, so we started to make our own nonsense of everything. We panicked, and tried to put an end to the pain any way we could."

Ms. Bonner was describing the early adjustment of her family to their most terrible crisis of all, the loss of a family member. She described what can happen to a family when that family cannot make sense of what is happening to it, desires an end to the pain of crisis at any cost, and often elects a short-sighted and panic-motivated pseudosolution. Her comments show her family's attempt at what I call "calming closure" rather than a solving step and true progress toward family resilience.

Just as taking sleeping pills fails to treat the actual cause of insomnia, the true underlying problems are never confronted when a family elects "calming closure." In the rush for any end to the emotional and cognitive imbalance experienced by everyone in the family, the family adopts a type of sleep state, a false sense of coming to grips with their problem, when in effect the family is reacting to life, rather than sharing in a common process of giving life more meaning.

When families possess "calming closure" rather than the fifth Rx of healthy family life, resilience, everyone in the family begins to work within the artificial confines of pseudosolutions to transitional life crises, never really attempting to learn from their problems and to ask each other the difficult questions about the meaning of life, crisis, and death. Family resilience is the ability to play any hand life deals us, to learn to enjoy the game even when our hand is poor, and to avoid folding too soon.

When a family is resilient, that family can "hang on." More accurately, the family is able to "hang open" for a sufficient period of time to develop new coping systems and to apply their belief system to new problems. The resistance of premature closure to problem situations in favor of a continued struggle through the realities of problems, and the continuing evolution of a new family problem-solving and life-interpreting system is the meaning of family resilience. Ms. Bonner's next statement is an example of this fifth Rx, resilience.

"Once the panic phase passed, we just stopped. We had to go through that part. We had to stay in a pain state, like trying to hold your breath longer and longer under water until you just have to breathe again. Like the quiet after the loud slam of a door, when everyone seems to listen for another slam, when everyone sort of tries to figure out what the loud noise was and what caused it, we just stayed upset. We tried to bear it. We sat for hours together, just the three of us. We didn't talk, we just sat together and seemed to be trying to get our energy back. Then we seemed to be thinking and feeling together, but not really talking out loud. Then we started to talk about how we were just drifting together in uncertainty, and then sometimes falling back into panic. Then we remembered together how we used to be. We remembered that we never before thought that things just happened to us, like the wind just slamming the door in our face. We had to turn back to our family beliefs, to our family faith, to our idea that my husband, that all of us, would always be family in some way. We had to turn back to our conviction that life does make sense, our sense. We decided to do nothing, to just wait. We decided to heal, like you want to just rest when you are sick."

Ms. Bonner's son remembered his father answering his question about what fire fighters do when they first get to a fire. "My dad said that, first, they run off their truck, look at the fire, and then they don't do a thing. They wait first, so they don't do something to screw it up. He said they try to make sense of what's happening first, even when the fire is roaring and everybody can feel the heat and everybody wants to do something quick. They have to get a plan first, and they have to think about what they did before. They have to figure out what type of fire it is before they can do what they have to do to put it out."

The key steps in family resilience are seen in this boy's story. Resilience involves a clear view of the nature of the problem affecting the family, intense and open sharing of all family members of their feelings about the problem, communication about the comparison of the immediate problem with past challenges the family has faced—the key step of interpreting the problem in the context of the family's belief system about the meaning and purpose of life—and finally the development of family coping strategies that deal with the everyday survival needs of the family.

"My dad said," continued the son, "that you just don't go pouring water over everything and everyone. When you do that, you only hurt people and make the problem worse. Sometimes the water doesn't work, and sometimes the firemen just have to watch the fire burn and try to prevent other fires as best they can." The father's advice emphasized the key component of family resilience, family ability to tolerate a sometimes prolonged period of uncertainty and instability, while the family gives itself time to integrate the present problem into its emotional and intellectual history as a group.

Ms. Bonner compared her husband's message to her young family's present struggle. She knew that her family had resources to draw on, and that they would all have to take time now to understand their own mortality, their resentment of their father for leaving them, and their sense of helplessness that would either cripple them or draw their attention to their inner strengths. The fire in their souls would have to burn itself out and be replaced with a rekindling of a new family spirit, a spirit ignited by their mutual faith in the strength of their family energy.

"Life's not fair," said Ms. Bonner's daughter. "It's not fair, and Dad used to tell us that. He said he went to car accidents, and that it seemed that usually the person who was the innocent victim was the one who would be hurt the worst. Now I know that life's not fair. We all know it's not fair. But we know we have to stay together, not separate just because it seems easier right now to do that. Dad said life isn't fair, and that you can only grow up when you accept that and try to be as fair as you can to your own family and to everyone else as a way of balancing out the unfairness. If you don't get more fair, even when everything seems unfair, you just get more and more unfairness. Dad said you don't stop driving because car accidents aren't fair. Instead, you drive as carefully as you can."

The Bonner family has stayed together and resisted the temptation to yield to their pain. Their statements reveal their own family resilience. They resisted the urge to jump at the first apparent solution to their crisis; they withstood their eagerness to do anything at all that would seem to ease their suffering.

They turned back to explanatory systems that had worked for their family before, and they allowed the family cycle of resilience to play itself out.

It is only time that heals all wounds, but also togetherness, tolerance, and time in combination with the faith that the family will be able to come up with an explanation for what has happened to them and put that explanation in the context of their overall family belief system help to heal. The Bonner family knew, as all families must learn, that life will either be seen as chaos or coherence, a coherence of what researcher David Reiss describes as ". . . the world as governed by an underlying and stable set of discoverable principles."[1] Dr. Reiss sees the family as the primary source of our learning to organize and make sense of our external and internal experiences and the place where our personal resilience, the principles that guide our life, is formed.

Strong families show the endurance to wait through crises for the reemergence of the family's system for making life meaningful for all of its members. Family resilience is the continued unity of optimism and family commitment to an appraisal of life as ultimately meaningful, controllable, and challenging.

The Family Resilience Test

To help you see how the elements of family resilience apply to your own family situation, take the following test:

0	1	2	3	4	5	6	7	8	9	10
ALMOST NEVER		SELDOM		SOMETIMES		A LOT		ALMOST ALWAYS		

1. ———— Does your family seem able to separate major crises from less significant problems, avoiding overreacting to setbacks?

1. Reiss, David. *The Family's Construction of Reality* (Cambridge, Mass.: Harvard University Press, 1981), p. 249.

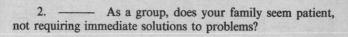

2. ———— As a group, does your family seem patient, not requiring immediate solutions to problems?

3. ———— Can your family tolerate disorganization and disruption without starting to argue and blame one another?

4. ———— Can your family make sense of the things that happen to it, even when events seem unfair and overwhelming?

5. ———— Do problems in and for your family seem to make your family stronger?

6. ———— Does your family have "family confidence," a sense that they can handle almost any problem together?

7. ———— Can your family find enough energy to deal with several problems going on at one time?

8. ———— Is your family as a whole optimistic regarding its future, feeling in control of their own destiny?

9. ———— Does everyone in your family try to take their fair share of the responsibility for things gone wrong and for trying to make them right again?

10. ———— Can your family "just let things go" once in a while, allowing some problems to go unsolved and just proceeding along with life without complaining, worrying, and harping about unresolved issues?

———— TOTAL FAMILY RESILIENCE SCORE

If your family scores over the arbitrary 90 points on this test, it is very high in the fifth Rx, resilience. Less than 90 and you may want to look at the particular single items that resulted in the most lost points and focus on that factor in your daily problem-solving attempts.

Resilience in a family depends to a large extent on the family's appraisal system, its way of understanding and interpreting major life events. The meaning of love, sensuality, justice, injustice, parenting, dying, death, working, and a sense of what is right and what is wrong, why things happen, and what life is really for are all components of the family appraisal system. If your family is currently going through a crisis, I hope you will read the rest of this chapter carefully and slowly, sharing your reactions with your family, because I will be describing ways that healthy families develop their appraisal system, their shared understanding of life, loss, and loving to make it through the worst problem times.

HOW THE FAMILY CONSTRUCTS ITS OWN REALITY

The first four Rx's of family living, ritual, rhythm, reason, and remembrance, are prerequisites for strong family resilience. They allow the time, priority, rational thinking, and honoring of family precedent necessary to cope with challenges to the family system. Strong resilience involves first and foremost the avoidance of the apparent ease of the short-term comfort of denial and avoidance, in favor of the attempt by the family to make sense of what has happened to them, to involve every family member both in the understanding process, and in the search for meaning in daily living crises. Such resilient families are able to continue to use their problems as building blocks as they, as Dr. Reiss writes, "construct reality" together.

The basic purpose of families is to help their members construct reality, to learn a system of appraisal of life events, and ultimately to help their members make the choice between a "self" and an "us" view of living. I have already pointed out that we make our own world by making choices about how we will think about that world. It is the family appraisal system that is the collective thinking of the family, its collective way of feeling and reasoning about life. The system of appraisal that is learned within the family will be the core of inner knowledge of every family member for the rest of each of their lives. When a resilient appraisal system is taught and learned by each family member, one that contains the steps of tolerance of disruption and a family way of appraising life problems and finding solutions, it is a family gift more valuable than any other.

To maintain this resilient appraisal system, the family

must understand what happens to them as a group when crisis strikes, when life seems unfair and doors are slammed in the face of the family by the winds of life. Families must understand the problems they face and the stages of their family problem appraisal system that can carry them through the most difficult of times. These two aspects of family resilience, clear understanding and interpretation of family problems and clear awareness of the family coping phases, are the core of this chapter.

FAMILIES IN CRISIS

More than one out of five families experience some form of violence within their own home as a repeated occurrence. At least two out of five marriages will end in divorce. More than half of the families report regular unhappiness in their daily family living. Four of ten children are raised in single-parent homes. Almost fifty percent of this year's marriages will likely end in divorce, and more than eighty percent of teenage marriages that take place this year will end in divorces that will pressure the families of the two married children.

There has been a seven hundred percent increase in divorce since the turn of the century, and the divorce rate is only slightly on the decline in some parts of North America. While almost eighty percent of persons who divorce will remarry, almost half of these persons will divorce again, leaving stepfamily members scattered throughout the country.

According to the Carnegie Council on Children, forty-nine out of fifty of the more than fifty-five million children under eighteen years of age in the United States will experience some change from the traditional two-parent married family. Three of five children of divorce live with stepparents. Although the U.S. Census Bureau reports that three quarters of all children live with at least one parent, only two of three homes have a husband and wife living together within them. One quarter of our children are born out of wedlock, starting their lives from relationships that are basically unstable.

Our children continue to have children. Births to children in the age range of eleven to fourteen have increased more than ten percent over this decade, and children with the least financial resources behind them and without social supports of their own are the most likely to have their own children while they are still children themselves. One of four children lives in poverty in the United States. More than seventeen million children, most of these under age six, live without the most basic of life's essentials, and most of these children are being raised by women living alone and in poverty, themselves unhealthy and underfed.

More than thirty million children live in homes where both parents work, and less than one third of homes have only the father working. More than three million school-age children must take care of themselves while their single parent or both parents work. There is only one place in a day care center for every six children who need such a place, and many of these places are subpar in quality and care.[2]

The family system is being overwhelmed by the pressures of change and by living in a world that seems without a direction toward intimacy and shared responsibility. Urie Brofenbrenner, professor of human development at Cornell University, states, "Our society does not treat families very well," and he writes about the contradiction between the societal emphasis on family while almost everything in society interferes with the family's survival.

What are the pressures that are overwhelming the family system? Here are the most often mentioned sources of problems for the families I have seen over the years.

THREE CONSPIRACIES AGAINST THE FAMILY

Three of the major influences that are disrupting family systems are our educational, religious, and medical institutions. Consider each of these influences as they may serve as the source of many of the problems affecting your own family.

2. Statistics on the family reported in this chapter are a compilation of data from an article in the *Detroit News,* Sunday, May 14, 1978, and U.S. Census reports from that period to June, 1988.

SCHOOLING IN SEPARATION

"Look how beautiful Lorrie's picture is. It's the best one I've seen as I've been walking around," said the teacher as she continued to patrol between the desks of the competing artists. The little boy sitting next to lucky Lorrie looked down at his own drawing. It had taken him hours, and until this moment, he had thought it was the most beautiful thing he had ever done. Now, he felt suddenly embarrassed as he looked at his own creation. Certainly nobody could ever do a better picture than Lorrie. She never colored outside the lines and she always colored in exactly the same direction. Her art looked like grown-up art. The little boy wrinkled up his creation and threw it toward the wastebasket.

The teacher had taught a powerful lesson in separation. The teacher was making quite clear the fact that art, like all activities in which to be engaged in school, was individualized, separate, competitive, and based on some arbitrary hierarchy of approximated perfection. As with most things done in school, the teacher was teaching for the individual, not the group, and for the future of the person rather than the power of the system.

"What group are you in?" the little girl asked her friend. "I'm in the fast reading group, but I see that you are carrying a yellow book. You must be in the slow group." This statement, too, shows how any grouping that is attempted in schools is known by the students to be based on discrimination, evaluation, and competition, not on caring, nurturing, and support. No one is put in such groups for support from the other members of the group. Students are put in groups to be "dealt with," to be more easily taught to become a successful individual. Groups are seldom used in schools to teach how to "group well" or to illustrate how families form and flourish.

You will be hard-pressed to name one group you were in during your school day that was a school-sanctioned collection of kids that existed just for the purpose of caring about the welfare of kids. You learned very early in school that groups were convenient ways of labeling people and discriminating, not ways of joining together to love and to live. Groups in school are the circles you run in, not a form of family you learn to live with.

Not much of what we learn in school about the social issues of the day deals with the family system. What does hunger really do to the family structure of the millions of persons who suffer without food every day? What is happening to the families trapped in the street fighting in Northern Ireland, in Beirut, or in the complex struggle in the Middle East? Are families in these war-torn areas huddling together in fear? Are these families nurturing reactive hate and developing lifelong prejudices in their members?

We learn to focus on a global "them," a vague image that makes it easier for us to watch the death and suffering on television. We watch a mother crying at the loss of her child, but our schools do not teach about the "now what" of the crisis impact on family and about what happens to our world when most of our families are hurting. There simply is no true family curriculum in our schools.

NORMAL AND ABNORMAL FAMILIES?

Since our schools are not teaching the process of "familying," or dealing with most of the ten family Rx's I am describing in this book, the schools are contributing to a dangerous dichotomy. They are teaching that family is a mother and father with two children and that there are "other" arrangements. The possibility of different family systems related to different sexual preferences and life orientations is seldom considered. What families look like or should like is emphasized at the expense of teaching about the feelings of familying that transcend any one limited view of the "normal" family.

Imagine the distress for the little girl or boy whose parents are contemplating divorce. These children must sit in the classroom and wonder and worry as they hear about "families" and "stepfamilies," or "real parents" vs. "legal parents," about who will come to parent/teacher night, but hear very little about the ritual of life of a group of people sharing life, the rhythm of living in harmony with others, rational approaches to problem solving in the home situation, the dignity and the importance of the history of their own family and families, or the wonderful resilience of all types and forms of families that have learned that the concept of "us" goes beyond mere legal definition.

WHEN SCHOOLS DON'T HELP THE HOME WORK

Recently in Detroit, Michigan, there was a terrible automobile accident. A driver lost control of his car and drove into a crowd of students walking on the sidewalk. When word of the tragedy spread, family members flocked to the school. Days later, in another crisis, a disturbed woman took a class full of young children and their teacher hostage, and again parents rushed to the school.

The concern of these family members is easy to understand, yet we tend to rush to our schools only when some crisis interferes with our daily life and out of family obligation. Seldom do families rush to school for positive reasons, other than prescheduled ceremonies and obligatory parent conferences, confused now by whose parent is a stepparent and whose child was a child of a former marriage twice removed.

The family itself is beginning to see the public school as a necessary evil, at best an irrelevant obstacle to be overcome in the child's struggle for success and independence, and at worst a dangerous, even life-threatening place where the only hope is for survival. This lack of reciprocal family-school integration renders much of our childrens' education at best irrelevant for daily living and at worst counterproductive for the establishment of loving and enduring relationships.

Schools are not only failing to teach the family view of living, they are pressuring the family system by their institutional ineptitude and insensitivity. Pressures for achievement by prematurely identified "talented students" is resulting in growing depression and even suicide attempts by the so called "gifted and talented . . ."

Neglect of students who experience attention deficit disorder, learning disability, dyslexia, or other problems that interfere with their school experience and education, is resulting in family conflict and panic over finding some program, any program, that could help. Schools seem to teach for the slightly above average, that statistically rare and often nonexistent group which probably needs less help than the majority of students, who fall elsewhere on our schools' abnormal curve.

Schools forget that everything they ask of the student, every homework assignment, every teacher lecture, directly impacts the family system. "When my daughter gets a big homework assignment," said Ms. Bonner, "we know we aren't going to be doing much as a family that weekend."

"I remember fearing that my son would get Mr. Baker," said Mr. Johnson. "He's the Scrooge of the school. He's mean, unfair, and a real tyrant. Everybody knows it. He's an institution onto himself. Well, my son got him, and we had hell in the family for that whole semester. You really wonder if he knew what he was doing to the kids and to their families. It makes you wonder if he ever really was in a family of his own. I think he just goes and hides in the classroom closet and waits for the next day to harass the kids."

Mr. Johnson's statement illustrates the fact that school plays a major role in the life of our families, in pressure on the single-parent family, in implied dependence on intact family systems that will be "home to help," when in fact, as the numbers presented earlier in this chapter illustrate, most students will go home to families in trouble, divided, or in a state of change. Can true learning take place without acknowledgment of the family, accounting for the family, and direct family-and-school interaction and cooperation? There really is very little true community education.

We need a new view of education that emphasizes an orientation of learning about and as family, a curriculum about how to appraise life from a family point of view. Here are a few "family education" recommendations, some concepts for discussion about an idealistic approach to designing a family curriculum. Of course, devising a family curriculum is a complex educational task, but any such endeavor will begin with families themselves giving serious consideration to reclaiming their schools.

Ten Steps for a Family Takeover of the Schools

1. Less "age" division of our students, with a return to the old country-school style of many ages learning together. No more adult-education courses offered at night. Kids and adults could attend classes at any time of the day and in the evening,

resulting in the benefit of exposure to several different learning styles.

2. Less focus on individual achievement and more focus on group projects and cooperation. The group mural-art project should be as least as important as the school individual art-fair competition.

3. Inclusion of family education in all classes in place of the one special family-education course offered in most schools.

4. Examination of all curriculum for family content. Does the course material refer to various family systems and interpersonal relationships? Do examinations take into account the family issues in all learning objectives?

5. Replacement of our current school counseling program. It is now based on three functions: testing, scheduling, and the treatment of what counselors see as problem students (actually almost always students with family problems). The new school counseling would include home visits and family histories of all children. No counselor should be certified who has not been trained in family systems theory and cognitive psychology. Counselors would become facilitators of school-and-family interaction instead of attendance-enforcement officers and plant managers.

6. Replacement of "parent-teacher" conferences with regular involvement of families in the curriculum. Parents could come to class at any time, take the tests, hear the lectures, correct examinations, and become involved in the learning and teaching process. Even with current time pressures and career obligations, shorter and more regular visits to school by parents and family should replace the once-a-year obligatory meet-the-teacher nights (referred to by some students and parents as "meet-the-creature nights") or parental response to problem calls.

7. Redesign of the school calendar and school day. Currently, the school system competes with all other nine-to-five systems and then closes down for the summer, leaving students, whose lives are dominated by school, without direction and formal educational opportunity for one fourth of the year. All-year schools, with the broader hours and some classes held off-

campus in factories and real-life work situations as suggested earlier, including an emphasis on cross-age education, would allow more family involvement, the opportunity for children to see how adults appraise their world, and perhaps a reduction in school violence that can result from the isolation of developing young people from the so-called adult world.

8. Complete redesign of the school curriculum and its emphasis on early determination of "college preparation and other." The old English eleven-plus exam, which determined an industrial career or an academic opportunity, is still seen in a more subtle form of "cutoff counseling" that places students in slots. Our schools must confront their biases in favor of what they view as the "academically able," and the fact that more than fifty percent of students do not fit well in our present school system. We seem to be attempting to teach our students to be teachers rather than citizens.

The majority of real training of our children takes place outside of school, because the curriculum offered in the school is almost entirely irrelevant to the daily life activity of most students. A broader definition of the educated person, one that includes all of the intelligences (interpersonal intelligence, appraisal intelligence, assembly intelligence, etc.), would allow more children to become involved in the school system and to see it as a path, rather than a prison with passes, truancy, and retention. This new relevancy of education could remove some of the pressure on families to "make it through" the currently irrelevant curriculum.

9. Required parental involvement in all curriculum design. Currently, only a few parents direct the curriculum. Sometimes, ultraconservative or ultraliberal but loud and expressive parents dictate school policy. School administrations live in fear of the "trouble-causing parent," rather than actively enlisting the majority of parents as an active curriculum committee.

No curriculum should be implemented without representative parental input. We must make families more than audiences at school plays. Even if all families would never be involved, a change in the view of curriculum as teacher-and-family-directed rather than "administrative curriculum com-

cred, as if we can find the spiritual in everyday life, as if the ritual of religious worship really means something to the family and not just to the individual concerned for his or her own rebirth, is a basic feature of family life that is being ignored by our religious institutions.

"I think about the only time we all go to church is on Christmas Eve," said one of my patients. "My wife goes almost regularly, but she goes alone. I just can't seem to get up on Sunday to go. I'm beat from the workweek. Even God had to rest one day out of the week, and that's my one morning to sleep. Anyway, the church leaves me cold. It just isn't relevant to my life. I believe in God, but I don't believe in churches. I guess I'm not too good at being a part of the flock. I was born to be a lion and not a lamb."

SLEEPING THROUGH SERVICES

I seldom take a family history that does not reveal the diminishing role of attending church or synagogue. What used to be the one time families dressed up together and went to sit and listen and pray has been replaced with, perhaps, one member going to church or synagogue or watching religious services on television, while one family member sleeps, and the others are off and doing their Sunday or Saturday things.

I pointed out earlier how important ritual is to the health of the family. Our religious institutions have failed the family in this regard as well. To paraphrase a well-known statement, going to church has not been tried and found failing. Going to church has been found difficult, and abandoned as a common whole-family activity. We criticize "blind faith" as if there were really any other kind of faith. We think that seeing is believing, when what we see is the result of what we believe, how we live, and the ritualization of the sacred in our daily living.

IMPERSONAL RELIGION

Many religious services are now characterized by performance on the part of one or a few "truly religious" lions leading their flock, raging at flocks numbering in the thousands about dangers that only the well-fed lion can lead them away from. Our religious institutions have adopted the "jungle view." Sermons about our failings and weaknesses dominate the agenda, as if we need to be reminded at least once a week of how short we fall from what God expects.

In a misguided attempt to find God inside us, we have turned to so-called "new age religions," new and improved spirituality that can be practiced "individually" through some mixture of metaphysical concepts, workshops and awareness training programs, star charts, crystals, channels, and out-of-body experiences.

"Religion is a personal thing" has been accepted as fact, even though the opposite is true. Religion is a group thing, the ultimate form of becoming the body of one another and God. Religion, if it is to be divine, must be a religion of closeness and active unity with others. Unfortunately, the ritual of gathering together to worship continues to diminish.

Our greatest religious leaders have not been models of family men and women. Most religious books emphasize and even worship the family, and then proceed to discuss individual spiritual growth and the worshipping of those persons who themselves gave little time to their own families, or surrendered their own family life to become a "church leader."

For some families, going to church has become similar to going to school. It is seen as something that ought to be done, even must be done, if we are to graduate to higher levels. We practice prophylactic education and religion; we learn so we won't starve and we worship so we won't cook. Neither of these negative motivations is sufficient to get us out of bed in the morning to go to the institutions where the scolding, warning, anonymity, and continued acknowledgment of our own failures takes place.

Here are some recommendations for altering our religious institutions to better serve the family. Again, these suggestions are idealistic and intended to initiate discussion of the interaction of religious institutions on the family. Talk some of them over with your own family and friends and see what you think about your place of worship and the family relationship, and how that bond might be strengthened. I am using the term "church" inclusively to refer to places of worship for all religions.

Ten Suggestions for a Family Church

1. De-emphasize the individual spiritual leader and the "guru" approach to religion. In its place should be "family" ministerships, rabbiships, and priestships, where families direct the religious services. Groups leading groups may set a better model than the "lions and flock" approach. We need a change from the model of the religious leader who doesn't "need" a family. As the old saying goes, if you don't play the game, you don't get to make the rules.

2. De-emphasize discussions of our obvious failures at religious services, in favor of regular celebration of our perfection. Religious sermons should celebrate God as "us," not as some humanized and therefore diminished view of a being in remote control of everything, or as some existential interpretation of nature. We must return to the metaphor of our immortality, the metaphor of our perpetual spiritual energy and unity, in place of the emerging practice of worshipping somebody or something "out there" or the self as God.

3. Discontinue Sunday school. Religious leaders should be smart enough, spiritual enough, and creative enough to provide familial celebrations that teach and appeal to everyone. Following the schools' practice of grade assignments for worshipping purposes only serves to divide the already divided family. Going to church should be a form of coming together, not of sending someone to "get religion."

4. Discontinue the "once-a-week service" approach in favor of open scheduling of religious services. Providing a sacred place for families to go together anytime to be with other families, with the availability of religious teachers and discussion facilitators, could be as important as providing a once-a-week celebration.

5. Churches should provide homework. The only part of the school experience churches should copy is the practice of sending their students home with something to do. Family volunteer work, readings, prayers, or any activity that models unity and system over "me and I," could help the family integrate spirituality with daily living.

6. Incorporate the general principles of health and holistic health practices into religious activities. If medicine has divided the mind from the body, the church has tended to divide the spirit from the self and the body. The spirit is not more separate from the body than the mind is. When we are using our body during our spiritual development, our body is very much "us" and influences our mind and spirit, just as our mind and spirit directly affect our body. If churches would incorporate holistic health care into their attempts at spiritual care, church attendance would increase. Just as hospitals neglect the spiritual side of healing, so churches tend to neglect the physical dimensions of health.

Research has documented the fact that persons who attend church regularly enjoy better physical health than persons who do not do so.[5] In 1897, French sociologist Emile Durkheim published his finding that what he called "social cohesion," the existence of a strong sense of group and belonging, correlated with lower suicidal rates.[6] Social organization around spiritual beliefs, on a regular and ritualized basis, is one of the healthiest things we can do, and I suggest that churches should offer health care education, even diagnostic testing and referral, as a part of their services.

7. Develop multimedia approaches to the religious ceremony. Integrating meditative techniques, music, slides, minidramas and plays, could add to the involvement of every member of the family. To entertain means literally to hold someone's attention, to admit to and hold in the mind. If the

5. Studies of Mormons and Seventh-Day Adventists indicate that these groups show lower instances of cancer, coronary artery disease and myocardial infarction. Certainly, the life-style of these groups, with reduced consumption of unhealthy substances, contributes to their healthier life. It is also true, however, that their faith and commitment to their religion contributes to their healthier life style. See E. L. Wynder and L. I. Bross, "Factors in Human Cancer Development," *Cancer* (1959) Vol. 12, p. 1016. See also G. W. Comstock and K. B. Partridge, "Church Attendance and Health," *Journal of Chronic Diseases* (1972) Vol. 25, pp. 665–72. See also T. W. Graham, et al., "Frequency of Church Attendance and Blood Pressure Elevation," *Journal of Behavioral Medicine* (1978) Vol. 1, pp. 37–43.

6. Durkheim, Emile. *Suicide* (New York: Free Press, 1951).

message of our religious institutions is to have an effect, that message must truly be entertaining for everyone in the family.

8. Church "services" should really provide family service. The church could serve as facilitator of social service, well-trained and experienced clerical counseling for families in distress, and as a clearing house for family direction and support. Too often, the church has become the most beautifully landscaped and peacefully empty place in the neighborhood. Going there for service to the family could again draw the family back inside the church.

9. Abolish as many "rules" as possible that serve to exclude church members from taking part in rituals or services. Many of my patients report lifelong emotional scars from being excluded from participation in some aspect of their religion. Universal and unqualified participation in church rituals allows those who most need the rituals to return for help; and with appropriate follow-up counseling, the church can serve as a place for redemption and comfort.

10. More social awareness in the church, and in church or temple services, with more use of family discussion groups, can again draw all members of the family together at church to debate issues of conflict that are universal within families and in our society. Social awareness refers not to political activism but to world responsibility, the inclusion of discussion of the issues of divorce, homosexuality, incest, and substance abuse as processes and not "failures," and to seeing the church as a place for the sharing of the development of the family appraisal systems that underlie family resilience.

THE FAMILY AS THE PATIENT

Neurophysiologist Candace Pert sees the "body as the outward manifestation of the mind."[7] If you take a good long look at each member of your family, at how they sit and walk, at what types of illness they suffer, and at what parts of their body seem

7. Pert, Candace. As quoted in *Brain Mind Bulletin,* January 20, 1986, p. 2.

to give them the most trouble, you are really seeing how these family members are appraising their world.

"My husband started to walk as if he had the burden of the world upon his shoulders," said Ms. Anders. "He slouched when he sat, shuffled when he walked, and his allergies started to act up on him. All of this happened when our daughter seemed to be getting worse and worse. He was talking about being helpless, and his body showed it. When we finally got into that treatment room with our daughter, when my husband started to feel he could actually do something to help, his allergies improved and he walked with his shoulders back."

Whenever families come to meet with me, I teach them to watch every family member, to look for what their bodies are saying about their thoughts and feelings. All illnesses from the most life-threatening diseases to everyday aches and pains, are really mental metaphors, signals about what our living has done to us. Good health care depends upon reading these metaphors and seeing illness as taking place within the family system, not inside an individual person. Mr. Anders's statement below indicates that it is whole families, not persons, who are healthy or unhealthy.

Mr. Anders said, "My wife was good at pointing out how I was walking and sitting and getting sick, but she seemed not so aware that she was walking faster and faster, getting up and sitting down, always on the move. She seemed to be trying to outrun our daughter's illness. She was thinking fast, looking for solutions, and that was what her body was doing."

THE CARETAKER'S COLD

I caution every medical student I train to pay attention to the family context of illness and wellness, to read the family body as well as the body of the patient. I warn the students about the risk to the health of those in a family who are caring for a very sick person. I have even noticed "caretaker's cold," the tendency of family members who are coping with another family member's illness to develop lingering head colds and upper respiratory infections.

In the case of very serious family illnesses, such as cancer and Alzheimer's disease, the burden of taking care of a sick family member creates a serious risk to the health of the care-taker. Ms. Muller's statement demonstrates this point:

"Now that you mention it, I don't think a day has gone by since Gramps got real sick that one of the rest of us hasn't had a symptom of something. Of course, we're all tired, so I guess our immune systems are weak. But I also think that our runny noses and our runny eyes are just another way for us all to cry, our body's way of grieving."

Popular psychology continues to attempt to help us con-quer stress, when in actuality stress is not the cause of any illness. Our health or our illness is the direct result of our appraisal of our world, of the meaning we give to what happens to us, and our system of appraisal is developed within the family system. All illness begins and ends within the context of the family, yet modern medicine has not seen fit to deal with an "us" approach to disease.

While the family is where we learn to give meaning to our life and to everything that happens to us, our so-called health care system has ignored the family in favor of the singular patient pathology view. Until medicine learns to look at the "appraisal effect," at how the family system teaches its mem-bers to make sense of what happens to them, medicine will never be able to deal with the challenge of illness or the magic of wellness. Sickness is an appraisal, the way our mind and body have decided to deal with some challenge. How we think and what we think can make us sick, and how the whole family learns to think together, the "family appraisal effect," can be one of the most significant health risks for any family.

Hippocrates stated that "those things which one has been accustomed to for a long time, although worse than things which one is not accustomed to, usually give less disturbance."[8] We learn to acclimate to a family system, a family ecology, and when change occurs, even change for what seems like the bet-ter, illness can result.

When American Indians were forced off the plains, with the accompanying severe disruption to their family systems, the outward situation seemed better. There was a higher standard of living and of sanitation, and health care was much better on

8. Hippocrates. *Works of Hippocrates,* Vol. 3 (New York: Medical Classics, 1938).

reservations than in the Indians' chosen home—the one to which they had become accustomed. Nonetheless, the rate of tuberculosis increased dramatically.[9] When thousands of Irish moved to the Eastern Seaboard of America during the last century, deaths from tuberculosis increased significantly.[10] Although these immigrants were better housed and fed in their new land, the forced migration resulted in one hundred percent more tuberculosis than in Dublin, where health conditions were significantly worse. There are several other examples of the impact of the meaning of change as related to health, and the influence of negative family appraisal on the health of the individual.

The family can teach hope and optimism, an appraisal system of faith and a sense of control. It can also teach surrender, despair, and pessimism. When the physician attempts to treat the singular patient, she or he neglects the single most important predictor of health and healing, the family appraisal system.

Some families teach such negative appraisal that their members learn only to "play dead," to hold their collective and individual breath until hope magically returns. Research has shown that persons who appraise their situation as hopeless experience excessive conservation of oxygen, as if they actually stopped breathing.

A neurological reaction occurs because of a vagal nerve reflex, and in turn, the heart rate slows potentially to the point of cardiac arrest and sudden death.[11] Real health care depends upon the identification and, if necessary, the modification, of the way in which a person learns to appraise their life experiences, not on radiation, surgery, and sublethal dosages of potentially lethal drugs.

Here are ten suggestions for the development of a true family practice of medicine:

9 Moorman, L. J. "Tuberculosis on the Navaho Reservation," *American Review of Tuberculosis* (1950) Vol. 61, p. 586.

10. Adams, W. F. *Ireland and Irish Emigration to the New World.* (New Haven: Yale University Press, 1932).

11. Wolf, S. "The End of the Rope: The Role of the Brain in Cardiac Death," *Canadian Medical Associaton Journal* (1967) Vol. 97, pp. 1022–25.

Ten Suggestions for a Family Medicine

1. All medical histories should focus on the "appraisal style" of the patient as the key factor in health. "Optimistic cognitive appraisal" is the healthiest human behavior, and the physician should be looking for it, modeling it, and helping to teach it.[12]

2. When families appraise events as stressful, their chances of illness, particularly of upper respiratory infection, increase.[13] All physicians should take careful histories to look as much for strain in the family as for a strain of virus. Regular records should be kept of family strain patterns, trends and styles of appraisal that may predispose family members to illness.

3. Physical examinations should include as many family members as possible. Physicians should avoid the solitary exam, even using the physical examination itself for family teaching. For most of the physical examination, there is no reason that the entire family can not be examined as a group. At the very least, physicians can hold family meetings to review the results of each family member's physical examination and help the family look for common sources of health risk.

4. Hospitals should provide direct counseling regarding appraisal styles within families, and all hospital staff members should be aware that family visits can either be immune system boosters or damaging to immunity and healing.

5. Before any medical procedure, the patient's, and the patient's family's, appraisal of the procedure should be elicited and, when necessary, modified in a more favorable direction. Hope and naive optimism is not enough. The actual direct effect of positive appraisal on body cells should be discussed with patients.

12. Kobasa, S. C., S. R. Maddi, and S. Courington. "Personality and Constitution as Mediators in the Stess-Illness Relationship," *Journal of Health and Social Behavior* (1981) Vol. 22, p. 368.

13. Meyer, R. J., and R. J. Haggerty. "Streptococcal Infection in Families: Factors Altering Individual Susceptibility," *Pediatrics.* (1962) Vol. 29, p. 539.

6. Families should be advised that illness is not the fault of the family or the person, and that the role of thinking and images in illness only demonstrate the multifactor aspect of getting sick, not a blame for disease.

7. When a family member is diagnosed as ill, immediate attention should be paid to the entire family system. It is a fact that illness is never a singular process, and the stress of being sick affects the entire family. Family life-style changes are necessary whenever one of the family members "gets sick for the family."

8. Medical schools should require courses and direct experience in "family life appraisal diagnosis." Complete psychological family histories should be taken of all medical students, and counseling and education of each student should be offered when needed. There is now an abundant and growing library of research in this area, and courses should be built around the new field of psychoneuroimmunology, or, the study of how thinking and feeling affects health and illness.

9. Physicians should be taught that we all carry "germs" and viruses within us. We will either learn to live peacefully with these internal factors, or will do something that lowers our defenses against them, and thus allow an invasion from inner space. They should be taught about the new field of "molecular psychology," concerned with how our thoughts change our molecules and brain chemicals and how our brain molecules affect our thoughts. The existence of communicating and learning molecules of health is no longer a subject of conjecture, and the way in which a group of people learn to appraise their life together is translated immediately into an internal molecular language, a pharmacopoeia of internal psychochemicals.

10. Less than twenty percent of our population will ever benefit from the so-called "medical marvels" and "breakthroughs." Trauma and some chronic illnesses can often be dealt with effectively by our modern medical approaches, but most illness is never helped by modern medicine. True medical intervention must take place by helping improve the family system of appraisal of daily life.

We think that aging is related to increased chances for getting sick. Actually, as we age, our style of appraisal of life changes, and these changes are as important to our proneness to disease as the aging process itself. We think that change causes illness; rather, what we make of change, and how we relate that change to the meaning of our living, are the key factors in staying well. Physicians would be well advised to look into how the family is, at least as often as they look into body orifices.

TEN PHASES OF FAMILY APPRAISAL

My clinical work with families has resulted in the identification of ten phases of family appraisal of life events and problems, of adjustment to change, of responses to challenges of and from within the family system. Consider each of these ten phases in terms of problems your own family may be having at this time or may have had in the past.

FAMILY APPRAISAL STEP ONE: DISORIENTATION. "When my husband died," said Ms. Bonner, "we were just totally at sea. I didn't know the first thing to do. I just froze." Ms. Bonner's statement illustrates the initial disorientation that takes place as families attempt to deal with crises.

Whenever change occurs, the system is thrown "out of whack." The family system, including the body systems of each family member, and even the community in which the family lives, is affected by even subtle changes that take place in everyday life. Even seemingly simple changes, such as a school board deciding to close a small local school due to low enrollment, can directly affect the health of every family in that community. Children may now ride buses instead of walking to school. Parents' schedules are changed, and new worries over safety and distance from children arise. A sense of lack of control of the child's education can evolve into parental protest. Issues of discrimination and power can result in confrontations, protests, and even the decision to move entire families.

One of the most frequent comments I hear in my clinical work is the comment "Nothing is simple." Family appraisal, indeed all learning, begins with disruption and disorientation;

the occurrence of hopefully safe emergencies that require family and individual adjustment. Learning to expect such disorientation may reduce some of the panic and rush to premature closure on problems that can destroy family resilience. Healthy families can live for long periods of time in a state of disorientation and are able to see challenge at such times, even while the family members are afraid and confused.

I stated earlier that tolerance of long periods of disorientation while avoiding "closure comfort"—coming up with a quick, convenient, but not thoroughly thought-out and family-shared solution—is a key to family resilience. Such tolerance requires the family faith that, eventually, sense will be made of whatever problem is confronting them.

FAMILY APPRAISAL STEP TWO: GUILT AND BLAME.

"I can still remember it," said Mr. Steiner. "Whenever something happened at home, whenever something went wrong, the first thing my mother would say was 'Who did it?' I always wondered why we didn't worry about what was happening more than we worried about who made it happen."

Guilt is a very healthy emotion. Psychologists have cursed guilt as the basis of neurosis and mental illness, but in actuality, there is such a thing as "good guilt." Like pain which signals us when something is wrong with the body, guilt is the spiritual signal that we are doing something, or have done something, that is incongruent with who we really are and how we want our higher self to be every day.

Good guilt can be a feeling that motivates us to correct our behaviors to be more in keeping with how we really think we should be and how we feel our family expects us to be. Bad guilt is accusatory guilt, a message sent to us or sent to ourselves about our shortcomings and inadequacies. Bad guilt teaches a lesson of avoidance and withdrawal, that we should stop doing something because we might get caught or suffer emotionally later. Good guilt teaches us to turn to others for help, and that we are behaving in ways that are not in keeping with who we really are and what we really can do. Ms. Steiner, in reflecting about how she raised her three now grown and independent children, commented about the difference between the good and bad guilt orientation to parenting.

"It wasn't until my third child that I learned the difference between what you call good guilt and bad guilt," said Ms. Steiner. "I used to yell at my kids that their dirty rooms were more evidence of what slobs they were. It took a while, but then I saw how different it was when I asked them if their rooms looked like they really wanted them to look. I would say things like 'I'm surprised at how your room looks. You're usually such a neat person.' It's a big difference. I won't say their rooms were always cleaner, but the atmosphere in our home was."

In Chapter Five, I discussed the importance of a rational approach to family living. Rational thinking teaches us that there is never a simple and direct causation between one behavior and the feelings and behavior of someone else. To feel guilty and withdraw is to begin with the assumption that people intend to harm or to do their worst instead of their best. Aside from criminal acts of intent, most pain is caused by error and oversight, by failure to listen and to see, by failure to be what we can be with those persons we love the most.

Blame and guilt are a natural phase of the family appraisal system. They are ways of assessing progress and comparing what is with what could be if all family members put forth their maximum effort at caring for the development and happiness of every other family member. The key at this step of family appraisal is to be sure that good guilt, the guilt of learning about the strengths that are not being used, is guiding this stage of problem solving. Good blame is sharing the good guilt within the family, and making sure that no single member of the family is held exclusively accountable.

FAMILY APPRAISAL STEP THREE: BARGAINING. "When we had problems," said Ms. Muller, "we would sort of feel like we were only supposed to have a preassigned number and severity of problem. When we got past that point, we started to feel gypped. We would sort of bargain with God. We would say, 'OK, now we really have a problem. Enough already. Give someone else the rest.' Or we would say, 'OK, we get the point. We will be good from now on, so don't give us any more problems. If we behave, will you stop sending more problems?' We started to bargain with God."

We often seem to think that problems are measurable. We think that our problem is "more" or "worse" than someone else's, that we can bargain or pay our way out of strife and challenge, or that by doing more we deserve more. This "bad bargaining" is a superstitious style of knocking harder and harder on wood to protect us from bad luck. All we accomplish is bruised knuckles.

Good bargaining during the family appraisal sequence is a bargaining with ourselves, not a bartering against evil. We decide to do something about our personal growth, about our own objectives and the meaning we ascribe to life in turn for the spiritual energy from within that results from such a decision. We seek meaning in everything that happens to us, and the bargain we strike with God is really a promise of commitment to integrity and redoubling of our efforts to love, tolerate, and forgive in exchange for the guidance and strength that will result from such self-responsibility.

"We said that my husband's passing was going to be a part of growing together," said Ms. Bonner. "The bargain we struck was that we would try harder to be us if God would help us with the pain. At first, we wanted to bargain with tangibles such as no more problems if we were willing to live through this one unbearable problem. That was no bargain at all, because that assumes that problems are parceled out according to who deserves them. That would mean that persons who are really hurt are all bad people, and that just doesn't make any sense."

FAMILY APPRAISAL STEP FOUR: FACT-COLLECTION PHASE. "When you are working, you try to get as much information as you can before you make a decision or try to solve a problem," said Mr. Anders. "When the family has trouble, you sometimes seem to try to solve problems on impulse and without any information, or with information that is incomplete."

Mr. Anders is describing the fact-collection phase of family appraisal, the period during which family members select and file the facts about what is happening to them. They gather more and more information about their problem, about alternative solutions, and about the possible need for amendments in the overall family appraisal system.

In some families, this fact-collection phase is so biased, so careless and rushed that it is as if a file clerk were trying to arrange information by using only the first four letters of the alphabet. Effective appraisal requires prolonged and nonprejudicial openness to the receipt of information about life events, as unbiased by the individual assumptions of each family member as possible.

"Did you ever try to listen when you're really mad?" asked Ms. Muller. "You don't want to hear anything that calms you down. It's sort of like a big slide, and once you're on it, you just don't want to stop. I can actually remember saying to my sixteen-year-old daughter, 'Don't tell me what you think, because I don't care.' Can you imagine that?"

All of us can imagine that, can remember when our anger developed a life of its own. Being angry is addicting, easy to do, and results in intense psychochemical changes that cause an emotional high. While prolonged anger damages your health, it actually feels good; in that the body systems buzz from head to foot. Like the seductive taste of junk food, junk feelings get us high even as they tear our bodies down. To be receptive, to listen and collect information with an open mind and without rushing to conclusions, is hard work that requires discipline, and being receptive does not create an immediate high. We must work to become comfortable with "plateauing" and not always "peaking."

Once the family has begun to tolerate disorientation, has learned enlightening self-blame and guilt, and has bargained within itself for movement toward its agreed-upon higher purposes, fact collection can be the phase that nurtures the problem-solving process. Open, nonprejudicial, shared, and slow-paced gathering of information, feelings, facts, comparisons, and precedents related to the problem at hand can only take place if someone in the family isn't busy trying to rush everyone else to a quick decision and solution of the problem.

Optimism and confidence in family strength during the fact-gathering phase of family problem solving allow the family to do an educated and informed appraisal, based on cooperation and goodwill rather than self-righteousness, ego-protection, or self-vindication. True open family fact-gathering requires maintenance of the sense of "us" while the data collection for problem solving is going on. Anybody can be family at fun times. Staying family at angry and difficult times is the true test of a healthy family and of an enduring family point of view.

To paraphrase William Shakespeare, smooth seas do not a sailor make.

The highest life expectancy in the world is recorded in Japan. It was thought that this longevity was due to genetic superiority, but Japanese who migrate to the United States and adopt our living and health—or unhealthy—habits, succumb to heart diseases and other diseases of civilization just as often as any other nationality. Japanese longevity is due to their receptiveness, their valuing of cooperation, goodwill, and group problem solving as fundamental to the welfare of the individual and the society.

Epidemiologist Leonard Syme, at the University of California at Berkeley, reports that we have assumed that the fast pace, smoking, fatty diet, and industrialized society in which we live are what cause us to get ill. The Japanese have all of these problems in their own culture, yet they live much longer on average than we do. The Japanese pollution problem is worse than North America's, and Japanese smoke much more than Americans, yet the Japanese have the lowest heart disease rate in the world and a low rate of death from all of the chronic illnesses.[14]

The Japanese value what they call "Amae," an emphasis on "us" over "me." They stress cooperation and receptiveness among families and all people. In place of our emphasis on "narcissism" is the Japanese emphasis on Amae, on the priority of the family.[15] Receptivity requires this emphasis on "us," on being able to allow ourselves to be penetrated by the feelings and needs of others, even when we feel threatened and stressed.

FAMILY APPRAISAL STEP FIVE: PROGRAMMING PHASE. "We always fall into the same trap," said Ms. Anders. "No matter how many times we promised ourselves that we were going to try this new parenting effectiveness training, I

14. Syme, Leonard. "People Need People," *Series on the Healing Brain Cassette Recording. No. 12.* (Los Altos, Cal.: Institute for the Study of Human Knowledge, 1982).

15. Doi, L. T. "Amae: A Key Concept for Understanding Japanese Personality Structure" in *Japanese Culture and Behavior,* T. S. Lebra and W. P. Lebra, eds. (Honolulu: Honolulu University Press of Hawaii, 1974).

still ended up yelling, going upstairs, and slamming my door
when I was mad at the kids. Some example, wasn't I?"

Ms. Anders is describing a phase of family problem solving and resilience that is unique to Western culture. We have
"programmed" almost everything in our life. We have exercise
programs, television programs, financial programs, and even
programs for "deprogramming" people who have been programmed by programs we don't like. We often find ourselves
trapped between a rock and a soft place; the rock of the real
problems with which we must cope, and the softness of popular
psychology "how to do its" that never really work.

Ms. Anders continued, "You're supposed to communicate.
So I communicated. The more I communicated, the madder I
got. Then, the program says, you're supposed to stay calm and
politely say that you are a little upset. At about that point, I'd
usually sooner say that I would like to declare my parenthood
over and return the children for a deposit. All the damn program did was make me feel even less adequate and give me
something else I couldn't do well with my kids."

The program phase of family appraisal can provide some
new ideas, some suggestions and guidelines for dealing with
transitional life events that are drawn from the experience of
other people. The problem with much of the programming
available in our society is that it is based on the individual and
not the family. There are few family self-help books, and programs are designed to help the individual and not the "us."
Programs are designed for how to be, to get, to do, and to
overcome. Programs are not designed to teach about meaning,
wishes, dreams, and spiritual struggles with the meaning of
problems in the context of the overall collective life experience.

Constructive family appraisal requires a program phase of
selective use of material available from every other person's
experience. Such selection must be a family process, not the
prerogative or assigned responsibility of one family member
who reads "the book" and tries some new program out on the
family. Family programming is family research, family searching for precedents within their family's own history, as described in Chapter Six, and family exploration of available
nonfiction books, films, poems, novels, even television shows
and plays, that may offer insights for problem solving that
freshen the family appraisal process.

In our society, there seems to be a more direct road to divorce court than to the library, church, or the theater. I ask families in distress to read classic works about other families who have struggled with life. One little girl asked her family to go the movies to see the Disney film *The Swiss Family Robinson,* a simple, silly, happy film about a family who struggled to survive being stranded on an island. The little girl said, "See, Mom, their mother doesn't stay mad. But she gets real mad. I wish you wouldn't stay mad."

Seeking out external stimuli for promoting better appraisal of problems can involve family programming that allows for a relaxing of tension and endurance through the "hot" phases of family conflict. Even if the whole family goes to the movies and sits quietly in anger as they watch, at least the family has bought some time for "us," and may discover even one lesson that can help them.

FAMILY APPRAISAL STEP SIX: SUCCESSFUL SURRENDER PHASE. Our society views surrender in negative terms. The successful surrender phase is a step in family problem solving that allows for the acknowledgment that many problems will never be solved, a step in the direction of forgiveness of self, family, and the acceptance of the lack of consideration and insensitivity of some people. In a society that tells us every day that "We can do it, just keep trying, you can conquer your problem, and never give up," it is difficult to learn to accept, to gracefully and graciously give in and move on.

To be able to accept as a family is to be able to free the family from struggling to try to solve every problem. Ms. Steiner, the mother struggling to cope with the leaving of her three children, stated, "I had spent a lifetime raising those kids. I was used to doing for them, taking care of them, getting them through school, helping them grow and develop. I was always solving their problems or helping them learn to solve their problems. Now, I have to learn just to accept, just to let them find their new life. It's hard to let go, to just let life happen after you've spent more than half of your own life trying to make life happen."

If you are driving your car and an unreasonable, mean, obnoxious person cuts quickly in front of you, looking back over their shoulder to call you and your family every vulgar

name imaginable, you have a choice. Hans Selye, the father of
stress research, said that it is not what stresses us that counts,
but the way in which we choose to react.[16] If you elect to fight
back, to yell at and threaten the thoughtless driver, you turn
your body, your health, and the health of your family over to
this thoughtless person. You are allowing this person to poison
your body with stress chemicals.

Remember the "as if" response.[17] Your body can not do
anything "abnormal." All body responses are natural, but every body response can go awry, over- or underreacting to too
much or too little stimulation. Everything your body does
"works," and is designed to be adaptive. Nausea and severe
diarrhea are adaptive when you have eaten something you
should not have, but not when you are attempting to rid your
system "as if" your boss were a form of food poisoning.

Even a disease such as diabetes is adaptive, in the sense
that the body "saves" glucose in the blood at times of severe
starvation so that the brain can use this glucose for energy and
survival. Some researchers believe that some forms of diabetes
result from persons behaving and thinking "as if" they were
starving for love. The close connection between food and loving
nurturance in our society may establish such a connection for
some people.[18]

The entire family health pattern is an "as if" pattern of
psychological and physiological reaction. The choice is always
yours; to overreact or underreact, that is the question. Acceptance is underreaction, the realistic appraisal of events that
starts with the assumption that we choose and conceptually
create our own heaven or hell.

"I have struggled with my weight problem since I was a
little girl," said one of my patients. "I have been almost twenty-
five pounds overweight all my life. I am now an obesity expert.

16. Selye, Hans. *Stress of Life,* Rev. Ed. (New York: McGraw-Hill,
1976).

17. For a discussion of how natural body responses can go out of
control, and the concept of "as if" body responses, see S. Wolf and
H. Goodell. *Behavioral Science in Clinical Medicine* (Springfield, Ill.:
Charles C. Thomas, 1976).

18. Hinkle, L. E., and S. Wolf. "A Summary of Experimental Evidence Relating Life Stress to Diabetes Mellitus." *Journal of Mount Sinai
Hospital* (1952) Vol. 19, pp. 537–70.

You name the diet book, and I could rewrite it. Finally . . . finally, I just broke. I said that I will now accept my weight. Maybe there's just something about me, about my true self, that is never going to be a hundred and five pounds. I'm a hundred-and-forty-pound person. I told my husband that I am writing a new book called *Pounds as IQ Points*. I now believe that you get one IQ point for every pound you weigh, and that people who are trying to lose weight all the time are actually getting dumber and dumber."

Certainly, good health habits and weight regulation are important. The patient above, through her joking, was making an important point about life appraisal. Accepting is not "less" than "solving." We must learn to make active choices between solving and accepting, between going "with" and going "against." The decision is never a simple one. The person who is dangerously heavy and seeks valid medical advice regarding the need to lose weight must examine effective strategies to do so. The struggle itself, however, may be unhealthy, and all of us must decide between the options of where we would like to be and the price we ultimately pay for the trip.

The patient with the weight problem continued, "Now that I'm forty, and after more than thirty years of thinking about scales, weight, food, and my body, I have only found out one real lesson. If I eat ten times my weight a day in calories and exercise a lot, I will lose a few pounds. If I eat fifteen times my weight and don't exercise much, I gain weight. I have found a plan where I eat about twelve times my weight a day in calories and exercise a little. That's it. I have been doing that for months. I'm still too fat, but I'm not as fat as I was. I refuse to waste the rest of my life trying to lose weight so everyone who passes by my casket will say, 'Doesn't she look trim?' "

The successful surrender phase of family appraisal is the most difficult of all twelve phases of family coping, for it requires clear life philosophy, spiritual strength, and a balance between needs for acceptance by others and a sense of self-celebration. Remembering that we have a choice, that we do not always have to be on a self-improvement program, is a key step toward a healthy family living. People who are in a "self acceptance" mode are sometimes easier to live with than persons who are forever trying to get some place other than where they are.

Mr. Johnson, the father in the new stepfamily I have been describing, said, "We stopped going to therapy after several months. We were trying to make this new family like some type of clone of our other families. We were being commended by our therapist for working hard, making progress, and really going and growing, but we weren't any happier. We finally learned to accept the fact that there would be differences, sometimes big differences, between this new family and our prior experiences. We finally exhaled and said to ourselves, 'OK, we agree to disagree. We'll fight sometimes. We're done trying to become. Let's start just being.' Once we stopped trying to make a family out of ourselves, we started to let us start to happen as our own unique family."

The five families I have selected for most of my examples in this book showed remarkable appraisal strengths, and you can see by Mr. Johnson's statement that he and his family learned to accept, to be, and to evolve rather than solve. I suggest you take some time to ask yourself and your family if you are giving yourselves enough credit for just how good you already are. Family fights and pain are natural indicators of family love when such distress is balanced with the recognition and mutual acknowledgment within the family that, like individuals, families can be perfect without solving all of their problems.

FAMILY APPRAISAL STEP SEVEN: TOLERATING IN-EFFECTIVENESS. Family resilience requires the endurance and tolerance of ineffectiveness on the part of individual family members and the family as a whole. Our society is too complex and too demanding to allow for complete and constant success in coping. Sometime in the family appraisal cycle, all family members will feel that their best efforts are not enough. To be ineffective sometimes is the underlying motive for learning, because self-efficacy is a primary human need. We all need safe emergencies, events in our life that challenge our effectiveness without demolishing our self-esteem. The drive for efficacy is the energy of life, but we must also be patient enough to allow ourselves to be just plain bad at doing some things.

"I cannot, no matter what you tell me, be this calm, easygoing type mother," said Ms. Bonner. "I was a little more easygoing before my husband was killed, but I can't be what I can't be. Maybe I'll just have to learn how to throw more efficient, less harmful tantrums."

Ms. Bonner's statement illustrates the ineffectiveness phases of family problem solving, of going through periods when we knowingly are not doing as well as we might. When families panic at times of ineffectiveness, fail to allow the time I mentioned for new solutions and strategies to emerge, they may only succeed in finding false solutions and in temporarily avoiding the central problems the family should be confronting.

Persons who truly believe they can be collectively effective in managing their problems have been shown to experience direct health benefits within their bodies.[19] Higher levels of suppressor T-cells, which keep the body from producing antibodies against itself, are shown in persons who have a sense of self-efficacy. Mothers who were taught pain-reduction techniques to assist with natural childbirth and who believe strongly that they will be able to effectively use these techniques, report less discomfort during childbirth and require less pain medication.[20]

What psychologists call a "belief in self-efficacy" is a key to personal health. When the family has its own sense of family efficacy, the family is healthier. To develop such a sense of efficacy—the sense that even when external events are beyond our control, our "reaction" to such events is under our own control—requires a toleration of prolonged periods of the opposite feeling of ineffectiveness. People are not "born" with a sense of effectiveness; this sense is learned in the family setting, by families allowing one another time enough to mess up, make mistakes, and take the necessary time to develop the self-efficacy we all so desire.

Psychologists Ellen Langer and Judy Rodin gave one group of nursing home residents potted plants to care for, and told the recipients to take their own responsibility for the plants and not to allow the staff to take over the responsibility for them. A second group of nursing home residents which received the usual amount of nursing home care was given plants, but the staff members announced that they would take respon-

19. Bandura, A. *Perceived Self-Efficacy and Health Functioning.* Paper presented at the annual meeting of the Society of Behavioral Medicine, San Francisco, March 1986.

20. Ibid.

sibility for the care of the residents' plants. Within three weeks, the first group improved significantly in health over the second group. Eighteen months later, the death rate in the first group was one half that of the second group.[21] A feeling of effectiveness had apparently been translated to effectiveness of physical health.

During the naturally occurring times of family ineffectiveness, an important decision must take place. Family members and the family system must decide whether they are controlling their life or being controlled by it. Psychologists call the feeling that life controls us a sense of "external locus of control." The sense that we cannot control the world, but that we can control our response and reactions to our world, is called "internal locus of control." Resilience of the family depends upon the development of a collective sense of family internal locus of control, of mutual responsibility for reactions to a world that we must create by our perceptions and not succumb to by our surrender to an "out there" that randomly impacts upon ourselves and our loved ones.

Mr. Anders stated, "Every time I feel overwhelmed, when I feel that nothing I can do will make any difference, I know I am reacting to me. I know I am creating my own hell. I try to use as many of these times as possible to focus my attention back in to me and my family. We are our own world, and our words are spiritual instructions and prophecies."

How we talk about our world is really a description of how we intend to make our life. "When I'm feeling inadequate, it's like I'm using a screwdriver to pound in a nail. I have to think of using different tools, but I guess first I have to use the damn screwdriver enough to know that I really need to learn how to use the right tool," said Mr. Anders. Mr. Anders's statement demonstrates the turning around of periods of ineffectiveness to times of learning about new paths to self-efficacy.

When I work with families, I make every effort to congratulate them on their failures. I tell them that it is a natural part of learning, a sign that some very important lessons are on the

21. Langer, Ellen J., and Judy Rodin. "The Effects of Choice and Enhanced Personal Responsibility for the Aged: A Field Experiment in an Institutional Setting," *Journal of Personality and Social Psychology* (1976) Vol. 34, pp. 191–98.

horizon, and that we must be careful not to change too quickly, because there is much in our old and seemingly ineffective behavior that may still be valuable. Such a warning takes the pressure off the family, seems, paradoxically, to motivate families to look even harder for new strategies of problem solving, and in most cases promotes an intrafamily tolerance during periods of frustration with slow rates of behavioral change.

FAMILY APPRAISAL STEP EIGHT: FATIGUE. "Sometimes I'm too tired to think. I'm even too tired to think about how tired I am. I'm thought out," said Ms. Bonner. "Can't the brain get tired? Your arms can, your body can, so I'm sure brain cells can get cramps too. I think I might have pulled a brain cell somewhere."

Ms. Bonner's statement illustrates another natural phase in family resilience, a period during which almost all psychological and even physical energy seems to be gone. Under chronic change or challenge from a problem family member, we can come to feel that there is no energy left within us. This feeling is a signal that we are not in fact thinking too much at all. What is really happening is that we are trying to "do" too much and not really being contemplative enough.

"I have worked for hours with my son on his math. He just doesn't get it," said Ms. Bonner. "My husband used to do it, and now I have to do it. I have tried to figure out why he can't get it, and I just get frustrated trying to help him. We tried a tutor, a new book on modern math, even my uncle tried to help, but nothing works. For my son, numbers are a foreign language from another planet."

You can see from Ms. Bonner's statement that she is trying to solve her son's problem with a flow of different strategies. If she were really thinking instead of tiring herself out trying to "do," she would listen to what she was saying to herself. Examine Ms. Bonner's statement, and you will see that the answer to her problem is in her own words.

Ms. Bonner states "My husband used to do it, and now I have to do it." She is trying to figure it out, and she is "trying a tutor," but the problem is really not her son's math difficulty. Her problem is feeling overwhelmed and trying to do everything herself to compensate for her husband's absence. When I asked her to sit down and write down exactly what she was thinking about the math problem and then on another day to read over her statements for the answer she would surely find in her own words, this was her report.

"I heard me as overwhelming me. I wasn't thinking clearly. Why was I taking on this problem anyway? This was the school's problem. Maybe a different math class, maybe a different math teacher, maybe no math at all was the answer. I asked the question you asked me to ask. 'What am I tired of?' I wasn't tired of math. I don't even know math. I hate it. I was tired of having to do everything. I called the school and said that they should do something about this problem of theirs, their unsuccessful attempts to get my son to learn math. They did switch him to a different teacher. My son still hates math, but he doesn't have the homework anymore. I'm out of the math maze."

When you feel "tired of thinking," remember you are really tired of "not thinking clearly," tired of what and how you are thinking, and not giving yourself enough time to think rationally and reflectively. You are really not taking time to just sit and think at all. Your brain is calling you, and you are mistaking that call for mental fatigue.

As I pointed out earlier, no one gets tired of "being." We tire of too much "doing." Resilience requires time to sit down, look in, and clear up your own private thoughts, feelings, fears, and aspirations. Cognitive fatigue results from mental and spiritual neglect. Our brain cells are not suffering from overuse, they are suffering from neglect and the boredom of day-to-day fixation on junk thoughts about obligations and "doing."

FAMILY APPRAISAL STEP NINE: REENERGIZING. "I always seem to get my energy back. Just when I think I'm at the end of my rope, I find more rope," said one of my patients.

I will be describing the concept of family energy in a later chapter, but for now, remember that being aware of family energy, and of disruptions in its flow, is another key to maximizing the resilience of the family system. The energy we feel we are lacking in our daily life is not just an energy of bodily metabolism, it is an energy of the human spirit, and all families feel an ebbing and flowing of this energy as they confront the problems of daily living.

Our vocabulary should tell us that we know we are energy,

and not just the stuff of bones and tissue. We say we feel drained, that we have no energy, that someone is taking all our energy, or that we have to be "reenergized." Learning to sense our own energy is more than trying to build our physical and emotional stamina. Being reenergized is learning that there is always energy available from our relationships with others, and from taking the time to seek out that energy at times of conflict and stress, by connecting with our family members, telling them how we feel, and telling them what we need.

As you will learn later in this book, some family members and other persons in our world are actually energy leeches, who consciously or unconsciously rob us of our energy because of their own inner turmoil, feelings of despair, and over-self-involvement. I will discuss how energy leeches affect the family later, but family resilience requires at least the acknowledgment that such family members exist, and that they play a major role in our feelings of being exhausted from our family living.

A second source of loss of family and individual energy is referred to by some writers as "divine discontent."[22] Such discontent and energy change results when we sense that we are not following our inner direction, that in some way we are not living day-to-day in the way our spirit, our innermost sense, seems to be asking us to live.

Sometimes we feel as if we are not flowing with our energy direction, and we sense a friction, a disruption from within. We may sense an energy that is available but without direction, and we may feel that we should be making a career or location change or some other fundamental shift in how and why we are living. Divine discontentment results from being out of tune with who we really are and how we really want to live.

Divine discontentment is very subtle, and may be causing us to be annoyed, to be curt with our own family, to experience physical symptoms, such as constant headaches or stomach upset, and almost constant fatigue. You may feel "just a little off," or "not quite with it." You may feel sad with no apparent

22. Gerber, R. *Vibrational Medicine* (Sante Fe, New Mexico: Bear and Co., 1988), p. 462. Dr. Gerber discusses the complex concept of multidimensional energy fields with respect to human beings and how these fields interact. He also explains the concepts of energy leeching and divine discontent.

reason. You may go from doctor to doctor to find out what is wrong, because again, in our mechanistic view of daily living, we think something physical or something "real" must be wrong when it is in our spirit rather than in our body that discontent has been brewing.

Many people find the concept of psychic energy to be mystical and unscientific, yet the concept of universal energy is well-documented fact. All of the recent discoveries in modern science support the existence of energy being emitted from our thoughts, feelings, and behaviors. These discoveries must be applied to the human experience or we will continue to behave like robots, while a much richer life experience goes on without our awareness.

Mr. Anders said, "When my son would get very upset, we would all feel the energy just go out of us. Then I begin to sense that I didn't have any energy at work or at home. I just wasn't living the way I wanted. I was always discontented and complaining about paying for things I didn't want and wanting things I couldn't pay for. We all had to reexamine what we were all about and where our energy was going, where we wanted it to go, and where we could find more energy."

Mr. Anders's statement is typical of most of patients. The discussions of energy, its lack of direction, its absence, or the thrill of feeling reenergized, are always at the base of therapy. All families are energy fields, attracted and repulsed much like poles of two strong magnets. Developing our ability to sense the type and amount of spiritual energy we and our family members emit and respond to is a key step toward healthier family living.

FAMILY APPRAISAL STEP TEN: INTEGRATION. When problems arise for the family, the phases of resilience I have described to this point will always take place. Think of your own family when problems strike. Think of the initial disorientation and sense of helplessness that often is followed by guilt and blame. Remember the bargaining within the family and with whatever system you feel runs your world. Think of your family's capacity to be sensitive and receptive to one another at times of challenge and of the programming that can help or hinder family progress. Think of the successful surrender phase, where your family learns to tolerate, forgive, and apply its own system of explanatory rules and source of meaning. Think of the ineffectiveness that can serve as motivation to higher levels of feelings of self-confidence and efficacy. Think of the cognitive fatigue that results from attempting to do and solve rather than be and develop. Think of the concept of constant family energy and of tuning in to that source of collective group energy for the development of the individual family member and the family itself.

When you learn to see this family resilience cycle in your own family, you have moved on to family integration, a sense of family peace in the knowledge that all life is a flowing energy cycle, and that the family system is where the meaning of this cycle is born, develops, is challenged, and is changed. If your family is under pressure now, try to place the phase of your family somewhere within this family resilience cycle.

Remember that these are not just steps in problem solving but recurring phases of the life cycle of daily family living when problems affect the whole family system. Knowing where your family is in this cycle, and in the context of optimism, hope, control, and effectiveness, helps to give a universal and shared perspective to times in your own family living when your problems may seem yours alone.

FINDING YOUR OWN FAMILY'S PHASE OF FAMILY APPRAISAL

To help you understand more about the development of your own family's appraisal system, read over the following questions. Find the question or questions that seem the closest to representing your own status regarding family problem solving. Check to see which phase of the family appraisal cycle matches up with the question or questions that you identified. Remember, nothing in life is totally separate, so your family may be in more than one phase at a time or moving back and forth between two or more phases.

1. Is your family feeling helpless, confused, and overwhelmed about a problem or problems it is trying to deal with? **DISORIENTATION PHASE**

2. Are members of your family name-calling and criticizing each other?   GUILT AND BLAME PHASE

3. Are family members trying to trade off behaviors, agreeing only to do things if another family member will do something first or in return?   BARGAINING PHASE

4. Are family members pointing out what other families are doing to solve their problems?
FACT-GATHERING PHASE

5. Have members of your family tried what seem like gimmick solutions from self-help books and talk-show television?
PROGRAMMING PHASE

6. Is your family becoming more comfortable with their daily life, seeming to adjust together even though several problems are still bothering daily family living?
SUCCESSFUL SURRENDER PHASE

7. Does your family seem to be learning to "work around" some problem behaviors by someone in your family, becoming more tolerant and less overreactive to some prior annoying behaviors?   INEFFECTIVENESS PHASE

8. Are members of your family feeling tired even though they are getting plenty of sleep? Do you hear statements such as "I've had it" and "I give up"?   FATIGUE PHASE

9. Have you noticed that your family seems a little closer together lately, trying to do more things together and to talk calmly more often?   REENERGIZING PHASE

10. Has your family just come through a difficult period of problem solving to feel a sense of victory, completion, and optimism for the future?   INTEGRATION PHASE

When families learn that problems are the seeds for all family growth, and that the family way of understanding and giving meaning to living is in a constant state of change through the phases I have outlined above, each family member may become more optimistic about the future of the family. Each member may develop a new faith in the family's capacity to provide him or her with a sense of control over their world, commitment to their growing family and to the family way of viewing life, and the confidence to be challenged rather than overwhelmed by the problems all of us must face.

CHECKING FOR THE FIRST FIVE RX'S

You have now read about the first five of the ten family Rx's for healthy family living. You have been asked to make a choice between seeing your world as a mechanical, I/me/mine, here and now, individual struggle to survive or to see your life as related to everyone and everything, in terms of the shared energy of us/we/ours, and a broader sense of the meaning of living in a way that shows your awareness of your connection with the cosmos.

A family view of life teaches us that healthy living demands that we find ritual and consistency in all that we do so that the natural rhythm of living will be given a chance to evolve and direct our life. Without rhythm and ritual, our lives are directed by external schedules and the constant roar of traffic and airplanes.

A family view of life teaches us that healthy living requires us to think in a new way that accepts many levels of reality and that "knowing" is different than perceiving. We create our world just as the experimenter creates the results of his or her own experiments because he or she is always a part of that experiment. Remembering and honoring the history of our family is a tangible way of showing our value and understanding of the importance of how all of our family experiences become a part of our world and of the whole world.

In this chapter, you have seen that the resilience of the family depends on the understanding of a cycle of adjustment to problems, and that the successful progress of this cycle depends on toleration and patience within the family for prolonged times of adjustment and change, rather than surrender to society's demand for quick solutions that keep the social machine running while the spirit of the individual and his or her family becomes stagnant. The following six steps suggest ways in which you may enhance the resilience factor in your own family.

SIX STEPS TO FAMILY RESILIENCE

STEP ONE. Remember that the family has a potential for loving that transcends mere romance. The most obvious indicator of family love is family optimism. When we talk optimistically, even if we have to "fake it," we issue subtle psychochemical commands to our own and our family's internal health maintenance system.

STEP TWO. Remember that your family has a potential for tolerance that transcends mere patience. Giving the family time to grow, adjust, and even to suffer is another act of family love. When in doubt . . . wait!

STEP THREE. Remember that your family has a potential for faith extending far beyond mere hope. Your family is your source of faith, where you learn to make sense of living and what is important to believe in. If you listen carefully and feel intensely, your family energy will guide you.

STEP FOUR. Remember that your family has a potential for forgiveness that is far more than just forgetting. We forgive our family members just because they are our family members, and the art of forgiving is an art of healthy living.

STEP FIVE. Remember that your family has a potential for renewed vulnerability and energy in the face of the most painful changes. We are energy, not objects, and the family is an evolving energy field of love. It is this loving energy that fuels our family resilience. It is always there for your use.

STEP SIX. Remember that your family has a potential for resilience and growth energized by its problems, and by the way in which your family learns to give meaning to its problems. Problems are family soul food.

Remember, above all, that your family can offer unquestioned acceptance of each of its members and guidance for each of their individual quests for meaning, based totally on the fact that all family members forever will be together, even as the process of family growth makes each of them strong enough to be free.

CHAPTER EIGHT

Family Resonance: Making Good Family Vibes

"You know how when you put your hand on something like a radio that is plugged in and you can feel the energy going through it? That's like our family. You can feel our energy when we're together."
MR. STEINER

FAMILY RESONANCE: The ability to tune in to, feel, and share spiritual energy with all family members, to provide family members with the energy to move freely between individual development and family unity, and to see the family as a system of flowing energy rather than a set of separate people.

FAMILY FUEL

The family is an energy system that provides the fuel for all of our growth. Everything that happens within the family, from arguments over curfews for teenagers to the meaning of the death of a family member, give energy to and take energy from the family and its members.

When we say that we are losing our energy, fatigued, overwhelmed, or drained by our daily obligations, we are really identifying an energy leak from within the family itself. When we feel invigorated and refreshed, we have become aware of the family energy within us.

The Family Resonance Test

As a starting point for understanding the family as a life energy source, take this family resonance test. Use the following scoring system to assess your family energy flow:

0   1   2   3   4   5   6   7   8   9   10

ALMOST NEVER   SELDOM   SOMETIMES   A LOT   ALMOST ALWAYS

1. ——— Does your family seem rested and ready to begin every day with new energy and commitment?

2. ——— Does your family intentionally speak positively to one another and about one another, believing that words are actually units of energy that can hurt or heal?

3. ——— Is your "FEP," or family extrasensory perception, improving so that you can actually feel what is happening to your family members even when they are not with you?

4. ——— Does each family member seem to feel energized by just being with the family?

5. ——— Are reactions within the family balanced, with no overreactions or ignoring of family member needs and concerns?

6. ——— Does your daily family vocabulary contain words that refer to the family's energy system, such as "good vibrations," "feeling uplifted" by someone else, "sensing" one another's feelings, and "with" or "out of" the energy flow?

7. ——— Can family members sometimes feel the

presence of family members who have died or left the family? Does just being in the room of a family member cause other family members to "feel" that family member's presence?

8. ———— Can you feel positive energy at a family gathering, with every family member adding to rather than subtracting from the good energy flow of the occasion?

9. ———— When you are sick, do you feel healing energy coming from your family?

10. ———— Do all family members seem to be making deposits to rather than withdrawals from the family energy bank?

———— TOTAL FAMILY RESONANCE SCORE

Use the arbitrary 90-point score as an indication of how your own family is currently dealing with the resonance of family energy within it. Your score on family resonance is like measuring the vibrations of a tuning fork. As soon as you have made a measurement, the measurement has changed, and the same is true for your score on this and all of the tests in this book.

For discussion purposes, however, if you scored over 90 points, your family is aware of, and behaving in terms of, the positive energy available within the family system and is benefiting from such energy in everyday life. If you scored less than 90 points, or if you had difficulty understanding the questions because the concept of family energy seemed strange or even meaningless to you, then your time would be well spent in trying to find your family energy.

FEELING THE FAMILY

"Just being in the same room with my son seems to take all my energy away," said one mother. "I feel drained by the time he leaves for school, and I begin to feel drained even before he comes back in the front door. He's like a vampire to me. He saps me of every ounce of energy."

Another mother reported, "My son is like a battery

charger plugged right in to me. I don't know what it is, but just being around him gives me strength. I feel good vibrations from him, and so does the whole family. Even our friends can sense it."

Each of these mothers is experiencing the effects of family energy. They are describing the everyday ebb and flow of life energy that influences all of us. Some families refer to the resonance, the movement of family energy, as good or bad vibrations, mood shifts, atmosphere, or even the effects of a full moon, but all families, in their own unique ways, know that there is energy flowing within them.

The family is where life energy is transformed into personal growth, given meaning, and harnessed for the development of the individual family members. Resonance is striking the family tuning fork, setting in motion and reacting to the vibrations of the energy that flows within all families. Families help their members to new levels of human development through the channeling of family life energy into the spirit of each person in the family.

FAMILY FRICTION

Listen to people talking, and you will hear the language of universal energy. Phrases such as "I'm drained," "good and bad vibes," "out of sync," "poles apart," "drawn together and apart," "energy spurts," "burning out," "momentum," "buzzing with activity," a "live wire," and several other phrases expose our inner knowledge of the energy that we know is at the core of all life. Once we take the family view and begin to talk openly with others, particularly with our own family, about energy rather than about single events and individual people, we begin to see the full power of the family.

"One argument—I mean, just one argument—and we all seem to lose our spark," said Ms. Johnson. "We may start out the day happy and full of energy, but if we get into one battle, we all just seem to have a big hole punctured in us and lose our spunk."

Ms. Johnson's statement illustrates how family friction can result in energy loss, overheating of family interactions, or depletion of the family energy supply. Like finding where something is rubbing in a machine to cause energy loss and eventual breakdown or burn-out, learning to identify where the major family friction points are and correcting them, or learning to avoid them, is a major step in keeping the family energy system flowing.

"We have learned that we don't talk about our former families yet," continued Ms. Johnson. "There's just too much friction there, so we're better off staying out of that area, at least for now. I used to blame my new husband and his family for this problem, but it helps just to see it as a problem in protecting the family energy from unnecessary friction points while we learn to live together."

Ms. Johnson is demonstrating how one simple change in conceptualizing a family problem can provide less blaming, less conflict, and better coping strategies. Viewing the Johnson family's problem in terms of shared family energy and friction, rather than trying to assign responsibility or blame to those we see as problem family members, leads to a solution that the whole family can work on together.

MOVING IN A FAMILY ORBIT

Like the planets around the sun, the electrons within an atom move in their own orbits. Energy is required for these electrons to move to higher orbits. Too much energy and there is danger of an explosion. Too little energy and an implosion can occur. Just the right amount of energy is needed for the electron to progress, and physicists call this exact amount of energy the principle of resonance. Families, too, must be able to provide the right amount of energy, not too much pressure or too much support, not too much caring but plenty of loving in amounts that don't smother but help us grow.

"We just seem to be going in circles," said one father. "We are going around and around, but we are going nowhere." If we think about this father's statement in terms of separation and isolation, we see helplessly rotating individuals stuck without clear direction. The family clock is seen as broken. If we choose to see the father's statement in terms of a family energy view, we see that this particular family lacks resonance, and is blind to the spiritual energy required to move to different and higher levels of experience as a system.

A CAUSE FOR EXPLOSIONS OF THE NUCLEAR FAMILY

If a family member is propelled to an orbit of life, to independent challenges for which they are not yet ready, he or she will experience "dis-ease." Scientists know the danger of an electron experiencing the wrong resonance and the potential for explosion that exists when energy fields get out of balance. When family members feel that they don't fit the family system, when their own energy flow seems different than that of the family system, their family orbit will erode, and they are likely to crash back into the family nucleus, disrupting the energy of all other family members.

If a family member simply circles endlessly and without progress or growth, their personal orbit can decay, resulting in possible illness and family problems derived from a true burnout of the family spirit. The ultimate challenge to the family is to keep everyone growing without too much pressure or too little encouragement.

"After we started talking about this energy thing, we really saw things differently," said Ms. Steiner. "We used to talk about our anger, our impatience, new discipline techniques, parent effectiveness training, and all kinds of labels for one another like depressed, hostile, or just plain crazy. Once we looked at how our family worked from the point of view of energy we all shared, it was more like we were on a trip together and we all had to pay attention to our energy, not to who did what to whom or what was wrong with one or the other of us. Every single time we had family problems, we could see that the problem always started with us not sharing positive energy together, not just being together and connecting together enough. We really had this problem when the kids got ready to leave. We are still trying to get our family energy back, sort of change the family orbits for all of us."

Ms. Steiner's statement reflects her newly emerging view

of family life. In her family therapy, she had come to see how the family energy concept was more constructive and instructive than trying to look for the family member or members who were causing or having problems.

THE FAMILY ENERGY METER EXERCISE

Try the following exercise to see just how real family energy is. Find a picture of someone in your family, sit down, and look at the picture for a few minutes. Try to feel the amount and type of energy you sense about that family member. If you take sufficient time and try to sense energy rather than "think" about the person or the picture, I promise you that you will feel what I mean by flowing family energy even in the absence of a family member.

Another exercise you might want to try is to stand next to a family member for several minutes. Perhaps in the kitchen while cooking or while the family member is busy doing something else, go and stand right next to that person. Try to feel the energy they are giving off. Try to feel if it is positive or negative energy. Check in with others to see if you are right. More times than not, and unless your family mocks or is reluctant to speak of such things openly, you will have sensed the energy system accurately.

BOUNCING IN ONE ANOTHER'S WAKE

The family may be conceptualized as several stones tossed in the stream of life, with each stone causing an "energy ripple." Each of the ripples from each family member will eventually overlap and collide. We are influenced by the existence and energy of all of our family. When one member is "over-energized" and sensitive only to individual development, his or her energy "wake" can rock and even sink another family member.

The two mothers discussing their children at the beginning of this chapter illustrated the effect of the energy waves on the family. We all must work in two ways to promote more effective family resonance, more balanced and healthy energy. First, we all must be aware of the energy we send and demand, thinking about and feeling for a balance in the sending and receiving process. We have to keep our family point of view alive and be vigilant in perceiving how what we do and feel affects the entire family.

Do we ask too much of our family and give too little? Do we ignore our family now that we may be distant from them? Do we turn to our family only in need, for an energy "fix," while providing little reliable energy input into the family's energy storage system? Do we really take the time to "sense" each of our family members, feel their energy, and enhance the energy with them? All of these questions relate to family resonance, the process of maintaining good and shared energy flow in the family.

Being aware of our own family energy is to make the effort to sense the family energy, to be aware of family "brown outs" or the waste of precious family fuel on petty arguments and old grudges. The question "How much family energy am I willing to spend on this issue?" is a good question for keeping our energy sensors in the "on" position. We cannot just jump into the stream of life without paying attention to the energy wake we create, or our splash will capsize those around us.

Ms. Anders said, "Sometimes I think people are either energy takers or energy givers. The givers seem to end up in therapy trying to understand why they don't give enough or why they feel that they have given all they have. The takers are out somewhere, spending their energy everywhere but where it is needed. It is needed most by those from whom you got that energy in the first place, in your own marriage and in your own family." Ms. Anders is describing clearly the concept of the need for appropriate family resonance.

SALAMANDERS, SEEDS, AND FAMILY ENERGY PATTERNS

Research in the 1940s began to show the existence of energy fields related to living things. Harold S. Burr, at Yale University, demonstrated that the electrical field around salamanders' unfertilized eggs did not resemble that of the eggs themselves, but the field of the future adult salamander.[1] He surmised that an energy field template for the later development of the salamander was in place.

When Dr. Burr measured the energy field around tiny seedlings, the fields were those of the adult plant and not of the seed itself. Again, there seemed to be an "energy template," a source of life energy that directed the development of these living things. Burr called this energy "bioenergetic growth fields," and I suggest that the family has its own growth field that profoundly affects family members throughout their lives and beyond.

"You can tell when someone is a family member," said Mr. Johnson. "You can sense who is family and who isn't. Sometimes you can't tell it so easily in your own family, because I guess you're too much a part of it yourself. You are growing in the thing. But you can see the family in every family you meet. You can see how they are connected, how they walk, look, feel, and talk. You just take it for granted in your own family, but you sure see it in others. It even seems to start when people are together for a long time, even at work or other places. The family is just in you. You can feel it within you, acting on you, influencing you, directing you, even helping you and giving you energy when you need it the most."

Mr. Johnson is describing the "family growth template," the energy patterns of our family that become permanent parts of who we are. The pull of this infinite family energy can be felt even as you read this sentence. How you interpret what you are reading, how you feel right this moment is in part due to a family energy template that is forever within you, dictating your actions and reactions. When you feel pity or anger, joy or

1. Burr, Harold S. *The Fields of Life* (New York: Ballantine Books, 1972).

sorrow, these and all of our emotions are manifestations of how your family might react to a given situation. You never react alone.

Instead of looking at how the "self" develops, the lesson of family resonance, of the vibrations of family energy, is that we must learn to look for the patterns of energy that determine our family development. We must learn to think not only about the experiences of our mother and father, of all of our relatives, but the energy imprint or the "growth template" that their experiences have imposed upon our family system. We must look beyond what these people said and did to how they really "seemed" to be, how they felt to us, and how their life energy influences us now.

Here are some "resonance" questions, some inquiries about family energy and "us," rather than "self" and a mechanical approach to living:

What type of life energy did your own father and mother seem to have, and why? Do or did you sense positive family resonance, what some people call "good vibes"?

Did you sense positive, resonating energy that made the family grow and move, or did there seem to be an energy loss?

What seemed to drain your parents' energy or spark them to new levels of energy?

How much energy did your parents seem to have for you and to give to you, and how much energy do you still have from them?

How much energy do your parents need now, symbolically or in the form of tangible supports? Remember that memories have their own energy and impact strongly upon you, giving and taking strength for daily living.

Do you feel like you are experiencing an ever-expanding spiral of life and development that was initiated by the energy you shared with your parents and other family members? Or, do you feel trapped and restricted, without the power to move on, because of some chronic energy leak in your own family?

Has one family member taken too much of the family's energy?

How has your family energy template, the quality of family energy, seemed to direct your life up to now and how is this template impacting on you at this time in your life? What type of family energy is drawing you forward or backward in your own development?

What type of energy seems to be buzzing around you, your children, and your family as you read this sentence?

Looking to your own family energy template is more than looking to blame or explain away some problem behavior. You are looking for the type or quality of energy your family has given you. You are looking for the energy you shared and share with them.

"You can only hope that you have sent them off with all that you have to give," said Mr. Steiner, who was struggling with his wife to deal with the empty nest created by their children's maturing. "You hope you have left some of you, a lot of you, within them. You hope that they take what their family was right along with them into life, and that you have made them strong."

Mr. Steiner is describing the strong influence of the family energy template, the strength of spiritual energy we all attempt to provide one another within our families. Families do more than teach right or wrong, or pass on genetic or behavioral characteristics. If we choose the family view of life, we see that families provide the resonance of energy needed by all family members to grow through life, and that we need never feel alone again.

"We have really become aware of the little sparks that happen when we interact with one another," said Ms. Muller. "We learned that, by the time a blowup occurred, there may have been dozens of little explosions, little energy confrontations that didn't seem to register on the family Richter scale. We now have a more sensitive scale, and we have far fewer explosions."

Ms. Muller is describing a major step in reducing family strife. Families must learn to resensitize, to be alert for sparks before a family fire breaks out, and to lower their threshold of sensitivity to good and bad family energy. Immediate disclosure, continued empathy, absolute integrity, and spontaneity of thought and feelings make up the only family spark extinguisher you can really rely on.

Healthy family resonance requires all of the first five family Rx's and all of the last four Rx's I will be discussing in the last four chapters. When families fail to maintain their rituals, family members are left on their own to seek energy outside the home. When families lack a shared and natural sense of rhythm in family activities, family members feel out of step and drained of energy needed just to keep going day-to-day in their own independent rhythm. When families or family members become irrational and lack family reason, ascribing responsibility for feelings and thoughts to others, rather than taking self-responsibility, they create the negative energy of blame and conflict. When families lack a sense of their history together, the remembrance of all they have experienced together, they fail to draw on energy banks established by prior family interactions. Finally, when families lack resilience and a patience to learn together through family problems, their energy is used up in mere survival rather than in family celebration of life together.

ENERGY FOR ARCHETYPICAL FAMILY BATTLES

Archetypical family battles and problems are those conflicts in family life that are really problems common to all human families. An archetype is something we share because we are human, problems and feelings common to all human experience from the beginning of time. Archetypical family problems, the common transitional crises that take some form in all families, are better resolved if they are viewed as metaphors, challenges that each family fights for the good of everyone, for the evolution of their own family system, and for the further refinement of the human spirit.

The minor family skirmishes, the major family conflicts, the anger, the sense of helplessness, the substance abuse, the immaturity, the selfishness, and a range of other family problems are really calls for the mobilization of total family energy to move to a new and larger orbit of energy, to resolve some spiritual deficit in the family's evolution.

THE FOUR "S's" OF FAMILY PROBLEMS

My clinical work indicates that all family problems are different manifestations of the same four unresolved universal human conflicts. Families who take a family energy view of their problems will find more energy and therefore more tolerance and patience available for family development, because they will be less distracted by the more obvious and petty interpersonal arguments, accusations, and struggles for control that are always based on "me" instead of "us."

The four family archetypical problems, the four "S's" at the root of every single family problem, are sexuality, substance abuse, self-esteem, and safety. Think of the one problem that seems to be burdening your own family the most at this moment and you will see that at least one of these universal problems is at the root of that problem. From our ancient ancestors to humankind today, we have just not been able to solve these universal problems of sexual fulfillment, healthy use of various of the world's substances, a consistent sense of self-worth balanced with caring for others, and an enduring sense of security and serenity.

Here are four statements by members from some of the five families that illustrate how each of these family members were able to find the family archetypical problem at the root of a family conflict:

Ms. Muller: "I fought with my teenage daughter every weekend about the issue of time. I would set a time for her to be home, and she would try to extend it. I thought I was too strict, then I thought I wasn't strict enough. It was our big battle, and we really got bitter and verbally really hurt each other sometimes. I was afraid to talk with her about what was really bothering me. It was sex. We just hadn't talked about sex openly. We hadn't talked about making out, masturbating someone else, intercourse, oral love, what boys might want from her. We had just talked about birth control. Once we got down to it, the negative energy was gone and we got to really share what we both felt about sex, and what I expected and she expected."

Mr. Muller: "You wouldn't think it would be possible, but

Gramps was on eleven different prescription drugs. We hadn't noticed how these were affecting him and our family. We were always trying to either fight with him, control him, ignore him, or work around him. We were beginning to resent him. We resented him, not the eleven drugs. We finally found a doctor who said that four of these drugs were useless, two were dangerous, and one pair should never have been given together. We were fighting about drugs, not Gramps. He finally dropped all the drugs but one—aspirin."

Ms. Bonner: "My son got hold of my credit card. My son! He put about two hundred dollars worth of clothes on the thing and never told me. I told him that I never thought I was raising a common thief. I really got mad when he said he may have been a thief but he wasn't common. I didn't think that was funny. I cried. I thought I was really failing as a parent, particularly now that my husband was gone. I was so frightened, so upset, so insecure that I didn't think about why he was buying these clothes, or why he found it necessary to lie. We finally got down to talking in therapy about how bad he felt about how he looked, his body image, and his lack of friends. It sounds so obvious now, but I never saw it when I was so afraid I had raised a crook. I was just seeing him, not my insecurity and fear about being a single parent and his low self-image. I had to think about 'us' instead of 'him and me.'"

Ms. Johnson: "I kept on criticizing everything my first husband did. I kept trying to find more and more reasons to divorce him. I started yelling at him and even at the kids. We fought about everything from household chores to sex. I didn't see the obvious. We were fighting because we were afraid. We were afraid to divorce, to end our family. I was afraid to be alone, to go out at my age and start again. I noticed how afraid I was when I heard myself screaming at my husband because he didn't put the toilet seat back down."

The louder and more intense the argument, the more helpless your family feels, the more immediate these four factors are and the more pressing they may be on one or more family members. Here is a chart to help you get started thinking about family energy systems being used up by failing to cope with the collective, rather than individual, and more universal issues. Each of these examples was provided by the five families you have been reading about in this book, but you can add your own examples by sitting with your own family, going over this chart, and trying to add other examples that seem to fit under each category. Remember, the same examples may fit under more than one category.

SEXUALITY

- ☐ Arguments about restrictions and privacy
- ☐ Complaints about being misunderstood
- ☐ Complaints about being "babied" and not treated as an adult
- ☐ Parental feelings of being overwhelmed with the constant presence of the children and their demands
- ☐ Arguments over the type of friends family members have
- ☐ Battles over type of clothing worn and the fit of the clothing

SUBSTANCE ABUSE

- ☐ Complaints about moodiness of one or more family members
- ☐ Obvious mood changes
- ☐ Arguments taking place at mealtime and disagreements over type and quantity of food in the house
- ☐ Frustrated attempts to get a family member involved in family activities, followed by arguments and further withdrawal
- ☐ Ganging up against one family member when conflicts take place
- ☐ Arguments about sneakiness and obvious lying

SELF-ESTEEM

☐ Arguments about one family member being embarrassed by his or her family

☐ Lectures, and rebellion against such lectures by family members, about how the family should be run

☐ Repeated lying when the family can not figure out why such lies would be necessary or what purpose they serve

☐ Physical conflicts, slapping and fighting among the children

☐ Complaints about favoritism

☐ Disagreements about how money should be handled; or someone in the family always seeming to want or need something

SAFETY

☐ One family member seemingly constantly in tears

☐ Conflicts over what are seen as too-strict rules and restrictions

☐ Complaints by one member that they have to take care of everything and to carry too much of the family burden

☐ Complaints that a given family member is unable to talk to another family member about anything

☐ "In-law" conflicts over who spends how much time for and with whom

☐ A family member constantly testing the family limits by taking risks or engaging in behaviors that frighten the family

Ms. Steiner said, "I didn't see why my husband thought that our arguments over the in-laws were about safety. Now I see it. We're getting older, and I think we are both afraid of who will take care of us. Maybe we were fighting then about the in-laws because we were really afraid of our own future." Ms. Steiner's clarification of the fifth item under the safety heading illustrates how your own family can try to relate each item to the major heading. This exercise will help teach your family to look for the real energy leaks, instead of the easier, but more destructive, confrontations over more transitional life events.

If one member is struggling with any of the four family universal family problems, the whole family is struggling with that issue as well. The problem member is only sounding the alarm. If one member is abusing substances, then look to the way in which the entire family deals with substances. If one member abuses alcohol, look to see how food or other substances are dealt with by other family members. Look to see how the family deals with the "goods" of the family, the "stuff" all families must learn to manage. Look for the metaphor of the family problem as a whole that reveals the universal problem, because that is where you will learn where the energy is seeping away.

HATE IS FOR ILLUSIONS

Hate, whenever it occurs, is an example of the lack of family resonance, the lack of balance in energy flow between family members. Hate in the family is the fire of chronic and unresolved family friction. When this happens, energy leaks away, the "us" perspective is lost, the metaphor of a family member's problems has not been found, and problems are seen as "belonging" to an individual.

I have noticed that my patients can speak of hate only in the abstract. When they come face-to-face with the source of their hate, the person they may hate, that hate immediately turns to different emotions. A sense of fear, withdrawal, helplessness, confusion, and sometimes even deeper understanding and empathy may take place when the person who hates realizes that all struggles between people are ultimately "for" people, for the dignity and caring that we all so badly want and need. If we always saw our enemies standing with their families, hate would not come as easy.

"My mother says she hates our next-door neighbor," said one daughter. "She says she really despises her. Then, when she sees her at the store, she either runs the other way or acts real, real friendly. She can only do a good hate when Ms. X isn't right there in front of her." This mother's behavior is typical of the "abstract hate principle."

Ms. Muller, whose father was dying, stated, "We could never make it through this thing with Gramps. We couldn't make it if we thought that all this suffering and time and fatigue was just for Gramps or just for us. We would start to hate Gramps if we thought that all of this was just for him. We feel like we're fighting for everyone, for everyone who will age and get sick and be frightened and alone. Ours is a battle against loneliness. We'll let death take Gramps' body, but never him. He will never be alone and we will never be without him, and it is all of us who are going through this, not just us helping Gramps." Ms. Muller cried as she joined hands with her family and added, "We're fighting for all of us."

THE PHANTOM FAMILY

To further understand the concept of family energy resonance, and how your own family energy growth template affects all that you do and feel, consider yet another discovery about life energy from modern science that applies to the family. Utilizing electrophotography, sometimes called Kirlian photography (photographing objects with high-frequency, high-voltage, low-amperage electrical fields), a leaf with the top part cut away will show an image not of a leaf with the top third missing, but an image of the whole undamaged leaf. The amputated leaf is seen in its entirety, with the energy of the missing piece left in place. The amputated portion of the leaf still appears in the photograph, even though that part of the leaf is mechanically "not there." Of course, the missing piece is "there" in energy, just as family energy is always with us.

Skeptics of this so-called "phantom leaf effect" say that moisture left by the missing piece of leaf on the photographic plate accounts for this remarkable finding. Researchers at California State University, using clear Lucite panels to prevent moisture during photography, have ruled out this possibility.[2] The leaf, all living things, are energy; and I suggest family energy, and our sense of us, can not be destroyed.

Work by another researcher in Rumania supported the "phantom leaf effect." This researcher photographed a leaf with a hole cut from its center. When the electrophotograph was examined, a small leaf was seen in the hole. This leaf was a perfect image of the entire leaf. In effect, we see a leaf within a leaf, an indication once again of the omnipresence of the energy unity of living things.[3]

If we learn to understand our family and ourselves from the point of view of the energy within us and of the infinitely connected nature of that energy illustrated by the experiments described above, we free ourselves from the perpetual struggle to redundantly relive family strife. Mechanistic and individualistic approaches to our problems will only cover up the true disruptions that retard family evolution and development.

WHAT IS A FAMILY MEMBER, ANYWAY?

"Whenever I hear the word 'family member,' I think of some unique body part, a member," said Ms. Bonner. "I guess that's really right, because when my husband was killed, it was like a part of us was cut off. We were actually dismembered."

When therapists utilize their hands to heal and massage the body, they caress the entire body. If that body is lacking a leg or an arm, such therapists learned long ago to symbolically caress the area of the missing limb, the missing "member." They run their hands around what they sense to be an energy field, a remnant template of the limb. These therapists know their science. Energy can not be created or destroyed. We are always "one" on an energy level, even when we may feel most alone.

2. "The Ghost Effect," *IKRA Communications* (Brooklyn, N.Y.: International Kirlian Research Association, June 1978).
3. "Life Energy Patterns Visible Via New Technique," *Brain/Mind Bulletin* (August 23, 1982) Vol. 7, No. 14.

Loneliness is an illusion. When we feel alone, isolated, or separated, we are forgetting the family view. The word "personality" comes from the Latin word "persona," which means "mask." When we focus on our individuality, self-accomplishments, and feel as if we are lonely victims when we have problems, we hide behind the mask of "self." We forget that we are tied together by the family energy resonating around us. It is when we feel most alone that we must struggle to reestablish our family view, drop our mask and share our every feeling and fear, or find help to get our family energy back.

"Who do you think I am?" asked the pressured and stressed man. "Two people? I can't be two people at once." "You can't?" asked the person who knew about the power of family energy. "I was sure you could be at least that many if you paid attention to what you can really do and feel. You have a lot more people within you than just one or two."

SIX STEPS TO HEALTHY FAMILY RESONANCE

To review and clarify the major points about family energy resonance, and to learn how to apply these points to your own family's daily life, take the time to sit with members of your own family and try to explain to them the following summaries of what you have just read. Remember, the following points only make sense if you elect the family view of daily living. The more a person chooses the individual and local view of living over the connected and universal view, the more strange these concepts will seem.

STEP ONE. GETTING A SENSE OF FAMILY ENERGY. Try to think and speak about energy and change rather than about personalities and inevitabilities. Matter and energy are the same. Your family is much more than a house full of people.

Mr. Anders reported, "You sort of see the family as a collection of items, a mixed and matched set of people living together. When you change that view, everything changes. When you see all of you, the whole family, as a system of energy that vibrates between all of you and in the world, you end up with a more cooperative orientation to daily problems. It isn't just the people anymore, it isn't the family doing things to or for you anymore. You start thinking about much more meaningful things, like you as part of the problem, not someone who has to deal with it. You see yourself as process more than as object, and you feel your impact on people and their impact on you. You even feel the people who are gone. You get a real sense of the energy of the family, when it is up and down. The family isn't like the family car that goes good and bad. Instead, it's like a whole feeling together. You just relate to your family as an 'us' more and more."

STEP TWO. GETTING YOUR FAMILY INTO ORBIT. Make an effort to provide energy for everyone in the family, not just to the one family member who seems to demand the most energy at a given moment.

> "You have to give everyone in the family a boost sometimes, but it can't be a kick."
> MR. ANDERS

We can begin to see the family as the first "spinner" of the top, the source of direction and energy of the spin in our daily life. When we think of our family as the place where we are given our life energy, we are freed from the "stage" or "passage" theory of individual human development, the old linear "if-then-next" cycle, to move toward family life and family member maturation.

"When we first started talking about providing energy to and for each other," said Ms. Bonner, "we began to understand what happened to my husband in a completely different way. We came to see his death as change, and not as ending. We always gave lip service about people dying and 'passing on,' but I think what we really meant was that people were dying and passing away, not really passing through a different energy with us. Now that we see ourselves as energy and our bodies as only temporary manifestations of that energy, we don't see the passing of my husband as so final. It still doesn't help us stop crying, but it helps us to start understanding our tears for the endless journey of the evolving spirit, and that nothing stays

the same. By getting past our hate and grief, we can try to feel
him again. I think we know more now what God is."

Ms. Bonner is discussing one of the most profound implications of the family energy and resonance point of view. Since
energy cannot be created or destroyed, all life process is
change. Life never ends, because family energy can never end.
Family grieving is helped by the family energy view, by the
view of changing forms and dimensions of our existence, rather
than a simple "here and gone" view of living.

Even when a family member is spinning in an orbit different from the other family members, the spirit of that member is
infinite, and is within every family member, as the leaf within a
leaf I mentioned earlier. No matter where they are, all family
members can be sensed by all other family members. We find
those we have lost by looking in, by looking to our souls instead
of the heavens. Our loved ones have passed on, but they are not
"out there." Our family is always "in here."

STEP THREE. LOOKING FOR OUR FAMILY HISTORY.
Look intensely today into the eye of every one of your family
members. Listen intensely to your family members, and you
might hear the whispers of your ancestors and all of our ancestors.

> "I can look in my daughter's eyes and see my grandfa-
> ther."
> MS. STEINER

Within each family member rests the entire image of his or
her family. One of the miracles of being "us," the true magic of
family, can be experienced by taking the time to pause, gaze
deeply into the eyes of someone in your family, and look into
the history of your entire family. If you look carefully, you will
see a grandparent, an uncle, an aunt, a sister, a brother, or a
parent. They are all in there someplace. Take a good, long look.

STEP FOUR. KEEPING THE ENERGY FLOWING. Try to
sense messages from your family members when they are away
from home.

"You don't have to go out on a limb if you pay attention
to your family roots."
MR. MULLER

Mr. Johnson reported, "We know we could sort of read
what was happening to our children, even when they were in
school. We always had a secret sort of sense about each other.
My grandmother always talked about that sort of stuff, and she
was sort of psychic. We used to laugh at her, but it really makes
sense to me now, that if all parts contain the whole, if the
universal plan is inside every cell, then we can communicate
with each other on levels we never thought possible. We can
sense when the family is out of order, out of its plan, out of
sync, and running low on energy. There does seem to be a 'way'
for us, and when we get too far from that 'way,' we just get all
out of whack. You don't have to be some kind of nut or some
sort of channel or whatever they call them to be aware of how
your family is doing and feeling."

We have misunderstood psychic phenomenon, or what researchers call "psi," as some type of special talent, as some way
in which the rare person can read the future or see things that
others will never be able to see. Nothing could be further from
the truth. Science, not superstition, explains "psi." Viewing and
sensing the family is a matter of developing your innate skill for
communicating with and sensing energy. We are all "psychic,"
because we are all connected. If we make the effort and take the
time to pay attention to our unity, there is a symphony of
messages from within just waiting for the concert to begin.

**STEP FIVE. APPLYING THE PHANTOM FAMILY
PRINCIPLE.** Try to view family losses as family evolution,
with the most painful losses experienced as the most profound
steps in the evolution of your family spirit.

"I think we have it wrong. My uncle is not 'gone but not
forgotten.' He's too often forgotten, but he's not really
gone."
MR. ANDERS

In the family view of life, all disconnection is mere illusion.
What we see as beginnings and endings in families are short-

sighted views of infinite processes without beginning and end. We never leave one another, we only rearrange the family energy patterns.

Ms. Muller stated, "Gramps is going to die soon. He knows it, and we know it. We have to face it, and we have to understand it. The overwhelming grief we have felt when other family members have died has been related to our inability to make any sense out of it. We just kept asking, like other people, 'Why, why, why?' Now, when we really think about it from this new perspective, we can see that we didn't look at the deaths in any type of system or order. How could Grandpa ever be gone? Of course, he never will be. He is us, he is our energy, and his energy is us. He's within us. We have to cry about his changing, about our changing, but never about his ending."

Family birth may be seen as family energy reentering the present family system, a remanifestation of the lives of all family members who have gone before. Death in the family in the family view becomes change, transition, and transcendence rather than loss and ending. We all make our mark on the family energy template, but it is the energy itself and not the mere presence of the family member that has true meaning for the miracles of "us."

STEP SIX. PAYING YOUR FAMILY THE ULTIMATE COMPLIMENT. Beware of self-fulfilling prophecies. Your family will be what you say it is.

> "Clouds, like us, are always changing from within and being blown by the wind. Just when you think you can see some shape to a cloud, just when you get someone else to see an elephant up there, it becomes a mouse."
> MR. MULLER

If we no longer have to think in terms of good/bad, up/down, in/out, and beginning/end, then we are freed from the constant pressure of evaluating all of our human experiences. We are freed to live our life and not be led by it, to celebrate and enjoy our family rather than always trying to improve or change it.

"When our kids were little," said Mr. Anders, "we made an effort never to say that they were good or bad. Somehow, as time went by, we fell into the trap of evaluating people instead of behaviors. Our kids were now good in school or they weren't. Our kids were nice or they were being bad, and our kids started to talk about us as good or bad parents. We finally learned that what you say seems to make things happen. We learned to watch what we say, and to talk about behaviors rather than personalities or good and bad characteristics."

Mr. Anders is describing the fact that there really is no need to "resolve" differences. Differences are a natural part of our life experience. No child, no parent, no relative is good, bad, fair or unfair. To label behaviors or people in an either/or fashion is similar to describing the moon as half full. It's always all moon. We choose to see the moon and label it by its reflection.

Can you feel some of your family energy right this moment? If not, as the Queen encourages Alice in her Wonderland, close your eyes, take a very deep breath, and try again. Your family is right there within you.

CHAPTER NINE

Family Reconciliation: Getting Back Together Again

"Parenting is disruptive, with the possibility of harm, but also the possibility of growth."
FREDERICK GROSSMAN

"I take my children everywhere, but they always seem to find their way back home."
ROBERT ORBEN

FAMILY RECONCILIATION: The ability to forgive, tolerate, and love even at times of family conflict, never allowing any family problem to scar the family soul so deeply that attempts to understand, accept, and love are discontinued.

TOO LATE FOR LOVE

The tears flooded his eyes, but he couldn't cry. His father was gone, and as he looked down at the man who had thrown him his first ball and had held him up on his first two-wheeler, he was unable to talk or to move. He wanted to talk to his father, to have one more chance to hug him, to tell him how much he loved him. Even though he had his own children now, he wanted to tell his father how afraid he was, now that he would never again have his dad to help and protect him. He felt as though every last ounce of energy for living and loving had been drained from him.

One of the most tragic and yet most immediately correctable crises facing the family today is a crisis of loving left undone, of the reluctance or fear of loving our family members openly and demonstratively, even as we struggle with them over daily life issues. Too many of us wait too long to reconcile, strangely shy and uncomfortable with actually hugging our own parents, or too angry or hurt to re-embrace a problem child, too proud to attempt reconciliation with a family member with whom we have broken our energy bond.

We can not disown what we have not purchased, and the love within a family is the experience of the sharing of the infinite energy that is common to all of us. Such love energy is not purchased, earned, or chosen, it is assigned through your humanness, through your evolution, to and within your own family. You can never truly disown or be disowned by a family member, because you never owned them in the first place. The energy that is the universe bonds you all together forever, and a failure at reconciliatory loving only causes needless and endless pain in your soul while you lead a life in the illusion of separation.

The Family Reconciliation Test

To assess your own family for the seventh Rx of healthy family living, reconciliation, take the following test. Remember, reconciliation in the family is a form of persistent and demonstrated loving that transcends any problem experienced within your family. Use the following scoring system:

0   1   2   3   4   5   6   7   8   9   10
ALMOST NEVER   SELDOM   SOMETIMES   A LOT   ALMOST ALWAYS

1. ———— Are your family squabbles resolved when they occur, rather than lingering on as constant sources of aggravation?

2. ———— Does your family have a wide range of what it considers to be acceptable and tolerable behaviors by family members?

3. ———— Is everyone in your family proud of everyone else?

4. ———— Do your family members seem to have short memories regarding conflicts, moving on to new issues rather than bringing up old and lingering grievances when new arguments arise?

5. ———— Is the most troublesome and problem-causing member of your family shown love, respect, and understanding?

6. ———— Do quiet and undemanding family members get their fair share of the family attention, even when another family member is very demanding?

7. ———— Is your family free of long-standing conflicts that have resulted in the exclusion of relationships with certain relatives?

8. ———— Does your family spend as much time apologizing as they do accusing and arguing?

9. ———— Is everyone in your family honest about their feelings for one another?

10. ———— When family members feel good about each other and feel like hugging, holding, and expressing love to each other, do they do so immediately and without reservation?

———— TOTAL FAMILY RECONCILIATION SCORE

Remember that the 90-point arbitrary cutoff is used to indicate where your first efforts at enhancing your family life should be spent. If you scored over 90 points on this test, your family is strong on the seventh family Rx of reconciliation, and may want to begin work on one of the other family Rx's first. Have all of your family members take these ten Family Rx tests. You may want to average the scores into one family score. You may also want to look at individual family scores as they compare with the family average score. Sometimes, one member's score will stand out as extremely low or high as compared to other family members, and when this happens, the need for reconciliation with that member is indicated.

FIVE FAMILIES IN SEARCH OF RECONCILIATION

Each of the five families you have been reading about in this book had their own challenges for reconciliation. As a starting point for understanding the importance of this seventh family Rx, I have presented the words of members from each of these five families regarding what they saw as a need for reconciliation in their own family:

The Anders family: "As much as we were concerned with our sick daughter, our ten-year-old son was feeling totally left out," said Ms. Anders. "He started to get so demanding that none of us could stand him. Every argument was an argument with him, or at least about him. We saw in therapy that we resented him for demanding time away from our daughter. He was becoming just another burden because we were always burdening ourselves. He was being left out, and we had to get him back in because part of our burden was the fact that our family wasn't unified."

The Bonner family: Ms. Bonner said, "With my husband being gone, we had to regroup. We tried to pay more attention to one another, but someone was missing. We learned in therapy that we had to fit my husband back in to our family even though he was physically gone. We had to put his memory back in with us somehow. None of us were talking about it for a long time, but when we were forced to talk about how my husband

and their dad could be a part of us still, we started to feel whole again."

The Steiner family: Mr. Steiner said, "When my son got married and didn't even ask us about it or talk about the girl he was marrying, we pulled away from him. We didn't talk to him and we just pretended that he was not a part of the family anymore. We didn't talk to his wife or her family. That didn't last long. The stress was too much. We finally faced up to it, and to our own feelings about the girl; and how our son had been afraid to involve us in his decision, because we were so sure we knew what was good for him or because we would reject his wife because she is white. I'm glad we made up. We could have carried this on forever, and every damned holiday, even the simple things, like speaking on the phone, would have been ruined for nothing."

The Johnson family: "I had to make up with my first husband," said Ms. Johnson. "I learned in therapy that I couldn't just leave him out of who I was. I got a divorce, but we never said good-bye. We had to hug, to hold, and say good-bye. We had to talk about how and when we would talk, even though we weren't together anymore, how we would relate when he came to see the kids. We just had to get sort of a semiremarriage instead of carrying on the cold war. You just can't carry on in a hostile way with one family member without dragging the whole family in to it."

The Muller family: Ms. Muller said, "I can't tell you how I hated my mother-in-law. She was always so right, so perfect, so patronizing to me. She criticized everything I did. She never liked me from the first day we met, and I felt it and didn't like her. One day during an argument she called me a useless bitch who was ruining her son. Can you imagine that? I hated her, and the hate colored everything our family did, every family plan or get-together. We learned in therapy that, like it or not, we had to make up. I won't kid you. We have a long way to go. But we do talk now, and that's something, because at least the family can communicate and get moving again."

These five families each came to my clinic with problems not immediately related to the issues raised above. The

Anderses were dealing with a very sick daughter, the Bonners with their grief for the loss of the father, the Steiners with the empty-nest syndrome, the Johnsons with the problems of forming a stepfamily, and the Mullers with the presence of a dying grandfather in their home. These more obvious problems were made worse by each family's failures to reconcile, to love through other problems that were also taking place. The phrase "Life is too short" usually reflects our error to lead a loving life free of unresolved conflicts, each of which will someday seem unimportant in the overall scheme of living and dying.

ROMANCE VS. RECONCILIATION

Family love is the love of reconciliation and not romance, a loving consisting of conscious attempts to maintain harmony and share a common acknowledgment of life energy with a family member, particularly at times of stress upon that relationship. Reconciliatory love is the purest love of all, for it requires forgiveness and toleration, not just surrender to strong impulses. It requires the acceptance of every family member as a part of "us," and as created by and with us. Reconciliation involves helping a family member share responsibility with you for how the family is developing.

Persons who attempt to seduce us, enhance our self-esteem, flatter us, and who show constant concern for our every whim, are easy to love. It is much more difficult to attempt to continue loving family members with whom we live every day, and who are a part of our everyday emotional experience of life. These persons are bound to frustrate us, hurt us, and even insult us by their occasional disregard for our feelings and their taking for granted of our love. Family love is a reconciliatory love of constant effort to accept, forgive, and understand. Family love is keeping the family point of view, no matter how strong the temptation for separation.

HOW SEX HAS TAKEN THE SENSUALITY OUT OF THE FAMILY

Our sexually immature and hypereroticized society dictates that we withdraw our physical demonstrations of our love from our children and teenagers at just that time in their young lives when they need that energy, the power of reconciliatory love, the most. The awkwardness of trying to reformulate the family system as its members resonate to different orbits, become bigger, louder, more selfish and independent, may make us pull away when we should all be pulling together.

The ability to show love, to talk of love and shared life energy, has become a casualty of a sexual revolution that has guaranteed only our freedom to "make" love, not to experience and share loving. Touching, talking gently and sweetly, hugging, and kissing have become casualties in the de-sacradization process of our society.

Romantic physical contact is now seen almost exclusively as prelude to genital interaction, rather than an intimate and profound way of connection with those we love the most and the longest. We have only succeeded in limiting our romantic capacity to sexual encounters rather than broadening it to tenderness with those we love as family. The sexual revolution has resulted in the involution of loving, a narrowing of our ability to show our caring.

On the one hand, we have made love the almost exclusive prerogative of heterosexual interactions related to eventual intercourse with someone new to us and not a part of our family. On the other hand, we have made love into some form of de-eroticized and nondemonstrated toleration or acknowledgment for those persons within our own family. Somewhere between "incest" and being "in love" is the path of mature family loving that allows intense embracing and closeness without eroticizing our tenderness.

SEXUAL MIS-LOVINGS IN THE FAMILY

Morally, socially, psychologically, and genetically, incest is one of the most destructive examples of love gone wrong. Unable to develop a mature family relationship that allows for intense love and closeness through the life process with all ages of family members, the adult who engages in incest, or any form of sexual abuse, has failed to learn how to love family members intensely and sensuously without genitalizing that loving. Such persons are casualties of a societal pressure for "sex" and a social taboo against romantic tenderness within the family system.

Sexually abusive persons do in the family what millions of persons do outside the family; they "use" someone for the "act" of love in a misdirected and desperate search for a sense of true loving and for safety from their fear of true intimacy. All sexual abuse is a form of a corrupted attempt to connect and share with someone else.

The most frequent form of incest is between brother and sister. The second most frequent form of incest is between father and daughter or male family members and younger girls and women. The least frequent form of incest is between an older female and a female child. I have never encountered female-female incest in my clinical practice. The frequency of male-initiated incest suggests that sexism, power and control are at the base of these corrupt interactions. Fearing intimacy, the male seeks shelter in the control of the vulnerable and overwhelmed younger female, thus escaping the adult responsibility of mutually responsible and shared loving. Being in control lessens the chances of the feared rejection by a mature and sexually competent adult woman.

Statistics on incest are difficult to compile, but estimates suggest that at least five of every one hundred persons has experienced some form of sexual interaction with an adult family member.[1] At least three out of every one hundred children are

1. Gebhard, P., et al. *Sex Offenders: An Analysis of Types* (New York: Harper & Row, 1965).

sexually abused.[2] Almost all research into the topic of incest and sexual abuse indicates that something went wrong in the family system as well as in the adult involved. To see sexual abuse as exclusively a sexual issue is to misunderstand the fact that loving has more to do with who and how a person thinks she or he is than what happens on a genital level.

Incest and sexual abuse occur when, somewhere in the family system, loving reconciliation has not taken place. The sexual energy of the family member who cannot direct his or her physical and erotic loving to the appropriate partner, who can not reconcile with that partner because of insecurity, distrust, and fear within that adult bond, becomes focused on a vulnerable and less powerful family member. Because reconciliation has not taken place within the basic and central bond of the family, loving energy becomes misplaced, misdirected, and corrupted. As a result, a vulnerable family member becomes the target of a fearful loving.

This statement by one of my female patients illustrates the fear and control issues raised above:

"It wasn't actually the sex that was the big deal, as I look back at it. I don't remember, or I won't let myself remember, what actually happened sexually. I do remember the sneakiness, the guilt, the fear, the helplessness. I remember carrying this terrible secret for years and years. It was like I was used, and that was the thing that got to me the most. I just didn't seem to have any options. I was trapped. I could feel my father's fear when he snuck into my room late at night. It was like he was not only sneaking in to see me but sneaking away from my mother. I can still see his shadow coming through my door at night, and I shudder. He was always nervous, shaking, like he was afraid of me even while he was making me so afraid."

If you yourself have been sexually abused, you must remember that there *was* love involved. It was a corrupted and fearful love, a panicked, immature, hurtful, and ignorant attempt to find pleasure and comfort through control, power, and exploitation, but there was a frustrated loving energy that motivated this terrible act. You have all of your family love within

2. Hinds, M. "The Child Victim of Incest," *New York Times*, June 15, 1981, p. 9.

you now, and even the pain and humiliation you may feel are really symptoms of the strength of that love trying to come out in more healthy ways. Don't allow the hurt and confusion of a misguided family member to distract you from your own capacity to love and be loved, to rob you of your family view of living.

LOVE PARALYSIS

We sometimes experience a type of love paralysis, and are unable to share our love, even when the energy of that love draws us so strongly to a family member that we shudder from its power.

"I wanted to hold my mother against me," said Ms. Anders. "I wanted to hold her and cry with her, but instead I just gave her a quick kiss. It was like the power of that love was too much, and I couldn't deal with it. It was like looking directly at the sun. You want to, but you can't. We just don't come from a hugging family."

It is no accident that we use the phrase "turned on" to refer to sexual excitement. We have made sex so mechanical that we speak of sexuality as an on-and-off mechanism. When we feel love in the family, we are not turned on like a machine, but "tuned in" to the loving energy within our family, and our loving energy is set in motion through our regular contact with our family.

Unfortunately, we have been taught that genital response is the ultimate response to being "turned on," so we may draw away from family members when strong feelings of closeness tell us to hug and hold. We may have failed to learn that what is "turned on" is an awareness of connection, the energy to reconcile all differences, conflicts and stored-up pain, allowing us to almost lovingly crush our family in our arms.

LOVE SIGNALS

Prolonged anger for a family member is not a signal that there is no love between you and that family member. Anger within families is an indication of intense frustration in attempts to love, the presence of a love barrier, and a symptom of the fear to openly share, give, and connect. Anger signals that reconciliatory love is needed to harness loving energy, to direct it back between family members.

The angrier you are feeling with a family member, the more the energy of love is demanding expression and family forgiveness, sharing, and reconciliation. Ms. Steiner's statement illustrates the close relationship between intensity of anger and intensity of love:

"My son could get me so mad I would actually bite my lower lip until it bled. We fought, slammed doors on each other, threatened each other, and wouldn't talk to each other for weeks. Now that he's married and gone, I miss him even more than my other children. He was so much a part of me. I love him so much, I guess I was trying too hard to control him and to run his life. We had this real bond together, and even though I said dozens of times that I wished he would get out of my life, I would give anything now if he were more a part of it."

If you ignore the loving demand sometimes experienced as familial anger, you may seek compensatory emotional intensity through a variety of serial relationships, total involvement in work, or even promiscuity and sexual abuse of yourself or someone else. We sometimes seek pseudofamily bonds when we are too lazy, too afraid, or too distracted to reconcile with those family members with whom we find ourselves in conflict.

To love freely, to be able to enter into mature relationships with others outside your primary family, you must first reconcile your family love and seal the leaks of family energy. It is not true that we cannot love someone else until we can love ourselves. To love anyone, we must first be able to reconcile the loving within our own family and learn to love within the context of a group of people going through life together.

When we have not resolved issues of safety, self-esteem, sexuality, and the balanced and healthy use of the various substances that make our world, our family will continue to struggle with each of these issues in the form of anger, fear, and constant conflict. Family reconciliation requires direct discussion of these four key components of family life, and the willingness and family energy to continually grapple with these issues.

"Until we finally had it out about how he felt about himself, we just couldn't really talk," said Ms. Steiner. "My son and I finally talked about how he felt like a failure as a son because he upset me so, and how I felt like a failure as a mother because I let him upset me. Instead of fighting about how he swears at me and how a son is supposed to listen to his mother, we talked about the real issue; our own feelings about ourselves and how we felt badly about how we were."

Ms. Steiner's statement indicates the way in which we argue right past the issues that really need addressing. To look for the family archetype that is causing our conflict is difficult, because our anger is so intense that we take little time to look for the real feelings at the base of our conflicts. My years of clinical work indicate, however, that we will continue to argue in circles until we look for one or more of the four basic family archetypes at the root of all family conflict.

TAKING A LOVING RISK

When I ask some of my patients to hug their parents, to say out loud the words "I love you," they often respond as the following woman did. "Oh, I couldn't do that. I hug her at Christmas and on her birthday, but I couldn't just hug her for no reason and say, 'I love you.' She'd be embarrassed and so would I. We fight all the time, and hugging just would seem strange to us. It would seem out of place, even ridiculous."

I promise you that you will regret not having hugged your own parents enough and not having told them you love them often enough. I promise you that you will regret not healing a family rift or attempting to seal off a family energy leak. I promise you that if you do not take the time to meditate and pray for reconciliation with a family member who is not with you, you will never know the completeness of true family love. Someday, you will feel helplessly sad that you didn't take a loving risk to reconcile, to hug, to kiss, and to share your love more intensely and more often with your family.

For your own good, and for your own health, you must learn to break whatever degree of love paralysis exists in your own family system, find the energy leaks that limit your loving, and make every effort to seal those leaks. Don't wait. Reconcile with your family members now. At the very least, call your parents and tell them you love them or, if your parents are nearby, give them a hug. You'll never regret it.

FINDING FAMILY ENERGY LEAKS

There are two primary sources of family energy loss that I have noted in my work with families, two reasons why families fail to reconcile. Living with someone who is an energy leech, who draws our energy from us, is one major source of depletion of the energy needed to fuel our loving. Secondly, spiritual seepage, the loss of energy that results from living day-to-day in ways which are not in keeping with what we sense is our way of being connected with the world and our true destiny and direction in life, can result in an almost total lack of the necessary energy to resolve the inevitable conflicts of daily living.

"I have never been more tired in my life," said Mr. Anders. "I was fighting with my own mother every day about the fact that I wasn't spending enough time with her and was forgetting her. If that wasn't enough, I was totally unhappy at work. I hated my job. I didn't want to work in an office. I wanted to help people, work outside, and do something to help the less fortunate. I wanted to go to the third world to help, not to the office to type. In therapy, I saw that the combination of both of these frustrations just robbed me of my energy."

Mr. Anders is describing the most deadly combination of health risk factors, family stress and disenchantment with our own life's purpose in career or other life activity. Both issues require our immediate attention. We must work toward risk taking to move toward the purpose of living and cosmic connection we feel within us, and we must work toward reconciliation with the family member or members with whom we are in conflict. These two challenges are the most important life tasks, and each requires the maintenance of the family view, the connected and cosmic view of our living.

The remainder of this chapter focuses on the first of these two major health risks, living with the family member who is sapping the family energy. The following chapter will consider the issue of spiritual energy loss, spiritual development, and living in harmony with a shared family purpose. Both sources of energy loss must be addressed if we are ever to know what true emotional, spiritual, and physical health really mean.

THE FAMILY ENERGY LEECH

One of the major causes of love paralysis, of stifling of loving energy flow in families, is the presence of the aggravating and aggravated family member who consciously or unconsciously leeches or drains our loving energy. Since reconciliatory love is the type of love that takes the most spiritual energy, this type of love is the first to suffer when there is an aggravating, energy-draining family member present.

Unhappiness, agitation, hatred, low self-esteem, resentment, and narcissism are emotional states which severely disrupt energy states within the family, just as the high tension electric wires humming outside your window can affect your physical and emotional state. Thoughts, emotions, and memories are energy too, as much electromagnetic and spiritual energy as any other source of energy, and we constantly are sending out "thought waves." Some family members' appraisal of their world is so negative and their thoughts so selfish that the waves they send are disruptive to their entire family, to other families, and particularly to the sensitive members in the family who have very low thresholds for the detection of negative energy.

Here is a test of the potential "family energy leech." Answer each question in terms of your own behavior or the behavior of a member of your family.

Energy Leech Test

Do you or does a family member:

1. Complain much of the time?

2. Share "negative" stories about other family members?

3. Sulk as a means of getting attention and control?

4. Behave selfishly, ignoring the needs of other family members?

5. Follow a schedule of sleeping and eating that shows disregard for the schedule of other family members?

6. Frown or show other negative body gestures to make a point or to get family attention?

7. Use "the silent treatment" for the whole family or someone in the family when things don't seem to go your way?

8. Try to teach others a lesson by "going to extremes"? (Such as the "Oh . . . so you want me to be quiet? I will never speak again" ploy.)

9. Have tantrums and act out frustrations by slamming doors, throwing things, or yelling?

10. Talk about other family members' flaws or characteristics with other family members as if the true facts of the matter were only known to you (him or her)? Does "family gossip" start with you or this person?

11. Try to manipulate family members by devising strategies of what to tell and not tell different family members?

12. Avoid sharing your (or his or her) true feelings by a "pseudoniceness" that explodes into anger and attacks?

13. Feel as if only you (or he or she) can do things the way they are supposed to be done?

14. Threaten to leave the family?

15. Always remember every detail of an argument and contentiously bring up past mistakes by other family members?

16. Attack or demean a family member's friends or associates as a means of hurting or controlling that family member?

17. Use sarcasm to make your (or his or her) point?

18. Act as if you (or he or she) are the only one who suffers in the family?

19. Lie as self-protection, under the erroneous assumption that you (or he or she) is only trying to keep peace in the family?

20. Violate the privacy of other family members?

21. Act or feel unhappy with his or her (or your) own life and goals and take that unhappiness out on the family directly or indirectly?

22. Use the family as a "dumping ground" for aggravations and feelings that are not expressed elsewhere? Treat the family in ways that you (or he or she) would never treat a stranger?

23. Compare other families to your (or his or her) own, seeing them as happier or "better," and pointing these alleged flaws out to the family?

24. Require the family to make adjustments "around you," (or him or her), forcing the family to avoid getting him or her (or you) upset?

25. See the family often reflecting his or her (or your) moods rather than trying to sense and reflect the mood of the entire family system?

The more yes answers on the above test, the more energy you or the person being tested is draining from the family. Remember that such energy leeching can be unconscious, so accusing family members of energy leeching will only make matters worse.

EIGHT CHARACTERISTICS OF THE FAMILY ENERGY LEECH

"My own sister is a complete lunatic," said Ms. Steiner. "She's selfish, she's sneaky, and she seems to love to stir up trouble. She's the kind of person you love to hate. If she wasn't a family member, I would never, ever let her in my house. I hate it when she even calls me. But I'll tell you this. I don't have to put up with all of her foolishness, but I will never disown her. She's my sister, and whyever or however she is suffering, she is suffering to some degree because of me and for me. I see her not as just 'her,' but as a part of me. It's us that's the problem."

Ms. Steiner's description of her sister reveals some of the major characteristics of the family energy leech, the family aggravator. Here are the eight most frequent characteristics of such a person:

NARCISSISTIC. The family energy leech seems completely selfish. Energy leeches tend to say hurtful things, to gossip and slander without any apparent regard for how much damage they are doing. Their own needs seem to come first in almost every case, and they are quick to anger or to feel wronged when fulfillment of their own needs is blocked in any way.

IMMATURE. The family energy leech is developmentally retarded, acting and even talking in childish ways. They tend to sulk, to throw temper tantrums, or to try to get even with what they feel to be unfair actions by other family members.

DISHONEST. The family energy leech will lie about even the simplest issues, such as where they have been or where they are going, things they may have purchased, and particularly about what they have said to other family members. It seems as if the energy leech does not even know they are lying, withdrawing to a type of dream world of their own creation and distorting facts to fit that world.

VINDICTIVE. The family energy leech is typically in the process of getting even with someone in the family for some real or delusional misdeed. Strangely enough, the energy leeches are usually vindictive about behaviors they see in others that are exactly the negative behaviors they themselves are engaging in. Energy leeches are not above embarrassing anyone in the family, and may spread rumors that paint other family members in the worst light. They may say things in public that hurt a family member. Their approach seems to be "There, now you know how I feel." They are right, of course, because how the hurt family member feels at this time is indeed how the aggravator feels most of the time.

DISASSOCIATED. The family energy leech seems to have lost touch with reality, and tends to absent himself or herself from the realities of day-to-day family life. They offer little help to the family system, and their distortion of reality renders them almost useless as an effective part of the family coping system. They fail to convey accurate messages, seem to hear things said that were never said, or things promised that were never promised. They react to family events in a highly idiosyncratic fashion, and they bemoan their sense of exclusion from the family system even as they seem to do everything possible to guarantee such exclusion.

UNFAIR. The family members of the energy leech complain about what they see as the blatant unfairness of this energy leecher. When the energy leech's own behavior is copied by another family member and turned against the aggravator, the aggravator is incredulous and indignant that anyone could treat anyone else in such a thoughtless fashion.

SECRETIVE. Energy leeches are hiding what they consider to be a major secret or secrets about their life. This secret may be something they did several years ago, or something they are doing now, or even the fear of what they might do or have fantasized doing, but the energy leeches are burdened by the need to protect what they view as some deep and damaging secret about themselves. The secret, in fact, may not be secret to the other family members, and the secret may not be as major as the aggravator feels it is. Burdened by the need to protect this deep secret about who they are or what they have thought or done, the energy leech acts like a criminal in the family court, expending all of their energy to avoid judgment and prosecution, a punishment that would likely never come if they could mobilize their own reconciliatory love.

INADEQUATE. The energy leech tends to brag, to over-assert themselves socially and within some family settings to cover a low self-esteem that is readily apparent to everyone else in the family. Constantly experiencing their own energy leakage, family leeches themselves feel as drained as those around them. Like a person drowning, they thrash out wildly at attempts by the family to rescue them, hurting and endangering the energy of the very people who could save their life. The energy leech is heading toward a terrible crisis, and can be saved only by family love and strength. To be rescued, he or she will have to stop grabbing and flailing and allow themselves to be pulled gently and lovingly to the safety of the family hearth.

The combination of these eight family energy leech characteristics creates the most severe form of family stress. Almost all of the family energy is consumed by just the day-to-day requirements of living with and talking with such a source of energy loss. Mr. Anders indicates how he dealt with some of the stress within his family:

"I just wasn't getting any rest there. We were really at each other. It was easier just to go down the basement and work in my wood shop. I could see how bad things were getting in the family, because I think I made enough new furniture to start my own store. Whenever I start turning out a lot of furniture down the basement, I know I'm having family trouble."

The family energy leech can be the parent, the children, or any member or members within the family. Even when such members leave the family, their influence can be felt, just as a sprained muscle may hurt weeks after the initial injury, and may be a source of pain for life. When an energy leech is present, communication becomes forced and awkward, sometimes sarcastically polite. Family members begin to feel that they are walking on eggs, afraid that even more disruption of the energy flow will occur if anyone tries to confront the problem person.

Even simple activities involving the whole family tend to result in conflicts, and simple phone calls can lead to family war. The smallest conflicts escalate to major verbal, even physical, conflict and abuse. Long periods of silence and withdrawal may occur, and there is often a sense of negative energy that can be felt even by visitors to the home. The family tree is sapped right down to its roots.

THE FAMILY GEIGER COUNTER

As I mentioned in Chapter Eight, I have found that one particular member of the family tends to be the energy leech "sensor." These family members are the beacons that can guide the
family system to the energy leak. This family member is extremely sensitive to the energy leaking and to the draining of
the family energy to replace the lost energy. They may sense
that problems are on the horizon, and they may even show
actual physical symptoms that serve as metaphors for the impending strain. The following statement illustrates that physical reaction by one family member to family energy problems.

"When our daughter's symptoms seem to act up, we know
that it is not always just her illness that is the problem," said
Ms. Anders. "She is the one in the family that shows the reaction to stress first. She's our alarm system, bless her, and she is
the most sensitive one of us. We have to pay more attention to
how she feels, because she is feeling for all of us. When I argue
with my son, she's the one who gets upset."

The "energy leech sensor" may experience allergies, perhaps symbolic of the overwhelming and emotionally suffocating
nature of the leeching family member's behavior. Stomach upsets may be the symptom of the "sensor," a metaphor of being
unable to "swallow" the constant poison in the family system
or being unable to digest the spoiled love and general lack of
family nurturance. Headaches may symbolize fatigue from constant thinking about problems with the aggravators, and the
"splitting headache" may represent the family ambivalence of
love and hate for the aggravating member.

You can make your own list of metaphor symptoms of the
sensitive person in the family by looking at your own health
and how it serves as a family energy Geiger counter for the
radiation that not only follows but precedes explosions of the
nuclear family. It is important to heed the message sent by this
sensitive person's or perhaps by your own body's "talk" about
how the quality of family energy or lack of family energy is
affecting you. Such messages are the barometers for impending
family storms and emotional drafts.

THE SILENT FAMILY PARTNER

A word of warning about the family energy leech is in order here. The family "sensor," the person who seems to be reacting the most severely to the family energy leech, is not typically the person in the family who will "be next," who will become emotionally or physically sick or follow in the footsteps of the family aggravator. If the energy leech leaves, the chronic stress the family has experienced will result in further energy leaks. Someone else will likely fill the leech role, but that person is typically not the "sensor."

The family member at risk of falling into the energy leech role is the family denier, the family member who seems oblivious, or behaves as if they are oblivious, to the energy leaking from the family. Sooner or later, the leakage will catch up with this person, their denial will no longer be effective, and like a ship whose captain has neglected a major leak in her boat, the denying family member may be swamped by the overwhelming swell of helplessness that can result from years of denial that no longer offers a safe port.

When I work with families in my clinic, I always keep my eye on the family member who sits quietly or seems to be unaware that Rome is burning. This "silent partner" has lost more energy than even they know; and the quieter such "silent partners" are, the more denial they tend to use, the more I know that the family aggravator has been causing them the most severe energy loss. In your own family, remember that silence speaks loudly about where energy leaks in the family may occur next.

Look to the silent partner, and the weaker, the more denying and oblivious they seem regarding the aggravating family member, the more likely that they will be the family member to react most profoundly and negatively to the family problems. The silent family partner may be next in line for depression or illness, and, like an ignored gauge on the control panel in an airplane cockpit that is reading dangerously low, the silent partner may be the most meaningful reading of all.

SOME GUIDELINES FOR FAMILY RECONCILIATION

To effectively reconcile with the problem family member, the following steps are necessary. I have illustrated each step with a statement from one of the five families.

STEP ONE. FINDING THE ENERGY LEAK. Who is the member or are the members causing family energy loss? Seldom is there only one family member responsible, so be sure to take some time to look beyond your obvious choice for family energy loss. You yourself may be the cause of family energy depletion.

One technique to help you see the family energy leech more clearly is to draw a "family-o-gram." Draw circles on a paper with the name of each family member inside. Draw arrows from each circle, representing positive behavior sent from one member to another. Next, draw lines with a reverse arrow on the end to indicate rejecting or hostile behaviors sent from one member to another. When you're finished, you should see that each family member sends and receives the same number of arrows and that, if there are rejection lines with reverse arrows in your family drawing, they should be few and equally distributed within the family drawing. If one member stands out as a "reject" or "rejector," or perhaps a family "isolate" with family members sending neither positive behaviors nor negative behaviors toward them, that person is likely to be the source of an energy leak.

Ms. Anders stated, "We seem to pass the family energy leech role around between us. We have family problem-causer terms of office that we each serve. When we draw our family-o-grams, they are always different. It's best to look for whose turn it is to be causing trouble than who the person is who is always causing the trouble. We keep a file of the family-o-grams we do just to remind us how we change."

STEP TWO. EMPATHY WITH THE ENERGY LEECH. How do you think the person who is causing all the family trouble feels? Take plenty of time to try to experience that person's disappointments, frustrations, and view of the family system.

A technique for promoting empathy with a family energy leech is to spend some time looking at the individual history of that member. Look at family pictures, schoolwork from past years, projects done, or just watch the family aggravator walking some distance from you as you watch out the window. Try to feel how they feel, and trust your FEP, or family extrasensory perception.

Ms. Anders continued, "I could really see how my son felt. Everything was being done for my daughter. I would have felt like he did, even though he showed it by being a pain in the ass."

STEP THREE. DISCOVER WHEN THE ENERGY LEAK FIRST STARTED. As I stated above, try to look back to the family history for even minor changes in the family system, even discussions about change, that may have aggravated the development of a family member. Even though the problem family member may be using present-day issues as their point of contention or complaint, there is almost always a historical development crisis experienced by the person now draining energy from his or her family.

One technique that helps families find the time when the leak began is to draw a family lifeline. Draw a long line on a piece of paper and have as many family members as will participate suggest significant events that should be placed on top of that line. Write these down until you have a family lifeline sketch of significant events. Then, have family members list their personal reactions to these events under the line. Look for differences in reactions as clues for not only what seem to be emotional overreactions but underreactions as well. Sometimes the apparent lack of reaction by a family member to a family lifeline event in comparison to other family members' reactions is a clue to the start of an aggravation or family energy leak.

"I would never have thought that having Gramps move in with us years ago would have caused my daughter problems," said Ms. Muller. "Now that we've looked back at our family development, I can see that Gramps moved in just when my daughter was worried about her period starting, boys, her body, and other preteen problems."

STEP FOUR. SHARING WITH THE ENERGY LEECH.
Tell the family energy leech about your empathy. Don't accuse
them of causing trouble. If nothing seems to be working, suggest professional therapy for the family, not just the problem
person. If they reject professional help, suggest at least one test
visit as a group. Keep inviting them for professional help. It
may pay off. Tell the energy leech that even though you can
never know completely how they feel, you have thought about
how they might be feeling. Don't expect immediate results and
appreciation. You are simply trying to create more family energy, not solve all of the problems draining energy from your
family.

Since communication with an energy leech is difficult, it
may help to send letters and audiotapes through the mail. This
may sound silly, but the families I have worked with have
sometimes had more luck sending a caring letter or tape than
trying to sit down and talk face-to-face with the family energy
leech.

Mr. Muller said, "When Gramps was more rational, I
used to tell him how I thought he must be feeling sometimes.
Before that, I just felt anger. Just talking to him with empathy
made me feel better and sort of defused things a little bit. Even
now that he can't seem to understand, I still write him letters
about how I know he must feel. I don't know if it helps him,
but it really helps me."

**STEP FIVE. KEEPING CONTACT WITH THE ENERGY
LEECH.** No matter what, don't allow further emotional or
physical distance to take place between you, the family, and the
person that seems to be taking so much of the family's energy.

As frustrated as you may feel, keep talking, keep touching,
keep inviting, keep forgiving, and most of all, keep the family
together. If you withdraw physical and emotional contact from
the energy leech, you will only worsen the family energy leak
by creating more distance between family members.

Mr. Johnson said, "My son got to me like a bee sting. It
hurt, then I got even more inflamed and puffed up. I would stop
talking to him and even get mad when other family members
talked to him. In therapy, I learned rule number one was to
keep contact, like holding on to someone in a storm. The more

I tried that, the less the infection from the conflicts. But I still got stung plenty."

These five steps are not final solutions to the family energy leech problem, but they provide the outline for reconciliation, for keeping the family system alive even when there is dis-ease within that system.

LONELY ARGUMENTS WITH LONELY PEOPLE

No matter how illogical, the narcissism of the energy leech is related to their own feelings of being deprived of what they see as their fair share of love and family energy. Remember that there is no concrete measure for family energy and love, so the following arguments used regarding the narcissism of the family energy leech are invalid:

—He or she got more love than anyone else in the family. How could he or she feel deprived of love?

Sometimes, the loving overload provided in the earlier life of the narcissistic family member makes any future love pale by comparison. They may feel deprived now because nothing compares to the indulgence they may have received before, or because there was an early lack of loving, resulting in a loving energy deficit that seems insatiable.

—He or she was actually spoiled, and got more things and favors than anyone else in the family.

It may have been the actual spoiling that resulted in the love addiction manifested by the narcissistic. Having had too much loving at one time, they now feel a love starvation when there is the slightest appetite for caring. It may also be true that the family was so overburdened by early demands from this narcissist that what the family saw as indulgence was really only impatience with having to give even a little loving.

—As a matter of fact, he or she was really the favorite in the family, so how could he or she feel jealous or resentful now?

Being treated as the "favorite" always breeds future resentment, because there is something within us that senses the "us," that knows that we should not be singled out for extra loving and family energy. The jealousy shown is a jealousy of equality, of longing to be just a part of the family rather than its center. The resentment may relate to being isolated, even if such isolation is placement on a lonely pedestal or being singled out for special attention.

—If anyone was deprived of love, it was the rest of the family. He or she took all of our time, all of our tolerance, and it was the rest of us who were really deprived. How could he or she feel deprived?

The energy leech is narcissistic partly because they do not feel the "us," or feel little welcomed as a part of the "rest of us." If the rest of the family members were busy trying to accommodate the aggravator, he or she ends up feeling like a target rather than a person. However obnoxious and intolerable the energy leech may be, they are really protesting their exaggerated or illusory sense of eviction from the family, their sense that they are an object, a project, or a problem to be solved rather than a part of the family problem-solving processes.

—He or she was born selfish.

No one is born selfish. We are conceived through the "us" process, developed within someone, and born into a system from a system. Any selfishness or narcissism results from energy disruption, from some leak in the family energy that stems from incomplete loving, distraction from loving in favor of everyday coping with self-imposed or external stress, or from some deficiency in the ability of one or both parents to love and be loved.

—He or she is the most arrogant and self-absorbed person in the world. How could he or she feel so inadequate?

It is because these narcissists have withdrawn to self that they do feel so inadequate. Alone, or at least feeling alone in the struggle for life, the narcissistic family member feels inadequate because of being without the resources of "us," without the sense of comfort and strength that comes from enduring family belonging. The narcissistic family member withdraws because of feeling inadequate; and he or she feels inadequate because of having withdrawn; and the negative family circle continues to wind around such narcissists, strangling rather than freeing them, entrapping them and separating them even farther from the loving energy that can break this sick family circle.

CHANGING SELFISHNESS TO SHARING

Our love maps, the way we learn to love, are determined not only by our family system, but also by genetic, prenatal, and biological factors. The combination of prenatal factors and family system is complex, so no one really knows how love maps are drawn, just as no one really knows what intelligence or creativity is or how they occur. Recent research is beginning to suggest that genetic factors are much more important in certain personality traits than once suspected. Even a trait such as shyness is now known to be due primarily to genetic rather than social influences.

Prenatal factors are not factors that take place only before birth. They continue to interact and develop with the experiences of the person over time. You must accept the fact that the family aggravator has an acquired love addiction, a need for more family energy and more family loving than is actually necessary for their own health and the health of the family. Like the heroin addict who needs more and more heroin to get the same degree of high, the narcissistic person needs more and more attention and love to keep even, to experience and maintain any slight sense of being loved.

Unfortunately for the narcissist, being selfish does not lead to loving behavior on the part of others. Being selfish only provokes an encapsulizing of the self that says, "OK, if I can't get the loving and energy I seem to need from you, I'll just have to keep drawing love for and from myself. I will gorge myself on me." This self-deception results in the energy depletion that causes family energy to flood in to fill the void. As a result, everyone loses their energy for love.

THE CARTHAGE COMPLEX

Mr. Johnson said, "I was the oldest, and I think all first children suffer from being expected to do more, to sort of allow themselves to be used. I just felt sacrificed for the good of the family."

Mr. Johnson is describing what I call the Carthage Complex. Carthage was an ancient city-state in North Africa on the Mediterranean Sea near Tunis. It was eventually destroyed by the Romans, but before its fall, it was common practice for the Carthaginians to sacrifice their firstborn. Sometimes five hundred or more children were sacrificed at one time while music was played to cover the cries of agony. Persons who feel that their cries of despair and pain were ignored by their family, that they were sacrificed by the family, tend to turn their resentment inward, pulling away from the family and tuning out any overtures for reunion and reconciliation.

THE NEW "LD": LOVING DISABILITY

To relate with someone who experiences the Carthage Complex, who feels sacrificed and is now sacrificing their family loving, it is necessary to see such persons as having "LD," a loving disability. Just as learning disabled children require special attention and remedial help, so do family members with their own unique loving disability, their own Carthage Complex that blocks them from learning to receive love with grace and give love with generosity.

If we can learn to see the narcissistic family member as loving disabled, we can begin to offer remediation as we would to a learning disabled person. We will teach by example, we will love more slowly and more obviously, we will show more toleration for failures and patience for setbacks. We will learn to see the effort to love as a beginning, just as the effort to learn is a beginning for the learning disabled person. The first step in helping a learning disabled person is unqualified acceptance and absence of comparisons, and the first step in helping a loving disabled person is that same acceptance.

To reject the selfish family member because of their selfishness only reaffirms the aggravators' worst fear and belief, the fear that they have been sacrificed and that no one in their family really cares about them. Like telling a dyslexic person that they are stupid, when we tell the narcissistic person that they are not lovable or loving, we are making a person's nightmare come true.

Dyslexic persons have trouble reading, but they are as bright as anyone else and perhaps often much brighter from their creative if unsuccessful attempts to compensate for their disability. Loving disabled persons are capable of intense loving, perhaps because they have felt the pain so long of so little loving. As dyslexic persons cannot perceive the written letters accurately, so narcissistic persons are blind to the more subtle signs of loving messages that never seem to filter through to their soul.

Helping the learning disabled learn and the dyslexic person read requires immense patience, creative approaches, and the celebration of the smallest signs of progress. These same characteristics are required of the family members attempting to help the narcissistic family member learn to see and give love.

The first words most dyslexic people I have worked with learn to read are the words "I am." When the connection is made between these two words and their meaning, the new reader may cry with the sudden recognition of the printed confirmation of their self-worth. The words that impact strongly on the narcissist are the words and the true recognition of the feeling "we are." You can help the narcissist with his or her journey into "us" by never losing your patience with their attempt to travel what for them is a new and unfamiliar road.

SEASONING THE IMMATURE FAMILY MEMBER

One constant pressure on the family is the fact that families, like water, have a tendency to seek their lowest level. When one family member is immature, explosive, accusatory, sulks, or has temper tantrums, the entire family can come to adopt such a style of daily interaction. The five families I have been describing in this book were able to avoid this phenomenon, instead helping the immature family member to season, to make progress toward more mature interactions with others.

The immature family member suffers from an inability to grow with the family, to benefit from the loving energy available in the family system. Immature members have become stuck in an orbit that is not evolving larger and larger around the family nucleus. Instead, like a spaceship that is losing power, they slow down in their development, becoming trapped in the same redundant and uncomfortable orbit of experiences and negative appraisals of their world.

"My wife's daughter was sixteen when we got married," said Mr. Johnson. "She was more like five or six years old in her attitude and behavior. She dominated all the kids in the family. If things didn't go her way, she would scream or hit. She would have a fit if the other kids went in her bedroom, but she would bother them anytime she wanted. We talked it out, and it just seemed obvious that she was stuck. It was like not having to face her mother's divorce and remarriage, if she could stay at the age she was when things seemed to be going fine between her parents."

The key to dealing with the immaturity of the problem family member is to clearly identify the actual emotional stage at which the person seems stuck. Describing in detail the behaviors of a child or adult family member, and then trying to match these general characteristics with a developmental stage or prior time in their family life, helps the rest of the family focus on the time that is psychologically "preferred" by that family member. The family can then look back to that time and see what aspects of life then are missing from the family life now.

As I pointed out earlier, the energy leech is confronting problems on behalf of the family. If this member is having trouble with substance abuse, self-esteem, sexuality, or feeling of security, then the whole family system likely has some form of problem in one or more of these areas. "What's our problem?" should replace "What's your problem?" as a key family question.

There is almost always something in the problems that the energy leech is experiencing that the entire family should ad-

dress. The stage where the immature family member is stuck
may signal something lacking within the family system. In the
case of the Johnson family, the immaturity of Ms. Johnson's
daughter was signaling her family that they were making too
many changes too fast. They had to go back, to allow a period
for stabilization before expecting the two families that resulted
from this remarriage to merge as one.

The developmental stage preferred by the immature family
member may have seemed safer, more supportive, more atten-
tive to the needs of that person. As Mr. Johnson pointed out
regarding his new stepdaughter, "She seemed to feel that her
behaviors at age five or six seemed to work for her. They, in her
mind, kept her family together. What she was doing at five or
six seemed lucky to her, so she just kept doing it. We had to
show her that more mature behaviors could be lucky, too."

Most immature family behavior is superstitious behavior.
When medical or the more classical psychiatric problems have
been ruled out, chronic immature behavior on the part of a
family member is behavior that the member feels "worked before," a type of desperate and usually fruitless struggle to
regain or maintain a "better" prior time in family life, and
sometimes a time that the family itself should be looking back
to for clues in solving present family distress.

Sometimes, the energy leech is attempting to direct the
family's collective attention to issues that need raising for and
by the family. Something may be lacking in the family energy
system, and this one person may be the beacon, the hypersensi-
tive person I mentioned earlier. Before trying to deal with the
troubled family member, be sure that he or she is not seeing
something that the rest of the family is missing.

Don't turn off or ignore a family alarm unless the family is
sure it is false. Sometimes the tearful eyes that see our history
are more accurate than glazed eyes that are always turned to
the present or future. The majority of the family is not always
right in their appraisal of family situations. Immaturity can be
a call back to a healthier family future.

Ms. Johnson reported, "When I used to fight with my first
husband, I would go into my daughter's bedroom and try to
comfort her. I guess I might have been trying to comfort myself. I knew our fighting was terrible for her, and she would curl
up like a little baby in my arms as I stroked her. Sometimes she

would demand hours of comforting and want me to hold her for what seemed like forever. She would come into my room whenever she wanted and ask to sleep with me. Now I see that she had reversed things in her own mind. She thought that if she kept me busy dealing with her, comforting her, then my husband and I wouldn't argue as much. In a way, she was sacrificing her own maturity because of our immaturity. It was all she knew to do, and now she still acts childishly, maybe to prevent arguments between myself and my new husband from starting. Of course, she was right. Our arguments were terribly destructive to the whole family. We really all were behaving like babies. We should have looked into the mirror she was holding up to us. We should have been comforting each other in the same ways she seemed to need so badly. We were really the immature ones. We were fighting while she was trying to love."

This mother was able to see the true source of energy leeching, to talk with this little girl about her fears, resentments, and superstitions. The family took her immaturity as a warning, as a sign to avoid the mistakes of the past. The discussion between the family members about the immaturity did not stop the immaturity at once, but making the problem an "us" problem changed the focus entirely.

The family's acknowledgment of their shared responsibility for the energy loss helped to reduce the frequency of the daughter's superstitious regressiveness. The style of daily interaction of the new family was enhanced in the process, and more energy seemed available to confront the challenges of forming one new family from two.

Immature adult family members may show their immaturity in this same "superstitious manner," believing on some level that the best way to avoid their worst fears (rejection, violence, isolation) is to maintain behaviors that in their own view "worked" historically. They see themselves as safe from clear and present dangers because they are not living in the present, and their immaturity gives them the false security of presenting what they consider to be a less clear target.

The family energy leech is usually correct in their perceptions of what is wrong in the family system, through painting broad and exaggerated family caricatures. The problems become more severe because this family member exaggerates, sometimes to absurd levels, the nature of family problems. As a result, the family system can not clearly see the problem at the root of the aggravating and energy-draining member's distress. The family is distracted from their real problems by the overwhelming and even frightening nature of the problem family member's family caricature. If we can learn from the messages being sent by the distressed member, and not become trapped in trying to cope with the behaviors without seeing their cause, we can help everyone in the family to reconcile together.

EXPOSING LIES FOR LOVE

Lies by family members are almost always lies for love. When we distort the truth, we typically do so because we either do not feel worthy of love or we fear the withdrawal of love. Aggravating family members experience strong needs for love, and their lies for love can be equally oversized.

Ms. Bonner said, "I never understood how my youngest daughter could lie so easily and so often. She lied about things that I could not see any possible reason for lying about. She seemed to lie just to lie. Then I asked myself one question. 'If she's such a big liar, what is the equally big truth she is attempting to cover up?' I had been just thinking about the magnitude of the lie and not the impact of the truth that she may have been frightened of. I thought and thought, and after really looking at things and talking to her, I still couldn't imagine what big truth she couldn't share with us. Then, in our therapy, I realized that she wasn't keeping things from us. She was keeping something from herself."

Ms. Bonner had difficulty, in her therapy, facing a major truth in her own family life. She felt that, in some way, she had caused the death of her husband. "I felt I should have done more, done something to keep him home that day he was killed," said Ms. Bonner. "I know intellectually that I couldn't have done a thing, but I guess I still felt I should have done something, even if it was paying more attention to him, loving him more, when he was alive."

"Then," continued Ms. Bonner, "I faced up to the worst truth of all. Our marriage wasn't always the best marriage, and I was mad at him a lot. He wasn't around enough when he was alive, and now I hated my husband for being killed, for leaving us. I just couldn't face that at first, and I started to wonder if my daughter was carrying some of the same 'false truths' within her that made her use lies to keep her distant from her pain."

During therapy, it was discovered that the daughter indeed felt responsible and angry about her father's death. It seemed easier for her to distort everyday life, to keep lying about almost everything, to save her from having to face this one "big" thing. The daughter was expending her energy on lying, rather than reconciling herself with her father's death and the terrible truth that none of us have, or will ever have, loved someone who leaves us intensely enough or often enough.

Once the daughter faced up to the "big thing," the angry feelings she had about her father dying, the lying decreased. Energy was freed up for loving, for integrity, and for turning to the family for support and the mutual sharing of the grieving process. This girl, as every family member does sometimes, turned to lies as emotional shortcuts to avoid confrontation of basic family issues. As with many shortcuts, more energy was consumed in this circuitous emotional route than the energy that would have been required for a more direct line to the family facts of life.

Another factor contributing to the chronic dishonesty of the family energy leech is "role-model lying." If the family system incorporates "little white lies," so-called convenience lying, into daily living, the vulnerable family member simply extends what they see as the family falsehood custom to bigger and bigger lies. If little lies seem to work, then big lies must work even better.

Integrity in all that we do or say is not the unrealistic goal that some of my patients seem to feel it is. Telling the truth requires much less family and loving energy in the long run than dishonesty. However, lying is a "quick high," immediate relief from the pressures of an intimate situation that may require resolution, disclosure of true thoughts and feelings, and a new level of personal responsibility. In a society that sees quick as better, lying fits right in, by providing for emotional acceleration right past issues that are bound to come back to haunt us. "Tell two lies and call me in the morning" seems to be an all too frequent family medicine.

Lying provides a type of pseudocontrol over our immediate situation, but sets us up for the expending of constant energy in the perpetuation of our own deceit. It is impossible to tell just one little lie. I tell my patients that lying is like the behavior of the most common mammal on earth, the shrew. These little animals cannot control themselves. They eat until all the food is gone, then they eat each other, and finally they start to eat their own tails, finally eating themselves up by chewing into their own vital organs. Lying is a "shrew" phenomenon, and we end up eating ourselves up by our own shortsightedness and unwillingness to see what we are doing to ourselves and others in our family.

I suggest that my patients consider lies to be wishes. I suggest that we listen to lies because they can tell us much about the fears and desires of the liar. "My son's lies were interesting, once I got by my anger about them," said Mr. Anders. "Like you said, I found wishes in them every time. Even when he said he cleaned his room when he really didn't, I could tell that he wished he did, and that he wished he had my approval for doing it. On more important things, like the time he lied about a low grade on a test, it was obvious what he really wished for. He wanted to do well for me, and his lie was giving me what he thought I wanted."

It has been said that facts are the enemy of truth. When families get caught up in interrogation and conflicts over who did or did not tell the truth, they spend insufficient time and energy in looking for the feelings, fears, hopes, and dreams of family members. The aggravating family member drains less energy from the family when feelings take on as much as, or more importance than, facts.

TAKING THE MOTIVE OUT OF REVENGE

The vindictiveness of the family energy leech stems from their own feelings of injustice, of being hurt severely over time by one or more family members. The vengeful family member feels like a scapegoat, the recipient of all of the anger and impatience of the entire family system. Often, there may have been some basis in fact for such feelings.

Mr. Anders said, "I'd just had it. I worked hard, and I provided for my own family, for my own parents, even for some people at work. I did right for everybody but myself. I started to resent the happiness that I was bringing to others, almost wishing that things would go wrong for them. Sometimes I would sabotage something for them, like intentionally not showing up for a family activity or ignoring someone at a family wedding. I wanted to punish them in some way. Sometimes my biggest protest just went unnoticed, which only infuriated me more."

Mr. Anders was expressing his own feelings of injustice, but just as in many cases of family energy leeching, the injustice had two sides. First, Mr. Anders himself had not developed the ability to act on behalf of himself, feeling that everything he did was for someone else, and that he was valued only for what he did, and not for who he was. Secondly, this martyrdom yielded only more usury by the family, which became accustomed to his selflessness and upset when any selfishness surfaced.

Family martyrdom and feelings of vindictiveness go hand in hand. Martyrdom elicits the family counterreaction of resentment at the perceived attempt to control by demanding sympathy or pity, and as a result even more expectations are placed on the self-martyred person. The only way out of the selflessness-martyrdom-resentment-usury-vengefulness cycle is what is called "enlightened self-enhancement," a balance between altruism and self-interest.

"When we saw this pattern in our therapy together, when we saw that my husband was so resentful, we were able to tell him that what we really wanted was for him to be happy too. We told him that we loved it when he would do something just for himself, and that we hated it when he always seemed to be giving up his life for us. Instead of admiring him for his sacrifice, we resented it. He finally learned that doing some things just for himself was doing something for all of us. His happiness made us all happy," said Ms. Anders. "It was difficult at first, because he did things for himself in an almost angry, 'I'll show you' manner. He'd say, 'In case any one cares, I'm going to play golf. I'll be home when I feel like it.' Finally, he learned that we all wanted him to enjoy himself, and that he didn't have to demand his right to be himself. We loved his 'self.' It really freed him up when he saw how happy his happiness made us. He's more to us than what he does for us, and I think he has learned that now."

When working with families, I tell them about "positive parasitism." Parasitism is a healthy, natural part of our world, and parasites live within every one of us. We ourselves are parasites of our earth, and the earth is a parasite of the sun, and on it goes. We all use one another and are used by each other.

Feelings of vindictiveness in families occur when family members disregard the positive parasitism principle, that we all take and give, use and are used. Such feelings usually fester beneath the surface, as the family member feels that he or she is giving and giving while others only take. Sulking, manipulation, and threats of leaving the family, or doing something that will totally upset the whole family, all indicate the feelings of revenge that have been building within the vindictive family member.

Vindictiveness by any family member is usually a signal that the delicate balance of usury in the healthy family parasitism is out of whack. Instead of becoming angry or reacting to the attempts at revenge by the aggravating family member, it is wiser and more constructive to openly and frankly examine and renegotiate who is using whom for how long and in what way. I tell the families I work with to assume that the vindictive person is right and is being taken advantage of. I tell the families to use this information to renegotiate a better responsibility and caring balance within the family.

If you yourself feel that you have given the best years of your life to your family, what about the years that are left? The revenge or "getting even" that you may attempt will never bring the appreciation and love that you feel was lacking in the first place. The best you can give to your family is your own enlightened, responsible self-fulfillment, a balance between doing for, doing with, and getting your family to do for you.

Your own unhappiness is your problem, not the fault of an unappreciative pack of individuals who happen to be going through life together and competing to take the most that they can from one another. We are all parasites of the universal energy of the world; we must give that energy back and take it again with grace and concern for our own development, and see that development as a responsibility to, and not in competition with, the welfare of the whole family system.

BRINGING THE "OUT OF IT" BACK IN

When family pressures are experienced as excessive by the family energy leech, he or she will tend to disassociate themselves from the family system. They are ultimately successful in just the opposite effect, as the family overreacts to the withdrawal by overindulging the withdrawing family member. All family conversation may be about this member, or to and with this member, and family plans may come to center almost exclusively on the family's perception of the needs of the withdrawn member.

"Our oldest son just pulled away from us," said Ms. Steiner. "He married a girl we just didn't like, but we thought it was his choice and that we were trying to get along. I guess we didn't mask our feelings very well, and we almost lost our son in the process. He stopped calling, never came to birthdays or holidays, and just left us. He would be polite enough when we did see or talk to him, but you could tell that he wouldn't let us back into his life. He would just look right through us."

When our self-created version of our family's treatment of us becomes so negative that we feel that we can no longer function within the family, everything that happens in the family seems to verify our perceptions of the family's unfairness or rejection. We hear things that were not said, do not hear things that were said, and say things we feel are so often not heard that we just stop saying them. The only way to break this cycle is to accept the withdrawing family member's feeling of rejection as fact, and act to draw them back in.

"We learned in therapy," said Ms. Steiner, "that we all need to try harder to behave ourselves, to not say the negative things we've been saying. We could sure behave ourselves in front of you, the therapist. We behaved better in the clinic than at home. We tried to be tolerant at the clinic. We learned to try the same thing at home. We tried to keep reaching out, to stop being critical, to call our son even when he didn't call us and keep writing him even when he didn't write to us. It finally worked, in small steps. He's back in now, and we're all more careful not to take liberties with our family feelings."

The most bitter of family arguments I have heard in my clinic come from prejudice, impatience, and intolerance for the individual choices made by family members. To an outsider, the issues over which each of the quarreling families battles often seem insignificant, even trite. Someone doesn't like somebody else's attitude, or the way someone dresses; or someone is upset at not being consulted before some decision or invited to some party; or some other issue will dominate the family feud. I often wondered, as I sat helplessly by, observing what seemed to be a silly family conflict turned bitter, if anyone in the family thought about what really matters. What matters is the love, the "us-ness" of the family system, and the "us" gets quickly lost in a shower of "You saids," "How could yous," or "Why didn't yous."

Sometimes we have to set aside some very basic convictions to keep our family together. We must allow our family members to love as they will, who they will. We must make every effort to stretch the range of what we will accept in the name of the family, in the name of "us." We do not have to change who we are, what we do, or even how we feel about major family issues, but we must be able to allow all of our family members the right not to change who, what, or how they are. And maybe, just maybe, we might be able to look beyond some of our own prejudices to the lessons a family member is trying to teach us.

We can only guide one another as family. We cannot determine one another's destiny. We can only give our family members a strong and dynamic family view of the world, not a complete way to live. Families are the crucible in which the lives of their members are forged, but families can never be the container that holds the final product. Energy spent in fighting over compliance is wasted, and much more needed for reconciliation.

I remember one father who would not accept his white son's marriage to a black woman. He said, "When he did that, he stopped being my son." The family never reconciled, but the mother secretly visited her son and daughter-in-law. The mother cried often about the permanent family split imposed by this father's stubbornness and blind prejudice. On the day of the birth of the son of this young couple, the mother could not convince the rejecting father to see his new grandson. The father died recently, never knowing the thrill of holding the tiny hand of his new family member. I often think of this sad family when I write about reconciliation and tolerance in the family. Don't let a similar crisis happen to your family. Make sure, no matter what, that everyone is still in the family ark.

FAIR FAMILY PLAY

The family energy leech demonstrates little sense of fair play. Expecting attention, appreciation, and family response, he or she shows little of these behaviors by his or her own example.

Ms. Bonner said, "My son complained constantly that I was always butting into his business. I was always asking about drugs, about sex, about his school and career plans. I guess I overcompensated when I tried to be both parents to him. Now that his father is gone, he wants to know where I am at all times, if I am going to date, and what I plan to do with my life. He has his eyes on me all the time. Where's the fairness in that?"

The contradiction pointed out by Ms. Bonner illustrates the dual ambivalence that dictates to most families. Both child and parent desire independence from one another on the one hand, and fear and resist such separation on the other. The aggravating family member wants privacy but constant attention, concern by the family but at the same time complete autonomy, and everyone's time while giving little time in return. This ambivalence relates to the fear on the part of some family members of losing their identity. Their insecurity and low self-esteem causes them to demand that which they cannot seem to give, asking others to make up for their own deficits by doing everything they themselves seem unable to do consistently.

The Bonner son said, "Yes, I know what she's talking about. I just don't know what to do. I want to just be on my own, but I worry about my mother, now that Dad's gone. I guess I want two sets of rules. I don't want her bothering me, but I want to be with her when I want to or need to, or when I think she might screw up or get hurt. She's kind of out of it, kind of naive because Dad used to do so much for her. She's the parent, but I feel like I have to take care of her now."

"We finally had it out," said Ms. Bonner, "not just one time, but many times. He cried, and I cried, and my daughter cried. I never saw it until you pointed it out. I was leaving everything to my daughter. I had her start supper for me, make my calls, generally handle the house. I was exploiting her and ignoring him. I expected very little of him, and that is exactly what I got. He was unsure of his new role, and he felt left out, so he took on the best role he knew. He tried to become my husband, probably because I was treating him like my husband and showing my anger for my husband to him."

Unfairness by one family member typically relates to the poor definition of rules and expectations in the family system. Failure to reconcile new roles in adjustment to family change or loss typically is followed by this type of unfairness and inconsistency.

Fairness cannot be demanded; it must result from a clear and dynamic code of conduct in the home. This family system must include rules that are not aimed at any one family member, but a code that applies to the family system. Such little but consistent steps as requiring knocking on doors before entering, not opening other people's mail, honoring the privacy of others, and balancing accountability must be clearly stated, equally applied to every family member, and renegotiable as the family system changes. When the rules need changing because of one member's needs, then all members' needs must be considered in the formulation of a new family code of conduct.

THE SECRET OF AN UNHAPPY FAMILY

The family energy leech, whether an adult or a child, is characterized by a secretiveness that seems unnecessary. There is an exaggerated need for privacy, and a resentment when the aggravating member is pressed for details regarding their feelings or behaviors.

Mr. Anders said, "My oldest boy just acted suspicious.

Every time I asked him something, I got either no answer or a shrug of the shoulders. I could never find out what was happening in school, about his friends, about anything. I started to wonder if he was on drugs, but when I asked him, he just clammed up more. It bothered all of us in the family. None of us seemed to know where we stood with him."

Mr. Anders was describing the "problem focus" of today's family. We come to deal with day-to-day life with a vigilance for "what's wrong now?" Some family members are particularly sensitive to this "imminent disaster" orientation, seeming to fear family overreaction to their feelings or behaviors. They have developed a psychological flinch, and they may jerk away from the slightest perceived challenge. It seems better to them to just "keep things to themselves," because there is a sense of negative family energy just ready to explode at some problem.

The Anders son said, "I couldn't tell them anything. They go ape. If I would get a low grade, they would think that I've ruined my career. I don't have any big deal to make them real happy either, so I just don't say anything. It's like they're looking for land mines or something. It was better to just keep my mouth shut."

In families where most discussions are problematic, it is difficult to talk only of simple feelings and events. We focus too often on what was done, and consider talking about feelings as "idle chatter" or small talk. We scan for problems rather than listen for people. One of the reasons the family ritual I discussed earlier is so important is that it allows for regular sharing without the pressure of problem focus.

Secretiveness can, however, mask more serious underlying suffering. Substance abuse, chronic depression, or other personal problems may be overwhelming a family member, resulting in their feeling that they are unable to share their burden with their family. The aggravating family member is losing energy every moment, and may feel that the family system is incapable of helping them to reenergize.

The best way to determine the difference between a temporary quietness of choice and necessary rest from the buzzing confusion of daily family life, and the more chronic withdrawal that signals serious distress, is to continue to reach out to the family member. Even when invitations and inquiries are rejected, gentle but consistent reissuing of invitations to join the family group should continue. Keep coming on to family members who seem to be turning the family off.

When continued attempts to bring the secretive person out of their shell have failed, professional help should be considered. Professional help is not sought because one person in the family is upset, crazy, depressed or emotionally disturbed. Psychotherapy or medical evaluation, as I said earlier, must be considered as a family process. The approach to professional help should not be "You need a shrink." Rather, the phrase "Let's all get a checkup to see if we can be of more help to each other." No energy leak in the family can be sealed by just attempting to repair one part of the system.

I suggest that the families I work with ask the following ten "signals of secretness" questions. By asking these questions, it is possible to begin to determine whether or not the secretiveness on the part of a family member means more than just a desire to be left alone for a while. I have included after each question a few of the factors that emerged in the super families when the ten questions were asked.

Ten Questions for the Signals of Secretiveness

1. Are there apparent changes in physical appearance, alterations of complexion, posture, body weight, and general body appearance? (Possible depression or substance abuse.)

2. Are mood swings severe and frequent, standing out from the mood changes in other family members? (Depression, severe anxiety interfering with thought processes, external social pressures, substance abuse.)

3. Is there resentment and anger at attempts to draw the secretive person out of their shell? (Depression, sexual fears or concerns, rejection by peer groups.)

4. Are there dietary changes, such as a severe decrease or increase in amount of food eaten? Are there cravings for sugar or junk foods that go beyond prior eating patterns for this individual? (Depression, substance abuse, food reactivity, eating disorders.)

5. Does the secretive person have a good knowledge base regarding sexuality, including specifics as to masturbation, courtship, and the art of "making out"? Have issues of what it means to be, and feel like, a woman or man in our society been openly and tolerantly discussed? (Guilt regarding masturbation, gender-orientation confusion, sexual confusion.)

6. Has there been a relatively immediate change in friendship group, with old friends disappearing? (Substance abuse, engaged in illegal activities.)

7. Is there some problem between two of the family members that has been going on for a long time, and that the whole family cannot seem to get involved in? (Abuse of a family member, carrying a secret on behalf of another family member, one family member seriously mentally impaired.)

8. Is the secretiveness just in the family, or is there a general reticence with friends and other family members? (Hiding something regarding the primary family, abuse outside the primary family.)

9. Is there any family precedent for the secretiveness? Have grandparents, uncles, or aunts shown this same behavior in the past? Have these secretive people experienced serious emotional problems? (Manifestation of prior family problems, metabolic or medical problems.)

10. Do you yourself have secrets that you are afraid to discuss? Remember that secrets are different than lying. "Signal secretiveness" is a subtle call for help, for more and more reaching out until the energy block in the person is exposed and help is found. Sometimes, the person who complains the most that someone else is keeping secrets is really talking about their own secretiveness. If one member is choosing "signal secretiveness," it is likely that more than one family member is in distress. (Hiding personal feelings by modeling another family member's secretiveness, family difficulty with disclosure, vulnerability, and unqualified family acceptance.)

The answers to the ten questions above are not simple, and the sample discoveries about a family member do not necessarily represent what you may find in your own family. You may want to pose them to the person who seems too secretive.

Problems with gender orientation, substance abuse, sexual confusion and fear, and ambivalence about the future are common in all families, and seeing secrets as signals, rather than as lack of cooperation and withdrawal, is a starting point for mobilizing the "us" factor for family problem solving.

BEING A COMPETENT FAMILY MEMBER

The family energy leech generally feels incompetent. You read earlier in this book about the importance of a sense of competence and positive appraisal of family life. The family member who feels incompetent may mask that feeling by bravado or arrogance on the one hand, and helplessness and sulking on the other. The first sense of personal competence comes from a sense of being a needed, respected, and valued family member, and if that feeling does not develop early in family life, it is difficult for anyone to feel worthy and self-confident in any situation.

"It worried me so," said Ms. Steiner. "Our middle child never seemed to feel good about himself. He showed it by acting out sometimes. He drove us nuts with his harebrained schemes. He tore apart everything, ruined his clothes, and from the time he was a little boy, he was just generally an accident waiting to happen."

Ms. Steiner's statement shows one typical pattern of reaction to a sense of family incompetence. If a family has a narrow definition of competence, relying on external measures such as academic and professional success, some of its members will always fall outside that definition. The "throwaway child" is the child who is unconsciously discarded by the family system by definitions of competence that do not include what that child can do and who he or she is.

"I loved to make things and take things apart. It didn't bother me when things were a mess or if I couldn't get what I took apart back together again," said the Steiner son. "Nobody in our family ever did stuff like that. They were readers, I was not. They liked music, I liked engine sounds. It's still true, but I think my family and I finally worked it out. I think they can see me through my pile of clothes, machine parts, tools, and grease, and I can see them through their books, magazines, and the printer's ink on their fingers."

When I met alone with the Steiner boy during therapy, he reported that he felt he was a disappointment to his family. He felt they really wanted a professional person for a son, not a mechanic. He said one day, "They seem to be more concerned with what I'm doing than who I am." This statement illustrates the impact of a sense of competence, and how important it is for families to broaden their definition of competence to include the personality characteristics of altruism, caring, respect, and integrity in place of an exclusive emphasis on success, compliance, achievement, and being "like everyone else in the family."

If you want to do something, right this minute, that will help every member of your family, write down two or three things about each family member that are unique and special to that person, and that make the whole family a better place to live. Write down some competence areas for everyone, free of societal expectations for status, education, and money. You may be surprised to see quite a range of capability in your family, and it's the family's job to protect and enhance the unique genius of all of its members.

SIX STEPS TO FAMILY RECONCILIATION

Before moving on to the concept of reverence, consider each of these six simple affirmations regarding family reconciliation, a loving of tolerance and acceptance:

STEP ONE. OPEN CHANNELS. No matter how angry or hurt I am, I will never miss the chance to talk with a family member. What I say and how I say it goes far beyond words. My effort to speak and act with tolerance and caring will help the aggravating family member to contribute rather than take energy from the family system.

STEP TWO. CLOSED ANGER. No matter what a family member has done, I will make the conscious effort to limit my anger. I will remember that anger breeds anger, both within me and within those toward whom I express my anger. My anger only confirms the hurting family member's worst fears.

STEP THREE. SHARED STRUGGLES. I will look for my family in every family member, and when that member frustrates me, I will remember that they are struggling for me and not with me. I will remember that I must make peace with family members who are gone, through looking inside myself for their memory traces and making peace between my soul and theirs through meditation, introspection, and prayer.

STEP FOUR. FAMILY NEED. I will remember that every family problem represents the expression of some unmet need for every family member. I will translate the problems of one of my family to expressions of needs on behalf of all of my family.

STEP FIVE. SIGNALS OF CHANGE. I will try to view every family conflict as the first step to more family growth. There can be no true growth without some level of crisis, because crisis initiates energy change.

STEP SIX. FAMILY LIFE GUARDS. I will try to fill the role of family guardian of the family system, doing what I can individually to keep the family system together, even when negative energy forces pull at the seams of our family unity.

If you know of one major rift, one unresolved family conflict that has gone on for a long time, make every effort now for reconciliation. You won't get far on your journey for a happy and fulfilling life if your family energy is leaking during the entire trip.

CHAPTER TEN

Family Reverence:
Protecting the Dignity
of "Us"

"A single glimpse of heaven is enough to confirm its existence even if it is never experienced again."
ABRAHAM MASLOW

FAMILY REVERENCE: The sharing of a common family belief system regarding the purpose of life, and an enduring commitment to the eternal unity of the family shown through the daily behavior of every family member.

FACING THE LIGHT OF OUR OWN BRILLIANCE

Ecstasy, awe, deference, tenderness, wonder, amazement, loyalty, candor, generosity, and joy. All of these concepts are too often mocked as Pollyanna, soft-headed, having little to do with the real world. Many people feel that they describe an unrealistic, childlike relationship to the world; yet each of these emotions can take place daily in the family, if we will try

272

harder to look beyond the frustrations of living so closely together to the magic of experienced life as a loving group.

Earlier, I mentioned Mircea Eliade's term "de-sacradization," the diminishing of the sacred in our daily living. If we are not careful, we stand the chance of surrendering the one gift unique to human beings; the ability to sense and communicate with one another about the sacred nature of life, a daily awe of the experience of our own existence. The reverence factor of the family relates to paying attention to how fantastic the simple things really are, the stealing back of our sense of the truly wonderful from the corruption of commercialism that tells us we can only really love a new brand of floor wax.

The family is a miracle because it allows us to confirm our experiences and sometimes, even without words, sense from someone else that they too are amazed by the grandeur of just being alive. We are naive when we think or act as if miracles are rare, extraordinary events parceled out by a judgmental God only to deserving people. The true miracle of loving people sharing every aspect of life, every pain and pleasure, every smile and tear, the birth of a baby and the passing of a grandfather, is right under our noses, circling around us like the aroma of turkey roasting on Thanksgiving day.

Look around you. Your family can surround you with the loving cloth of the miracle of unconditional love, but you must first learn to experience that unconditional love, learn how to revere the family life experience and to feel family love, even when all the problems of living seem to distract us from that loving. Family reverence is not based on "I'll love you if . . . ," but rather, on "I love you no matter what." Reverence of the family system is a behavior, something you learn to do, and not an automatic emotional reflex, the result of being related by blood or adoption.

Like the first seven of the ten Rx's of healthy family living (rhythm, ritual, reason, remembrance, resonance, resilience, reconciliation), the eighth Rx, family reverence, requires active choice, effort, patience, courage, and a new sensitivity for the miracle of family living. Family reverence requires the choice to value the family over all else; the effort to continue to show that choice for the family and its members, even at times of severe stress and conflict; the patience and sensitivity to allow the miracle of family love to evolve; and the courage to transcend the conditional love that society emphasizes in favor of the accepting and unqualified loving of family life.

The Family Reverence Test

To help you understand the concept of reverence for the family system, take the following test. Once again, you may want to average your family scores and compare individual and total family reverence scores. You may also find it helpful to look back at your first seven family Rx scores as you examine the reverence factor, because each of those first seven Rx's constitute one step toward family reverence, and family reverence is required to fully experience each of the first Rx's.

Each of the ten items on this test represents one component of "reverence behavior," of treating your family with reverence in all that you do. Use the following scale to score yourself on this test:

0	1	2	3	4	5	6	7	8	9	10
ALMOST NEVER		SELDOM		SOMETIMES		A LOT		ALMOST ALWAYS		

1. ——— Does everyone in your family seem to care about being together and sharing experiences as a group rather than as individuals?

2. ——— If asked to rank elements of living, would all of the members of your family list the family as their number one priority?

3. ——— If given the choice, would all family members elect to live together or near one another for life?

4. ——— Does your family enjoy staying home as a group to do just the simple, everyday things together, rather than each family member heading out on his or her own away from the family?

5. ——— Does the pace in your home seem slow,

quiet, and peaceful, with voices quiet and mannerisms gentle and tender?

6. ———— Does everything in the house belong to everyone in the family, with each family member showing respect for family belongings?

7. ———— Does everyone in the family take care of the house, pick things up around the house, and try to make the house a clean and comfortable place to live?

8. ———— Are you proud of your family (not just individuals in the family), and do you tell others how proud you are of the whole family, rather than complain about family conflicts?

9. ———— Does the whole family laugh together loudly and often?

10. ———— Do all members of the family share a common belief system regarding the purpose of life and translate this belief to behaviors, such as volunteer work, helping less fortunate people, and adhering to whatever religious traditions have evolved within the family?

———— TOTAL FAMILY REVERENCE SCORE

If you scored over 90, the arbitrary cutoff point on this test, your family is high on the eighth Rx of family life, reverence for the family system. If you, or someone in your family, or your family when its scores were averaged, scored less than 90 points, you should look at the items where points were lost on this test. Too many families surrender their reverence, feeling that "once it is gone, it's gone for good" or saying that "we never had it anyway" or that "reverence can't really last in this society."

Family reverence, like all of the ten family Rx's, is a skill. Family reverence is not earned; it is the active choice to assign the highest respect and priority to family life. This chapter will describe the many aspects of reclaiming or establishing the reverence factor in your own family.

REDIRECTING OUR FAMILY REVERENCE

You have learned that the family is where our energy, our life force and life resonance, begins. You have learned that the family "happens" at the juncture of the waves of energy emanating from each family member. If you will sit down quietly with your family, spend some time just "being" together, you will feel that merging of energy ripples, and it will be a sobering life experience. You will feel that "being" together physically, emotionally, and spiritually.

The sacredness of family unity requires that we take the time to direct our full attention away from television screens and blaring stereo players to the energy that holds the family together. It is the awareness and development of this sobering experience of energy merging and evolving, even through crisis, that is the major step toward family reverence.

Family reverence requires the daily intentional effort to attend to the family energy system, to hold that system in the highest esteem, and to defer to its prominence in our life whenever possible. Our society spends much time telling us all just how bad families can be. There is little more than token discussion of the sacred, the tender, or the concept of treating life experiences with a sense of awe and deep spiritual awareness. Yet when we show our respect for our family, we defer to a universal spirit that bonds all humans together forever.

Church is not someplace you go. The family is where church and our beliefs about the meaning of life are translated to daily living, and we must not be afraid of being accused of uttering platitudes or being "corny" when we talk of the celebration of the spirit of the family rather than the failures of family life.

"I took my two sons to a football game the other day," said Mr. Anders. "They really needed to just have some time away as brothers with their dad. Their sister's illness was just becoming a total focus. When we got to the game, a touchdown had been scored, and all of the cheerleaders were on their knees moving up and down as if to worship their football team. For some reason, I guess because of all this problem with our daughter, it seemed kind of ridiculous. Worshiping a football team just was so removed from what I was feeling with my two sons and what I was feeling as we all dealt with our daughter's illness. Now these feelings are worth worshiping."

Mr. Anders's statement indicates the underlying simplicity of the concept of family worship, of reverence for family. He made time to solidify a part of his family, to attend to one of the links in the family system, and when he felt that special closeness with his sons, the intensity of dozens of cheerleaders worshiping a touchdown seemed a mock worship, paling in comparison to the meaning of his family in his own life.

In my clinical work with families, I have heard all of the arguments against family reverence. "It sounds corny," "There's no time for it," "I have to work," "I have to study," "Teenagers don't care about families anymore," "I have two jobs," "The family takes care of itself," "My wife and I both work," and the most common statement of all, "We're not that religious," are some of the ways some families attempt to explain away their failure to pay attention to themselves and to their importance to one another.

If you choose to view your family as our hurried and demanding society would have you view it, then reverence is indeed much too time-consuming and distracting from more important issues, such as working, television watching, shopping, and self-development programs. If you choose to attempt to employ the ten family Rx's in your own family life and to elect the family view of living, reverence will become the way in which all of the family Rx's come together into a way of living more easily, more peacefully, and more lovingly every day.

THREE PATHS TO FAMILY REVERENCE

Norman Cousins writes, "Human beings have been able to comprehend everything in the world except their uniqueness. Perhaps it is just as well. If ever we begin to contemplate our own composite wonder, we will lose ourselves in celebration and have time for nothing else."[1] When members in a family take the time and make the effort to comprehend what they have created and experienced together, they bring the joy of reverence for humanness to every day of their lives.

There are three specific things you can do to begin to return a sense of the sacred to your daily living, three paths to take to the experience of family reverence. You must take control of your own sense of time, space, and self.

Path Number One to Family Reverence: Family Savings Time

> "If our time together isn't sacred, then what is? The ultimate loss is the loss of our time together, and we all must struggle to protect it."
> MS. ANDERS

The first path for learning to revere our uniqueness is to understand that time isn't flying, we are. Every day of our life, every moment, is less a part of our life than the moment before. Have you ever felt that time seems to be going faster and faster, and that your life seems to be passing by quicker than it did when you were younger? This fleeting-time feeling is our conscious reaction to the fact that the first year of our life is one hundred percent of our life, but our fiftieth year is only two percent of our lifetime. Each year that goes by represents an increase in the percent of our life that is gone and a decrease in the percent of lifetime we have left, and it is that acceleration that we truly experience.

The only way to take more control of the metronome of personal and family life experience is, as I have asked you to do in other chapters, to take the time to sit down, pray or meditate, and just "be" with your family. Time only goes as fast as you do, so slow down together and go on "family savings time," and try to maximize family moments as they are before they go right past you. Just "being" aware of the reverence factor of families, and taking some time to think about that

---

factor are key steps toward more reverence of the family. You don't always have to "do" something to "feel something."

"When you told us to sit down and just 'be' together for a while, I thought we could never do it," said Ms. Johnson, the mother struggling to merge two stepfamilies into one new family. "Can you imagine a whole new family, two families trying to be one, trying to sit down and be quiet? It seemed embarrassing, awkward, and time-wasting. We were too used to 'doing' to just 'be.' I just couldn't get everyone together, so we started by twos. Then we combined two people being together quietly with two more and made a group of four. We finally got all together and decided that time was making us and we weren't making time. It really works to get you feeling closer, but you just have to make the time."

Ms. Johnson is describing the difficulty most families have with trying to go on family savings time. Even if you keep failing at this exercise of family time control, try having each member of the family pause once a day at a given time to think about the family for just one minute. Even if you are not all together as a group, you will feel the family unity at what one of the families called the "daily pause for the family cause."

Path Number Two to Family Reverence: Finding Space for the Family

> "Now that Gramps is so sick, we have to stay home more. And you know what? It made us realize that we were hardly ever home together before."
> MS. MULLER,
> SPEAKING ABOUT HER FAMILY'S
> ADJUSTMENT TO THEIR
> DYING GRANDPARENT

To the baby, looking at the mobile rotating over her crib, the whole world stops at the little characters rotating round and round above her. The rocking chair in her room is in another dimension beyond her life. When she is an adult, she may travel to Europe and see the world, but she has not yet become aware of the meaning of the distance of a light-year or a parsec.

Staying home and doing nothing together is as important

as constant motion, going, and "doing." Two key words for family reverence, then, are "slow" and "stay." I use the term "family innings" to replace the concept of "family outings," suggesting that the families I work with learn to spend as much time together in their own space, in their own home as a group, as they do as a group going out, or as individuals spinning in such separate orbits that the family seems to be a satellite rather than an Earth base.

Path Number Three to Family Reverence: The Self as a Cell

> "It struck me at the airport, when I looked at all the lonely people there. No one was smiling except the people who were greeting someone coming home. It sounds funny, but there was no 'us' at the airport, only a bunch of 'selfs' on the move.
> MR. STEINER,
> DESCRIBING A TRIP TO THE AIRPORT
> TO PICK UP ONE OF HIS SONS FOR
> THE HOLIDAYS

Philosopher Teilhard de Chardin, in his book *The Phenomenon of Man,* suggested that there is a "thinking layer" around the Earth, what some writers call a noosphere, or layer of consciousness, created by our collective thinking and appraisal of the world. All of our own individual thoughts contribute to that layer, just as our tears are eventually found within the clouds and the chemicals in our hair sprays float up to help destroy the ozone layer around us. Thoughts can contribute to a healthier atmosphere or help pollute that atmosphere, and each thought is a choice we make regarding what we are doing to our family and our world. Each thought sprays the atmosphere with joy or junk.

Learning that we control our experience of time and space by how and what we choose to think requires that we understand that "self" really means a profound awareness of "us," of family, a reverence for our collective magnificence as spiritual beings. The third path to family reverence is understanding, as I have emphasized throughout this book, that "we are us," and acting and speaking every day as if that premise was the single priority that guided our every act.

I ask family members to carry pictures of the whole family with them at all times. I ask them to be sure these pictures are easy to view and not tucked away in the back of a wallet or purse. I ask family members to take time, when they sit alone in an airport or during a business meeting, to take out their family picture and try to feel their family with them. We seem to have many more pictures of babies, children, and couples than we do of entire families, so you may have to take some new pictures. Good luck in getting the whole family together for a photography session!

THE MAGIC WORDS OF FAMILY LIFE

Listen to the language we use when we describe the family, and you will hear the basic reverence, the equating of family with living, that characterizes each one of us. We speak of the family tree, as if that tree were in the center of a confusing forest of life experiences. We speak of our family roots, as if we were nurtured and held in place by the family itself. We speak of the family constellation, as if the family were at the same time within us, nurturing us, and all around us, protecting us and giving us stars to reach for and to guide us. We speak of "home base," the family hearth, and the family circle as places of safety, security, refuge, and sanctuary. There is something within us that knows the reverence of family, that knows that there is no place like home.

"Just watch sometime," said Mr. Anders. "Watch a family together, and you will see what I mean. There is something religious about the whole thing. There is something holding a family together, and you feel awe when you see it. We have that sense in our family, but we come close sometimes to letting our society steal all of our best words for sacred things. We start to feel silly or corny even talking about the word 'sacred.' It was awkward talking with you about it at first."

Mr. Anders is confronting one of our major developmental problems today. We may experience reverence and awe, but we shy away from talking about these experiences openly and freely. We are embarrassed by our own grandeur, and shy about our own glorious nature as beings who can merge, share, and be a part of one another's consciousness. Our society has almost succeeded in making our sense of the sacred suspect, viewing it as a symptom of confusion or temporary dizziness or delusion. We seem to want our people bent over, not in obeisance to the grandeur of family, but because our noses are to the grindstone and our shoulders to the wheel. In such a posture, no one else can join you and you will never know where you are going.

A father in one of the families I was treating felt awkward when his family began to talk of time, space, and the family system in spiritual terms. When his wife spoke of her strong feelings for the family tree and her own roots, he attempted to joke away his discomfort. "Well," he said. "If we have a family tree, then your mother is our Dutch elm disease." He laughed loudly, but stopped when he saw that no one else was joining in his laughter. He really did not need to feel so awkward about the natural sense of reverence that will emerge in families when they allow themselves a more sacred language.

The father who initially mocked the concept of family worship and reverence was moved by his participation in the three family reverence paths I have outlined here. After months of being with his family more, of doing things with his family at home in a gentle and quiet manner, and of spending time just looking at the new family picture his family had taken, he stated, "You know what? Maybe our gross national product is just too gross. Maybe we had better learn to look at our gross national process and how and why we are doing what we are doing."

MAKING THE SACRED SILLY: DE-SACRADIZING DAILY LIFE

Mr. Anders said, "I would be embarrassed to talk about this sacredness I feel with anyone but my family or maybe my minister. I think it makes me sound strange, maybe even drunk, or like a member of some cult."

Mr. Anders is describing the same type of psychological defense used by the man who joked about his mother-in-law's impact on his family tree. We use a de-sacradizing defense to avoid the intensity of our direct confrontation with our own divinity. We turn away from the brilliance of the human experience, perhaps because we are aware, on some level, that if we ever really paid attention to all that we can be, we would indeed do as Norman Cousins suggested, and spend all of our time in joy and celebrations.

De-sacradizing is our defense, our attempt to escape from our potential to wonder at almost every moment of our own living. We seem to need to hide from our greatness and perfection through working, loving, playing, and traveling as hard as we can, constantly trying to "spend" our family time as if it were won in a lottery, rather than given to us as a precious eternal gift to be guarded and saved.

We are running away from the single most intense human psychological and physical experience we can ever have; the sense of reverence for "us." We may find that sense of awe sporadically, in religious services and at weddings and funerals, but we seem afraid to think that we can in fact be reverent every day of our lives. Dare we think that miracles are simple, common, and right there around us at the family dinner table, or a phone call away from contacting a family member who lives far away? Can we take a risk to rediscover the miracle of "us"?

The family offers the opportunity to overcome our de-sacradization, to learn to revere life every day. The intense spiritual energy emanating from the family system is strong enough to draw us back to the reverence experience, but we first have to listen for it, look for it, and sense for it.

If you stop right now, as you read this chapter, and think about your own family, or try the three paths of intentionally restricting your activities to allow contemplation, prayer, or meditation about your family and your true sense of "us," or take time to think about what you have shared with your family, even when times have been difficult, and to think about who and where your family is, you may sense just a little spark of the family reverence factor. Don't worry about losing control. Your schedule and "more important things" will no doubt distract you back to the non-sacred everyday obligations that crowd out this special sacred sense. But for just a moment, you will have had a brush with family sacredness.

Even in our work, we seldom talk of the sacred. We do not emphasize the real purpose of our work, to help others and share our skills. We too often think of "getting the job done" and meeting deadlines. "I once got carried away," said one of my patients. "I started talking about this clay model of the car I made with my staff in the engineering department at work. I don't know what happened, but I started talking about making something of nothing, about making an idea touchable, about how the car we were creating was coming from a combination of all of us as a family, about the car not really being there and the car existing within us and being conveyed to others who would mold the illusion for others to drive. I said we were dream makers. I was gone, man. Then I looked around and blushed because everyone was laughing at me. I quickly joked that the pressure had gotten to me, and I laughed with them."

Try it yourself. The next time you are at work, talk seriously about the underlying sacredness of what you do. Talk in a voice of reverence and deep respect. Does what you do facilitate idea sharing, promote the well-being of others, improve the life of someone in some small way? How does your job fit the overall scheme of the world? Even the question may sound strange to you or to those you work with, and if you talk like this with your fellow workers, you will see how awkward they begin to feel. Many of them will have "de-sacradized" their work. If you change to talking about wages, unions, complaints about management or about other employees and policies, everyone will fall right in line with you.

De-sacradization is one of the most common psychological defenses in our society today, and reverence is the only hope of rescuing our sense and experience of the sacred within our families. Reverence for all of living begins in the home.

THE NUMBER ONE CAUSE OF THE MOST SERIOUS DISEASE OF OUR TIME

A classic study of the relationship between the family system and proneness to disease was conducted by Dr. Caroline Thomas at The Johns Hopkins University Medical School.[2] Dr. Thomas followed thirteen hundred Johns Hopkins Medical School students for several years, gathering information about the family history of each student and administering a complete battery of psychological and physiological tests to each student. Her findings illustrate what I have found to be the number one cause of the most serious disease of our time: family alienation as a major cause of depression.

Depression is at the core of almost every disease process. We are not able to document that depression causes a specific disease, and many factors go in to making us sick and making us well. Depression, however, clearly impacts upon our immune and healing systems, affects our loving, working, playing, thinking, and every aspect of our daily living. If you are depressed as you read this sentence, you will sense that depression within yourself even as you read, think, and relate to what I am writing. Depression seems to have a life of its own that takes its energy from your own living, and the genesis of depression is in our lack of sacredness in our family experience.

Family alienation is a sense of isolation from the family, a falling or jumping from the family nest. Remember, your family is as much a feeling as it is a group of people, a sense within you of being connected to others, no matter how much strife your family may have experienced. Even if your own family has been afflicted by alcoholism, abuse, or other factors that have torn at the family fabric, there is something within it, some feeling for being an "us," connected with others, that came from your family, however hurt that family was. It is that sense

2. Thomas, Caroline, and D. Duszynski. "Closeness to Parents and the Family Constellation in a Prospective Study of Five Disease States: Suicide, Mental Illness, Malignant Tumor, Hypertension, and Coronary Heart Disease," *The Johns Hopkins Medical Journal* (1973), Vol. 134.

of "us" you must hang on to, even as you turn away from some of the pain of family struggles.

Sometimes, the alienation takes the form of a sense of being thrown from the nest, or even the sense that there was never a sturdy nest there in the first place. In Dr. Thomas' study, family alienation was measured objectively on psychological tests and questionnaires. Many students revealed that they felt distant from their families and that they sensed distance between some or all of their family members. These students stood the most chance of developing serious illness.

Every beginning psychology student knows that depression relates to the turning inward of our own anger. I suggest that the most frequent source of the anger that gets turned inward is anger at ourselves for not climbing back into the family nest. We may resent our parents or our siblings, but my clinical work indicates that when we blame them, we are really blaming and punishing ourselves for not maintaining a sense of "us" and not having sufficient toleration, understanding and forgiveness to benefit from a sense of family, even if our own family was one of much conflict. We all know, on some level, that our family is sacred and basic to our physical, psychological, and spiritual health; and no matter the degree of family strife, we forever blame ourselves when we emotionally leave the nest and sever (or try to sever) our ties to our family system.

You can't fool with Mother Nature, and you can't fool with the sacredness of the family. The energy of the family system is just too strong. It has a hold on you right this moment. No matter how many times you may say things such as "I have severed all ties with my family" or "My father is not my father any more," you are only fooling yourself and issuing orders to your immune system that something sick is going on and you don't care. If you don't care, then your immune system won't care either. Your immune system will cease to work as a family of protective cells.

Remember, your immune system is literal. It takes you seriously, no matter what you say and how wrong you may be. If you say you are out of your family, your immune system hears you saying that you are withdrawing from living, that you are not a "part" anymore, and that you don't need defending. Your defenses against disease lower, and, over time, serious illness can result.

When you emotionally pull away from your own internal sense of your family, when you give up the struggle to overcome emotional rejection by a family member, you pull the plug on the energy source that powers your physical and emotional health. Immune energy is ultimately family energy, and belonging and loving are the bonds that help the immune cells mass together for your defense.

Dr. Thomas found that those students who had scored low on tests of closeness to parents and to the family in general were those students who were more prone to develop cancer. The "familial alienation factor" was exactly the same factor that, in her study, predicted suicide. It appears that persons who feel a break with their family system, and sense a break between their own parents within that system, become depression-prone, even suicide-prone, because they are not at peace with their internal sense of family. Such persons are vulnerable to cancer and other diseases that are cooked up over a faulty family hearth.

In Dr. Thomas' study, more students who developed cancer reported negative family associations than did any other group in her study. Since Dr. Thomas' work, other researchers have confirmed the relationship between chronic depression, disease, and family alienation.[3] If, as I discussed in Chapter Eight, the family is the ultimate source of our life energy, then it is also the possible origin of the basis of the depression that dominates our time. The energy leeching and spiritual seepage that I described earlier are correctable only if we can learn to "re-sacradize" our family life by allowing our sense of family to grow within us, in spite of the pain we may have experienced in our daily family living.

We need a model of the healthy family member, a family system that is basically healthy and sacred, not problematic and secular. We need a model of the family member who flies from the nest, returning to give and take with all other family members, even as his or her own flight becomes higher, wider,

3. LeShan, L. "Psychological States as Factors in the Development of Malignant Disease: A Critical Review," *Journal of the National Cancer Institute* (1959) Vol. 22, pp. 1–18.

and stronger. We know only too well what the pain of families gone wrong can do, but we also must have a vision of what can go very right in the family process.

WHAT DOES A VERY HEALTHY FAMILY MEMBER REALLY LOOK LIKE?

Our model for family health, the image worthy of our sense of awe for the power of the family, must be clear, before we are able to experience a legitimate sense of family reverence and sacredness. What are the characteristics of the family member who shows the good that family life can do?

The five families you have gotten to know in this book contained family members whom I called "us" actualizers. The famous psychologist Abraham Maslow wrote about "self-actualizers" who were able to have their own "peak experiences" of intense individual awareness of the meaning and purpose of life.[4] I suggest that strong families produce members with a profound sense of "us," who have the ability to volitionally function in a state of "plateau experience," a prolonged sense of serenity and peacefulness with others in everyday life.

When we work hard to get "high," we will find ourselves more often than not busy with the processes of either going up or coming down from temporary highs, busy with attempts to maintain and protect our "high," or with the inevitable dissatisfaction of never getting high enough. Much of the depression and drug abuse in our society is related to the pursuit of the illusion of being high and to a conditioned disappointment with reality that results when we fail to learn and practice the reverence of the plateau experience, the celebration of the ordinary and the everyday.

4. Later in his work, Abraham Maslow did recognize the "plateau experience," likening it to the mother who sits and gazes for a long period of time into the face of her baby, feeling awe and peacefulness simultaneously. Most psychologists, however, focused on Maslow's "self" actualizers and "peak" experiences. See Abraham Maslow, *Religions, Values, and Peak Experiences* (New York: Penguin Books, 1976).

We need a model of daily elation to replace our attempt to "treat" what is becoming a chronic societal depressive state. We need to develop our "us-ness," and the joy of being and doing together. We will be trapped by inevitable depression if we see human development as the individual struggle to be higher and higher and to eventually "peak." If we indeed have a peak experience, there is no place to go but down when we are at the "peak." Like the tightrope walker who attempts more and more dangerous tricks, we only succeed at setting ourselves up for the inevitable fall. When we learn to walk on the ground and enjoy the stroll with our family, depression vanishes. It's wonderful to be ordinary, just so long as you have a family to be ordinary with, to share with as a part of the order of the cosmos.

THE ARTIFICIAL "SACRADIZING" DRUGS

When drugs are used to treat depression, the idea behind such drugs relates to the attempt to replace the emotional state of surrender with its perfect counterpart, reverence. In effect, psychiatrists who prescribe antidepressants are attempting to induce a pseudoreverie to take the place of depression.

There is no question that some types of depression are biochemically based.[5] Antidepressant drugs work by altering neurotransmitter patterns in the human brain. Serotonin and norepinephrine are two neurotransmitters found, among other places, in the limbic system of the human brain. This is the part of our brain that governs our emotions. When serotonin and norepinephrine are at normal or healthy levels, we can experience elation in daily living. When serotonin and norepinephrine are at high normal levels, we can experience reverie, the emotional component of reverence. Antidepressant drugs work by allowing serotonin and norepinephrine to remain at normal or high levels.

The limbic system is a cap (*limbus* comes from the word

5. Snyder, S. H. *Biological Aspects of Mental Disorder* (New York: Oxford University Press, 1980).

cap in Latin) over our primary mammalian brain.[6] The mammalian brain is where the roots of our sense of "us" is, where our sense of our archetypical universal family is stored. I suggest that we become depressed when the "cap" on our sense of family falls out of balance, blocking our vision and sense of family.

The top third of our brain, the neomammalian brain or cortex, only thinks about the business of living day-to-day. The lower two thirds, the reptilian part of our ancestry and the limbic system that gives emotional significance to our sense of that ancestry, must work in balanced tandem for us to maintain our sense of "us" and reverence for our collective existence.

By using drugs such as MAO inhibitors (monoamine oxidase inhibitors), which block an enzyme which destroys serotonin and epinephrine, or by prescribing the tricyclics, a class of drugs that prevent the inactivation of serotonin and epinephrine at the synapse or gap between the limbic cells, psychiatrists are actually keeping our channels open for reverence of our human existence. They are, in effect, using artificial drugs to allow our instinctual drive for family to remain intact, to allow our ancestry to connect with our emotions, so that we can function daily in consideration of who we are and not just what we have to do.

Antidepressant drugs, then, are really drug "sacradizers," artificial and short-lived chemical boosts of our innate ability to enjoy the natural mellowness of our connection with everything, with the infinite family experience. We can write our own prescription for this mellowness. We can keep our own primal neural connections with our sense of family intact, by telling our brain to think differently about life, by appraising life from the point of view of "us" rather than "me," by emphasizing the not-so-little things that happen, rather than by seeking out the big experiences that are always just some distance ahead of us. We can write our own natural prescription for the neurobiological family response.

In my more than twenty years of working with depressed

6. For a detailed description of the three levels of the human brain and the relationship of these levels to our experience of our world, see P. Maclean, "The Triune Brain," *American Scientist* (1978) Vol. 66, pp. 101–33.

patients, I have come to learn that, no matter the cause, some-where the depressed person is experiencing a disruption of their natural family reflex, their internal sense of family and "us." Depression seems to be a form of internally experienced discon-nection. As I suggested earlier, pulling away from the herd by showing depression may be a way of getting the attention of the herd, the family. Some of us may run far ahead of the herd, neglecting our family by being too busy, too fast for them. Others fall far behind, hoping the family will see them back there and come back to get them. If we conceive of emotional problems in the metaphor of a disrupted reflex for family, for "us," we begin to understand just how central to our health our internal sense of family truly is.

HOW TO BE A BETTER FAMILY MEMBER

Here are twelve characteristics of the very healthy family mem-ber, the family member who has learned to write their own prescription for the natural family drugs within our own prewired neural family template and to help their own family be a happier and healthier place to live. You will see in each characteristic the strong influence of energy from the family constellation.

I have included the actual reports of members of the five families, so that you will be able to see how they exemplify "us" actualization in place of "self-actualization," how they show reverence for the family system in ordinary daily life. You can use each of the following characteristics of the healthy family member as steps to helping your own family stay healthy and to showing your own reverence for your family.

BEING AN ACCEPTOR: "TAKING IT" FOR THE FAMILY

"My husband is remarkable," said Ms. Muller. "Even when Gramps is a mess and just gets out of control, my husband accepts it. I know it sounds impossible, but it's as if he absorbs the problems we have, dissolves them, and then goes on. He's a rare person. He is almost never in conflict over anything that happens in our house. I know it sounds like that must mean he doesn't care, but really, he seems to care so much that he will accept what happens as part of loving us so much. He tries to send out positive energy all the time."

Ms. Muller cried as she talked about her husband. She was being almost overwhelmed at this time in her life by the serious illness of her father, and her husband was providing the center, the comfort, the energy and steadiness she so badly needed. She kept telling me how unbelievable her description must sound, as if her husband were too good to be true. I told her that I knew of many family members who were extraordinary "us" actualizers, rare family participants who have such a profound sense of family that they can accept the crises that are inevitable in close families, without aggravating or escalating these problems. One of the greatest gifts you can give to your own family is to show the discipline and continued effort to take some of the "stress blows" for the family without exacerbating and adding to that stress yourself.

"Family acceptors" seem to be able to serve as family buffers. They absorb the negative family energy, purify it in some way, and give new energy back to the family. Their steadiness in the line of family fire is central to the families' survival. At a time when so much is written about the problem family member, the acceptor stands out as one of the most important features of the super family.

When I interviewed Mr. Muller, it was easy to see the "acceptor" within his character. "I don't know," he said. "I made a decision a long time ago to be more like my own dad. He had a temper and he was no saint, but he could go with the flow. He never really exploded at key times. In fact, my dad would get madder about a football game on television than he ever could get about anything that happened in the family. I modeled myself after him. I learned that the key question to ask when things are really rough is a very simple question. I always ask myself, 'So what?' Now, I don't mean that nothing matters to me. I really mean that everything matters, even the bad things. I just mean that, when everything is going to hell, you have to try then to see that everything happens for a reason. When Gramps craps all over the couch after we all tried to get him to go to the bathroom for an hour or more, it would be easy to go nuts. But you have to ask, 'So what? What does it really matter in the long run of things?' And when you think in that perspective, some funny answers occur to you. I got answers like these. 'Well, Gramps is going to die soon, and I'll bet after a while we would have traded crap on the couch for Grandpa still being here.' You just have to keep your perspective by talking to yourself when you're upset, keeping the question about 'So what?' in your mind."

Mr. Muller describes the central component of the family acceptors. They are the "perspective keepers." They can keep their heads when everyone around them is trying to cut off someone else's head and, in the process, losing their own. They keep their perspective through effort, not some divine gift. They have a sense of reverence for family life that they refuse to allow to be diminished by the hassles that impact on all of us.

The acceptor is aware of their role in the family and he or she actively pursues that role. Acceptors seem to know and sense that someone must be accepting, absorbing the negative energy so that this energy will not spill all over the family. This analogy was mentioned by Ms. Muller about her husband.

"I call him Scotty sometimes. That's not his name, but he's like that character in 'Star Trek' who could always provide more energy for the *Starship Enterprise*. When Captain Kirk called for 'Warp speed three,' good old Scotty could always find more energy somewhere to get the ship out of trouble." You can see the energy metaphor that repeats itself in the super families, as well as the wit and humor that seems everpresent, even at the most unlikely times.

"I never knew that, Mom," said the Muller daughter. "I thought you called him Scotty because he was like a Scott brand paper towel. You know, like he can absorb all spills." The whole family laughed at the daughter's statement, and it was a laugh of acknowledgment that this wonderful man was a true "us" actualizer.

"OK, Mom," continued the Muller daughter, "I see what you mean about 'Star Trek.' From now on, when we are fighting or something, I'm just going to look at Dad and say, 'Beam us up, Scotty.' "

SHOWING AUTONOMY:
PULLING MORE THAN YOUR OWN WEIGHT

Although it may seem a contradiction at first glance, the "us" actualizer shows autonomy within the family system. He or she is responsible for their behavior, feelings, and daily living, and places very few demands on other family members. Balanced with the autonomy, however, is the capacity to be vulnerable and to turn to family members for help and support at times of change and challenge.

"My youngest son really amazes me sometimes," said Mr. Anders. "Ever since he started school, he just takes care of everything himself. He gets up on time, heads for school, does his homework, and asks for help when he needs it, and even takes a shower and goes to bed on his own. I can't remember telling him about taking care of himself. He's a rare kid."

Mr. Anders's son shows the individual responsibility for everyday living that characterizes the autonomous familial member. In contrast, some family members require regular care, prompting, and reminding. As I described earlier, they become energy leeches for their families, who must monitor even their most simple daily activities.

"Now you take my nephew," continued Mr. Anders. "If you didn't tell him to flush the toilet, he never would. You have to tell him when he stays with us to do the most basic things. He has what we call the 'C-I-G-I' syndrome, the 'Can I get it?' approach to life. He wants something all the time. We have to tell him to go to bed, and we repeat it a thousand times. He needs support all of the time. He's always upset or almost upset. We're all dead tired by the time he leaves, and we even start talking to each other like we talk to him. It takes us days to get back to normal."

Ask yourself if you are an autonomous family member. How much of your family's energy do you drain through your own needs and inability or unwillingness to take responsibility for your own life? Even if you no longer live with your primary family, how much of your family's energy do you take by your own failure to take control of your life?

One mother said to me, "I think my son thinks I have

superhuman powers of finding things he loses, picking up things he drops, and sending his clothes to the right drawers in his room by some form of clothes psychopower. He is more of a puppet I have to direct than a person sharing life with us. It really takes my energy away." If you compare this mother's statement with Mr. Anders's description of his son, you can see that the autonomous "us" actualizer is a special and valued contributor to the family energy bank.

BEING A SPONTANEOUS FAMILY MEMBER: LETTING IT ALL OUT FOR YOUR FAMILY

Another significant characteristic of the "us" actualizer is his or her spontaneity, the ability to immediately express positive affect. Spontaneity in family living refers to the complete absence of manipulation, dishonest emotional expression, or holding back of feelings to punish, make a point, or get the attention of family members. When you read about the energy leech, you saw the opposite of this directness, the containment and manipulation of feelings for purposes other than for sharing and enhancing the family ecology.

"Boy, you can really tell how she feels," said Mr. Muller. "My daughter is an open book. Her feelings are always honestly expressed. She smiles when she is happy and she frowns when she is sad. Now that may sound obvious and that everyone does it, but I can tell you that you just can't read some people. Smiles hide resentment and frowns are signals that somebody wants attention or is trying to get you to ask or do something. With my daughter, you sense that what you see is what you get. She's just real, as corny as that may sound."

Family members who are manipulative, hold their feelings within them, or are afraid, unwilling, or unable to be spontaneous in the expression of feelings, leave the family in a state of suspension. Family members are uncertain, never knowing exactly how the feelings are flowing in the system. Left only to guess, the family guesses wrong as often as they guess correctly. Feelings are hurt or misunderstood, and conflicts result.

Being spontaneous with feelings and thoughts is not being irresponsible and explosive. "Letting it all hang out" can become a process through which a family member "uses" his or her family to scatter emotional debris, not caring who gets hit or what happens in the aftermath. Being spontaneous means being "real" and immediate with all thoughts and emotions, and avoiding the saving up of feelings for later explosion.

"You could tell when we were in for trouble," said one mother. "You just knew that when Ginny started acting a certain way that she wasn't being herself. She went into what I call her neutron bomb state. She would be on the verge of destroying all the people around her, leaving only the furniture and the house. You knew something was going on, and you had to start playing the emotional guessing game. Would saying this upset her? Would saying that upset her? You just never knew. It was like a teapot on the burner whistling away, and you are too afraid to go and take it off the stove."

This child was constricted in her emotional expression, for some reason turning in to self rather than out to family at the most crucial emotional times. In your own family life, it is important that you work toward an awareness of what you are feeling and thinking and try to say it, share it, and listen, watch, and help with the vulnerable reactions of your family.

Spontaneity in family life is a major life luxury. At work, at school, and with strangers, complete emotional and communicational spontaneity is risky. In such situations, you are not protected by guaranteed unconditional love. The family is where you may, indeed must, be all that you can be as immediately as you are able to be. Families have a more difficult time firing their members than most businesses, so it is safer to take your developmental risks in the home.

APPRECIATING THE SIMPLE BEAUTY OF THE FAMILY: HOW TO BE "AWE-FULL"

There is something about our humanness that requires beauty and order. We may corrupt our environment, pave our forests, and pollute our air during the week, but after we have wreaked this environmental havoc for five days, we often long to head for the mountains, the woods, and the water for a quiet, clean, and beautifully natural place to rest.

The increasing pace of life in Japan, with all of its crowding and competition, has resulted in the spread of "oxygen stores" where busy Japanese executives go to breathe clean air on a break from work. There are now "executive fishing ponds" in the middle of Tokyo, small tubs of water surrounded by dozens of Japanese businessmen and -women fishing for twenty minutes at lunch. There are "rent a scene" stores where executives go to sit in a chair and listen to sounds of birds and animals, while looking at pictures of trees and mountains. These fast "soul food" approaches reveal our attempt to avoid confronting just how far we have gone from the natural beauty of our existence. The healthy family member is able to bring an appreciation of life's beauty back to family living.

Perhaps if we made vacations illegal and closed all of our luxurious resorts, we would have to do something about where and how we live day-to-day. Perhaps if all of us, instead of just some of us, had to stay in the mess we are making without retreating to what is left that is still beautiful and natural, we would treat our world more like our home.

The "us" actualizer finds the beauty of family life in the simple things; through shared responsibility for the maintenance of the home, respect for the property of other family members, and an effort to enhance the ecology of the family whenever and wherever possible.

"My son will straighten the books on the shelf when he walks by," said Ms. Bonner. "Some mothers can not believe that he would do a simple thing like that. He seems to care about how the house looks, the image of himself that we see. He even cleaned the garage one day while I was shopping. Can you imagine a fifteen-year-old boy cleaning the garage because it just looked like it needed it? He straightens up the family room before he goes to bed at night, and I have seen him stand at the door and just check to see if things look right before he turns in. He bought a small shrub at the nursery last week because he thought we needed one by the front door. His own money, and he buys a shrub! Now this is a son."

When I had one of my students listen to the tape of Ms. Bonner's report, she could not believe it. She said that the report sounded too idealistic, in her words, "just too good to be true." I told this student that this was why I was collecting this material on members of families who were extraordinarily healthy and good for the health of their own families. Like the self-actualized person of Abraham Maslow, "us" actualizers are rare. They are so rare because too few of us take the risk and make the effort to be all that we can be for ourselves and for our family.

I assure you that "us" actualizers exist. They are persons who see the potential beauty and order in family life and in the world, and who attempt to facilitate such beauty wherever and whenever they can. They are keenly aware of what their presence in this world does to this world.

There is a danger to the aesthetic nature of the "us" actualizer. Such people are so rare that they may come to feel alone, unusual, or alienated from those around them and from the society in general. "Us" actualizers are vulnerable, for they care so much about others, about the family, that they are easily hurt by conflicts that their more hardened and less sensitive counterparts may not be aware of at all.

It is all too easy to corrupt and damage the aesthetic sensitivity of the "us" actualizer when we yell and scream, clutter our homes, and rush through family life without rhythm, ritual, remembrance, reason, and the gentle resilience that can come from a constant awareness of the resonance of the magical energy within us.

"We have to be careful with my son," added Ms. Bonner. "He gets upset so easily. What doesn't bother us can really hurt him. He really got upset when I asked a lawn company to spray our lawn. It never occurred to me that a young kid would care. He said it worried him that we were putting chemicals around our house. He asked me to cancel the call and let him try to weed the lawn by hand. I never thought it was such a big deal to him, but I know now that everything means a lot to him. I have heard of earth mothers, but this kid is an earth child."

Ms. Bonner's son resembles other "us" actualizers who seem forever vigilant for the world, for the environment, for the basic ethics of respect for our emotional and physical environment. These "us" actualizers are the keepers of the family flame, and are sensitive to the ill winds that threaten to snuff out the family energy while most family members do not even feel the breeze; and you too can serve this role for your family. You must make the time and effort to break away from society's expectations of a more mechanical, uncaring approach to living, but anyone can be an "us" actualizer if they are willing to reconsider the basic ways in which they behave in their family everyday.

TRANSCENDING THE HERE AND NOW: FEELING THE FAMILY

"Us" actualizers have tuned so intensely to the family energy system that they can sense the family, and each of its member's feelings, beyond the see-and-touch world. Sometimes without knowing it, these persons practice the three paths to family reverence I mentioned earlier in this chapter; slowing, staying, and sharing. They have finely honed extrafamilial perception, read very well the family holographic image I mentioned earlier, seem aware of the growth template of the family, and go beyond their own narrow self-image to a broader picture of the entire family's welfare.

"The kid is like a historian," said Mr. Steiner of his college-age daughter. "Out of the blue, she will describe something Grandma said, or something we all used to do years ago that we may have forgotten. She is like a psychic. She senses all of us, and she will ask if we are OK well before any of us is aware that we may be on the way to not being OK. She goes beyond herself and into us almost all the time. We find ourselves asking her what's going to happen next. She's the unpaid family astrologer."

Mr. Steiner is describing the transcendency of the "us" actualizer. Such persons have learned on some level that their own self-welfare cannot be separate from the welfare of those around them. They know that their orbit in life falls in juxtaposition with others' orbits, and they sense other people, like a police car's radar detector reacts to invisible sound waves bounced from cars going too fast to be safe.

We all have the capacity to be transcendent, to tune into our holographic image of our family and maintain our internal sense of and for our family throughout our life. We have but to look long enough and intensely enough at each member of our family, and we will see pain before it hurts, healing before the healing crisis, love before it happens, and illness before it strikes.

Our transcendency is our early-warning system and our

early hope system. The true sense of "us" is the language of living, our means of interpreting life's purpose even as life is taking place. The transcendent person is a projected image of the entire family, and if we watch him or her, he or she will tell us where the family is going based on that ability to compare our direction with where we have all been and would like to go. Selfish people lead us only into themselves. "Us" actualizers lead us to "us."

The altruism that underlies transcendence is the reward for the effort to read and help others. Altruism carries with it immediate and measurable positive effects on the human immune system. When we attend to the needs of others and extend ourselves on their behalf, we are following our genetic imperative, our evolutionary destiny to keep the human family alive. When we do so, our immune system seems to know that we are important for the system, important enough to be defended and to be kept alive and well.

Our healing potential is activated when we think and feel in altruistic fashion, perhaps because there is something within us that knows that we are acting on behalf of what really matters. In studies of nonhumans, almost all instances of altruism occur between immediate family members.[7] Altruistic acts assure the survival of those genes that we have in common with others. Anything that keeps the family unit alive, that helps human beings in general to survive and thrive, is in keeping with evolutionary principles of the survival of the fittest. In this case, the fittest is similarity and "us-ness," not some narrow view of millions of individuals competing against one another for survival. Family survival is a survival of the sharing-est.

There is absolutely no value in one person surviving if all other persons are gone or corrupted in the process of their survival. Transcendence is going beyond self, and the "us" actualizer is behaving and feeling in accordance with a sense of the evolutionary directive of keeping as many of us all as possible here, happy, and healthy.

7. Hamilton, W. D. "The Genetical Evolution of Social Behavior," *Journal of Theoretical Biology* (1964) Vol. 7, pp. 1–52.

UNDERREACTING TO FAMILY PROBLEMS: THE ART OF SUBTLE CONTROL

The "us" actualizer approaches family life in a balanced fashion, treating family members with equanimity and fairness. They do not attempt to control others and they do not require firm control and direction from the rest of the family. They model patience and understanding, offering encouragement and guidance to other family members. They do not attempt to direct and coerce their families, and make no claim to being in charge or being the center of family control.

"My dad runs things, but then he doesn't," said the youngest daughter in the Johnson family. "He doesn't act like he's in charge or anything, but he helps us get things done. He organizes us, but he doesn't boss us. When we all cut the lawn Saturday, I saw our neighbor screaming at his kid to watch out for the lawn sprinkler. Sure enough, he hit it with the lawn mower. The father threw a real fit. He said that if anything was going to get done right, he would have to do it. When I hit our sprinkler, my dad asked me what happened, and how it happened. I knew I screwed up, and he had warned me to be careful. I was ready to get my head chewed off. He just said we would try to fix it together next week. I got his point. That meant I would be out there with him fixing it and not going to the beach with my girlfriend. It wasn't like he was grounding me or anything, but I won't hit the sprinkler again."

You may remember that the Johnson father is attempting to reassemble a stepfamily with his second wife. He is modeling the egalitarian approach of the "us" actualizer by underreacting to problems of daily living within the family. His response to his daughter illustrates the egalitarian orientation, the intentional underreaction to family problems and the removal of the problem of struggling for power from the issue of struggling with problems.

"Well," he said, "I did what I could do. I told her about the sprinkler, she saw the boy down the street hit one, and she forgot to pay attention and went right ahead and hit ours. You don't think I wanted to send her to her room for about a decade? It wasn't a test of me or my authority. It's her lawn sprinkler too, you know. I just don't make things an us-them, me-them argument. When you demand something of your family, the only demand you really place is on your own heart and vessels. I have one challenge to my children. I ask them to be like me. I work to be what I want them to be, even when I felt terrible about the inconvenience and the expense of the sprinkler problem. The whole house is much more peaceful when you don't get caught in power struggles. She broke the sprinkler, not me."

"Us" actualizers are able to see even the subtle power problems within families, the constant testing of arbitrary rules and the struggle for independence through rule-bending and limit-stretching. "Kids pull you like a rubber band," said Mr. Johnson. "They don't mean to, but they pull and pull to see if you will break or snap back on them. They are testing the limits, I guess, and you just have to let them know that they will never be able to break the bond of your family. You can't get into a status or control thing. You just can't take problems seriously. You take people seriously. You will never win. When they break a family rule, it is a test of the system, not you."

The egalitarian environment in the healthy family home prevents strain from building to levels where explosions are inevitable. When families talk about things and behaviors instead of personalities and power positions, they focus on what a unified family is doing, not on who is breaking or enforcing what rules made by whom.

A SENSE OF THE WORLD: FITTING YOUR FAMILY WITH ALL FAMILIES

The "us" actualizer conveys a sense of social responsibility to the family. He or she does not teach discrimination or prejudice, modeling instead a nonjudgmental orientation to living. They have learned early and clearly that all discrimination is ultimately discrimination against oneself. Discrimination and prejudice, modeled while driving the family car or discussed in the family setting, even in jest, is an indirect way of teaching the family members that love is conditional and predetermined by narrow definitions of who is worthy of loving. When we talk or act prejudicially, members may come to feel that, at any time, they can fall into one of the categories that is targeted for dislike or exclusion.

"Even at big parties at our house, my parents never get into talking race or religion," said the daughter in the Anders family. "They never put down white people, and I have seen them both walk away when anyone says things that are discriminating against another person. It sounds real strange to me at school when anybody tells jokes about white people. It just isn't the way I was raised. And my parents are really sensitive about comments about hurt people or impaired people. Maybe it's because I'm hurt with my disease, but my parents really care about everybody."

The Anders daughter's comment illustrates the impact of the social consciousness of the "us" actualized family member on all other family members and the way in which healthy family members can extend their own experience of a family problem to more universal questions, or what I have called the "archetypical issues" of sexuality, self-esteem, security, and substance abuse.

The Anders daughter's next statement shows how the universal issues of security and self-esteem can be guarded by the extremely healthy family member. "When someone really hates somebody because of their color, then they could hate you for anything at all. I wouldn't feel safe if I lived with some of my friends' families. They always put down white people or black people or some religion. It gets kind of weird and it can scare you."

"When we would go out for a drive, my dad would never speed, throw paper on the highway, or waste gas," reported the Johnson son. "My mom and dad will pick up other people's trash and throw it away. One time after I had a Coke, I was playing with my straw and I shot it into a bush. My mom just looked at me, and I went and got it and put it in the trash can. They really take this stuff seriously. When I was in the school cafeteria, I didn't even realize it when I picked up after the other kids at lunch. I guess you sort of pick up what your parents do."

The concept of family I have been describing in this book is a broad concept, one that sees the small family as metaphor for the more universal sense of the family of humankind. Social consciousness starts as family consciousness, and the "us" actualizer's grasp of the integration between all families and the shared responsibility of these families for the world condition contributes greatly to a super family system.

THE GLOW OF FAMILY WARMTH: TEACHING YOUR FAMILY TO CELEBRATE

"You just look at my son, and you have to smile," said Ms. Bonner. "He's always happy, and he looks it."

Our society suspects anyone who is too happy for too long. We accept the pathology of the average, the idea that hard-earned happiness comes only after spurts of effort. To carry oneself with a sense of celebration is to provide a portrait of joy for the family to see and experience every day. The "us" actualizer is happy for himself or herself and for the privilege of family membership, and shows this living pride every day.

Try this experiment with your own family, and you will see the immediate impact of what I call "behavioral happiness." Smile almost all day. Say positive things, even if you have to work hard to keep up the act. Pretend that you are being videotaped for a national prime-time television show on super families, and that the whole world will be seeing how you treat your family. Act like you probably do when strangers are around, and watch the immediate positive effect on the energy level of your family.

"Mom just always smiles," said Ms. Bonner's daughter. "Everybody teases her about it, but she has smile pits at each side of her mouth because she has smiled so long that she has dented her face in there."

Ms. Bonner responded, "Sure I have what the kids call these smile pits. Sometimes I have to force myself to smile, to laugh, to show my happiness. It's easy to get lazy and drop your face. When my husband was killed, I wasn't smiling. But everyone said how strong I was. I noticed a long time ago that how I act, how people act around people who really don't matter as much as their own family, is usually better, and takes more effort, than how they act with their family. When visitors came, I used to talk nicely and politely. When they would leave, I would turn into a drill sergeant, ordering the family troops into clean-up detail. All the charm left with the last guest. When I started trying to find the same humor in our private life that I could always find with visitors, things really lightened up in the house."

As I pointed out earlier, one comes to feel as one behaves. The "us" actualizer consciously attempts to find humor in the everyday, to laugh with his or her family at the silliness of much of what happens in our life. One family I have worked with had the joke-of-the-day requirement in effect just before dinner. Every family member had to tell a joke, requiring, in this four-person family, twenty-eight new jokes a week. This sent the family members scurrying to books and tapes and television to find their joke of the day.

"I ran out," said Ms. Anders. "I couldn't think of another joke, and I had forgotten to look for one. So I bluffed it. I asked the family, 'What can you sit on and brush your teeth with?' My son said in disgust, 'Oh, Mom, I heard that in kindergarten. A chair and a toothbrush. That doesn't count as a real joke.' The family laughed, though, and now I have the reputation as the teller of the worst and oldest jokes in the family."

It may help your own family to try this joke-of-the-day plan. Such an approach is much preferred over the problem-of-the-day approach that covertly finds its way into many family dinnertimes. Laugh, and your family will laugh with you. Cry, and your family will cry with you. Intentionally bringing humor to the family system helps to provide a balance between the tears of laughter and sorrow that run through our life.

PROMOTING YOUR FAMILY'S CREATIVITY: BEYOND THE NORMAL FAMILY

"Us" actualizers are able to extend creativity beyond its typical individualistic definition. They are able to include their entire family in a creative approach to daily living, in artistic endeavors and recreational pursuits that extend beyond the narrow boundaries of more traditional family activities.

"No one at school would believe it at first," said the son in the Anders family. "We painted the whole inside of our garage all around in a big mural. It was a collection of scenes from our family that we took from family pictures. The walls in the garage were a perfect white, so we could paint with magic markers, big ones that Dad bought. We did it for weeks and weeks. My mom really had a great idea when she thought that one up."

Ms. Anders reported neighborhood wonderment at this strange garage mural, and even more wonder at the basement walls which were covered with family-drawn cartoons and caricatures. The true definition of creativity is the ability to break out of long-established sets and ways of seeing and doing things. We too often see such creativity as only something the individual does, some gifted or naturally talented individual who outdoes all others with some remarkable new concept or approach to problem solving. The "us" actualizer starts from the premise of "us" being creative, and then brings the entire family on a journey into new activities and experiences.

What is the weirdest, strangest thing your own family has ever intentionally done together? All of us must live "in" our cultural boundaries, but we do not have to surrender to living "with" our culture's dark side and limitations. There are very few major works of art, writing, or music that have been completed by families. Our society celebrates genius as a solitary experience, and often requires our geniuses to sacrifice their family life for the pursuit of their great ideas. The "us" actualizer does not accept this limitation, and can see beyond the individual definition of creativity to "us" doing something new and wonderful.

Individual family members may become outstanding dancers, yet the family seldom dances together. Learning any new skill is typically seen as individual learning, and families are divided up for teaching purposes. What if we were able to use all of the talents and cognitive styles within a multigenerational family system, and apply this range of skills, viewpoints, and capabilities to a specific problem? What if we put "us" to work on finding new ways to make life worth living? These are the questions asked by the creative "us" actualizer.

PICKING THE RIGHT BATTLES: KNOWING WHEN TO GET UPSET

The "us" actualizer is a fighter, but sees his or her struggles as skirmishes for the entire family to enter into together. He or she is selective of their battles, choosing when and where to fight for principles that really matter, rather than scattering their forces in minor battles of inconsequential wars for self-enhancement or protection. Most often, the healthy family member chooses to fight for issues related to the basic archetypes of family living.

The following statement by the Bonner son illustrates how the Bonner family father chose to fight for a principle related to self-esteem and security that ultimately affects us all.

"One day, when my dad was alive, he came home, sat down, and called us all into the kitchen," said the Bonner son. "My dad hardly ever got mad, but when he did, he got us all involved. He said that anything that was worth fighting for should be worth all of us getting into the fight. He said that if only he was mad and fighting, then he was probably fighting out of selfishness and pride, and not about something that really mattered. When we got into the kitchen, he told us about age discrimination by the city. He said the city was not promoting the older firemen, and that even though he was going to get his promotion, he didn't think it was fair. He had us all work on writing letters, making up handbills, and calling people. It became a family fight. He said, 'The Bonners are going to war!' "

There would be far fewer conflicts if people would turn to their families for approval of any conflict. Perhaps we should use our families as a system of checks and balances and as a type of war council that helps us assess when we should and should not go to war. Much of our stress and pressure in daily living centers around our individual indignation, perceived damage to our always fragile self-concept, and our feeling that someone has encroached on our territory. Our family can help us decide if we are merely indignant over encroachment on some aspect of our own limited concept of self, or are concerned for the dignity of everyone.

By bringing our issues to our family, we accomplish two

things. First, we get input from our family about the relevance and perspective of our indignation. Our family may rush to our side to help, or point out the immaturity and insecurity that we may be showing in our anger. Second, when we take our battle to the family for consideration, we compare our concern for the narrow self-view to the "us" perspective. Is this an issue of consequence because it affects everyone in some way, or is this just one person feeling put out by some injustice? The super family provides perspective, guides us to a more measured response, and can calm us down when we need to be settled down.

It is a mistake to see the "us" actualizer as a passive, smiling, placid person who never gets upset. The uniqueness of the "us" actualizers is their collective response and approach to life. For them, everything is processed through the concept of the family, both the immediate family and family of humankind. Here is a summary of the characteristics of the "us" actualizers I met in the super families. How do you compare on these factors of the super family "us" actualizer? Try this " 'us' actualizer test" to see how you contribute a special gift to your family.

The Healthy Family Member Test

Use the following scale to score yourself on the ten basic characteristics of an "us" actualizer and to determine if you qualify as an extremely healthy family member. Each item represents a summary of the key characteristics of a very healthy family member.

0	1	2	3	4	5	6	7	8	9	10
ALMOST NEVER		SELDOM		SOMETIMES		A LOT		ALMOST ALWAYS		

1. ACCEPTING. ———— Are you a family member who offers your unconditional love to your family, and whose steadiness of emotional complexion settles your family, through its deflection of negative family energy?

2. AUTONOMOUS. ——— Are you a family member who tries to fit with your family, providing support and effort for the conduct of daily family business and minimizing obligations of other family members?

3. SPONTANEOUS. ——— Are you a family member who is immediate with your disclosure of feelings and thoughts, allowing an even flow of family energy free of indirectness, sarcasm, and manipulation?

4. AESTHETIC. ——— Are you a family member who is aware of the appearance of your family and its environment and who cares for that appearance respectfully and gently?

5. TRANSCENDENT. ——— Are you a family member who reads and senses all other family members, and is aware of your family energy and growth template? Are you well tuned to the family holograph, providing resonance to other members of your family for their own growth and personal expansion?

6. EGALITARIAN. ——— Are you a family member who is free of needs to dominate and control others in your family, flowing with the family and leading by example, caring, and teaching rather than judging, evaluating, and criticizing?

7. SOCIALLY CONSCIOUS. ——— Are you a family member who places your family within the larger context of the human family, modeling a respectful, tolerant, and nonprejudicial appraisal of others and a caring for the ecology of all families?

8. HUMOR. ——— Are you a family member who energizes your family through humor and constant awareness of the silly, ridiculous, and amusing in yourself and in the human condition? Do you try to defuse negative family energy through the use of laughter and joy, and are you able to help other family members find the laughter within their own souls?

9. CREATIVE. ——— Are you a family member who

sees achievement and problem solving as a collective issue, involving your family in a collectively aesthetic and original approach to daily living? Do you see your achievements in the context of your family?

10. FOCUSED FIGHTING. ———— Are you a family member who is basically peaceful and nonconfronting, who selects major issues to fight for based on their relevance to the collective whole, involving the entire family in the struggle for equal justice for everyone?

———— TOTAL "US" ACTUALIZING SCORE

Any score over 90 would put you in the rare category of "family 'us' actualizer" who is contributing to the health of your own family. A score below 90 indicates an opportunity for you to make changes in just one or two of the areas on this test that could greatly enhance the life of your own family.

The above list may seem idealistic and the behaviors difficult, but I assure you that the extremely healthy family members I have seen modeled such behaviors in much that they did and said. They showed a reverence for the family experience that translated to an emotional reverie for them and their family. Each of them subscribed to what I identified as twelve basic articles of family faith. In place of the six steps toward a super family that have concluded the chapters on rhythm, ritual, reason, remembrance, resilience, resonance, and reconciliation, I provide here the twelve articles of family faith. I hope you will discuss each one with your own family, and that you and your family will rediscover the power of family reverence in your own life.

Twelve Articles of Family Faith

1. Everyone in my family belongs in my family. Nothing will ever change this, and this article of faith is our first and most basic rule.

This family article of faith shows reverence for the family by preventing any form of exclusion or threat of exclusion of a family member, either in fact or in gesture. There is nothing that a family member can do that would isolate him or her from the family system, for all family members are forever a part of the family energy.

2. We will honor one another in all that we do and say.

Even at times when our family love is tested, we will show honor for one another by our words and deeds. We revere the family by our honoring of our family. The Fifth Commandment is not the fifth suggestion. "Honor thy father and mother" means that, even when our loving becomes difficult, we will work even harder to show our reverence for our family.

3. Our response to one another's needs will be immediate, and the major priority in each of our lives.

Families become super families through their immediacy of response to family requests. All of our other life obligations will be secondary to the requests of our family, and doing "now" for your family is an act of reverence, by not allowing any other factor to get in front of the family system, and by honoring the expressed needs of family members as legitimate and considered requests for help on their part.

4. We will ask of each other only what we need, understanding that a response to our need will be immediately forthcoming. By expressing only needs which are important to us, we will free our family members from an undue sense of obligation.

Knowing that our requests will receive immediate family response, we will intentionally limit our requests to our most important and immediate needs. We will make every effort to help our family in its reverence by limiting emergency requests and the number of our requests.

5. We will behave and talk knowing that our public image is not just our own, but the image of our family and all families.

As all energy, we are inseparable from the mass of our family. We will behave in accordance with our reverence for our family, avoiding any act or statement that reflects dishonor on our family. Even when we are angry or upset with a family member, we will remember that we speak for all of us when we speak of or to any of us.

6. We will defer to one another, realizing that family needs are more important than any other needs.

Deference is the key to reverence. Putting our family first means never allowing ambition or needs for status, success, or personal growth to crowd out the importance of the growth of our own family.

7. Our work and career will be at a lower priority than our family.

There is no meaning to work unless that work does good for everyone. If our work takes from our family, our work loses all meaning.

8. The recreation and celebration of our family will always come before our individual recreation and activities with others.

Our own enjoyment of life, our own re-creation, is fundamental to our health. The family should be included in our recreation, sharing, and not observing or accommodating to, our individualistic pursuit of the daily joy of living. Recreation does not have to involve "opponents" and competition. We can learn to recreate in cooperative games which emphasize the value of cooperation over conquering and defeating someone else. Try to name one adult game that is not structured on the idea of defeating or outscoring someone else. Apparently, to play is not the thing; individual competition is.

9. Every day, we will make personal contact with one another. No matter what the distance, or how heated the conflict, we will make a family moment for recommitting ourselves to our common family energy.

Our daily lives are becoming more intense and less meaningful. To counterbalance social pressures for speed and efficiency at the expense of spiritual growth, we will never allow a day to pass without taking time to "be" together in peace, joy, and silence.

10. We will worship together. We will work toward a com-

mon belief system based first and foremost on the primacy of the family, and we will work for the continued development of that belief system, in accordance with the changes all of us will experience.

The quest for individual spiritual growth is impossible. We can only grow as persons if we grow together. We must do the difficult spiritual, cognitive, emotional, and communicative work within our own families to move toward an enduring but dynamic system of explaining the purpose of our life.

11. We will never lie to one another. What we say and what we hear will be taken as fact.

Lying, even under the misassumption of protecting a family member, will always lead to despair and distrust. Even though the truth may be painful and require time and personal investment for its understanding, and for working with its impact, anything but the truth will allow energy to drain from the family system.

12. We will select a family day every month, one day dedicated to the renewal of family energy and connection.

Since the family is so important to our physical, emotional, cognitive, and spiritual health, we must make a special effort to find one day a month for a family celebration. This is not to be a formal holiday from the calendar, but a day mutually arranged by the family members for reenergizing the family system through shared time and closeness.

If there is one part of my clinical work that saddens me the most, it is our human tendency to revere our family too late, to learn what we missed of our family energy when we or one of our family is in crisis or is passing on. Say a prayer or make a verbal affirmation now for your family, with your family, and for your family's and your own spiritual strength, to work toward extreme health, rather than to merely avoid the conflicts and pain that we hear so much about as characteristic of families today. Reverence for the family is not a feeling, it is a choice to commit to keeping your sense of your family unconditionally alive within you through all of life's tribulations.

CHAPTER ELEVEN

Family Revival:
Quick Recovery from
Family Feuds

"The first half of our lives is ruined by our parents and
the second half by our children."
CLARENCE DARROW

"If you have never been hated by your child, you have
never been a parent."
BETTE DAVIS

FAMILY REVIVAL: The ability to move quickly beyond the
distractions of petty and redundant hassles of daily living and
to identify and work together to solve the core and universal
problems that underlie all family conflicts.

A SYMPHONY IN THE KEY OF F

"Just shut up," said the young daughter as she slammed her
hand against her own thigh. The slap must have stung, because
she winced and became even angrier. "I said shut up!" she
hollered, and this time her anger did not prevent her from
hitting the table instead of herself.

In unison, her parents responded, "You shut up, young lady!" The father allowed his wife to finish the passage, the next words that the family knew only too well from prior rehearsals. "Who do you think you are, telling us to shut up?" said the mother, as the father nodded in rhythmic accent to each syllable.

The younger brother joined in. "I have to go to the bathroom."

The father turned to his son and said, "You can just wait. This is more important."

"But, Dad," protested the boy, as the daughter yelled at her mother, "I can say whatever I want to."

As I sat listening to this difficult beginning to a family therapy session, I could hear the music playing through the sound system in the hall outside the door. Bach's "Fugue in G Minor" was playing, and I noticed the similarities between this family feud and Bach's fugue, the two or more themes enunciated by several voices, the complex contrapuntal themes underlying each statement and building to an inevitable and predictable climax.

This family "feud fugue" was without a conductor. It was composed of the pain and poor communication of a family energy system gone awry. It was an endless and damaging performance, and, slowly but surely, the performers of this work would find themselves unfulfilled and left emotionally drained. They would end their interaction out of tune and in a dreadfully incomplete minor key. Their performance would leave them devoid of their individual and family energy, without vigor for the enjoyment of family life or the identification of the more universal problems that underlay their feud.

Families who can revive themselves have the capacity to get back in tune, to find a center of family purpose and direction that can help them conduct their daily lives even after major arguments and conflicts. Families who possess the ninth of the family Rx's, family revival, are able to avoid the redundantly ineffective family battles that go nowhere but to further pain and helplessness.

To find life again after the struggle, to see that some family fights have to be fought for family growth to take place, is a key family characteristic of healthy families. Healthy families draw energy from their conflicts, reviving themselves through their awareness that most family feuds are natural steps in human development, and not signs that the family is failing.

All families fight and struggle, but families also have the capacity to avoid wandering too far from their main themes of love and caring, always energized by their capacity to revivify, to reenergize one another, even during and after family conflicts. It's not the arguments that hurt families, but the failure to listen for the main theme of family loving even as that theme is elaborated and embellished through the struggles of daily living. Family revival is the opposite of family recrimination, and represents family awareness of their shared responsibility to struggle together for health.

The theme of your family love is always playing, but you must make the effort to listen even harder when the volume of family life is turned up. Remember, there is something within the healthy family that is in tune with the real purpose of family conflict: to identify and help to promote the eventual resolution of the several manifestations of the four archetypical problems of the unsettled human spirit.

The Family Revival Test

To help you understand the behaviors needed for your family to revive itself after conflicts and to return to its main theme of family love, take the following family revival test. Remember that averaging family scores and comparing individual scores with these averages can help identify family members who may be having trouble staying in tune with the family. Use the same scoring system we have been using throughout this book:

0	1	2	3	4	5	6	7	8	9	10
ALMOST NEVER		SELDOM		SOMETIMES		A LOT		ALMOST ALWAYS		

1. ———— Is your family free of name-calling?

2. ———— Do family members avoid overgeneralizations such as "you always do that"?

3. ——— Do your family members avoid labels such as "lazy," "hostile," or "dumb," when arguing?

4. ——— Do family members request politely, rather than expect and demand of other family members?

5. ——— Are family arguments free of the attempt to find someone to blame or accuse, in favor of solving the problem at hand as a group?

6. ——— Is your family free of petty bickering and bartering over insignificant things, such as who does the dishes or who takes out the garbage?

7. ——— Can family members laugh and keep their sense of humor even when things get "hot" in family conflicts?

8. ——— Is there an absence of statements of surrender and helplessness in your family communication? ("I've had it," "That's It," or "Forget It," etc.)

9. ——— Are family arguments about new issues that evolve with your family growth, rather than the same old issues?

10. ——— Do family members feel that the family is growing and getting closer, even through conflicts and arguments, rather than getting angrier and angrier and drawing apart?

——— **TOTAL FAMILY REVIVAL SCORE**

If you scored above the arbitrary 90 points on the family revival test, your family is capable of being energized and re-energized by the natural conflicts that happen in all families. If your score, or your family average score with all members' scores included, is less than 90, it is likely that you and your family are failing to see the "real" problems that are affecting your family, and are distracted by trivial conflicts that are really only the symptoms of more basic family issues.

As you read the following material describing the details of the ninth family Rx of revival, remember that it is only the close, loving, and growing families that argue and find themselves in conflicts. As one mother said, "Families are for fighting, but only if everyone remembers that we all love each other forever, and only if we can learn to fight about things that really matter to us." When people don't care about one another and don't choose to spend the emotional and physical energy to try to revive the family system every day through conflict resolution, there are few problems, but there is also little lasting love.

SEVEN SINS VISITED UPON THE FAMILY

As I described earlier, it is helpful to view family crisis and conflict in the context of universal, archetypical issues that are being confronted for all of us by each family and family member. Every family argument is ultimately about sexuality, self-esteem, security, and substance abuse, and the most productive family conflicts are those which focus on the common threads of these issues as they show themselves in the seven family sins.

Ms. Johnson was struggling with her attempts to make the new arguments in her new stepfamily more tolerable and productive. Following therapy one day, her comment summarized what family revival is all about. She said, "It sounds like a joke, but we call our family arguments 'family revival meetings' now. That one day in therapy when you made each of us hold up one of our four cards—with the words sex, safety, security, and self on them—during the arguments, we could see what we were really fighting about, and that we sort of need to fight to revive ourselves and to grow."

A model for understanding the ways in which the four archetypical or common problems are dealt with daily by all families derives from what are referred to as the "seven deadly sins." These are the capital sins, forever recycling through the human experience and showing different aspects of the concerns we all have for our use of substances, our sexuality, our self-esteem, and our security. If we consider these seven sins metaphorically, and if we look for them in every family argument, we will begin to understand even the typical day-to-day family conflicts in a different, brighter light.

THE PRIDE OF THE FAMILY

The pride of self-accomplishments, an emphasis on what someone can do better or faster than someone else, has dominated our history. The words "pride and joy" seem connected, as if all happiness depended upon self-fulfillment rather than "us" concerns and responsibility. Arguments over pride in the family are arguments about self-esteem and security, not just who cleans up the best after dinner.

We have failed to emphasize an "us" pride in what the world can do for its inhabitants, while we have been busy seeing how much each inhabitant or subcluster of inhabitants within nations can do better than others. If we look at family conflict from the perspective of concerns about pride, we will see that, almost always, someone's "pride," someone's inordinate and dominant opinion of their own importance over someone else's, is at the root of many family disagreements. It is always a foolish pride that makes us attempt to see how much value the self can incur, while the idea of accountability and responsibility for others is neglected.

I often hear the complaint that "no one has pride in their work any more." The problem is really the reverse. There is too much pride in "my work" and not enough pride in "our work," and too much talk about "it's not my job" or "that's my job so don't interfere with my territory." Pride in self, concern for self-enhancement, has taken precedence over the concern for working for the welfare of others. The opposite of pride is caring, caring for what we do and how we feel as we impact responsibly upon others.

"I have done everything possible for this family," said one man. "What I do is done well, quickly, and reliably. The rest of the family does things when they get to it, and when the kids do something, it is done half-assed. They don't have any pride at all."

"You just think your way is the only way to do things," answered the son. "You're just trying to run everything. You don't think anyone should be proud unless they do what you want."

"I am not," said the father. "I have worked my way through college; I provide this great house and all the food. What in the hell have you done? Just look at what I have done."

"I'm doing harder work in school than you ever did," said the son.

"Then why have I done so well?" asked the father angrily.

The argument got more intense as each of the two family members engaged in their narrow self-pride protection. Both combatants were forgetting that nothing they have done or will do could be accomplished without others. As if trapped in a universally unresolved issue of self-pride that has prevented collective cooperation to solve key world issues, this family was fighting on a small scale about issues that continue to hinder world progress on the larger scale. This was a family battle between the "self" and the "us."

I asked these two bright family members if they saw any similarity at all between their argument and the recent summit between the Russian and United States leaders. At first, both father and son laughed. Then, the son said, "Well, it seemed to me that they were both trying to make themselves look like good leaders, rather than trying to solve the real problems of nuclear arms. They were taking care of themselves first before the people."

The father responded, "I get the point. It's very difficult to see beyond your own perspective when you get so upset. Maybe you can't see the forest when you're one of the trees. What we're trying to get done here is to get a cleaner house, or at least some agreement as to what a clean house really is, and who has to do what, and how to get where we want to go."

In your own family arguments, and whenever you feel indignant and disregarded, try to think of the still-unresolved universal, shared, archetypical problem of the dominance of pride over caring in our world. Think of how overinflated self-importance and an emphasis on "me" has for centuries resulted in corrupt leadership, shortsighted political policies, dishonesty in our public servants, and even the simple but destructive behavior of tossing litter from a car, as if to say, "I'm too important to care about this little matter of litter. Let someone else less important and less busy than I am pick this up."

Ultimately, pride is a lack of a developed sense of "us" and a sense of family. When the "I, I, I, and me, me, me" arguments start, the family is attempting to cope with the long-unresolved issue of human pride, working too hard to help family members become independent and not hard enough on helping them become interdependent. Your struggle to deal with this issue has universal importance, even if the family is really only arguing over who left a light on in the hallway.

CONSUMING THE FAMILY WEALTH

The second deadly sin, avarice, refers to the focus on acquiring and protecting what we wrongly see as "our own" goods, money, and the "things and stuff" that seem to dominate much of our purpose. The issue of "substance" use and abuse underlies family arguments over who has, gets, uses, or gives the most. As our world has tried unsuccessfully for centuries to overcome the prideful emphasis on self-promotion of the "I, I, I, me, me, me" orientation, so has it failed to move beyond the "mine, mine, mine, and yours, yours, yours" emphasis of daily living. We actually seem to think that we can own land and possess things and people. We are learning much too slowly that we are passing through this earthly experience as visitors and not owners.

Listen to the language of chronic and unresolved family conflict, and you will hear continued reference to "things" taken, broken, or lost, and things borrowed without permission. You will hear conflict over an ownership that is mere illusion. When the family conflict language, the family words of war, contain the "I, me, mine, and get" emphasis, we know that the "us" factor is missing.

"It's my car, and I will not allow you to use it if you don't take better care of it," said the mother to her daughter. "Every time you bring it back, it has scratches or damage, or you have driven it too hard. That car is mine, and not yours. Do you understand? I own it, and I paid for it with my money."

"That's stupid," said the daughter. "You can't drive a car

too hard, and I didn't see any scratches that really were any big deal."

"You can drive your own car, if you ever get one, the way you want to, but you can too drive my car too hard," answered the mother. "You don't respect your things. I respect mine. You don't see scratches because you don't care what anything looks like. Just look at your room. My room is clean, and yours is a mess. You don't take care of your things. I take care of mine, and I expect you to take care of my things when you use them."

The argument continued, becoming even more personalized, attacking, overgeneralized, and hostile. Both performers in this family feud were fighting over the issue of "mine and yours" instead of ours. Even though the mother had paid for the car, the issue of proper use would never be directly dealt with until both mother and daughter could see that they were dealing with avarice, the "mine-yours" issue that blocks the healthy evolution of a sharing atmosphere in our society.

The only constructive way out of this argument was for both mother and daughter to look for the unresolved family issue archetype, in this case the reemergence of the issue of avarice, and how substances and objects can take precedence over people. Not only were the mother and daughter speaking from the prideful point of view of "I do, you don't do," but they were dividing up what can never be divided, the issue of responsibility for the feelings, not the objects, of others.

Accusations, overgeneralization, name-calling, and slander are almost always symptoms of family archetypical problems of pride and avarice, selfishness, and the use or misuse of substances. Until our world purges itself of these continually emerging themes, all families will dance to a music that is out of key. Paying attention to the basic theme, looking for which of the seven basic archetypical issues is showing itself to the family, will help the family change the tune and see that they must argue about what is happening to "us" instead of what is being done by one person to another or to another person's "stuff."

LOST LUST

The third archetypical sin of our world that is visited upon the family is lust, the overmastering desire that results in the ultimate confusion of what is needed and what is wanted. Lust in this sense does not refer exclusively to overwhelming sexual desire that is deemed immoral by some religious or social mandate. The archetypical sin of lust is the absence of renunciation, the ability to forego immediate "want" gratification until a clearer understanding of the underlying spiritual need for tenderness and sensuality manifests itself.

"Come on, Dad," said the son, "I really, really need that stereo. I've got to have it bad. I've got the speakers. They're no good without a high-quality stereo. Just a little loan, and I can get it. I'll pay you back."

"You don't need the stereo," said the father. "You want the stereo. There's a big difference. Last week you needed the speakers. Now you need the stereo. You always need something. You seem to need everything. You want something so much that you don't have any needs any more. You wouldn't know a real need if it hit you in the face."

The pride and avarice archetypes are clear here, but the power behind these factors is the lust, the power of desire, of wanting so long, so often, and so intensely, that the "want" itself begins to have a life of its own. We become so addicted to the biochemistry of "wanting" that charges through our body that, when we don't want something, we feel uncomfortable and confused. We may begin looking through advertisements for something else to "need," when we are really looking for a new "want" to get us high again.

Advertisement agencies are in the lust business. They are dedicated to creating "wants" and to converting our sense of want to a feeling of need. Certainly, you must need what everyone seems to want. Do you want to be the only family on your block without a new videocassette recorder? It is not just the avarice that underlies such an approach, but a seduction into the psychochemical high of being in a "wanting" state.

If the language of pride is "I-me," and the language of avarice is "mine-yours," the archetypical language of lust is one of intensity, a language of "now-must." Listen for impatience in your family conflicts, and you will hear words such as "right this minute," "I must have," or "you must do." Lust shows itself as a constant stimulus away from patience and toward immediate and intense gratification.

In families struggling with this third archetype of lust, typically one member feels pressured to meet the "wants" of another member, resents such pressure, and may feel that this pressure of someone else's wants gets in the way of their own focus on their own wanting. We will never be able to identify our truly basic human and spiritual needs when we are consumed by consumption itself. We have become a world of consumers rather than providers, deal-makers rather than helpers, and many family arguments center around a sense of imbalance between who is using and who is giving.

The solution for dealing with our addiction to lustful states, states of intense wanting that can underlie substance abuse, is to see that all our wanting is ultimately a desire for connection, for verification of our humanness. Our need for connection may be corrupted, and we may think that some "thing" can help us find the feeling of connection and meaning, but ultimately, all addiction is a misguided attempt for the "high" of human connection.

The opposite of the archetypical pressure of pride is altruism and a focus on helping and doing for others in the family. The opposite of the archetypical pressure of avarice is sharing, and the realization that we can never truly "own" things are only illusions, images of transient energy, not objects to be stored in a bank. The opposite of lust is patience, and in the words of the Tibetan yogi Milarepa, "The shortest road to freedom is the path of patience."[1]

To illustrate this principle of seeing family conflict as archetypical attempts to revive and bring to our own family the evolving universal energy that is our universe, I ask the families I am working with to "look for where the shared sin is." What sin of humankind is playing itself out in your family system? What is it that all of us do, that is contrary to the welfare of all of us, that is now showing itself in this family as a ghost of families past? What is it that continues to haunt the future of this family, and all families, until the ghosts are exposed for

1. Evans-Wentz, W., ed. *Tibet's Great Yogi Milarepa,* 2nd Ed. (New York: Oxford University Press, 1951).

what they are, the continuing sins against the evolution of the spirit of "us"?

The issue is not one of who is the sinner, but what sin against the evolving universal spirit of family, of "us," is coming back to haunt the family and requiring its attention, time, and energy. All of our family quarrels are a waste of time if they are not seen in the context of a higher purpose than who takes out the garbage and why someone used up the last bar of soap.

Each of the first three deadly sins is deadly because of what that sin does to the potential miracle of "us." Pride steals the joy and freedom of empathy and glee in experiencing someone else's experience as our own. Avarice takes away the beauty to be seen in the fact that all that we experience comes from us, belongs to all of us, and is, in fact, "us." Lust drains our family energy, and, like a water spout left full on, lust saps the spiritual strength needed to get back to the most fulfilling experience of all, the shared meeting of the basic needs of life.

Psychologist Abraham Maslow described what he called the "hierarchy of needs," a pyramid of motivation.[2] He suggested that the basic human needs, such as hunger and thirst, were "prepotent," or stronger than the higher-level needs for friendship and love. Researchers have shown that, when a group of persons reduced their eating to such a level that they lost twenty-four percent of their body weight, their every thought, dream, and behavior had to do with food.[3] Hunger needs had become prepotent, or dominant, for these persons.

It is a mistake, however, to think that the personal and spiritual impact of meeting higher-level needs, such as the need for love, is more fulfilling than the meeting of the need for food. If we learn to want less, to focus less on the intensity of a wanting state in favor of allowing our true inner needs to emerge, we may someday rediscover the remarkable pleasure that comes from eating when we are truly hungry, drinking when we are truly thirsty, and feeling warmed when we are truly cold.

2. Maslow, Abraham H. *Motivation and Personality,* 2nd Ed. (New York: Harper & Row, 1970).

3. Keys, A., et al. *The Biology of Human Starvation,* Vols. 1–2 (Minneapolis: University of Minnesota Press, 1950).

Is it less an intense emotional experience to drink when we are extremely thirsty than it is to buy a new car? If we think that acquiring the car is the more significant and rewarding event, we are beginning to need what we want instead of wanting what we spiritually, personally, and collectively need.

GOING MAD WITH ANGER

Archetypical anger is one of vengeful passion directed against someone else. Anger is directly related to the degree that we are dominated by pride, avarice, lust, and the family archetypical problem of personal insecurity, because when these orientations to life begin to direct our daily living, we feel the need to retaliate against someone for our sense of helplessness.

The continuum of anger to rage to fury corresponds directly with the speed with which we move through the potent feelings of pride, avarice, and lust. All anger is based on our own lack of family skill, our own inability to show unconditional loving-kindness and to maintain a sense of "us." It is almost impossible to become angry and to act angrily when "you are they."

Psychologists know that frustration, when continued, leads to anger. Eventually, anger will always result in regression, in infantile, childlike impatience and competitiveness with others whom we blame for our original frustration. We come to see people as barriers to our selfish goals rather than as paths to shared joy. Remember the "FAR" formula of frustration-aggression-regression sequence the next time your family is "far out" in its arguing.

Author Deane Shapiro writes of the similarities between ancient teachings and modern psychological techniques for learning compassion and reducing the frustration, anxiety, and threats to self and perceived self-territory that almost always underlie anger.[4] Compassion and sympathy are the antithesis of anger and hate, because the only way we can feel anger toward someone else is if we do not see them as "us."

Psychologists sometimes use desensitization, relaxation

4. Shapiro, Deane. *Precision Nirvana: An Owner's Manual for the Care and Maintenance of the Mind* (Englewood Cliffs, N.J.: Prentice-Hall, 1978).

techniques, and cognitive restructuring to quiet the anxiety that leads to anger, while the Buddhist practice was to replace anxiety with loving thinking and behavior. Both approaches are attempts to establish some sense of connection for the person whose anger reveals a sense of indignation and resentment as a consequence of self-imposed isolation.

The language of the family feud that signals the archetypical struggle against anger is the use of the words "stop-do." When family arguments contain these words of demand, someone is feeling out of control and out of the family system.

"You have one minute to clean off that table," said the mother on a tape recording of a family dinnertime. "I said do it now, and stop watching television. Do it!"

Even if this son who was being ordered to respond immediately did comply with the demands he heard, he would only be yielding to and reinforcing the anger of the demander. He would be further isolating the angry family member. There was no "let's" or "start," only words of immediacy, dissatisfaction, and implied threats.

We live in a world that has become accustomed to anger. We drive, shop, and vote with anger because we feel disenfranchised from the "us," out of control and without effective means for maintaining a sense of who we are while we interact in a caring way with the world around us.

I have heard athletes say that they lost at an event because they were not angry enough. I have heard businessmen and -women being told to "get tough, get mean, get mad, get even" in a motivational speech to a sales force. Anger is seen as a healthy motivation, but in actuality it only blocks the effectiveness of any human behavior or thinking process.

When the family experiences anger, it is an anger that has been hanging around with us human beings for all of our days. The more we have tried to acquire, and the more selfishly we try to live, the more frustrated we have become. The more frustrated we become, the angrier we get. The angrier we get, the more immaturely we act. The more immature we become, the more we want things, and want people to do things our way. The more we want, the more frustrated we get, and the circle of anger accelerates and repeats.

Families are trying to get rid of some of this universal anger through their struggles to reduce it, but too often the helplessness and despair that underlie the anger response are overwhelming, and family arguments turn to rage and even fury. As a result, all family members spin away into their own orbits, away from the nucleus of the family, convinced that only they know the way things should be.

The opposite of anger is love, and every moment of anger within the family is draining love energy. Anger should direct our attention to love, not away from it. We must learn to invite, to ask, to request, and even to beg. We must try to stop demanding, expecting, requiring, and blaming our family members for our own frustrations.

When we demand by saying "do" or "stop," there are two negative results. First, a family member may comply out of fear, which leads to later resentment and withdrawal by that family member even if they do what they have been demanded to do. Second, any possibility of loving kindness, of sympathy and of doing out of caring for the "us" has been ruled out, because the complying family member can not do "for," in expectation of loving, when they feel they must do "because" of their fear of emotional or even physical retaliation.

EMPTY FEELINGS AND EMPTY FAMILIES

The fifth deadly sin impacting on the family system is gluttony, the continued theme of excess in our world and misuse of the substances of our world. As the main character in the movie *Wall Street* says, "Ladies and gentlemen, greed is good." We are living in a time of hostile takeovers rather than gentle surrenders, and the screaming and yelling on the floor of the New York Stock Exchange give testimony to what our society has come to see as "good greed."

Like the tiny shrew's gluttonous eating of his own tail when all the food is gone, we are eating ourselves alive. Our wild consumption of every resource we have is resulting in our eating ourselves out of our house and home, and the archetypical sin of human gluttony presents itself in every family for some small decrease in its magnitude. As with all of the seven family problems, perhaps if we can get just some of these problems solved in one family, the problems may reduce in the overall human family.

"Mom!" yelled the brother. "He ate up all of the ice cream!"

"So what?" answered the other brother. "I was hungry."

"Share next time," said the mother.

"Let him get his own ice cream. I need a lot of it when I'm hungry."

This simple family exchange shows the implied acceptance of gluttony in daily life. Every advertisement campaign is aimed at this gluttonous approach to life, offering the opportunity to go for the gusto, to have the Bud that is for you, or to get your piece of the rock. The language of family arguments that illustrates the impact of the gluttony archetype is "get-all," an emphasis of total and immediate possession, consumption, and almost constant comparisons of quantities.

"He doesn't give me all the love I want," said the wife. "I just want him to want to gobble me right up, to consume me." This statement illustrates how we want to consume and be the target of consumption at the same time, attempting to experience both gluttony and what it is like to be the target of such gluttony.

We seem to show less desire for making others feel good than for being sure we get our due. The Buddha pointed out that the positive spiritual effects of sharing with others and limiting and controlling ourselves for the welfare of others are so strong that, if we truly understood what sharing and generosity could give us, we would never eat a meal without sharing our food with someone else.[5]

Our own gluttony is really the opposite of generosity, of giving, of limiting ourselves intentionally so that someone else may have and do more. Even on the emotional level, we seem to want to feel it all. We want to get high, stay high, and then get higher, and the pursuit of such highs, of such doomed attempts at emotional satiation, results again in frustration, isolation, and loneliness. Just as starvation will cause a shrew to cannibalize his fellow shrews before he begins eating himself, we end up alone, beginning to consume ourselves through our ultimately fatal gluttony.

Think of the times your own family may have experienced

5. Goldstein, J. The Experience of Insight (Santa Cruz, Cal.: Unity Press, 1976).

conflicts over quantity. We will never be able to constructively deal with the universal sin of gluttony in our archetypical family battles until we realize that the family is the perfect place to give, to sacrifice, to provide for others without hesitation, expectation, or qualification. Knowing the simple joy of leaving ample ice cream in the refrigerator for a brother whom you know would love to share that ice cream may seem a simple gesture, but it is one small but significant step toward diminishing our evolutional gluttony and moving toward the reviviscence of the family system.

THE ENVY OF THE FAMILY

Envy is the sixth deadly sin, the continued human characteristic to want what others have, feel whatever positive feelings others have, and to avoid whatever distress someone else is experiencing. Envy is not only jealousy, but avoidance of a sense of "us." Almost always, envy reflects two of the four archetypical family problems, insecurity and low self-esteem.

Envy is passive, the waiting and expecting of some universal balance of distribution of favors and goods. Envy is the repeated questioning of "Why me?" or "Why not me?" The active involvement in "us" would make envy an evanescent sin, because when we are connected with others, we do experience and have what they have, the good and the bad and the highs and the lows.

The language of family arguments that reveals the archetypical battle regarding our historical human envy is "more-less" in place of "enough-sufficient." As long as we continue to see others as separate from us, we will forever be in search of, and jealous of, what they seem to have and do. We may live in fear of suffering from whatever we think they may be suffering from.

Just as pride, avarice, lust, anger, and gluttony sap the energy of the family and make it almost impossible for the family system to revivify, to reenergize through conflict resolution and effective argumentation, envy only furthers the distance between us. The word "share" comes to be a noun meaning "a rightful portion," rather than a verb that means "to demonstrate our family love."

"Why does he get all of the attention?" asked the son. "Everybody does everything for him. He gets all the good stuff, like he's a king or something."

"You get your share of attention. What's his is his, and what's yours is yours," said the mother. "You're just jealous."

I have seldom seen a family argument that was not constructive when the language contained terms such as "ours," "give," "allow," and "surrender," and "I understand just how you feel." Envy is a way of avoiding empathy, a way of externalizing the experiences of others so that we can either resent them for their good fortune or be glad that we do not share the negative experiences they may have.

Envy is a signal that there is something within us that wants to be a part of someone else. We mistake the feeling of wanting what others have or do for the spiritual imperative to join with them, to merge with their energy and spin with them in their family orbit.

ASLEEP AT THE FAMILY SWITCH

The seventh of the deadly sins, sloth, plays itself out in all family systems and in conflicts within these systems. We may be willing to enjoy with vigor the intensity of life's experience, but we experience a spiritual and mental sloth, torpor, and indolence when we must do the difficult work of tuning in to our spirit. Our society is suffering from severe spiritual underemployment, and it is our insecurity and low self-esteem that causes us to shy away from all that we can be.

I noticed in my clinical work with families that there was almost a unanimous reaction to one of my favorite family assignments. I ask all the families I work with to learn family meditation. I ask them to join hands, close their eyes, breathe deeply from the abdomen, relax every muscle in their bodies, and clear their minds. I ask them to allow the family mind to take over, to join with their family in a quiet, peaceful revivification of the family energy system. After extensive and repeated practice, some very special and intense spiritual experiences are reported by the families. However, when the families first attempt this family meditation, they tend to become tired or even fall asleep.

When our mind is deprived of its junk thought food, of being "on" by dealing with conversation and seeking constant stimulation, it is too lazy at first to keep awake. It's as if the brain says, "If I can't have junk food, then I won't eat." Researchers have shown that the inexperienced meditator experiences brain waves that resemble the first stages of sleep.[6] We fall asleep at the family switch that controls our innate family energy when we yield to a lazy brain that prefers the ease of intensity over the challenge of meaning.

Many families today are addicted to intensity, but slothful in their efforts for spiritual growth. It requires a great effort and "us" discipline to view family arguments as archetypical metaphors of the universal family struggle to grow through, and hopefully away from, the seven deadly sins. It is much easier, much more acceptable to our brains, to fight over who said or did what to whom than to understand that every family argument has been done before. Every family argument is either another step in the evolution of the family spirit, or a mindless, brain-directed exchange for the individual preservation of one or more of the seven deadly sins.

The language of sloth is "can't-won't" rather than "sense-feel." If we want to just survive family life, we can continue to argue and fight until our energy for family is totally misplaced and beyond reviviscence. Once we have lost our energy for family, we can then move on to other experiences, forever and mindlessly trapped in the repetition of the sinful archetypes I have identified here. If we choose instead to experience the miracle of "us," we can summon all of our available family energy, tune into the universal family mind, and thrive as family, because we spend family conflict time revivifying the human spirit and our family spirit at the same time.

If a family fight is due to individual wants, the family is in trouble. If the family struggle is for all of its members' needs, the family will help itself and its members to contribute to the evolution of the universal family spirit, promoting the enhanced and revivified reincarnation of "us" energy through every family conflict.

The following chart summarizes the archetypical problems

6. Shapiro, Deane. *Meditation: Self-Regulation Strategy and Altered State of Consciousness* (New York: Aldine Press, 1980).

that affect the family. When your family has a problem, enter this chart at the point that seems to characterize the communication style of your family during the conflict. Next, trace that style to the right on the chart to see the universal problem that is likely to be at the root of the family problem. Then move further to the right, to see what individual behaviors are needed to promote a more basic problem-solving approach that actually deals with the archetypical issues that may be showing themselves as mere petty squabbles.

Of course, family problems are complex, and several of the four basic problems of family life, and their seven family-"sins" manifestations, are usually operating at the same time. True family revival requires a commitment to the family system and a willingness to work toward what the Buddhists call "the perfections," many of which relate to the concepts in the column entitled "Family Revival" on the chart.

TEN FAMILY "TYPES"

Over the years of watching families struggle to find renewed energy and attempt to become reanimated in their progress toward a strong "us," I have noticed some commonalities in the themes of these family journeys. While no individual or family can be classified as a type, it is possible to look at clusters of family behaviors that characterize family systems at various times in their evolution.

Each of the following "types" of family is offered for your own discussion with your family. See if you can find characteristics of your family in one or more of the following categories. Revival as a family characteristic depends on a clear collective look in the family mirror, at the way in which your family is doing its spiritual share of the work on humankind's universal problems. Remember, each of the following categories contain positive and negative aspects of family life.

FROM FAMILY PROBLEMS TO FAMILY GROWTH

Family Problem	Language	Family "Sin"	Family Revival
Name-calling	"I-me"	Pride	Altruism
Fights over territory	"mine-yours"	Avarice	Sharing
Demands	"now-must"	Lust	Patience
Accusations	"stop-don't"	Anger	Compassion
Battering and bargaining	"get-all"	Gluttony	Generosity
Blaming and demeaning	"more-less"	Envy	Empathy
Sarcasm and surrender	"can't-won't"	Sloth	Commitment

1. THE ULTRALIGHT FAMILY

The ultralight family is a family that flourishes in the good times, but has very little family energy available for those times that all families must experience, the crises and confrontations with the family archetypical issues of selfishness, territoriality, immaturity, anger, and greed. The ultralight family is better at celebration than at dealing with the growth needs of every family member, and at least some members within this family system will feel isolated, even afraid that a personal problem they are experiencing would overwhelm their family if they were to disclose their true sense of despair.

One member of an ultralight family said, "We can laugh, play cards, or tell jokes. But if we really have a problem, you can't get people around here to listen. It's like we're playing a big family board game, and we're the game." For the fun family, life is to be taken easily and lightly, with the assumption that problems ignored are problems solved.

Some families lack the capacity to enjoy life together, and could benefit from the lesson of the ultralight family and its ability, as a group, to take pleasure in life. Sometimes, the ultralight family changes and becomes reenergized by a crisis, learning that it must face up to the pain and healing crises that characterize any growth. More often, however, the denial system of the ultralight family is so strong that problems are deflected back within each family member and seldom processed by the family itself.

If you find the ultralight family component in your own family, you will note a strong family defense system, intact against any "bad news." A type of family group denial is always in place. As one wife said, "You just don't fight or quarrel in our family like I used to do in my parents' family."

Someone in the ultralight family, perhaps yourself, might feel that problems should be handled by the individual who experiences them, and that sharing problems is a way of burdening the family, or of taking all the fun out of living. If a major crisis strikes, this family may find itself helpless, due to its lack of experience in living and loving through prior rehearsals of minicrises. However common, all denial eventually fails.

The ultralight family is usually under the strong influence of one strong and controlling family member who is unwilling or unable to face up to the natural frailties of being human. The rose-colored glasses worn by this family member do not allow the slightest hint of darkness to penetrate, and the rest of the family may feel intimidated by the ultralight approach to family life preferred by this person. Such persons seem to want everything to be "right," giving off the message that any negative is a hassle they are unwilling or unable to confront.

2. THE FAILING FAMILY

This is a family that is hanging on by an emotional string, stressed and strained to its energy limits by one or more of its members, who are abusing the family or themselves. Typically, one member of the family is holding and protecting that emotional string, feeling burdened and pressured to hold themselves together for the sake of family survival.

Unlike the ultralight family, the failing family has almost no fun at all. Fun and recreation are sought outside the family home, and each family member seeks their own "pseudofamily" of friends, or of colleagues at work, for support. Feeling the vulnerability of the family system, members in the failing family are as reluctant as those members of the ultralight family to discuss their own problems and worries. They see the family as a basket of problems that cannot support the weight of even one more family or personal problem.

"We know exactly where we stand around here," said one member of a failing family. "We stand on the cliff. One move, one problem, and we're over the edge." This sense of impending doom weighs heavily on the failing family, with everyone waiting for, even anticipating and expecting, the ultimate failure of the system or of the vulnerable member.

3. THE FAILED FAMILY

Perhaps the saddest and most helpless of all of the family patterns is that of the failed family. Due to chronic mental or physical health problems, substance abuse, unresolved problems in the basic marriage that should be serving as a base for the family, sexual addiction that overtly or covertly draws the primary relationship in the family apart, sexual lack-of-fulfillment in the primary family relationship, or the presence of a child or adult whose behavior is chronically aggressive and demanding, the failed family has lost almost all of its energy. As a result, everyone in the family feels hopelessness and despair, and the problems of each individual family member become worse and their coping ability less.

"You just can't live with someone like him for so many years and have anything left," said the mother, speaking about her troubled son. "He's always angry, moody, unfair, and even attacking. We're always a wreck when he's around. We don't know how to deal with him. We have come to hate him, and every day of our lives we just live in this prison camp called a home. He has us held prisoner."

As this mother cried, she went on to describe her sense of helplessness, surrender, and the despair shared by her entire family. As you learned earlier, this family is failing to see that no family problem is related to just one person, and the sense of "us" that is needed for this family to begin to deal with their problems is not present. If the difficult family member is using and abusing their family, the family is also using that member to avoid the direct confrontation of a system breakdown for which every member shares responsibility.

4. THE OPPRESSIVE FAMILY

This family leaves its members without freedom of spontaneous expressions of feelings of joy. The home is quiet, subdued and functioning on an overserious and highly reactive level. The slightest problem in daily living causes a family avalanche, with even the most minor of difficulties being viewed as family-threatening.

A little girl in one of these families suggested another name of this category of family to me, by saying, "In our house, everything is totally awesome. If you break a dish, everybody gasps and waits for a big discussion of the cost of dishes today." The oppressive family is awesome in almost all that it does and feels.

The antithesis of the ultralight family, the oppressive family finds little time for family recreation or celebration. Even putting up the family Christmas tree becomes a solemn, serious, and major event. Should the lights explode, or the tree fall, there is likely to be a major uproar with attempts to blame, rather than laughter and group acknowledgment of a tradition of family Christmas-tree-tipping that could become a part of the whole process of family celebration of this holiday.

5. THE FRENZIED FAMILY

"None of us goes to bed at the same time, we all get up at different times, and I don't think we eat a meal together other than on holidays," said the father. "It's like a family marathon. We don't stop. We can't stop. There's just too much to do in too little time, and now that the kids are getting older, we are really on the move."

This father's statement describes what many people have come to accept as a model of family living, with the family becoming a general operations center for family troop deployment. A visit to many family homes today would reveal that one major characteristic of the modern family is its assembly-line-like constant movement. Like promiscuous sex, the family process of contact is characterized by the foreplay of a quick shower while holding off other family members who are pounding on the bathroom door, instant and solo meals, the doing of each family member's "thing," followed by an almost involuntary refractory period during which the respective members collapse, spent and too often unfilled.

6. THE STAGNANT FAMILY

The stagnant family is a family unable and afraid to grow to new stages of family life. Unlike the failed or failing family, the stagnant family is not declining in function. Instead, it is dead in the water, just floating, without direction, but also without immediate danger of sinking. Sooner or later, various family crew members will jump ship one at a time, seeking renewal with new families of their own.

In the stagnant family, one or more members are clinging to what they view as "the way things should be done," and the other family members may be responding to patterns they see in other families. The conflict between the old and the new is avoided, however, because usually one family member dominates, and the absence of a true sense of "us" results in the family being stuck in its ways. Change would be viewed as a problem rather than as a stimulus for growth.

"My mom thinks she has to run everything," said the son. "She has her views of the way things were done in her own family when she was a little girl, and now she seems to be reliving her family in this one. We can't get her to change without upsetting her whole world, so we just go along and try to go around her whenever we can."

Almost clinging to an emotional imprint of a former family experience, perhaps because of unresolved problems there, or because a sense of safety from present pressures is sought by trying to keep things the way things used to be, one of the members of the stagnant family is unable or unwilling to allow family system growth. Even if the way things are done is not working efficiently, change and development are resisted.

7. THE FORCED FAMILY

"If things hadn't happened the way they did, this group of folks would never be living as a group together," said the mother in her third marriage. "I don't know really when it started, but the resulting group of kids, and even me and my husband, don't really make a family. It's like we have to be together because we ran out of energy to try again at a better family."

This mother's report is not infrequent in my clinical experience. Due to marital instability and the lack of family and marital aptitude, the resulting undeveloped sense of a growing and dynamic "us" leads to a family entrapment. So many changes, so many steps have been climbed in the stepfamily system, that the family energy is nearly depleted. While unhappy with the family system, each member seems to tolerate the forced family for fear of yet another disruption in an already overly-disrupted family history.

"You've heard of peace at any price?" continued the mother in the forced family. "Well, we sort of have a family at any price. It's easier to keep this family than try for another one." Like the stagnant family the forced family is not growing, but unlike the stagnant family forced families seem to collectively and actively share the decision to avoid any decisions that would mean yet another new family system.

8. THE FAZED FAMILY

In every family there are times when severe crisis will strike. A death, a divorce, the exposure of some deceit, or a major failure in the development of one of the family members will deal a hard and direct blow to the heart of every family during its development. The fazed family has not yet recuperated from the blow, has lost its collective breath, and is unable to conspire together for the necessary developmental and adaptive changes that are necessary.

"We just sit around most of the time, like we're all in a trance," said the father. "We talk in a monotone, and seem to be waiting for somebody to come up with an idea to get us out of our doldrums. We're stunned, I guess. After the kids found out about my affair and heard me and my wife talking, everything stopped. Just like a freeze-frame in a movie, we are right where we were on that day."

Even the stagnant family, trapped by prior precedents rather than crisis, can show some response to the pressure of individual family members for change. The fazed family has been damaged severely, becomes disoriented and may look to already weakened and suffering members for help, when in fact the entire system requires change as a result of the problem that damaged the family.

The question that must be asked by the fazed family is "What can we learn from this, and how can we all grow and contribute new energy to the family system?" When the fazed family stops and looks just to the problem or the loss itself, it ends up waiting for a rescue line that will never be thrown.

9. THE FIXATED FAMILY

Earlier, I described the general phases through which the family system evolves, the phases of family genesis. The fixated family has become stuck at one of the phases, when its members are so comfortable with where they are and so afraid of the next phase that they are unable to progress in their collective development. A form of family developmental retardation takes place.

"When Mom had Jennifer," said the boy, "everything

changed. Everything was the baby this, the baby that. Mom became a super baby mom, but she forgot all of us. Dad became a baby dad, and I became the big brother. Now, my sister still acts like a baby, and they treat her like a baby, and they expect me to treat her like a baby."

The fixated family has components of the stagnant and fazed families. It is not developing, and what might have been a stimulus for growth and change becomes a family energy leak, a point of focus, a heavy anchor on the family arch. This family does so well at the phase in which they are trapped that they become addicted to what they experience as a solution to family strife. However, the lack of growth and change will eventually catch up with every family member in the form of their own eventual regression.

Without development, everyone slides backwards. The necessary sense of a mature and mutually responsible "us" will not develop, leaving the younger family members unprepared for their new family systems, and at risk of progressing only to the phase of development in their new family that became the roadblock for their primary family.

10. THE GROWING FAMILY

It is obvious that all of the above family styles overlap, and represent segments of the family sequence of evolution. It is likely that these family styles are experienced by all families at one time or another. The troubled family is the family that becomes entwined in negative energy and lacks the resonance necessary to move on to other levels and experiences.

The growing family, on the other hand, is able to incorporate the styles mentioned earlier into a growing, dynamic system of an evolving sense of "us." The growing family does not panic when it senses itself at one of the earlier nine stages, and is able to see that families develop as the people within the families evolve and grow.

The growing family has all of the first nine characteristics within it, and, because it has the capacity to show ritual, rhythm, reason, remembrance, resilience, resonance, reconciliation, and reverence, it can revive itself through its knowledge that its struggle is about the evolution of life itself. Growing family members can burn up crises and conflicts as fuel for family energy and reanimation of family development.

When the growing family encounters one of the nine styles listed here, it is carried forward, because of firmly entrenched family rituals that are not abandoned at times of challenge and are the projection of every family member's needs and contributions, not just one member's fear of newness and experimentation.

The growing family is so in tune with its internal spiritual pulse that a skipped beat due to crisis does not cause family developmental arrest. The ability to be rational, and the invoking of long-standing optimistic and coherent family ways of appraising life events, result in a strong and responsible family esteem.

The resilience of the growing family is strong, and each member does indeed seem to grow with each change, resonating to higher orbits of energy in their own development. The reverence for the growing family system and the sense of "us" that underlies an enduring willingness to reconcile, even at times of the most severe pressures, carries the growing family through their encounters with the inevitable archetypical family problems.

Ultimately, the growing family is capable of saving its own life, of reviving itself and reenergizing the family system through, and not in spite of, the challenges it faces. The growing family finds a positive meaning in its existence and in all of the archetypical problems given to their family for work, remaining committed to one another through the worst of conflicts.

Consider these brief comments from a family member from each of the five families you have been reading about in this book. Look for the basic Rx's I have been discussing, and look particularly for the revival capacity reflected in each statement.

Mr. Anders: "When the boys were young, they were very close in age. We were overwhelmed by just keeping dry diapers on them, pee off us, and rashes off their butts. We began to argue and accuse each other of not doing things right. We finally realized that we were allowing the babies to be everything. We were becoming impatient with them and with us, and this wasn't our family anymore. We were starting a nursery. We had to work at setting up a more regular schedule, letting the little ones cry and stay wet sometimes, and we had to get back to taking our time to be together. We almost lost us for a while, but we got us back by remembering that what was most important to us . . . was 'us.' "

Ms. Bonner: "We were fazed, I mean, totally stunned, when my husband died. We couldn't move. I got mad at God and everything. I tried to take care of everything alone, and I panicked. I kept thinking about what I was going to do, what would happen when the kids were older, where I could possibly find the money we would need. Then, my daughter asked me why I wasn't letting her and her brother help anymore. She said she lost her dad just like I lost my husband. She cried one day and said, 'You know, Mom, I will never have another dad. You might have another husband. He won't be like Dad, but you might find somebody, choose somebody. I can't ever choose another Dad. You don't have him, we don't have him here, but he's here. He's us. We'll always have us.' That got to me. It got me . . . no . . . I mean, it got us, moving again."

Ms. Steiner: "We just kept trying to pretend that the nest wasn't empty. We kept the kids' rooms ready, just in case they divorced or wanted to bring their whole families home. We focused all of our attention on our son in college. He got enough parenting for three. We began to feel that something was wrong, and it was. We weren't changing. We were stagnant, just living in the past. We liked what we had so much, we were failing to see that we could have another part of our family, now that they were growing up. Growing up does not have to mean growing away, unless we thought that our family was only a geographical area. When we thought about us as something more than a place, we remembered that we were still a family. We would always be a family, even if we were becoming the major contributors to the profits of the long-distance phone company."

Mr. Johnson: "Trying to make a new family when you still have the pain of another family's end is not easy. Let me tell you, it is just a mess sometimes. You try to do it like you used to do it, and everyone resents being treated like you think you were in your other family. You have to begin by remembering that your former relationships are always a part of you. Those relationships would have had to change and adapt, too. You can't get stuck in what was. You have to help the new family find its own growth pattern as it needs to, not as you fear it won't, expect it too, or try to force it to be."

Ms. Muller: "Gramps died today. It's so quiet. It's so strange. We don't have anything at all to do now, it seems. We were so busy helping him, doing for him, getting ready to accept his death, that we just don't have anything to do now. I know we have to go through this. We have to just 'be' for awhile. We're not a new family now, but we're a changing family. We loved Gramps so much. We know he is within us, and we just want to sit still and let him, let his spirit, settle within us. We'll get moving again, but we don't want to move too quickly when something so very important is taking place."

If all of these reports sound remarkable to you, it is because these people have managed to keep their family view of life alive through the most difficult times. They have gone beyond the restrictions imposed by a society that sees life as individualistic, and in terms of local, here-and-now phenomena, to a cosmic view of living based on the principle of connection.

Some of the parents had alcoholic parents, some came from extreme poverty, some of the families had children or relatives with chronic disabilities, and some of them experienced sudden loss and marital disruption of their own, or in their earlier, family life. These families were not protected from the realities of living. They worked at remembering that they create their own reality by the choice they make—a life of "us" over a life of "me"—and through the power of their collective appraisal of life as a family process.

Family revival is a process of family hope, a vital optimism that we will not allow ourselves to be distracted by annoying, local, everyday problems. Family revival is finding your family's power to solve the real problems of living together. It is such a collectively constructive and optimistic appraisal that constitutes the main feature of healthy family living. Each of the five families you have been reading about has learned that joy is not a family mood, but an active choice of how the family will experience their life and perceive their life together.

A FAMILY PROBLEM-SOLVING GUIDE

Family revival requires a consistent system of dealing with the cyclical problem archetypes confronted, for all of us, by and with our families. The five families described in this book were helped in my clinic by the following problem-solving suggestions for reviviscence, for getting going again when problems arise. I suggest that you consider these problem-solving concepts when your own family is fighting for all of us.

Healthy Family Problem Solving
When Your Family Has Trouble,
Try to Remember:

1. All families have problems. It is one of the most important functions of a family to make it easier for each of us to solve problems that are common to being human.

2. Every problem has occurred before. Your family is fighting for all families about universal problems that are both infinite and indicative of the evolving common spirit that has yet to be able to resolve the seven major problems of life. Every family problem is one more attempt to promote the evolution of the human spirit in a small but significant way.

3. The first response of families to problems is to adopt "solutions" that are often manifestations of prior ineffective means of dealing with universal problems. These solutions are ineffective, but they are maintained as problem-solving attempts because better and more effective solutions do not seem available.

4. Unworkable family solutions continue to be attempted because the family sees no other way to solve their problems. If an unworkable solution is continued, it is only because it is "working" against the family, working in some counterproductive but habitual sense. Any behavior which continues must be viewed as working in some way, meeting some need, even if the

family is not feeling better and is failing to see the human problem archetype it is unknowingly attempting to resolve.

5. It will be difficult to understand how apparently uncomfortable and ineffective behaviors can be seen as "solutions." A key step in family problem solving is to confront the apparent contradiction, that the unworkable "solutions" are working only in that they are keeping the system going but not growing.

6. Unworkable solutions continue to be employed because they work only for some "self" want of one or more of the family members, not in the direction of meeting the "us" needs of the family system.

7. Ultimately, the family's "unworkable solutions" become themselves another form of problem, and the family begins to struggle, trapped with solutions instead of focusing on the basic archetypical problems. Ineffective problem solving continues to increase in frequency without addressing the underlying needs of the family system. The key question should be "what do we need?" and not "what does he, she, or they need or want?"

8. It is actually more difficult to get rid of "unworkable solutions" such as arguing, accusing, blaming, and withdrawing than to deal with the underlying "us" problems, because the unworkable solutions are intense, cathartic, and seem at least to be doing something. A form of "family superstition" results, with the whole family redoing the same unworkable arguments and conflicts "just because." The family begins to make its knuckles raw from knocking on wood, rather than looking for the leaks in the energy system that feeds the family tree.

9. All families have vastly underutilized resources. The energy available to families is infinite, and one and the same with the energy of the universe. This assertion is not based on romantic belief but documented scientific fact.

10. To get rid of the "unworkable solutions" that have become negative family habit, the family must first look to its resources and strengths, to what makes it a family. The ten Rx's of the super family are a shorthand for the basic ten family

resources, and the suggestions for applying each of the ten Rx's to daily family life will help your family mobilize its universal energy resources.

11. It will be difficult and even frightening at first for the family to give up its "unworkable solutions," such as accusations, judgmental confrontations, sarcasm, and threats, because when the unworkable solutions are removed, the real underlying problems will emerge immediately and with the force of centuries of struggle behind them.

12. The "real" problem that will emerge will always relate to one of the seven basic family archetypes of conflict, metaphors for the seven deadly sins of pride, avarice, lust, anger, gluttony, envy, and sloth.

13. Listen for the language of the seven archetypes, the "I-me" of pride, the "mine-yours" of avarice, the "now-must" of lust, the "stop-don't" of anger, the "get-all" of gluttony, the "more-less" of envy, and the "can't-won't" of sloth. When any of these words dominates a family conflict, look to the archetypical human struggle that is indicated by such family feud language.

14. The family may feel a lack of energy when first trying to solve the true family problem. More energy will enter the family when the real problems are confronted, because it feels better to the family to be working on the real universal spiritual problems. There will be a sense of "aha," that the family is finally doing something about their growth that really matters. There will be immediate emotional and spiritual rewards for struggling with the real human problems on the part of all humans.

15. It is so rewarding to confront the "real problems" of our humanness, rather than to be stuck in unworkable and more selfish pseudosolutions, that the family is likely to create all kinds of new problems to be dealt with. Family conflicts can be a sign of the strength and readiness of the family to deal with the universal issue of "us" on behalf of all of us. When this happens, the family becomes a healthier family, a part of all families in process, a part of the infinite "us."

Only the universal problems of human suffering are worthy of constant family energy investment. The revival of the family depends upon learning to differentiate between the significant struggles for the evolution of the human spirit and the meaningless and purposeless conflicts for the enhancement of the lonely self. When this lesson of the universal importance of the family is mastered, we will live in awe of our collective power and the significance of our family. If we try hard enough, we can accomplish a family renaissance that can enlighten the world, once again, to what "us" really means.

CHAPTER TWELVE

Family Reunion: Celebrating Life Together

"The rents, the tears, splits, and divisions, are mind made; they are not based on the truth but on what the Buddhists call illusion."

NORMAN O. BROWN

FAMILY REUNION: The ability to draw more strongly together through awareness of the power of the family and an energy for life and loving, derived through a common faith in the spiritual strength of the family.

A FAMILY REUNION

You could hear the screams of delight rising from the family baseball game. Grandpa threw his bat in the air, and screamed "I did it!" He was ninety years old, and the family softball game was one of his favorite parts of his family's annual reunion. He had played in every game, but no one could remember him actually hitting the ball out of the infield. This time, the ball soared into left field, and the uncle playing his position there did not have to pretend not to catch the ball as it looped over his head.

349

Grandpa moved slowly toward first base, his speed restricted more by his laughter than his age. The first baseman, his ten-year-old grandson, picked up the bag, moved it several feet toward his grandfather, and put it down to shorten the base path and ease his grandfather's way to his first base hit in family reunion history.

Everyone forgot the score and rushed out on the field. Hot dogs were left burning, as aunts, uncles, and everyone old and young celebrated as if the family had won the World Series. In a way, they had. The family had just finished one of their worst years. There had been three deaths in the family, one divorce, and two of the men and one of the women had been laid off from their jobs. No one said anything, but there were fewer hot dogs and less pop this year. There was a silent acknowledgment that the family reunion was more important this year than most, a time to comfort one another, to celebrate the survival of their loving group.

The final of the ten Rx's of healthy family living, reunion, is the type of strength for re-collection of the family system shown by this family. No matter what happens, the healthy family can reunite, get the system not only back together, but back to a celebrating, growing, thriving orientation to daily life.

Family reunion is the ability of family members to maintain family energy and cohesiveness no matter what forces impinge upon the system or its individual members. Reunion is a family counterreflex to the societal forces for family disintegration, the ability of the family to spin back to its core even as it continues to spin outward in its growth. No matter how strong the outside influences, families have the capacity to "stick together," clinging even more strongly to one another when events seem to pull at family unity. Perhaps because every human being is ultimately a family member of every other human being, the family represents a microcosm of the forces that unite all living things.

The Family Reunion Test

To help you see how the tenth Rx of healthy family living, reunion, applies to your daily family life, take the following test. As with the prior nine tests of the family Rx's, each item offers a specific way in which you may implement this factor in your own family living. Use the same scoring system that you used in prior chapters.

0	1	2	3	4	5	6	7	8	9	10
ALMOST NEVER		SELDOM		SOMETIMES		A LOT		ALMOST ALWAYS		

1. —— Do you feel close with all family members, as if they were a part of you while you seem to be a part of them, and do you make a point of talking about and showing your sense of connection?

2. —— Can you sense a connection between your own family and all other families, with family conversations characterized by talk of commonalities with others?

3. —— Does your family spend time together discussing world issues and trying to come to a common agreement on your "family politics"?

4. —— If you had to think of one word that describes your family, would that word be one that reflects togetherness and peacefulness?

5. —— At times of loss or major changes, does your family become more unified, mutually supportive, and able to put these events in a perspective that has meaning to every family member?

6. —— Is your family optimistic about its future, and does it show this optimism in its daily language?

7. —— Do all members of your family show economic restraint, avoiding addiction to getting more and more "stuff" and acting and talking with awareness of the danger of "using up" our world?

8. —— Does your family seem to be enjoying life

more now than it did earlier in your family history, by making a collective effort to enjoy the simple things and making moments together count?

9. ———— Do family members react to one another with tolerance and an attempt to "keep the family together," even when there are arguments and family crises?

10. ———— If the world would end today, do you feel that you have enjoyed being with your family often enough and intimately enough?

———— TOTAL FAMILY REUNION SCORE

If your own score or your family's collective score was over the arbitrary 90 points, you are showing a strong tenth Rx factor of family reunion. If you scored less than 90 points, you may be failing to work hard enough at keeping your family together in the context of the common purpose of celebrating the intensity of being alive together, the true meaning of the miracle of "us" that I have been describing with each of the ten Rx's.

FIFTIETH COUSINS THIRTEEN TIMES REMOVED

We are all ultimately united and influenced by the force of "us" to a much stronger extent than most of us would even imagine. In fact, none of us is less related than fiftieth cousins.[1] If we trace our family tree back far enough and with enough care and consistency, we eventually come back to a trunk that we share with every living human being. Doubling the number of our ancestors for each generation and going backwards, (two parents, four grandparents, eight great-grandparents, etc.) we would account for all mankind by the time we went back thir-

1. Murchie, G. *The Seven Mysteries of Life* (Boston: Houghton Mifflin Co., 1978), p. 345. Dr. Murchie's research, including consultations with leading geneticists, reveals that ". . . no human being of any race can be less closely related to any other human than approximately fiftieth cousin, and most of us are a lot closer."

teen times. We are all actually fiftieth cousins thirteen times removed.

It is not overstatement to say that this interrelatedness of all of us is the most important fact in the world. Even by mathematical calculation, we are all united, and when we pull away from each other, or allow crises to tear away at our family without intense and consistent effort at reunification, we break the first law of nature; that we are all family and we are all a part of "us."

Perhaps someday we will all be invited to the most important cousins' reunion in the world, the universal human reunion. Until that time, we must work toward the reunification of every individual family as a step toward a reunion of the overall "us."

THE FIVE FAMILY FRAGMENTING FORCES

My clinical work indicates that five major factors directly pull at that union of the family. Each of these factors is another family archetype, a common thread of the challenge for the refinement of the evolving human spirit and a reawareness of that spirit within all of us. All families must deal with these family fragmenting forces or stressors to varying degrees.

I will describe five of the most severe challenges that families experience as group, "wrongful" challenges only in the sense that the evolving spirit is stressed to the maximum by each of these extraordinary pressures, requiring equally extraordinary family reunion capacity. In a sense, all challenges to the family are "rightful" because they are at least symbolically universal and necessary to the evolution of the human spirit. The five fragmenting "wrongful" challenges are almost too intense, too difficult, too seemingly unfair for the family to deal with.

1. WRONGFUL FAMILY LOSS

Earlier, I discussed the issue of loss in the family. Ms. Bonner lost her young husband and the Muller family lost Ms. Muller's father during the time I was collecting my material from the super families. The Muller family's loss was painful and disruptive, but the grandfather had lived a full and rewarding life. The Bonner family loss was seen as "wrongful," in that the young father was in the middle of his most productive years and responsible for a young and developing family.

"Rightful" loss actually strengthens a family system, impacting on the family as a natural evolutionary aspect of the passing on and development of the human spirit and of the energy of the family. When older people die after loving and being loved, we grieve, we cry, and we feel anger. No matter how old or how sick, their leaving seems always to be too soon. We are eventually able to appraise such loss as natural and appropriate to the scheme of life.

"Wrongful loss," however, often seems beyond our comprehension, stretching our ability to appraise such loss with any sense of optimism and hope regarding the future. The loss of a premature baby is such a "wrongful loss," and society offers little true support or empathy beyond statements such as "you can try again." The final surrender to infertility seems to be a wrongful loss, with those persons with children never truly able to understand the pain of the sterile person and the constant reminders of the loss of a child never born. The loss of a child to a random gunshot, as a victim of the senseless violence of our society, is yet another example of wrongful loss. The following statement indicates how "wrongful" a loss can feel.

"Why would a just God take my husband while his father is much older and no where near as nice a man as my husband?" asked Ms. Bonner just after her husband's sudden death. "It's not fair. It's senseless. How could his father go to his son's funeral?" Ms. Bonner's sense of indignation, injustice, resentment, and torment is related to the "wrongfulness" of this loss in terms of our day-to-day experience of life.

Ms. Bonner struggled to make sense of what is ultimately senseless and only knowable beyond thinking and through faith. Ms. Bonner's feelings about her loss temporarily restricted the family reunification process, and only a renewed reverence and resilience of the family system carried her through this tortured time.

Religious platitudes will never soothe the suffering spirit of a family that experiences a wrongful loss. Only the reunion of the family, a full understanding of the universality and immortality of the human spirit and the relative lack of importance of the physical body in comparison to the spiritual energy of the loved one, will provide any sense of direction for effective grieving and deflection of anger into the intensity of need for reunification with the family.

"Wrongful loss" seems to have the following five characteristics:

FIVE COMPONENTS OF "WRONGFUL LOSS"

1. INSUFFICIENT LOVE TIME. By reason of age, distance, or time commitment, the person who is lost "wrongfully" seems to have fallen too soon out of love's way, preventing the family from loving him or her as intensely and openly as it wanted and needed to. Often, the loss itself draws the attention of the family to the fact that there is never enough loving going on within the entire family system, and it is this loving lesson that must be learned even through the almost endless pain from the wrongful loss. The issue is not to blame oneself or others for not having loved enough, but to see this loss as a stimulus for even more loving.

"I wanted so fiercely to wipe all that make-up junk off of him," said the woman at her husband's funeral. "I wanted to make him look like him, and to love him, hold him, tell him one more time what I never said enough. I love you, I love you, I love you." Most of us will know the agony of lost opportunities to love, so I urge you to build more demonstrative loving into your daily living.

2. SUDDEN LIFE EFFECT. Wrongful loss almost always seems sudden, even if an illness may linger. A diagnosis of a fatal illness or the eventual passing of a family member, however long the lingering, seems too sudden. No one seems really ready for the loss. Loss by heart attack, sudden infant death, accident or other unanticipated death slams to our attention the vulnerability of our own physical life, and we have an "into body experience," a type of "sudden life awareness" that results in feelings of vulnerability and fear. We are often too busy living our lives to pay attention to trying to have our life, and an unexpected death can draw the family to a reunion around the importance of daily living and a new sense of the sacred in even the most minor of family activities.

"When my uncle died of the heart attack," said the nephew, "I started to think about me. It could have been me. I'm not that much younger than he was, and I just never gave life much thought, or at least that much thought, until Uncle George died that day. Now I really watch myself and every single symptom of something." The "into body experience" of this man illustrates the sudden life effect of a sudden loss.

3. DISBELIEF SYSTEMS. Wrongful losses seem to happen more often to people who have inconsistent, too literal, or too narrow belief systems concerning what life and death means for their family. Without a sense of life's meaning, death is always senseless, because life seems senseless. When the family is not united around a common belief system, some way of appraising the major life events that affect all families, any crisis or loss will seem wrongful because it seems totally unexplainable within the context of the family disbelief system.

"You never think about what you believe until someone dies," said the man. "Then, at least for a while, you sort of promise yourself you're going to take a long look at what you're doing and why. Unfortunately, society isn't set up for long looks, just long hours." Most of us fail at our promise to pause a moment to examine our direction and purpose, and sudden or wrongful losses can bring the immediate need to do so directly to our attention.

4. LACK OF AN EMOTIONAL ESTATE PLAN. The family that does not have a plan of direction, of where they choose as a group to invest their emotions, will experience every loss as an interference, even an annoyance, that is unfair and without reason in the overall scheme of their life. The question "what is our life for" is the key question in emotional estate planning, and when there is no emotional life assurance policy, no family guidelines for what matters, what should matter and what should not matter as much, or the absence of unity of agreement on these factors, every loss will seem wrongful.

"Funny how you don't pay attention much to how you're feeling unless you are feeling really sad or really frightened," said the woman who had just lost her child. "I used to think I was feeling a lot, but I never knew what feeling was until this happened." Wrongful loss is an emotional attention-getter, a type of bank statement bringing to our attention the fact that we have been exceeding the limits of our account or investing in the wrong places for a long, long time.

5. MISPLACED PRIORITIES. When we experience the loss of a family member, or some major family change that is experienced as a loss, it can seem that such a loss is wrongful because we have for too long placed our priorities incorrectly. We may have spent too much time thinking about and dealing with work, with recreation, with taking care of the house or the car, or even involved in a hobby or other distraction, and, when a loss occurs, we learn suddenly about our soul's divine discontentment. When a loss occurs while our investment in life activities is in proper balance with our spiritual direction, our inner sense of contentment with what we feel on some level we should be doing, the loss seems "rightful" in that we can make sense of the change and take comfort in how we are living even as we grieve.

A man who had lost his father said, "I noticed that, after the initial shock, everyone who came to the funeral home started to talk about the purpose of life. That's what I'm thinking about from now on."

FAMILY PRAYERS FROM SOUL SCHOOL

Baha'u'llah, the nineteenth century prophet of the Baha'i faith, wrote, ". . . tests in life are not punishment but rather serve to recall the soul to itself . . . for the earth in essence is a workshop, a crucible for the making and refining of character." Scientist Guy Murchie refers to our earthly experiences as a "soul school," a type of workshop for the development of the soul. He writes, "Praise God, O humans, for your problems—the worse the better and look for more—because problems are what you are made of."[2]

Most major religions view our earthly experience as a time of refinement for the evolution of the soul; and the family system is the classroom itself, an advanced center for spiritual training. Where else could we find such variety and intensity of conflict, from the spilled glass at family dinner to the sudden loss of a loved one? Earth itself seems designed with the ultimate of variety, including disasters, pleasure, pain, joy, and sorrow, an infinite spiritual course catalog, and when we learn to see the family as the place for archetypical struggles for soul-searching and eventual soul-soaring, we learn to grieve our wrongful loss in the context of growth, rather than in loneliness of despair.

The ancient Hawaiians, the Kahuna, believed that chanting caused the palate, the roof of the mouth, to vibrate. They thought that this vibration in turn transferred to the bottom of the brain resting just above the roof of the mouth. The positive vibrational tones and words were believed to cause the brain to "vibrate" more positively and to create a more positive world and a healthier body for the person who chanted of "the sacredness of life." Whether the Kahuna were correct or not, it is true that we all make a choice about how we will see the world, and to say out loud that this choice is positive and a celebration of the family view can only be of help to all family members.

By speaking out loud about the hopes, prayers, and strengths of the family, we can affirm the ultimate unity of the family. Whether your own family calls it prayer, chanting, meditation, repeating affirmations, reflection, or contemplation, no matter what religious system you have embraced, and whether or not you consider yourself religious at all, the process of taking the time to talk with and to the higher power within you is the most powerful healing process in the world.

When I speak of family affirmations or prayers in this chapter, I am speaking of the effort to reunite with the power that makes us alive and unites us all, a way of making your mind pay attention to your own spirit and the spirit of your family. The affirmations I will include relate to affirmations of a reunion with our collective spirit, the infinite "us" that gives

2. Ibid., p. 621.

meaning to our living and provides the context for the ten family Rx's of rhythm, ritual, reason, remembrance, resonance, resilience, reconciliation, reverence, revival, and reunion.

Here is an affirmation, an appeal to the power of the spirit of the family for times of wrongful loss, words to help with family reawareness and reunification with the meaning of living, even when such meaning seems beyond our comprehension. You may want to design your own family prayers or affirmations, but by speaking to your own higher power, you have begun the process of reunification with that power even at times of severe crisis.

A FAMILY AFFIRMATION FOR WRONGFUL LOSS

Please help us all at this time of such painful loss.

Help us to love more deeply and broadly from Your call to loving that is heard by us as You summon our loved one and torture our souls in Your demand for our learning.

Help us to see what this loss means for our loved one and for all of us in our infinite development under Your teaching.

Help us to feel the strength shared by all of us that we may more clearly see how our suffering is not retribution, or a form of earned punishment, but a challenge for the refinement of the universal spirit.

Help us to know and to feel, now more than ever, that our family loved one is not lost or gone, but always growing with and within us, guiding us from within as we can no longer experience our loved one as external to us.

Help us see that, as our loved one only seems to have ceased to exist, we must learn to live with even more meaning and commitment to one another.

Help us to stay family forever.

2. DIVORCE AND THE FAMILY

Not all, and maybe not many, divorces are easy and simple. Few divorces result in the mutual growth of all persons involved. Divorce of mutual choice that takes place at the same developmental time in each person's life, for similar reasons, and that results in more freedom for growth for all concerned would be "rightful divorce." My clinical work indicates that the "rightful divorce" is extremely rare.

"Wrongful divorce" takes place when one or both partners feel helpless, when development has not been mutual, and when anger, blame, and a sense of injustice and lowered self-esteem in one or both members are involved. Wrongful divorce seems to "happen" to one or both of the partners, while "rightful divorce" is mutually chosen, a decision that evolves within the total family system over time and for clear and communicated reasons.

Here are the five characteristics of wrongful divorce that make it one of the five fragmenting factors for family systems, and make such a divorce process an obstacle to true reunion into new families in the future.

FIVE COMPONENTS OF "WRONGFUL DIVORCE"

1. NONSECRETIVE SECRETS. When a wrongful divorce takes place, both members have been struggling for years, sometimes from even before the marriage, with serious secrets about their own feelings and wishes regarding their own life and needs for their individual development. Both partners have been aware of the disparity in developmental direction, but have distracted one another from open disclosure and confrontation of this difference by focusing on career or children.

Unlike a "rightful divorce," where differences in development emerge and are discussed openly through to the acknowledgment of irreconcilable differences and the decision for separation, "wrongful divorce" takes the form of the "unspoken difference," the failure to say openly what both partners know and fear about the underlying and serious differences that have been present for so long.

"I've known it for the whole marriage, Doc," said the husband. "She never wanted to be married. She just wanted someone to take her out of her parents' home, and I was never interested in giving the marriage any attention. I just wanted a housekeeper while I worked. We both knew there were serious problems, so we just got busy with the kids. Now it's too late to do anything, and we both feel helpless and hopeless."

This husband is describing a situation common to many marriages I have seen in my practice. The problem really relates to "no marriage" rather than a bad marriage. The couple has been attempting a marriage that was never started, and both are trying to divorce someone to whom they were never really married in the first place. The only outcome from this situation is a wrongful divorce, unless both partners chose to marry one another for the first time.

2. SEXUAL SADNESS. Wrongful divorce typically involves two persons who have both been unhappy with their sexual life together and have failed to openly discuss this issue. In the rightful divorce, partners have clearly identified their sexual distress, and may have tried to seek help for a specific sexual problem such as erectile or orgasmic failure.

In the wrongful divorce, no help is sought and sexual activity and interest is reduced to a sadness and lowered sexual self-esteem on the part of both partners. Therapists often refer to such a situation as a case of "inhibited sexual desire," when in fact a more mechanical problem may have been present, long ago in the relationship, that was never confronted, resulting in withdrawal, resentment, and anger at self and partner.

Rightful divorce is associated with failed vigorous attempts to face up to and correct sexual differences or problems, a surrender to sexual incompatibility rather than a mutual withdrawal because of sexual sadness, a shared depression at the absence of sexual delight.

"For the whole marriage, you never did anything about your problem," said the wife. "You worked on everything but the problem. You knew you were coming too soon. We talked about it, and now twenty years later we haven't had sex for most of that time. You would get help with your taxes and look for every penny, but you wouldn't get help for our sexual problem. I feel so gypped, so empty, and so hateful for what's happened."

This wife is despairing over sexual years lost and her own sense of helplessness, now that the sexual clock seems to be stopped forever. I have never treated a case of sexual sadness that did not have, somewhere in its past, at least the beginnings of a mechanical sexual problem or lack of sexual knowledge that was not addressed.

3. MARITAL ROBBERY. Rightful divorce takes place when both partners see their problems within themselves, sharing clear and communicated responsibility for marital unhappiness that they can both trace to the marital interaction itself. Wrongful divorce happens to marital partners who have been fighting over in-laws, over unresolved family issues outside of the marriage, or over difficulties in one or both of the marital partners which relate to what happened to him or her in their primary family and continue now to play themselves out in the marriage. In effect, the marriage is robbed of its energy by the unfilled energy leak in the primary family system of the husband or wife.

"If he hadn't have been so damned involved with his mother's problems, maybe he would have seen ours," said the frustrated wife. "He was married to her demands rather than to our needs as a couple." This wife is expressing her sense of indignation that the marriage might have been able to grow if one or both partners would have saved some energy for that marriage.

4. FINANCIAL FEELINGS. Rightful divorce can take place when a disorder of love, an incapability in the way each marital partner has learned to love, is identified, worked on, and found to be irreparable in spite of intense effort and professional help. All divorces have the elements of the "love or money" issue, and the wrongful divorce involves differences not only in how money is spent but in what money really means. One partner may devalue money while the other sees money as a means of quantifying love or commitment. Divorce over spending is typically divorce over differences in life dreams, over whether or not two people can learn to dream together and not just earn and spend together.

"It's not that my wife spends too much money," said the husband. "It's just that she likes to get a lot of things, and things cost money, so her things addiction costs money. She has no idea what money means. She just likes to get, to acquire."

"I do so know what money means," replied the wife. "To you, money is your measure of everything. You think a balanced checking account is the same thing as a balanced life. You take all the fun out of getting anything or doing anything because you see dollar signs everywhere. You measure everything by money."

The debate between this husband and wife illustrates that it is not always the amount of money, or power struggles over who controls what money and how, but what money signifies for each partner that is at the root of a wrongful divorce.

5. LOW MARITAL APTITUDE. I will soon be publishing my just completed research on the concept of "marital aptitude," on the fact that some people, perhaps many people, never learn the skill of how to marry and stay married. "Maritability" is a learned skill, not a genetic trait, and I suggest that we can all be married to almost anyone if we learn marital aptitude. The romantic notion of the one and only is pure myth. Being and staying married requires marital aptitude and remediation of any "dysmatrimonia" that a person may suffer from.

Rightful divorce takes place when one or both marital partners acknowledge their own low marital aptitude and make the active choice to attempt to correct their own "marriageing" deficiency, identify the areas of their marital aptitude that are deficient, and try but fail to successfully remediate a marital disability.

Wrongful divorce takes place when marital partners see each other as "not worth marrying," or "not being able to be married to anybody," or "needing to marry someone more like himself or herself," or "just not the one for me." As I have pointed out, we can be and stay happily married to almost any one of our fiftieth cousins, but we must first learn what "marriage ability and aptitude" is, and where our own marital disabilities lie.

"He's not the one that was made for me," said the unhappy wife. "I'm not in love with him. I just don't feel the right feelings toward him. He's a fine man, but he's the wrong man. I feel like he's more of a father or a brother than a husband." This woman is failing to look at her own marital aptitude, her own inability to be the "marrying kind."

When we "wrongfully divorce," we drop out of soul

school without having understood why we are dropping out, or what deficiencies we have as individuals in our ability to learn marriage. The rare rightful divorce is sad but energizing, resulting in a new feeling of freedom and growth for both partners. Wrongful divorce results in confusion, unresolved guilt and blame, and lasting pain and alienation.

Here is an affirmation or prayer for the family system that encounters the wrongful divorce. As with each of the prayers provided in this chapter, modify the words to suit your own family's feelings about the meaning and context of our living. It is not the prayer itself that matters, but the process of the family unifying and reuniting at times of challenge to form a brief shared statement that can help focus the family on what it views as the nature of the evolving human spirit. The prayers presented in this chapter are intended only as starting points for family affirmation of unity.

AN AFFIRMATION FOR THE FAMILY OF A WRONGFUL DIVORCE

We will need new strength to be together now.

Even though we will be apart, we will always be a part of one another, and will need to help each other find our unity even as we are less together in our daily lives.

We need to help each other look at ourselves, to learn about our loving and our needs, to learn how to love one another even as we decide to separate to allow a different love to grow between us and within each of us.

We need to help one another find our shared energy within us, that we may take comfort in discovering that all love involves loss, loneliness, and change, and that not all love is shown in the same way for the same time.

We must help one another to know that we needed one another to learn this part of our loving, that we may love more fully now and in the future.

As some flowers do not flourish near one another yet still grow strongly when apart, we have decided to grow at more distance that we each may bloom more fully at each other's side.

We must work together to turn our pain to praise, our hurt to healing, and our pride to patience for one another, as we try to do at more distance what we could not do when we were close.

3. CHRONIC ILLNESS AND DISABILITY

Disease is as natural a part of life as health. Without illness, we would not be able to fully experience the true nature of health, and would be unable to make necessary adjustments to maintain our health. When we get sick, something is finally going right within us, something is getting our attention for more caring for our body and how we are living day to day.

Rightful illness and disability is an adjustment process in the human body that results in a rallying of our internal healing capacity. Rightful illness results in caring and comforting by our family, a time when the family becomes an intensive caring unit. Wrongful illness and disability, however, tend to tear at the family fabric, overstressing the caring capacity and resilience of the family so that reunion, a joining together to help, may be ineffective.

Here are the characteristics of "wrongful illness and disability" that can interfere with the family's reunification for its own health:

1. AGE-REVERSED ILLNESS OR DISABILITY. When a young child is stricken with disease, resulting in limitations on that child's behavior, in apparent aging before the child's time because of restrictions on movement, appearance, and capacity to flourish and grow, illness is wrongful and requires extreme family reunion and strength for family survival. When older adults are stricken with an illness or accident that causes them to regress physically or mentally, to act too young and to lose their deserved dignity and self-respect, again the family must find super energy to cope with this "wrongful illness."

Ms. Muller said, "Gramps is really just like a baby. He cries, he wets, he has tantrums, and sometimes he doesn't even know us. It takes all that we have and can do just to keep him at home."

Another woman stated, "My daughter's leukemia has made her a forty-year-old in a nine-year-old body. She's so serious, so mature, and she carries such an adult burden that we are sad every time we look into the old eyes looking out of that young face."

Both women are describing the "age reversal" aspect of wrongful illness, the distortion of the natural evolutionary process of youth to age. It is difficult for the family to understand the spiritual lessons being taught at such times of crisis, to know that the spirit is ageless, and there is something needed in the archetypical human evolution that is being manifested by this age-to-youth and youth-to-age distortion that requires such profound family adjustment.

2. THE VOYEURISTIC SOCIETY. Unfortunately, our society is not often enough a tolerant society. Limping with a cast on the foot elicits understanding and perhaps the assumption on the part of the casual observer that the limping person was injured in some athletic event. Limping, as a result of chronic disability, or shaking from the tremors of a disabling disease, too often elicits only stares, ogling, and curiosity, rather than support, acceptance, and empathy. A child who cannot speak clearly, an adult who cannot hold a cup, a family member who appears "unusual" in the eyes of a society that has too narrow a definition of what seems "normal," is viewed as more object than person.

Wrongful illness and disability is wrongful because society seems to need to make the disability "wrong" so that some safe distance from the hurt person is achieved. In the process of just watching, society fails to see beyond a deformity or handicap to the spirit and soul of the person who is limping, shaking, or slurring speech on our behalf. Remember, the hurt person is hurting for us, and we must do everything we can to be sure that they are not hurting even more because of us.

"Do you know what it feels like?" asked the woman with multiple sclerosis. "I look normal at first, don't I? Then, they look closer and see that I am skinny and I shake. Then they watch me shake and try to pretend that they aren't watching.

They need to see me shake, because if I'm doing the shaking, they can feel safe that they don't have to."

This woman's anger and feelings of isolation only obstruct the important channels for her healing from within. Society has failed to appreciate her battle on its behalf and has left her out of the overall family reunion.

3. INVISIBLE DISABILITIES.

Invisible disabilities such as learning disability, intellectual impairment, dyslexia, attention deficit disorders, and severe perceptual handicaps are wrongful disabilities because the person with such an impairment is forced to experience his or her problems alone. The family of such a person is forced to carry its burden anonymously and without empathy from a society that rejects what it will not take the time or make the effort to feel. Unless the family can summon extraordinary energy for reunion and demand attention and caring for the invisible problems, our major institutions will offer little help or understanding.

While persons may stare at an obvious deformity or physical restriction and thus interfere with the dignity of freedom to "be" without constant scrutiny and wonder, persons who have less visible or even invisible disabilities suffer no less and are likely to encounter rejection, impatience, anger, and little effort to look deeper for the hurt. While the curse of being pitied may effect the visibly impaired more than the invisibly impaired, invisible impairments are "wrongful" in that they elicit little help in healing and growth from others.

A newspaper recently reported the strangulation death of an eleven-year-old boy by his mother. The mother then took her own life. The police officer at the scene stated, "The motive was that the mother seemed to be obsessed with the fact that he had learning disabilities, and she seemed to feel he wouldn't be able to cope with things later in life."[3]

What the police officer and all of the officials quoted in the story above failed to understand was that the suffering within this family was imposed by a society that would never know how hopeless and alone the family may have felt in trying to help such a boy grow up in a world that could see nothing

3. Boyle, J. "Police Think Mother Killed Son Over Despair About His Future," *Detroit Free Press*, July 16, 1988, p. 1.

wrong but provided nothing to make things right. The police officer continued, "It appears a lot of it was in her mind." He didn't know that the suffering was in her soul as she struggled with a wrongful disability that destroyed her family.

4. UNDISTRIBUTED ILLNESS AND COUNTERHOSTILITY. Rightful illness and disability seems distributed over time. and families, without the seemingly unfair overwhelming of one family group by multiple illnesses. Wrongful illness and disability are impairments that seem to come in clusters or distribute themselves too heavily on one family system. Several suffering family members at one time can make the necessary reunion of the family at times of healing very difficult in terms of finances, time, and emotional energy.

"We have a poor track record," said the father. "Both of my daughters have been seriously ill, my wife is in a wheelchair, and my back is never really good. Just to go out somewhere is like taking a whole hospital ward. And you know what? When we all hobble through the zoo, everybody sort of gets mad. It's like they're all saying, 'Why don't you all stay home where sick people belong? You're in our way, and you are making us feel uncomfortable.' "

This father is describing the counterhostility that can be experienced by families overwhelmed with their disproportionate share of illness. Instead of eliciting caring, such families sometimes sense discomfort from those around them, even a sense of dislike, perhaps related to fear and guilt on the part of the nonimpaired persons for their own good fortune.

Once again, society fails to see the family with numerous health burdens as a group of people fighting our developmental battles for us. In place of condescending nods of sympathy and pseudoapplause for the courage of the overwhelmed family, we should be busy working with vigor to enhance the social system in which such families must conduct their life, attempting to make their world an easier place in which to live and be loved.

5. ILLNESS TOO SHORT OR TOO LONG. Illness and disability can be the ultimate teacher, and a rightful illness lasts long enough to provide lessons about adjustments to living that can promote future healing and result in life-style change. Wrongful illness either strikes so suddenly and lasts for such a short period of time that little can be learned other than help-lessness, or lingers so long that the energy system of the family dissipates into a chronic state of trying to survive rather than develop.

"Her illness was so sudden that it was like an explosion," said the mother. "We ran from doctor to doctor, hospital to hospital. We were so busy that we didn't even see her get better. Just one day, she wasn't sick. Now we don't even know what made her sick or made her well."

A father reported, "By the time my dad died, we had gone through so many years of problems, of money hassles, of con-stant hospital visits, of parking, visiting, going home, coming back for false alarms, that all we learned was to keep moving."

This man and woman represent the overwhelming nature of the pattern of some illnesses and the way in which the timing of disease can disrupt the capacity to learn about wellness in the family system.

"Wrongful illness or impairment" is sickness or disability that makes the lessons of living and healing difficult to learn. Instead of the illness teaching metaphorically about our living too fast, not caring for our body, or being inattentive to our loving, the apparent age-inappropriateness of the impact of the particular disability, the lack of social understanding and sup-port, the possible invisibility to others of the impairment itself, the seemingly unfair distribution of the illness or disability bur-den, and the severe acuteness or almost unbearable chronicity of the problems can make family reunion almost beyond family resources.

Here is another "starter" family affirmation for times of family impairment. Remember again that you should be trying to form your own affirmation statements or prayers as a family, perhaps using the prayers I have provided as points of depar-ture. Say the words of each affirmation aloud and as a family, and you will find the power of family is available to you.

A FAMILY AFFIRMATION FOR TIMES OF DISABILITY

This burden seems too much for us, even though we know we have been chosen to do this for everyone and on behalf of everyone.

We know that we have been given a challenge to learn, to love, and to grow beyond our bodies and the easily accepted gift of perfect health, but we must help one another to see and feel our energy from one another.

We need help with the small things that must be done every day but are made so difficult for us now.

We need help with the big things that seem to have lost so much of their meaning and take so much of our effort.

We need help to understand why this illness crisis is happening and to see that we are suffering for everyone because all of us suffer for each of us and for everyone.

We must help one another to hold in our minds the fact that our spirit only suffers if we all fail to keep our faith in our family energy to carry us forward through this lesson of life.

Please help us to be strengthened by our burden and see the way to spiritual wellness, even as we struggle with this challenge to the house of our Spirit's growth.

4. OUT-OF-STEP FAMILIES

When new families form from combinations of previous families, the adjustments necessary always involve a significant rearrangement of the family system. "Rightful formation of stepfamilies" results from rightful divorces, losses, or from the super family ability to overcome the wrongful family fragmentation factors, to make the necessary and constructive rearrangement of a life system for the welfare of the survivors of a major insult to the family system.

"Wrongful" formation of stepfamilies results when the bitterness and despair of wrongful divorce, loss, or illness causes the involuntary formation of a stepfamily. Here are the five characteristics of a "wrongfully formed stepfamily."

1. LACK OF FAMILY CONSULTATION. "Wrongful stepfamily formation" occurs when all members of the family have not been actively involved in both sides of stepfamily formation. The first side is consultation and involvement of both sets of primary family members, eliciting everyone's feelings and attitudes regarding the factors that changed the primary family. The second side is consultation with, not permission-seeking of, the primary family and new family members regarding the stepfamily. Assigning new family relationships is much different than actively involving everyone concerned in the process of new family evolution.

"We weren't told anything about the plans," said the daughter of a newly formed stepfamily. "We were sort of placed together and supposed to all be happy and become an instant family. They forgot that just because they picked each other, we didn't pick each other. We were just coming along for the ride."

This daughter is discussing the failure of meaningful involvement of all family members, not as permission-seeking but as productive planning, and as a request for help in the formation of a new family system.

2. PREMATURE PARENTHOOD. Wrongful stepfamily formation takes place when one or both new stepparents attempt to become instant parents, to gain perhaps more influence over their stepchildren than they felt they had over their own children in a prior marriage. Parenthood, like childhood, is a developmental process that requires time, tolerance, and patience. We can no more "force" a child to be our child than we can make ourselves be a parent, just because it seems like it is time to do so.

"I saw early in the thing that I was out of practice," said the stepfather. "I hadn't been doing too well before as a parent or a husband, and all of a sudden here I am trying to be superparent to a family that is still stunned by the changes." This father is expressing his premature attempts at control of a family system before he has allowed time for a family to form.

"I didn't have much of a father in my first family," said

the stepdaughter. "I don't know why they think I seem all of a sudden to need one now." This daughter senses the premature attempts at making a family rather than learning to "family."

3. MISPLACED HIDDEN RESENTMENTS. When resentment and blame based on primary family relationships are unresolved, the stepfamily may become the theater for the last act of an incomplete family drama. A stepfather, -mother, or -child may become the surrogate target of anger that was never dealt with in interactions with the appropriate person in a primary family. The new stepfamily feels "wrong," because there are conflicts that seem to have no explanation within the new family situation. The lack of reason relates to the fact that the conflicts are unresolved historical family imprints and not present interfactional problems. The following statement by a stepfather illustrates such an unresolved imprint.

"This kid was angry from the day I met her," said the stepfather. "I know that she's not mad at me, but it's rough not just spanking her. I know she's mad at her father, but finally she has somebody around who feels her anger, and she is taking full advantage of it."

4. THE WAIT-AND-SEE FACTOR. Wrongful formation of stepfamilies can result when family members within the new stepfamily feel as if it is emotionally risky to trust the durability of the new family. As a result, a family member may hold back from becoming a contributing part of the family energy system, adopting a "wait and see" posture regarding the workability of the new arrangement before investing their emotions. This wait-and-see orientation is revealed by the following statement by a stepdaughter.

"My new mother wants me to tell her how I feel. She wants me to really be open with her, but she doesn't understand that I have to be sure first. I have to be sure I can trust her. You can't just talk about everything right away like that. The last time I tried that, everything got screwed up."

5. THE FAMILY SURRENDER FACTOR. Wrongful stepfamily formation can result from family members giving up on the concept of family. Due to prolonged conflicts or imposed isolation resulting from a lack of an intact primary family system, the new stepfamily may be pressured by one of the new member's feelings that families just don't work out very well.

As one of my patients pointed out, "You can't really form a new family when you aren't sure if you ever had an old one. You have to learn from scratch."

The stepfamily is continuing to be a more frequent occurrence in our society, and rightful stepfamilies can represent the ultimate form of reunion, of coming together again as a new group of people to try once more to find the miracle of a family "us." Wrongful stepfamily formation, however, can be just another step down instead of up the family evolution scale. Here is a starter family affirmation for the stepfamily:

A STEPFAMILY AFFIRMATION

We are new together, so we must show patience for one another.

We still hurt from our past family life, so we must give one another the strength and wisdom to see the good that was in our old family, that may find this good in our new family.

We are tentative in our new roles, so we must give one another the comfort and courage to reach out to one another for love and to love.

We are not yet sure of one another, so we must give one another confidence that our prior pain has strengthened all of us to help and guide each other through our confusion and uncertainty.

We must help one another move together, be in step together, toward a new family love that will last forever even as the love of our former families still energizes our soul.

5. THE IMPOVERISHMENT OF THE FAMILY

All challenges to the family can lead to growth, and financial pressures can cause a reassessment of purpose, direction, and family dreams and goals. Such positive reassessment and reunification of the family for a new direction based on financial realities is a major aspect of family system evolution.

Wrongful financial pressures are based on the impact of an uncaring, irresponsible society that allows a situation in which most of the world's poor and hungry are children and single women, and unemployment results too often from lack of opportunity rather than lack of effort. Here are five of the characteristics of wrongful financial pressures on the family:

1. POVERTY WITHOUT OPTION. Rightful financial pressures that lead to growth and reunification of the family allow for the discovery of constructive and positive options in lifestyle. Wrongful financial pressures are imposed on the family without available options, forcing severe sacrifice and suffering, no matter what the family itself attempts to do to adjust itself to its changing economic environment.

Plant closings without notice, layoffs without planning for the welfare of the worker, and shortsighted business decisions that fail to see that the overall welfare of people is in the long term the most profitable business practice of all, can leave the family reeling from financial shock. Lack of resources to build even a beginning economic base can destroy the base upon which families are constructed, a predictable source of sufficient funds to live in safety, shelter and health.

"I wonder if you can imagine what it's like to not really know if you will be able to eat next week," said one father. "Do you know what it is like to count on a paycheck, to work and work only to be told suddenly one day that you're out and there is no more work for you? You don't just say, 'Oh well, I'll just start again.'" This father went on to describe his feelings when his family would look at him inquisitively about whether or not they could drink the last bit of milk.

2. MISUSED MOTHERHOOD. Psychologist John Romano, professor emeritus of psychiatry at the University of Rochester, stated that "When the history of the twentieth century is written, its hero will be the black mother."[4] Poverty strikes directly

4. Quoted in K. Fisher, "Gramezy on Genetics, Moms, and Social Support," *The American Psychological Association Monitor* (July 1988) Vol. 19, No. 7, p. 13.

and most severely at the heart of the minority family and particularly the black family. Many such families are the full responsibility of a mother who is left in charge of the family system and of caring for the total economical and emotional welfare of everyone in the home.

The extraordinary energy and resilience required of the black mother alone, or any mother or father attempting to raise a family alone while taking care of the family's financial security, can take a toll on the physical and mental health of these courageous and overburdened people who are trying to carry the load for our insensitive and unresponsive society.

Wrongful financial pressures are those which rob the parent and child of the opportunity for peaceful unity, comfort, and security in the parent-child interaction, because of the constant concern about where the next meal may come from or how the heat for the next winter will be paid for. Here is a statement from one mother who was caring for her family even without a home to live in:

"The school doesn't even know it, but we don't have an address. We keep moving to different parts of the projects here. When we find an empty place, we move in. I try to keep the money coming to get some clothes and food, and I have to watch for the cops. They got us twice and told us to leave because where we were living was condemned. We're the ones who are condemned."

3. LOSS OF ECONOMIC ESTEEM.

When the family as a whole shares responsibility for the financial base of that family, all members view themselves as contributing to the day-to-day budgeting and financial planning in the home. Wrongful financial pressures result when one person feels that they have failed the family in measurable terms, with lack of dollars totalled up as a measure of the degree of personal failure to provide and protect.

The man or woman who feels that it is they who are failing to provide, to live up to family expectations, to bring food to the nest, can come to feel anger toward self and misdirected resentment toward the family itself for making their perceived failure so abundantly clear. During the recent economic crisis in Detroit, Michigan, and the accompanying plant closings and layoffs, particularly in automotive related industries, suicides and family abuse increased dramatically. All self-respect and dignity seemed lost for those who felt the financial burden for their family. This man's statement shows how severe financial pressures can become in their impact on self-esteem.

"I felt like nothin'. I couldn't even make love. I felt like I was worse than nothing, because me just being in the family was even worse than me being gone. I drank too much when I could get some stuff, but it never helped. It just all fell apart. I didn't feel like a man anymore."

4. WITHDRAWING FROM YOUR FAMILY ACCOUNT.

The family experiences wrongful financial pressures when the family energy is used up almost solely on economic problems. The entire family system can come to feel as if there is no justice, no caring by society as a whole, and family members may rebel by pulling away from the family. On some level, family members may withdraw as a form of self-sacrifice for the financial survival of the family, attempting to lessen the family burden by finding their own way. Street gangs and other crime "families" may become a type of illegal "halfway home." A "Robin Hood" complex may evolve, which results in crime against those who are perceived as "having," so those who "aren't allowed to have" can survive.

Certainly, all crime cannot be explained because of economic disenfranchising of some family systems, but lack of financial security plays one key role in family disintegration. This woman's statement demonstrates this point:

"I know my son thought he was helping us by taking off. He would be gone all night, and then he would show up with some new clothes or something. He didn't even try to make up stories after a while. He was trying to help, I guess, but he only made us sadder, runnin' with that group of thugs."

5. DOLLAR DREAMS.

When financial pressures take precedence over enjoyment of closeness and the joy of daily living, the family can fall into a pattern of constant "negotiation," attempting to quantify everything and everyone. The family question "How do you feel today?" is replaced by "How much is it worth or what does it cost?" A bickering and bartering system of family communication results. A "How much do you do for me, what do I get for doing that?" orientation develops, and covert limits on the dreams of the family are set because of the implied quantifying of everything the family does, feels, or thinks.

"I can't even get my son to take his plate to the sink without getting bargained with," said the father. "Everything he does has to do with what is in it for him." This father and son find themselves in the conversion of sharing to dickering as the giving dimension of that family life is diminished.

All families struggle with and argue over money, and such conflicts are inevitable in a society that attaches dollar amounts to everything. Financial concerns can serve as constructive measures of some aspects of family planning. However, when finances dictate family life or the focus of one or more family members, wrongful financial pressures result. Here is a sample prayer used by the families I have worked with for times when financial pressures seem excessive and to be fragmenting the family system:

A FAMILY AFFIRMATION FOR TIMES OF ECONOMIC DESPAIR

We know that money has no meaning without a purpose of life motivated by love and caring.

We know that our economic suffering is not as severe as many others', and we care for all who need and for all who cannot find the comfort in daily bread.

We know that we all must hold together and see our pressures as belonging to all of us and less the intent than the ignorance of others who seem to have or want too much daily bread.

But we must help one another to find ways to limit our needs even further, even as we seek ways together to find the creativity, strength and necessary sacrifice to carry on.

We know that our lack is something we endure for others, and we must help one another to remember that we are never alone, even when we feel deserted and forgotten.

We must work even harder to stay together, even as the world seems to ignore the economic forces drawing us apart.

We must give one another in spiritual energy what we lack in economic security, so that we never allow our poverty to extend too deeply to our soul.

We must save one another from the theft of the value of our family spirit which belongs to us forever, and not to the material world.

COME TO THE FAMILY REUNION

The reunion factor of family life involves the integration of all of the prior Rx's described in this book. To illustrate the influence of these Rx's, I have selected each letter of the word "FAMILY" to summarize some of the major aspects of the features of the potential for healthy living in a family context. I have attempted to review some of the steps along the path to the miracle of "us" as each of the families I have been discussing moved along this path. Remember, the miracle of family reunification after any fragmentation is an individual path within each family household that ultimately leads to a beginning of the road to the ultimate reunion of humankind.

As I have pointed out, it is my belief that the majority of suffering in our world is related to a seriously eroded sense of "us," a failure of the development and endurance of our awareness of and accountability for our collective spiritual development. From the person who drives while drunk to the person who walks by without stopping to help an injured person, the failure of a sense of "us," of true mutual responsibility for the welfare of someone else and everyone else, continues to result in pain and world despair.

It is not a coincidence that sociologists have noted that people tend to help others when a group is around. When alone, a person will tend to look the other way when a stranger needs help. When the reality of our "family" is experienced, when others are there in body, we can not ignore our family responsibility to our fiftieth cousins. When we are physically alone, however, our underdeveloped sense of an internalized "us" allows us to leave a cousin lying by the roadside.

Each of the letters of the word "FAMILY" can serve as a daily reminder of the miracle of us and the message I have attempted to convey in this book. Each letter in "FAMILY" represents the incorporation of the ten Rx's of healthy family living. Perhaps you will post the word "FAMILY" on your refrigerator where everyone can see it as a reminder that your family is invited to come along to the new world family reunion. Charity indeed does begin at home.

F: FAMILY FREEDOM

Today we will take time to just "be" together.

The Rx's of Ritual and Rhythm

Whenever I interview a patient, I hear somewhere in their report or in the tone of their voice a sense of entrapment, a sense that life is leading them, even dragging them along, through a series of obligatory daily activities punctuated with a few vacations, "vacatings" from the world they have created for themselves and away from the reality of unchosen obligations. The reunion of family, getting everyone back together in ritual and rhythm together, allows for a new sense of freedom and control of our life.

When life becomes more predictable through ritual and more comfortable through a steady and reliable family rhythm, through family prayers or meditation and flexible but unanimously shared schedules for the simple aspects of daily living, a new sense of freedom results for every family member.

Freedom does not mean lack of responsibility. Freedom means self-fulfillment while promoting the fulfillment of others, and when everyone in the family senses a new control of time, a time to sit and to be together, a time to eat together, sufficient time to say a meaningful hello and good-bye, we begin to share life rather than to try only to survive it.

Mr. Anders said, "Now that we finished therapy, we have really felt a big family sigh of relief. We can help our sick daughter now, instead of just watch her suffer. We feel free, like it's our life, that it's our time, and that we aren't being domi-nated anymore. We have our family back, and we will never let the world take us away from each other again. Tell the people who will read your book that, if they're not careful, their home will be burglarized. While they are all out running around and busy doing, all of their what really matters will be taken from them. Tell them to lock the door, stay home sometimes, have dinner together, and say a little prayer together every day. It's the perfect home security system."

A: FAMILY ALTRUISM

Today, we will each do something for each other.

The Rx's of Reason and Remembrance

As I have said, the healthiest human behavior, not only in terms of spiritual and emotional growth but basic physical health and immunoefficiency, is altruism. To do for, to take care of, and to help are behaviors which inoculate the soul against infections from a society that is too cold, too poisoned with hate, selfishness, and the disregard for "us."

When we make the effort to be reasonable, to stay rational even at times of the most severe family conflicts and tests of our patience, we are behaving with altruism and remembering the concern for the welfare of the universal family system. When we take the time to remember the people who gave birth to our family, to remember that we are all at least fiftieth cousins with everyone in the world, when we focus on our family history, we begin to appraise the world in a way that is altruistic instead of only futuristic.

"Just doing the little things for each other changes the whole atmosphere in the house," said Ms. Bonner. "We have to help each other even more, now that my husband is gone, and we take more time and spend more energy on trying to be rational instead of just exploding, on trying to remember who and why we are, instead of always thinking about what is scheduled for later in the day or the week. Tell your readers to take care of each other in the family more. Tell them not to miss the chance to really love each other. Tell them to protect themselves every day from maybe missing the chance to do something for someone in their family before it's too late."

M: FAMILY MODERATION

Today, our family will do less, eat less, and rest more.

The Rx's of Resilience and Resonance

When the family makes the effort to sense and maintain a steady life rhythm, to maintain family rituals that have meaning to every family member, the family begins to experience a sense of moderation, of under- rather than overreaction. When we eat more slowly, we eat less, and when we move more slowly, we are in less danger of collisions. The ancient Greek warning of "moderation in all things" is still an important guideline for today's family.

When we are sick, we must rest. When the family is sick, it must be quiet and pause for healing and reenergizing. Moderation is the body's and spirit's way of getting back on track, of slipping into a more appropriate emotional and physical gear of life. We become resilient, and resonate with new energy, when we are moderate in our living. We can more easily resonate, move to new levels of peacefulness and loving energy, when we are less hostile, impatient, and competitive.

The family group can serve as the perfect moderator, the perfect place for everyone to calm each other down rather than to rile each other up, but constant vigilance and effort is necessary to maintain daily moderation in a world that beckons us to go faster and faster.

"Tell your readers to sit down together when they fight or argue," said Ms. Steiner. "Now that we are not together as much, some of our family visits when our children come home become problem-solving confrontations rather than enjoyable family reunions. We tried to get the Christmas tree up quick, the presents wrapped, opened, and then everything put away. For us, the Christmas rush became a description of our home. Tell your readers just to take it easy."

I: FAMILY INTIMACY

Today, we will touch, hug, and talk gently to one another.

The Rx of Reconciliation

To reconcile, to make up, get over, forgive, and re-embrace is one of the major functions of family life. The family is for forgiveness, an unqualified acceptance, toleration, and a short memory for error and thoughtlessness on the part of a family member. Intimacy in the family is an intimacy of closeness, even when anger and resentment results from the impact of that closeness and arguments start because people care so much and live so closely together.

"I would tell your readers to forgive, forgive, forgive," said Ms. Johnson. "When you try to start a new family, you have to really look beyond all the petty stuff that starts up right away. I guess you got used to some of the small stuff when you had big trouble in another family, so you really don't sweat about the small things in a new family. And since the new family members you get sort of stuck with are new to you, sort of distant from you, it's not as easy to forgive them. But you have to really try. Tell your readers that all they can do is try to forgive and always give a second, third, and hundredth chance."

L: FAMILY LEARNING

Today, we will learn something new about each of us
from each of us.

The Rx's of Reverence and Revival

"Tell the people who will read your book that real loving is tough learning," said Ms. Muller. "Just before Gramps died, I guess all that we went through started to sink in. You learn about you, about life and death, about what everything means, when someone in the family is struggling like Gramps did. We went through everything with him. We used to sing with him and play with him when we were all younger and when he was young, and at the end we were shaving him and changing his diaper. We went through his life . . . I mean we each went through all of life with him. We learned never to take life and living for granted."

The reverence Ms. Muller and her family showed for their grandfather and his long and painful illness was a reverence of learning, of coming to know each other in new ways. The revival and new birth of the family, even as the grandfather died, was due to the spiritual development of the family, their unyielding and dynamic adaptation through the crisis of a lingering death. The family worked through and learned through the universal family archetype of the birth/death cycle, of aging and change and passing on, and their learning gave them all a new sense of reverence for the significance of family and a new energy in each of their individual lives to carry on for the good of all of us.

Y: FAMILY YOUTH

Today, we will recommit ourselves to stay together forever.

The Rx of Reunion

I suggest that you take some time soon to sit down with your family and ask one very simple and very important question of each family member. Ask for short answers, just some simple and direct words in answer to this question about the factor of family reunion and the reenergizing of the family, the maintenance of perpetual youth of the family spirit. Ask each family member, "What is our family for?"

This book has been a plea for reunion, for a recommitment to a new awareness of "us," for a reinvigoration of the sense of family in everyday life. No matter what the form of your family, from single-parent household to the largest multi-generation family in your town, your work at keeping families together is the job of saving our world. Here are short answers from a member of each of the five families to the key question in my research on the miracle of "us," the reunion of the human spirit:

What is your family for?

Mr. Anders: "My family is for me, and we are all for each

other, no matter what happens. I think our whole family saved our daughter's life, so you could say that families are for saving lives."

Ms. Bonner: "My family is for keeping love alive. Even with my husband taken from us, we seem to be more of a family together. We keep my husband alive within us by keeping us together."

Ms. Steiner: "Our family is our safety place, our sanctuary, in a way our salvation from the world. Even with our children gone now, we have a family still, a family that gives a sense that there are people out there, even inside us, that will love us forever."

Ms. Johnson: "My family is a new family, another chance to have a family and stay a family, to have people who really care around me, who will always be there for me. Maybe we call it a stepfamily because, if you do it right, you take a big step toward being a healthier family."

Ms. Muller: "What's my family for? I guess I never saw it until we went through this with Gramps. What is my family for? My family is forever."

I hope you will discuss your own answers to this question about the importance of "us" to you. You will see that your answer to this question will change from day to day and year to year as your family system grows and evolves. You will see, however, that there is something within you that wants very strongly to be an "us."

FAMILIES AND MIRACLES

In Chapter One, I described the Anders family's attempt to unify to help their daughter to better use her medical treatment. Just before I finished this book, the Anders family wrote to me. They had flown as a group to a famous medical center to seek additional treatment for their daughter. The last part of their letter to me summarizes the message I hope you will take with you from this book.

"It's a miracle," wrote Ms. Anders. "She's not sick anymore. They tested her here again. There is no evidence of the blood disease. They ran the tests several times, and she is cured.

They called it spontaneous remission and they think the chemotherapy must have finally started to work, just about the time we all started joining her in her treatment. We know better, don't we? It was our family power that really started to work. We are the miracle."

Epilogue

I still hear from the five families you have read about in this book. They are all working to implement the ten Rx's of healthy family living into their daily lives, and in spite of experiencing the same setbacks and failures that all families must live with, they remain happy families who assign their number one priority to their relationship with one another.

The Anders family is celebrating today. The little girl continues to be free of any signs of the return of her disease, and the whole family has learned to treasure each moment together. They have come to appreciate the rhythm of their family pulse because that rhythm had become so disrupted by what had been the solo healing efforts of their daughter. They discovered that the ritualization of family healing, of allowing the whole family to heal together, can work miracles to help the family stay well.

The Bonner family still cries and protests the loss of the father, but they cry together now and they have moved on to their own different but intense celebration of their newfound dependence on one another. They have learned to show more reason during the inevitable arguments that take place in all families and are so intensified by prolonged grief, and they have shown remembrance not only for the fallen father but also for what being a family means to every family member.

The Steiner family has succeeded at finding more time to

talk together and meet together whenever possible, but the parents have learned that the physical presence of family members is less important than working to be aware of our own internal representation of our family. They have become more aware of the resonance of energy that transcends time and distance to keep their family together. Mr. and Ms. Steiner have shown the resilience to love their family even in the physical absence of that family group.

The Johnson family continues to evolve its own traditions as the two groups of children from prior marriages discover a new family connection with one another. The parents are learning to reconcile not only with their new family, but with issues related to their prior families that are still a part of each person's sense of family. The Johnson family has shown a reverence for the family system even when the pressures, discriminations, and expectations of society seem to focus only on the dysfunctions of family living.

The Muller family is still grieving the death of their grandfather, but they are congratulating themselves on the strength and loving energy they showed as a family that helped the grandfather pass with less pain and alienation. They have revived their family energy that was so extended in the care of their grandfather, and they have reunited as a group, not without their grandfather, but with the knowledge that he will be even more a part of each of them and all of them forever because their love was not stolen by the processes of aging and disease.

All of these families have chosen the family view of their world. They have found the power that comes from being "us." I hope this book will help you and your family discover your family power. I hope this book will help your family be more tolerant of one another, patient with the progress and setbacks of your family members and, during the joy of the best of times and particularly at times of the sorrow of the worst of times, to be more aware of the power of loving energy that flows within every family circle.

Bibliography

Ackerman, N. *The Psychodynamics of Family Life.* Cambridge, Mass.: Harvard University Press, 1974.

——, ed. *Family Process.* New York: Basic Books, 1970.

Adams, W. F. *Ireland and Irish Emigration to the New World.* New Haven, Conn.: Yale University Press, 1932.

Antonovsky, A. *Unraveling the Mystery of Health: How People Manage Stress and Stay Well.* San Francisco: Jossey-Bass Publishers, 1987.

Bandura, A. *Perceived Self-Efficacy and Health Functioning.* Paper presented at the annual meeting of the Society of Behavioral Medicine, San Francisco, March 1986.

Beck, A., A. J. Rush, B. Shaw, and G. Emergy. *Cognitive Therapy of Depression: A Treatment Manual.* New York: Guilford Press, 1979.

Berman, E. *Scapegoat: The Impact of Death-Fear on an American Family.* Ann Arbor, Mich.: University of Michigan Press, 1973.

Bowlby, J. *Attachment and Loss.* Vols. 1–3. New York: Basic Books, 1969.

Boyce, W. T., C. Schaefer, and C. Uitti. "Permanence and Change: Psychosocial Factors in the Outcome of Adolescent Pregnancy." *Social Science and Medicine.* Vol. 21, 1985.

Boyle, J. "Police Think Mother Killed Son Over Despair About His Future." *Detroit Free Press,* July 16, 1988. p. 1.

Brain/Mind Bulletin. "Life Energy Patterns Visible Via New Technique." Vol. 7, No. 14, August 23, 1982.

Briggs, J., and F. Peat. "David Bohm's Looking-Glass Map." In *The Looking Glass Universe: The Emerging Science of Wholeness.* New York: Simon & Schuster, Inc., 1984.

Brodey, W. *Family Dance.* Garden City, N.Y.: Anchor Books, 1977.

Burr, H. S. *The Fields of Life.* New York: Ballantine Books, 1972.

Capra, F. *The Turning Point.* New York: Bantam Books, 1982.

Clayre, A. *The Heart of the Dragon.* New York: Houghton Mifflin Co., 1985.

Comstock, G. W., and K. B. Partridge. "Church Attendance and Health." *Journal of Chronic Diseases.* Vol. 2, 1972.

Cousins, N. *Human Options.* New York: Berkley Books, 1983.

Dodson, B. *Sex for One: The Joy of Self Loving.* New York: Harmony Books, 1987.

Doi, L. T. "Amae. A Key Concept for Understanding Japanese Personality Structure." In T. S. Lebra and W. P. Lebra, eds., *Japanese Culture and Behavior.* Honolulu, Hawaii: University of Hawaii Press, 1974.

Dossey, L. *Space, Time, and Medicine.* Boulder and London: Shambhala Press, 1984.

Durkheim, E. *Suicide.* New York: Free Press, 1951.

Edwards, D. "ELF Under Suspicion in New Report." *Science News.* Vol. 132, July 18, 1987, p. 39.

Eliade, M. *The Sacred and the Profane.* New York: Harcourt, Brace, and World, 1959.

Ellis, A. *Reason and Emotion in Psychotherapy.* New York: Lyle Stuart, 1970.

Erikson, M. H. "The Identification of a Secure Reality." *American Journal of Psychology.* Vol. 55, 1942, pp. 270–73.

Esterson, A. *The Leaves of Spring.* New York: Penguin Books, 1970.

Evans-Wentz, W., ed. *Tibet's Great Yogi Milarepa.* 2nd Ed. New York: Oxford University Press, 1951.

Ferguson, M. *The Aquarian Conspiracy.* Los Angeles: J. P. Tarcher, Inc., 1980.

Fischer, K. "Gramezy on Genetics, Moms, and Social Support." *The American Psychological Association Monitor.* Vol. 19, No. 7, July 1988. p. 13.

Fosse, D. "More Years with Mountain Gorillas." *National Geographic.* Vol. 140, 1971, pp. 574–85.

Foundation for Inner Peace. *A Course in Miracles.* Riburon, California, 1985.

Freud, S. "On Narcissism." In J. Strachey, ed., *Standard Edition of the Complete Works of Sigmund Freud,* Vol. 14. New York: Hogarth Press, 1914.

Gebhard, P., J. H. Gagnon, W. B. Pomeroy, and C. V. Christenson. *Sex Offenders: An Analysis of Types.* New York: Harper & Row, 1965.

Gerber, R. *Vibrational Medicine.* Sante Fe, New Mexico: Bear and Co., 1988.

Goldstein, J. *The Experience of Insight.* Santa Cruz, Cal.: Unity Press, 1976.

Graham, T. W., B. A. Kapplan, J. C. Cornoni-Huntley, S. A. James, C. G. Becker, and S. Heyden. "Frequency of Church Attendance and Blood Pressure Elevation." *Journal of Behavioral Medicine.* Vol. 1, 1978.

Haley, J. *Problem Solving Therapy.* San Francisco: Jossey-Bass Publishers, 1976.

Hamilton, W. D. "The Genetical Evolution of Social Behavior." *The Journal of Theoretical Biology.* Vol. 7, 1964, pp. 1–52.

Henry, J. *Pathways to Madness.* New York: Random House, 1972.

Hinds, M. "The Child Victim of Incest." *New York Times.* Vol. 132, July 18, 1987, p. 39.

Hinkle, L. E., and S. Wolf. "A Summary of Experimental Evidence Relating Life Stress to Diabetes Mellitis." *Journal of Mount Sinai Hospital.* Vol. 19, 1952, pp. 537–70.

Hippocrates. *Works of Hippocrates,* Vol. 3. New York: Medical Classics, 1938.

Hoffman, E. "The Right to Be Human: Abraham Maslow." *East/West: The Journal of Natural Healthy Living,* May 1988, pp. 68–69.

International Kirlian Research Association. "The Ghost Effect." *IKRA Communications.* Brooklyn, N.Y., June 1978.

Jensen, E. W. "The Families Routine Inventory." *Social Science and Medicine.* Vol. 7, 1983.

Jung, C. "Conscious, Unconscious, and Individuation." In H. Read, M. Fordham, and G. Adler, eds. *The Collected Works of Carl G. Jung,* Vol. 9. Princeton, N.J.: Princeton University Press, 1939.

Keys, A., J. Brozek, A. Henschel, O. Mickelson, and H. Taylor. *The Biology of Human Starvation,* Vols. 1 and 2. Minneapolis, Minn.: University of Minnesota Press, 1950.

Kobasa, S. C., S. R. Maddi, and S. Courington. "Personality and Constitution as Mediators in the Stress-Illness Relationship." *Journal of Health and Social Behavior.* Vol. 22, 1981.

Laing, R. D. *The Politics of Experience.* New York: Ballantine Books, 1978.

————, and A. Esterson. *Sanity, Madness, and the Family.* New York: Penguin Books, 1954.

Lange, A., and O. van der Hart. *Directive Family Therapy.* New York: Brunner/Mazel, 1983.

Langer, E. J., and J. Rodin. "The Effects of Choice and Enhanced Personal Responsibility for the Aged: A Field Experiment in an Institutional Setting." *Journal of Personality and Social Psychology.* Vol. 34, 1976, pp. 191–98.

LeShan, L. "Psychological States as Factors in the Development of Malignant Disease: A Critical Review." *Journal of the National Cancer Institute.* Vol. 22, 1959, pp. 1–18.

Lewis, J., W. Beavers, J. Gossett, and V. Phillips. *No Single Thread: Psychological Health in the Family System.* New York: Bruner and Mazel, 1976.

Maclean, P. "The Triune Brain." *American Scientist.* Vol. 66, 1978, pp. 101–33.

Maslow, A. H. *Motivation and Personality.* 2nd Ed. New York: Harper & Row, 1970.

————. *Religions, Values, and Peak Experiences.* New York: Penguin Books, 1975.

————. "The Authoritarian Character Structure." *Journal of Social Psychology.* Vol. 18, 1943.

Meyer, R. J., and R. J. Haggerty. "Streptococcal Infection in Families: Factors Altering Individual Susceptibility." *Pediatrics.* Vol. 29, 1962.

Minuchin, S. *Families in Family Therapy.* Cambridge, Mass.: Harvard University Press, 1974.

———. *Families of the Slums.* New York: Basic Books, 1974.

Money, J. *Lovemaps.* New York: Irvinton Publishers, 1986.

Morowitz, H. J. *Cosmic Joy and Local Pain.* New York: Charles Scribner's Sons, 1987.

Moorman, L. J. "Tuberculosis on the Navaho Reservation." *American Review of Tuberculosis.* Vol. 61, 1950.

Moss, C. *Elephant Memories: Thirteen Years in the Life of an Elephant Family.* New York: Morrow, 1986.

Murchie, G. *The Seven Mysteries of Life.* Boston: Houghton Mifflin Co., 1978.

Napier, A. *The Family Crucible.* New York: Harper & Row, 1976.

Needham, J. *Science and Civilization in China,* Vol. 2. Cambridge, England: Cambridge University Press, 1962.

Ornstein, R., and D. Sobel. *The Healing Brain.* New York: Simon & Schuster, 1987.

Pelletier, K. *Toward a Science of Consciousness.* New York: Dell, 1978.

Pert, C. As quoted in *Brain/Mind Bulletin.* Vol. 20, January 1986.

Piaget, J. *The Moral Judgment of the Child.* Glencoe, Ill.: Free Press, 1960.

———. *The Origins of Intelligence in Children.* New York: International University Press, 1952.

Pincus, L. *Death and the Family.* New York: Pantheon Books, 1974.

Porkert, M. *The Theoretical Foundations of Chinese Medicine.* Cambridge, England: Cambridge University Press, 1962.

Reiss, D. *The Family's Construction of Reality.* Cambridge, Mass.: Harvard University Press, 1981.

Scjefem, A. "Susan Smiled: On Explanation in Family Therapy." *Family Process.* Vol. 17, No. 1, March 1978, pp. 59–68.

Selye, H. *Stress of Life.* Rev. Ed. New York: McGraw-Hill, 1976.

Shapiro, D. *Meditation: Self Regulation Strategy and Altered States of Consciousness.* New York: Aldine Press, 1980.

———. *Precision Nirvana: An Owner's Manual for Care and Maintenance of the Mind.* Englewood Cliffs, N.J.: Prentice-Hall, 1978.

———, and J. H. Shapiro. "Well Being and Relationship." In R. Walsh and D. Shapiro, eds., *Beyond Health and Normality.* New York: Van Nostrand Reinhold Co., 1983.

Shlain, L. Lecture at College of Marin, Kenfield, Cal. January 23, 1979.

Snyder, S. H. *Biological Aspects of Mental Disorder.* New York: Oxford University Press, 1980.

Sorotkin, P. A. *Social and Cultural Dynamics,* 4 Vols. New York: American Book Co., 1937–41.

Stuart, R. B. *Helping Couples Change.* New York: Guilford Press, 1980.

Syme, L. "People Need People." *Series on the Healing Brain: Cassette Recording 12.* Los Altos, Cal.: Institute for the Study of Human Knowledge, 1982.

Targ, R., and H. Puthoff. *Mind Research: Scientists Look at Psychic Ability.* New York: Dell, 1977.

Thomas, C., and D. Duszynski. "Closeness to Parents and the Family Constellation in a Prospective Study of Five Disease States: Suicide, Mental Illness, Malignant Tumor, Hypertension, and Coronary Artery Disease." *The Johns Hopkins Medical Journal.* Vol. 134, 1973.

Wolf, S. "The End of the Rope: The Role of the Brain in Cardiac Death." *Canadian Medical Association Journal.* Vol. 97, 1967.

————, and H. Goodell. *Behavioral Science in Clinical Medicine.* Springfield, Ill.: Charles C. Thomas, 1976.

Wynder, E. L., and L. I. Bross. "Factors in Human Cancer Development." *Cancer.* Vol. 12, 1959.

Zilbergeld, B. *The Shrinking of America: Myths of Psychological Change.* Boston: Little, Brown and Co., 1983.

Index

Absolute assumption, 99–101
Acceptance
    versus continued struggle,
        187–188
    practicing, 382
    of self, 100
Acceptors as perspective
        keepers, 291–293
Accusations, 113, 114, 321–
        322
Achievement
    absolutism and, 69–70, 100
    school emphasis on, 70,
        161
Age, deference to, 112–113
    See also Older parents
Alienation
    and depression, 285–288
    nature of, 285–286
    overcoming, 3
    of teenagers, 47
Altruism
    effect on immune system,
        300
    family, 380–381
    versus pride, 324, 334

of transcendence, 300
traps in, 260–261
Anger
    and anxiety reduction,
        326–327
    basis of, 326
    choice of, 90
    depression and, 286
    effect of, 183, 327–328
    language of, 327, 334
    reconciliation and, 234–
        235, 270–271
    relationship to love, 234–
        236
    revival strategies against,
        326–328, 334
    as a signal, 74
Appliance addiction, 80–81
Appraisal system
    nature of, 157–159
    phases, 179–196
    relationship to health,
        175–178
    wrongful loss in, 356
    See also Family resilience

Arguments
    rationality and, 109–110, 113
    reconciliation, 110–111, 225
    time-out, 109–110
    See also Conflict
Articles of family faith, 310–313
Assumptions, irrationality of, 113, 114
Attention deficit disorder, 163, 367
Autonomous family members, 294–295
Avarice
    effect of, 326
    language of, 321, 334
    nature of, 321
    revival strategy against, 334
    as a source of conflict, 321–322

Bargaining as a crisis reaction, 181–182
Basic bonds
    and divorce, 122
    elective, 121–122
    and family traits, 120–121
    nature of, 120–121
    types of, 123–143
Beauty
    environmental, 298
    in family life, 296–299
Belief system
    development, 312–313
    flawed, 356
    resilience through, 153–156
    See also Church; Religion

Caretaker's cold, 174–176
Caretaking
    defined, 32
    health hazards, 174–175
Carthage Complex, 252
Causation circles, 83–84
Change
    basicality, 93
    death as, 94, 220–223
    and perfection, 72
    and the phantom family, 222–223
    See also Stress
Children
    effect of ritual on, 48
    exploited, 132–135
    latch-key, 160
    limit-stretching by, 302
    needs, 106–107, 132
    as parents, 135–137, 160
    precocity, 77
    pressures on, 159–160
    role, 30
    sacrificing for, 106–107
    sexual abuse, 134, 232–234, 268
    shared custody of, 127
    See also Teenagers
Church
    attendance, 169, 172, 173
    current failures, 168–170
    and daily life, 276
    family leadership of, 171
    open scheduling, 171
    participation, 172–173
    revitalization, 171–173
    social awareness, 173
    See also Religion
C-I-G-I syndrome, 294
Closure comfort, 153, 180
Cluster response, 7

Clutter, 298
College students, re-
  embracement of, 51–
  52
Communal family, 142
Communication
  bartering system, 376–377
  and conflict, 110, 262–263
  cross-generational, 151
  daily, 312
  with energy leeches, 243,
    248
  errors in, 109, 113–114,
    223–224
  of feelings, 282
  labels and, 97–99, 223–224
  manners in, 316–317
  in marriage, 360–361
  during meals, 56
  overreaction, 265–267
  reconciliation through, 270
  spiritual, 23, 193–195, 210,
    222
  during stepfamily
    formation, 371
  underreaction, 301
Compensated family
  structure, 140–141
Competence
  nature of, 190, 269–270
  psychological impact, 190–
    191
Complementary family
  structure, 139
Conflict
  and apologies, 110–111
  archetypical issues, 318
  bases of, 318–334
  choice of, 307–308
  correlation to love, 16,
    110–111, 189

energy for, 211
energy leaks from, 203–
  204
with energy leeches, 243
growth through, 271, 347
patterns, 112
and rationality, 109–110
redundant, 315
See also Reconciliation
Connection response, 6–8
Control
  over events, 190
  external locus, 191
  internal locus, 191
  martyrdom as, 260
  overreactions, 187, 190–
    191
  through underreaction,
    301–302
Counterfamily movement, 47
Creativity
  in daily life, 305–306
  in problem solving, 306
Crisis
  appraisal system, 179–196
  calming closure, 153, 180
  connection response, 6–8
  effect of, 26, 179–180
  and the fazed family, 340
  growth through, 271
  isolation during, 3–4
  numbness toward, 162
  resilience and, 153–155
Cultural relativism, 128–129
Custodial family structure,
  141–142
Cynicism, 168–169

Daily schedules
  control over, 278–279, 379
  for family rhythm, 79–80

Daily schedules *(cont.)*
  for family togetherness,
    278–280
  ritualizing, 53–59
Day care, 125
Deafness, selective, 103–104
Death
  acceptance, 73, 353–354
  as change, 94, 220–223
  living through, 69
  natural role of, 67–69
  sudden, 152–156, 355–356
  talking about, 68
  wrongful, 354–355
Debt to family
  origin, 29–30
  repayment, 30–32
  scope, 31, 124–125
Demands, irrationality of,
    113, 114
Depression
  and disease, 285
  drug treatment, 289–291
  genesis, 285–286, 289–290
  sexual, 361–362
  as a signal, 74
  societal, 288
  See also Secretiveness
De-sacredization
  of daily life, 273, 282–284
  of society, 168, 231, 284
Detoxification method, 97–99
Divine discontent, 194–195,
    357
Divorce
  and the basic family bond,
    122
  and life style, 124
  nature of, 125–128
  no fault, 125
  pervasiveness, 159–160

  rightful versus wrongful,
    360–364
  See also Wrongful divorce
Dyslexia, 163, 367

Emotional estate planning,
    356–357
Emotions
  addiction to, 183
  dishonest, 295
  and energy states, 238
  junk feelings, 183
  manipulation through, 295
  reactions to events, 105–
    106
  responsibility for, 108–109
  and spontaneity, 295–296
Energy
  balance, 206–207
  burnout, 205
  depletion, 259, 325, 336
  family template, 208–211,
    217, 222
  fields, 208, 222
  immune, 287
  from memories, 209
  negative, 243, 266
  psychic, 195
  renewal, 311–313
  and resilience, 193–194
  spiritual, 193–195, 210,
    222
  See also Family resonance
Energy leaks
  archetypical categories,
    214–215
  effect of, 200–201, 209
  in the fixated family, 341
  identifying, 237–238
  and leech identification,
    245–246

symptoms, 200–201
and wrongful divorce, 362
Energy leeches
versus autonomous family
members, 294–295
characteristics, 241–243
effect on family health,
244
empathy with, 246–247
versus energy givers, 207
and family resilience, 194
and family stress, 243
immaturity of, 253–257
and love paralysis, 238,
252–253
narcissism of, 241, 249–
251
pinpointing, 245–246
self-justification, 249–251
sensors, 244–245
sharing with, 248
test, 238–240
versus us actualizers, 294–
295
Enlightened self-
enhancement, 260
Envy
language of, 330
nature of, 330–331
revival strategies against,
334
Ethics
current code, 168
environmental, 298
Extended family portrait,
34–36

Failed family type, 336–337
Failing family type, 336

Failure
economic measurement,
375–376
learning from, 191–192
tolerance, 20–21, 189–190
Fair play
by an energy leech, 264–
265
rules, 265
Faith, articles of, 310–313
Family
articles of faith, 310–313
attachment within, 21–22
cultural view, 11–12
defined, 7–8, 33, 35, 143–
144
developmental retardation,
340–341
developmental stages, 144–
150
exclusion from, 310–311
features, 19–23
financial pressures, 373–
378
growth, 338–339
holographs, 299
identification, 34–35
image, 311–312
lack of, 32
media portrayal, 10–11, 24
mutual responsibilities
within, 31, 86–87,
262–263, 316–318
negative impacts of, 25–26
phantom, 217–218, 222–
223
primacy, 19–20
problems within, 24–26,
334. See also Problem
solving
programs for, 184–186

Family *(cont.)*
  purpose of, 19, 22, 158,
    383–384
  scope, 8, 33–35
  as a source of neuroticism,
    9–10, 25–26
  structures, 120–143
  types, 333–342
  See also Family system
Family affirmations
  during divorce, 364–365
  essence of, 358–359
  for new stepfamilies, 373
  for times of disability, 370
  for times of economic
    despair, 377–378
  for times of illness, 370
  at times of loss, 359
  use of, 103
  See also Prayer
Family curriculum, 162, 164,
  165–166
Family day scheduling, 313
Family energy template
  phantom family, 217–218
  sensitivity to, 208–211, 222
Family extrasensory
    perception
  existence of, 23, 222
  of us actualizers, 299
  using, 247
  See also Family resonance
Family history, 151, 299
Family innings, 280, 313
Family lifeline, 247
Family maintenance
    activities, 79–84
Family medicine, 177–179
Family member
  ideal
    aesthetic nature, 296–298

altruism of, 300
autonomous behavior by,
  294–295
capacity for transcendence,
  299–300
characteristics, 291–308
creativity of, 305–306
extrafamilial perception,
  299
positive attitude of, 304–
  305
versus self-actualizers, 288
social responsibility, 298–
  299, 302–304, 306
spontaneity in, 295–296
stress absorption by, 291–
  293
test, 308–310
of the week, 82–83
Family reason
  perspective, 85
  practice of, 380–381
  test, 86–87
Family remembrance
  defined, 115
  development, 120–121,
    150–151
  practice of, 380–381
  test, 116–117
Family resilience
  aspects, 158–159, 381
  defined, 153–154, 155–156
  prerequisites, 157–158
  steps in, 153–156, 199
  test, 156–157, 196–197
  See also Appraisal system
Family resonance
  departure from, 205–206,
    211, 216
  exercises, 219–224

and family friction, 203–204

nature of, 202–203

need for, 207, 381

test, 201–202

See also Energy; Family energy template

Family reunion

importance, 349–350

nature of, 378–379

practice of, 383–385

strains on, 368

Family rhythm

death within, 67–69

defined, 60

discerning, 64, 71, 73–74

establishing, 79–84

freedom through, 379–380

and health, 64, 69

importance of, 60

loss of, 61–62, 73–79, 211

and rituals, 63–64

sex within, 67–69

in suffering families, 78–79

test, 62–63

Family savings time, 278–279

Family system

basic bonds within, 120–143

children within, 106–107

democracy within, 113

forms of, 136–137

functions, 22, 25

ritual within, 44–46

roles within, 291–308

rules within, 265

scope, 34

FAR formula, 326

Fazed family type, 340

Fear

of loving, 11–12, 226

problems stemming from, 215–216, 254

as a signal, 74

See also Security

Financial pressures

affirmation for times of, 376–378

crime and, 376

from disabilities, 79

growth from, 373–374

self-esteem and, 375–376

wrongful, 374–377

Fixated family type, 340–341

Forced family type, 339

Forgiveness

and health, 199

lack of, 226

practice in, 382

See also Reconciliation

Frenzied family type, 338

Frustration-aggression-regression sequence, 326

Gangs, 46–47

See also Pseudofamilies

Generalization assumption, 101–103

Gluttony

global, 328–329

language of, 329, 334

revival strategies against, 329–330, 334

as a source of conflict, 328–330

Gratification

immediate, 324

versus need, 323

Growing family type

characteristics, 341–342

Growing family type *(cont.)*
  ten Rx's seen within, 342–344
Guilt
  engendering, 107
  good, 180–181
  impact, 180–181
  regarding children, 31
  regarding parents, 31
  regarding sex, 268

Handicaps, 367–368
Happiness, learning to practice, 304–305
Hate, 216–217, 238
Healing
  elements in, 156
  natural capacity for, 73
Health
  alienation and, 285–287
  appraisal effect, 175–176
  through awareness, 64, 69
  family nature of, 173–179
  family re-embracement and, 50
  and family stress, 237, 286–287
  forgiveness and, 199
  and longevity, 184
  and religion, 172
  risk factors, 237, 286–287
  and ritual, 47–48
  self-efficacy and, 190–191
  work stress and, 237
Humor
  despite conflict, 111
  in the everyday, 304–305
  learning to practice, 111, 304–305

Illness
  age-reversed, 365–366
  alienation and, 3, 285–287
  appraisal effect, 175–176
  chronic, 365
  fatal, 355–356
  family context of, 173–179
  as a form of adjustment, 73
  isolation during, 2–3, 49–50, 366–367
  mental, 50, 367
  as mental metaphor, 174
  prediction of, 287
  stress and, 174–176, 237, 286–287
  wrongful, 365–369
Imminent disaster orientation, 266
Immortality
  effect of, 68
  family energy of, 220–221
  need for emphasis on, 171
Immune system
  effect of anger on, 286
  and family alienation, 286–287
Impatience
  in family interaction, 263, 326
  manifesting lust, 323–324
Incest, 11, 134, 231–234
Independence
  desirability of, 9–10
  maturity and, 92
  strength through, 4
  teenage, 74–76
  young adult, 77–78
  See also Individuals

ndividuals
  developmental theories,
      115–116, 129–130
  family roles for, 291–308
  normalcy in, 26–27
  priorities of, 310–313
  respect for, 263, 269–270
  spiritual development, 170
  See also Independence;
      Self
nstincts
  for family, 4–6
  herding, 7
  for survival, 4–5, 7
ntegrity, 258
ntellectual impairment, 367
nvisible impairments, 367–
      368
solation
  during illness, 2–3, 49–50,
      366–367
  myth, 92, 219
  response to, 7
  See also Alienation

apanese ethos, 184, 296–297
et lag, 54
oke-of-the-day plan, 305
unk feelings, 183
unk thoughts, 193
ust Being Test, 119–120

Kirlian photography, 217
Knowing versus perceiving,
      88–89

Labels
  avoidance, 98–99
  school tendencies toward,
      161

self-fulfilling prophecies,
      223–224
Layoffs, 374
Learning disabilities, 72, 367
Life
  changes during, 65–66, 69.
      See also Change
  creative approach, 305–306
  and death, 68, 94, 355–357
  false assumptions
      regarding, 95–109
  and immortality, 68
  jungle view of, 168
  meaning in, 45
  motivated orientation to,
      118–119
  perceptions of, 89–91
  perfection within, 70–73
  powerless view, 91
  rhythm, 64–66
  sacredness of, 168–169,
      272–273
  structure in, 45–46
Life styles
  alternative, 124
  hectic, 63–64, 338
  normal, 26–28
Limbic system, 289–290
Listening, selective, 104
Love
  and conflict, 16, 110, 189,
      234–236
  connection with food, 187
  disability, 252–253. *See
      also* Energy leeches
  fear of, 226
  insufficient, 187, 355
  nature of, 90, 93–94, 129,
      199
  paralysis, 234, 238

Love *(cont.)*
  physical demonstrations
    of, 231, 234, 236–237
  reconciliatory, 230
  unconditional, 273–274
  verbalizations of, 236–237
Lust
  biochemistry of wanting,
    323
  effect of, 325
  impatience and, 323–324
  language of, 323–324, 334
  nature of, 323
  revival strategy against,
    334
  as a source of conflict,
    323–326
Lying
  effects of, 313
  energy depletion from, 259
  by energy leeches, 241
  reasons for, 257–259
  role-model, 258
  versus secretiveness, 268

Malignancy assumption, 96–
    99
Manners, family test of, 316–
    317
Marriage
  aptitude for, 363–364
  and divorce, 124–125
  open, 125, 127
  perfection in, 71
Martyrdom
  control through, 260
  and revenge, 261
Maternal active family
    structure, 138–139
Maternal reactive family
    structure, 137–138

Maturity
  defined, 92
  independence and, 92
  lack of, 241, 253–257
Mealtimes
  breakfast, 56
  dinner, 58
  ground rules, 57–58
  prayer at, 58–59, 64
  rushed, 64
  sharing, 41
Medicine
  disruptive practices, 50
  revitalizing practices, 177–
    179
  See also Health; Illness
Meditation
  efficacy of, 358
  method, 331
  See also Prayer; Quiet time
Memories
  energy from, 209
  and family history, 150–
    151
  within us, 221
Mental fatigue, false sense of,
    193
Molecular psychology, 178
Money
  meaning of, 362–363
  as a source of conflict,
    321–322, 362–363,
    376–377
  See also Financial
    pressures
Monoamine oxidase
    inhibitors, 290
Motivation orientation, 118

Name-calling, 113, 114, 321–
    322, 334

See also Labels

Narcissism
of energy leeches, 241, 249–251
as a love disability, 252–253

Needs
communicating, 311
versus desires, 323
hierarchy, 325
identification, 324
individual versus family, 312
response to, 311

Neurotic normal, 27

New age religions, 170

Norepinephrine, 289

Normalcy myth, 26–28

Older parents
abuse, 30, 32
age reversed illness, 365–366
debt to, 30–32
guilt regarding, 31
parenting of, 30–32
reconciliation with, 236–237
separation from, 33, 236–237
See also Death

Open family structure, 142–143

Open marriage, 125, 127

Oppressive family type, 337

Optimism
and health, 176–177
practicing, 304–305
use of, 199

Parallel family structure, 140

Parent abuse, 30, 32
See also Older parents

Parental bond, 123–131

Parent/child bond, 132–135

Parenting
by children, 132, 135–137
demands of, 29–30, 375
forfeiture, 130–131
myth of, 29–30
of older parents, 30–32
single, 130, 136–139, 374–375
stepfamilies, 371–372

Paternal active family structure, 139

Paternal reactive family structure, 137–138

Patience
antidote for lust, 324, 334
lack of, 263, 326

Peak experiences
aftermath of, 288–289
desirability of, 288

Peer groups
influence of, 47
rejection by, 267

Perception
and emotion, 105–106
false, 89–91
versus knowledge, 88–89
of self-responsibility, 85–86

Perfection
and change, 72
family model, 24–25
of the human spirit, 94–95
image of, 14–15, 69–70
unattainability, 90–91
natural, 70–71

Permanence, sense of, 45

Perspective
    individual, 320
    keepers of, 291–293
    practicing, 382–383
Phantom family principle,
    217–218, 222–223
Photographs
    focusing through, 281
    Kirlian, 217
Physiological reactions
    to positive thinking, 190
    to psychological stimuli,
        186–189
    See also
        Psychoneuroimmunology
Plateau experiences
    nature of, 288
    versus peak experiences,
        288–289
Positive parasitism, 261
Poverty, 374–375
Power
    misused, 232
    over life, 91
    personal versus family, 85–
        86
    See also Control
Prayer
    allowing time for, 278–
        279, 283
    at bedtime, 59
    during divorce, 364
    efficacy of, 358–359
    at homecoming, 57
    at mealtimes, 58–59, 64
    for new stepfamilies, 373
    purpose of, 364
    for times of disability,
        369–370
    for times of economic
        despair, 377–378

for times of illness, 369–
    370
    at times of loss, 359
Prejudice
    within a family, 263–264
    role modeling, 302–303
Pride
    effect of, 325
    language of, 319–321, 334
    overweening, 320–321
    revival strategies against,
        324, 334
    as a source of conflict,
        319–321
    See also Self-esteem
Priorities
    in daily life, 310–313
    misplaced, 357
Privacy
    family rules regarding, 265
    versus secretiveness, 265–
        269
Problem solving
    appraisal system for, 179–
        196
    versus blind support, 107–
        108
    communication methods,
        104. *See also*
        Communication
    creativity in, 306
    detoxification of events,
        97–99
    guidelines, 345–347
    information sources, 185–
        186
    and premature closure,
        153, 180
    surrender, 186–189
    timing for, 58

Pseudofamilies
    attraction of, 376
    family conflict and, 235,
        336
    nature of, 46–48
Psi, 222
Psychic energy
    development, 222
    scientific support of, 195
    See also Family
        extrasensory
        perception; Spiritual
        energy
Psychoneuroimmunology,
    178

Quiet time
    allowing, 278–279, 283
    at bedtime, 59
    at homecoming, 57–58
    at meals, 45–46, 58

Reconciliation
    of arguments, 110–111
    defined, 225
    difficulty in, 226
    guidelines, 246–251
    necessity for, 228–230,
        234–236
    practice of, 382
    steps toward, 236–237,
        270–271
    test, 226–228
Reconstituted family
        structure, 141
Re-embracement ritual
    emphasis for, 52–53
    methods, 51–52
    need for, 51, 75
    occasions for, 51, 57

Religion
    blind faith in, 169
    and health, 172
    jungle view, 170
    new age, 170
    personal nature, 170
    practicing, 312–313
    revitalization of, 171–173
    See also Church
Responsibility
    for emotions, 108–109
    for family, 31, 86–87, 262–
        263, 316–318
    for oneself, 85–86, 294–
        295
    for other's feelings, 321–
        322
Reverence
    acts of, 310–313, 382–383
    for the family system,
        272–277
    paths toward, 277–281
    test, 274–275
Revival
    nature of, 315–316, 344
    need for, 314–316
    practicing, 382–383
    test, 316–317
Rhythm
    of life, 64–69
    self/other, 66–67
    See also Family rhythm
Ritual
    children and, 48
    church, 173
    during crisis, 49
    as an energy source, 210–
        211
    establishing, 53–59
    evening, 54–55, 57–59
    and family rhythm, 63–64

Ritual (cont.)
  freedom through, 379–380
  health and, 47–48
  importance of, 40–42, 44
  mealtime, 56, 58
  morning, 55–56
  nature of, 41
  re-embracement, 51–53,
    57–58, 75
  replacement, 48–49
  versus routine, 40–42
  substitutes for, 46–48
  test, 42–43
  types of, 43–44

Sarcasm, 113
Schools
  athletics in, 167
  competitiveness within,
    161, 167
  counseling in, 165
  effect on family life, 163–
    164
  family curriculum for, 162,
    164, 165–166
  family takeover of, 164–
    167
  hours of operation, 165–
    166
  labeling practices, 161
  parental involvement in,
    165
Secretiveness
  of energy leeches, 242
  handling, 266–267
  reasons for, 265–269
  as a signal, 268
Security
  anger and, 326
  basis for arguments, 318
  basis for problems, 212–
    215, 254
Selective assumption, 103–
    104
Self
  industrialized sense of, 118
  pride in, 319–320
  primacy of, 125
  respect, 269–270
  sense of, 93
  social, 94
  spiritual, 94
Self-esteem
  basis for, 90, 94, 102
  basis for arguments, 318
  basis for problems, 212–
    215, 254
  and financial pressures,
    375–376
  fragility of, 96, 99–103,
    269–270
  reinforcing, 260–261
  sexual, 361–362
  See also Narcissism
Selfishness
  destructiveness of, 68
  and family responsibility,
    86–87
  See also Energy leeches
Sensitivity
  aesthetic, 296–299
  to energy leaks, 244–245
  within the family, 23, 222
  See also Family resonance;
    Spiritual energy
Serotonin, 289–290
Sex
  absolutism in, 101
  basis for conflict, 318
  basis for problems, 212–
    214, 254

communication in, 361–362

failure in, 128

guilt regarding, 268

mechanization of, 234

natural role of, 67–69

talking about, 68

versus tenderness, 231

Sexual abuse, 11, 134, 232–234, 268

Sharing

antidote to avarice, 324, 334

with energy leeches, 248–249

of meals, 41

Silent partner, 245

Sins (Seven Deadly), 318–334

Skepticism, 168–169

Sleeping patterns, 54–56

Sloth

as a basis for conflict, 331–332

language of, 332

mental, 332

revival strategies against, 334

spiritual, 332

Social responsibility, 303–304

Spiritual awareness

development, 276, 284

efforts toward, 331–332

of us actualizers, 299

See also Family extrasensory perception

Spiritual development

individual, 170

lack of, 331–332

purpose of life, 357–358

Spiritual energy

and divine discontent, 194–195

family template, 210, 222

scientific basis, 195

Spiritual seepage

correcting, 287

defined, 237

See also Energy leaks

Spontaneity

desirability of, 295–296

lack of, 337

nature of, 295

SSAADD talk, 113–114

Stagnant family type, 338–339

Stepfamilies

affirmation for, 373

coherence in, 371–372

parenting in, 371–372

resentments in, 372

rightfully formed, 370

trust in, 372

wrongfully formed, 370–373

Stress

family buffers, 292

from financial pressures, 373–377

fragmenting effect of, 353

and health, 175, 177, 178, 237

reactions to, 174, 187, 244

sources, 243

See also Depression

Substance abuse

basis for arguments, 318, 321–322

basis for problems, 212–214, 254

daily life with, 140–141

Substance abuse *(cont.)*
  reasons for, 288
  and ritual, 47
  secretiveness and, 266–268
Suicide
  from financial pressures,
    375–376
  motives, 76–77
  prediction, 287
  school pressure and, 163
  teenage, 74, 76–77, 163
Superstitious behavior, 255–
    256
Surrender
  irrationality of, 113
  occasions for, 186–189
  and reverence, 289
  successful, 188–189
Symmetrical family
    structure, 139–140

Teenagers
  in gangs, 46–47, 167
  independence for, 74–76
  peer pressure, 47, 267
  rebelliousness, 47
  runaway, 74–76
  school dropouts, 167
  secretiveness, 265–269
  suicide by, 74, 76–77, 163
Ten Rx's
  basis for, 37–38
  integrated, 378–384
  test of, 38–40
Thought
  choice in, 280
  collective, 280
  irrational, 105–106
  junk, 193
  See also Mental fatigue

Three E's, 168
Time
  control over, 278–279,
    379–380
  for family togetherness,
    278–279
  as a gift, 283
  nature of, 89, 278
  use of, 278
  See also Ritual
Toleration
  versus absolutism, 101
  of failure, 20–21
  in family love, 230, 263–
    264, 270
  practice of, 382
Transcendence
  altruism and, 300
  capacity for, 299–300
Tricyclics, 290

Ultralight family type, 334–
    335
Us actualizers
  aesthetic nature, 297–299
  altruism of, 300
  autonomous behavior by,
    294–295
  capacity for transcendence,
    299–300
  characteristics, 291–308
  creativity of, 305–306
  extrafamilial perception,
    299
  positive attitude of, 304–
    305
  versus self-actualizers, 288
  social responsibility, 298–
    299, 302–304, 307
  spontaneity in, 295–296

stress absorption by, 291–293

test, 308–310

Vindictiveness
  of energy leeches, 241–242
  futility of, 261
  reasons behind, 259–261
Virgin syndrome, 70
Volunteer work, 171
Voyeuristic society, 366–367

Wait-and-see factor, 372
Weight regulation, 187–188
Work
  and family life, 107–108, 277, 312
  and health, 237
  sacredness, 284

Wrongful divorce
  components of, 360–364
  defined, 360
  family affirmation, 364–365
Wrongful illness or disability
  characteristics, 365–369
  clusters, 368
  counterhostility toward, 368
  defined, 365, 369
  family affirmation for, 370
  invisible, 367–368
Wrongful loss
  components of, 355–357
  effects of, 355–357
  family affirmation, 357–359
  nature of, 353–355

About the Author

Dr. Paul Pearsall founded and is the former director of the Problems of Daily Living Clinic in the Department of Psychiatry of Sinai Hospital of Detroit. He has worked with hundreds of families, helping them discover their own inner strength for hardiness and health. He is the author of three best-selling books and lectures throughout the world on issues related to extreme wellness. He is an adjunct assistant professor at the Department of Psychiatry at the Wayne State University Medical School, Professor of Psychology at Henry Ford College, and Director of Professional Education at the Kinsey Institute for Research in Sex, Gender, and Reproduction at Indiana University. He lives with his family in Franklin, Michigan, and Kihei, Hawaii.